Ordo Pluriversalis: The End of Pax Americana and the Rise of Multipolarity

Leonid Savin

Ordo Pluriversalis:
The End of Pax Americana and the Rise of Multipolarity

Leonid Savin

Translated from Russian by Jafe Arnold.

ISBN-13: 978-1-912759-36-1

Black House Publishing Ltd
Kemp House
152 City Road
London
United Kingdom
EC1V 2NX

www.blackhousepublishing.com
Email: info@blackhousepublishing.com

Dedicated to the 100th anniversary of the publication of

Europe and Mankind

by

Nikolay Trubetzkoy.

Contents

Foreword

When in the first days of January 2020 the US military assassinated by drone strike Iranian General Qasem Soleimani, who was at the time in Iraq on a diplomatic mission, tensions escalated and an international scandal broke out. Many countries harshly criticized the United States' actions, and even many US political and public figures condemned the White House and Pentagon's methods.

In the journal *Foreign Affairs*, an analysis of the connection between the murder of General Soleimani in Iraq, the ensuing demand by Iraqi authorities that American troops leave the country, and the White House's responsive threat of harsh economic sanctions, pointed out: "In turning financial relationships into a tool of empire, the United States follows in the footsteps of ancient Athens. The experience of this predecessor does not augur well for Washington. Athens used its financial power to abuse its allies and in doing so precipitated its own ruination. The United States risks doing the same."[1]

However, besides definite political risks for the US, the January incident also incited a sharp sense of *déjà vu* harkening back to the US' 2003 military intervention in Iraq, when practically all of the US' allies refused to participate in its adventure. The latter event sparked new discussions on the need for a more balanced international system and on the numerous threats posed by unipolarity. Now, 17 years since the invasion of Iraq, unipolarity has virtually disappeared, yielding instead to emergent multipolarity. One of the most prominent American strategists, Graham Allison, has since remarked: "Unipolarity is over, and with it the illusion that other nations would simply take their assigned place in a U.S.-led international order. For the United States, that will require accepting the reality that there are spheres of influence in the world today, and that not all of them are American spheres." Meanwhile, Allison noted, Russia and China are continuing to further

1 Henry Farrell, Abraham Newman. The Twilight of America's Financial Empire// *Foreign Affairs*, January 24, 2020. https://www.foreignaffairs.com/articles/2020-01-24/twilight-americas-financial-empire

strengthen their power through spheres of influence, as great powers have traditionally done.[2]

The director of the Brookings Institutions' Center on the United States and Europe, Thomas Wright, sees the reason behind the collapse of the US' Grand Strategy in the ruination of the bipartisan consensus on the US' global role, management of alliances, use of its armed forces, and the promotion of human rights and democracy. Wright remarks: "it would be wrong for the United States to pretend that the world has not changed, to deny that the unipolar moment is over and that great-power competition has replaced counterterrorism as the central objective of U.S. foreign policy. In acknowledging the new circumstances it faces, the United States can employ retrenchment selectively, carefully abandoning some of its post-Cold War and post-9/11 commitments." Wright thus calls on the US to be "disciplined enough to understand the distinction between the places and things that really matter and those that do not."[3]

But what exactly really matters? Former US State Department Senior Advisor Bruce Jentleson has spoken of major power rivalry in a non-hegemonic world, the pluralization of diplomacy, and of new rules in bilateral relations and contested global governance. Moreover, according to Jentleson, new ideologies are appearing, and not only is the old model of "good democracy vs. bad authoritarianism" no longer effective, but in a historical perspective is incorrect.[4] It is also likely that such characteristics will be acceptable to other states whose strategies and interests are different from those of the US.

---

2 Graham Allison. The New Spheres of Influence. Sharing the Globe With Other Great Powers, March/April 2020. https://www.foreignaffairs.com/articles/united-states/2020-02-10/new-spheres-influence

3 Thomas Wright. The Folly of Retrenchment. Why America Can't Withdraw From the World, March/April 2020. https://www.foreignaffairs.com/articles/2020-02-10/folly-retrenchment

4 Bruce Jentleson, That Post-Liberal International World Order: Some Core Characteristics. Lawfare, September 9, 2018. https://www.lawfareblog.com/post-liberal-international-order-world-some-core-characteristics

Nevertheless, a new world structure has not been formed, and states and decision-making organs are in need of new mechanisms and rules. Societies are in need of clear visions of possible paths of development, as are political parties and movements in need of alternatives to outmoded templates and dogmas. All the while, multipolarity is emerging as a desirable model for the future and as a process for the transformation of international relations. Multipolarity is now a kind of "umbrella" encompassing ongoing geopolitical shifts.

The present work is a contribution to the development of the theory of multipolarity. However, it might be more correct to say that it is concerned with analytical method since, after all, as the present work will show, the foundations of multipolarity (and various theories of such) have always existed, but have merely been suppressed by global Western hegemony, which has not allowed them to be fully revealed and blossom.

This book consistes of thirteen chapters. The first chapter is devoted to the current crisis of liberalism in the broadest sense - as an ideology, as an economic system, and as a philosophic-political tradition. The concept of unipolarity is analyzed citing the examples of its main apologists.

The second chapter examines theories of poles and the balance of forces in the international system, as well as theories of transition and hegemony as such relate to the trichotomy of unipolarity-bipolarity-multipolarity. Examples of historical attempts at establishing multipolarity are presented, such as the Non-Aligned Movement, the Organization of Solidarity with the People of Asia, Africa and Latin America (OSPAAAL, the Association of Southeast Asian Nations (ASEAN), the African Union, the Union of South American Nations (UNASUR), the Southern Common Market (MERCOSUR), and the Community of Latin American and Caribbean States (CELAC). We also analyze the international crises which have contributed to the transition to multipolarity, and the West's reactions to this process ranging from attempts at instituting a multilateral framework and institutional criticisms of the ideas of multipolarity to objective assessments of the situation seen as attempts at eliminating injustices and underscoring the need to develop a new global model.

The third chapter is devoted to the theoretical and practical efforts of a number of countries to create a multipolar system, in particular the roles of Russia, China, India, Iran, and Latin American countries, as well as to those conceptualizations put forth by representatives of European and Asian states which organically fit into the multipolar approach and give preference to new forms of international cooperation.

The fourth chapter contains a detailed analysis of such philosophic-political concepts as polycentricity and pluriversum (pluriverse and pluriversality) in connection with geopolitical theories of large spaces and cultural zones.

The fifth chapter undertakes an attempt at a critical analysis of the notion of the West and the mechanisms of its territorial-political expansion, racism, colonialism, and exceptionalism. Such phenomena as time and space are examined as scientific, ideological, and political instruments of influence.

The sixth chapter is dedicated to analyzing notions of law and justice. It is shown that the system of international law, including various supranational institutions, was created exclusively in the interests of the West. This chapter also examines as a case study the model of social formations found among the indigenous peoples of the Andes region in Latin America, whose attitude and approach to the surrounding environment does not fit into the positivist juristic model. Also examined are the African palaver tradition, the *azerf* system of Berber law, and the continuity of traditional juristic schools in India and Russia. The hypothesis is put forth of an opposition between the ideocracy of classical Eurasianism and Western nomocracy.

The seventh chapter focuses on sovereignty and security as foundational elements of statehood. How differences in the etymologies of different languages of different peoples yield different understandings of the principles of security, as well as new approaches to this question, are examined. The historical transformation of the notion of sovereignty and its varying interpretations and implementations in the field of international relations and domestic politics are illustrated in detail.

The eighth chapter considers the deep interconnection between religion and economics. It is shown how the prescriptions of various faiths influence labor relations, economic management, and exchange systems as the fundamental foundations of any economy. Judaism, Buddhism, Christianity, and Islam are analyzed in terms of their economic approaches.

Chapter nine is about the typology of power and state. Both concepts are more complicated than it seems and can not be implemented everywhere as one uniform pattern, especially in the context of historical developments. Three different cases of power and state are presented in this chapter.

Ensuingly, the tenth chapter presents a consistent overview of theories of ethnos, nation, and nationalism, including non-European versions. The interrelationships between such, the differing views that arise on given questions, and the contradictory nature of the term "nation" when employed in a non-Western context are identified and specified.

The eleventh chapter is devoted to the fairly broad concept of civilization and its interpretations in European, English, American, and Russian scholarly schools. Also examined are the views of Muslim authors from various countries on this question as well as perspectives from Latin American and Asian cultures. In addition, the concept of strategic culture, and the multiplicity of social formations in general, is analyzed as a special element of identification of importance to the perspective of statehood, and an extended interpretation of this notion is proposed.

In the twelfth chapter, we turn to alternative theories supported by the opinions and studies of internationally recognized scholars and authors. Beginning with a critique of unified world theory, we analyze the possibility of the application in international relations and global politics of the theories of neopluralism, synthesis, various non-Western theories of international relations, theories of aesthetic politics, and the Fourth Political Theory. The author's own contribution is proposed in the form of a theory of sustainable policy based on holistic conservative thinking.

The thirteenth chapter describes the practical experiences of establishing a multipolar world in the cases of different organizations, institutions, and projects which, previously being theoretical models (and some remain such), have over time become integral parts of the international system, such as BRICS, the G-20, N-11, VISTA, and others. Multiple examples are presented of scientific methods which might be used to describe a new type of world order, such as system of systems, neofunctionalism, complex adaptive systems, relationism, multiplexity, polylogue, systasis, and syneresis. Although all of these chapters proceed in a logical manner, each one can be seen as a separate text in and of itself.

Throughout this work, special attention is paid to the etymology of concepts, since the original meanings of words and terms have frequently been distorted over the course of history. The restoration of the deep essence of both famous, established concepts as well as forgotten ideas can be fruitful for giving adequate content to otherwise emasculated doctrines if applied from different points of view.

It is quite possible that at times the reader may intuit that some of the elements of this book are fragmentary or do not directly relate to the topic of multipolarity. However, the wide range of topics considered in this book was originally intended to expand the scope of perceptions and to demonstrate the interconnections and intertwinings that permeate the cultures of peoples and civilizations but which are not always obvious and explicit, especially for the rational perception of the Western man of the Postmodern era. Moreover, this approach has been taken as part of an attempt to overcome the positivist scientific approach that has long been the global "master frame" which has not allowed for different interpretations of reality, especially those harboring theological or metaphysical characteristics.

However the format and length of this book can cover all of the theories in current circulation, and only offer examples from and for far from all regions. For instance, ideas which might be used to develop multipolarity in Africa (such as Negritude, Afrocentrism, and African Renaissance) are not reflected in this work. At the same time, in the author's opinion, insufficient attention has been paid to Arab metapolitical projects and the Pacific region. This shortcoming will likely be corrected in future editions or additional studies. Nevertheless, the author hopes that this work will be adequately received in the scholarly community and in those circles engaged in international relations and the development of foreign policy strategies, will stimulate further research on multipolarity-polycentricity-pluriversality in the political sciences, and will inspire the new, creative solutions that are so needed in the current period of global geopolitical turbulence.

1

The Collapse of Unipolarity and the Crisis of World Politics

In recent years, the world has been experiencing a crisis. This crisis concerns not only the economic repressions ongoing in a number of industrial countries, and not only problems of a political nature and conflicts, but also a crisis of identity and ideology. On the local level, all countries are facing problems intrinsic to their regions, while on the global scale there is the glaring trend that is the destruction of the present world order as we have known it for the past 30 years.

Since the demolition of the Berlin Wall and the collapse of the Soviet Union, the whole world has been gripped by a wave of bloody ethnic conflicts accompanied by the destruction of entire national economies. Yet this process has also been bound up with the opening up of certain new opportunities for the expansion of contacts and for the redetermination of borders hitherto believed to be inviolable. Some states have preferred to remain on the sidelines and pursue their own paths of development. Nevertheless, it has been more than obvious to all that the end of the Cold War entailed the disappearance of not only the planetary confrontation of two superpowers, but also the accompanying bipolar world system. This system was replaced by a unipolar model headed by the victor: the United States of America. But its time has turned out to be short.

For instance, the economist Martin Wolf wrote in the *Financial Times* on January 5th, 2017:

> We are, in short, at the end of both an economic period — that of western-led globalisation — and a geopolitical one — the post-cold war "unipolar moment" of a US-led global order. The question is whether what follows will be an unravelling of the

> post-second world war era into deglobalisation and conflict, as happened in the first half of the 20th century, or a new period in which non-western powers, especially China and India, play a bigger role in sustaining a co-operative global order.[1]

Leading American experts of Liberal orientation have also begun changing their tone, whereas just a few years ago such a change in attitude was still unimaginable. In his article of January 2019, Joseph Nye, Jr. wrote: "'liberal international order', the phrase commonly used to characterize the period of American primacy after the Second World War, is somewhat misleading, for the order was never global and not always very liberal." Further, Nye writes:

> "The terms 'liberal international order' or 'Pax Americana' have become obsolete as descriptions of the US place in the world, but the need for the largest countries to provide public goods remains. An open international order covers political–military affairs; economic relations; ecological relations; and human rights, whether directly or indirectly…Promotion of democracy can be a source of soft power, but only if the means are modest. Overreaching intervention to promote democracy has in the past provoked a counterproductive reaction. The neo-conservative strand of Wilsonianism is not likely to succeed. Crusades for liberal values would not be supported at home or abroad."[2]

Another of this author's works poses the question in its title: "Is the American Century Over?"[3]

Over the years, a great deal of analytical work has been done on possible global trends. Although no one scenario was ever intended, based on the forecasts that came true and new facts, it can be concluded that an alternative is approaching the current world structure. And, perhaps, several alternatives that are interconnected with each other.

---

1 Martin Wolf, 'The long and painful journey to world disorder', *Financial Times,* 5 Jan. 2017.
https://www.ft.com/content/ef13e61a-ccec-11e6-b8ce-b9c03770f8b1

2 Joseph S. Nye, Jr. The rise and fall of American hegemony from Wilson to Trump. International Affairs, Volume 95, Issue 1, 1 January 2019, 63–80.
https://academic.oup.com/ia/article/95/1/63/5273551

3 Joseph S. Nye, Jr. Is the American Century Over? Polity Press, 2015

In early December 2012, the US National Intelligence Council officially released to the public its report on future threats, entitled "Global Trends 2030: Alternative Worlds."[4] This document, as is traditionally characteristic of such reports, presents the views of the American intelligence community on how the world will develop over the next 15-20 years, for which the report's subtitle, "Alternative Worlds", suggests genuinely global shifts in world geopolitics - or, in the very least, in the understandings of the document's authors. The content of "Global Trends 2030: Alternative Worlds" became the subject of discussions and analyses among numerous US analytical centers, some of which proposed efforts to preserve American power while others have spoken with a sense of fatalism on the inevitability of the processes described in the report.

Four potential future scenarios of world order are presented in the report under the allegorical names "Stalled Engines", "Fusion", "Genie-Out-of-the-Bottle", and "Nonstate world." The first scenario supposes that a new Great Game in Asia will lead to the outbreak of conflict, and since Asian countries are the driving force of the world economy, such would seriously brake global development. This scenario is seen as the worst one, entailing more serious consequences than the First and Second World Wars. The second scenario is completely opposite to the first, being a kind of "happy end" in the American understanding. In this scenario, the US, Europe, and China (where gradual political reforms are expected) will arrive at a convergence and find ways for cooperation, doubling global GDP and returning the "American Dream." The third scenario presents a world of extremes, in which social and political contradictions will escalate within many states, the US will no longer be the global policeman, and China will see a rift in incomes between its coastal zone and inland. Overall, in this situation, the world would remain wealthy, but not as safe as it is now due to the exacerbation of the negative effects of globalization on domestic and international politics. According to the last scenario, non-governmental organizations, transnational businesses, academic institutions, and the wealthy, alongside sub-national subjects such as megalopolises, will flourish and manage global changes. The basis for their support would be the formation of a growing global social consensus between the elites and the middle class on environmental

4 Global Trends 2030: Alternative worlds. NIC, Dec. 2012.

questions, anti-corruption, the primacy of rights, and the problem of poverty. The world would still remain imbalanced in such a scenario, as authoritarian and democratic regimes will experience difficulties in fulfilling their functions. States themselves will not disappear, but would organize "hybrid coalitions of state and nonstate actors."[5]

At the same time, the Council on Foreign Relations stated that it sees a reverse of the historic rise of the West that began in 1750, paralleled by a restoration of the role of Asia in the global economy.[6] The Atlantic Council, meanwhile, has presented its vision of the future in the report "Envisioning 2030: US Strategy for a Post-Western World." The council's president and executive director, Frederick Kempe, stated therein: "The United States has something rare among history's great powers—a second chance…The United States–unlike other great powers in history–has a second chance at molding the international system to secure its long-term interests. No other nation is likely to have as much impact in influencing the global future."[7]

It is telling that in a similar report published in March 2012 by the EU Institute for Security Studies, future multipolarity is seen in a positive context. The report itself bears the title "Citizens in an Interconnected and Polycentric World" and remarks that the future "depends on how the EU copes with the present economic crisis and uses its strengths to operate effectively in a polycentric world. If it rises to the challenge in a credible manner, the current crisis could be reversed by a new 'European renaissance.'"[8]

The previous Global Trends report released in 2008, "Global Trends 2025", observed a rise of new powers, the globalization of the economy, an historical shift of relative wealth and economic power from the West to the East, as well as growing influence of nonstate subjects.

---

5 https://www.dni.gov/files/documents/GlobalTrends_2030.pdf

6 http://www.cfr.org/united-states/nic-global-trends-2030-alternative-worlds/p29631

7 https://www.atlanticcouncil.org/in-depth-research-reports/report/envisioning-2030-us-strategy-for-a-postwestern-world/

8 Global trends 2030 – Citizens in an Interconnected and Polycentric World. Ed. by Alvaro de Vasconcelos. Institute for Security Studies. https://espas.secure.europarl.europa.eu/orbis/sites/default/files/espas_files/about/espas_report_ii_01_en.pdf

The 2017 report "Global Trends: Paradox of Progress", referred to the fact that the "unipolar moment has passed and the post-1945 rules based international order may be fading too."[9] Global Trends 2030 also pointed out:

> Just as important, the economies of other non-Western states such as Colombia, Egypt, Indonesia, Iran, South Africa, Mexico, Turkey, and others that are middle tier today could rise by 2030. Individually most of these countries will remain second-order players because China and India are so large. However, as a collective group, they will begin to surpass Europe, Japan, and Russia in terms of global power by 2030. Our modeling shows, for example, that this group of rapidly developing middle-tier countries—the Goldman Sachs "Next Eleven"will collectively overtake the EU-27 in global power by 2030.[10]

Thus, economic development is taken to automatically mean change in the political roles of international activities. At the same time, the report speaks of the onset of economic multipolarity:

> Some experts have compared the upcoming decline of US economic weight to the late 19th century when economic dominance by one player—Britain—receded into multipolarity. Other resemblances include an accelerating globalization, rapid technological development, and growing geopolitical competition among the great powers. The late 19th century was a time of relatively high real economic volatility with wide fluctuations in growth rates. The average growth rate of the leading country, the United Kingdom, in the 19th century was not high, while the growth rate of the rival—the US—was higher but variable. Just as now, intellectual property rights were in dispute with no government in a position to enforce them abroad. An added current complication are the differences over market liberalization and role of the state in the economy, which are likely to continue.[11]

---

9 https://www.dni.gov/files/images/globalTrends/documents/GT-Full-Report.pdf P. 6.

10 https://www.dni.gov/files/documents/GlobalTrends_2030.pdf P. 15.

11 Ibid, p. 46.

A similar study prepared by the European Parliament suggests: "In the most likely scenario, globalization patterns will be shaped less by politics and more by structural factors."[12] These trends, the report says:

> will have significant consequences for some of the more fundamental assumptions about the nature of the international system. They will likely add up to a continued evolution away from what might be known as the postCold War order, dominated by a unipolar United States, into a multipolar order, in which medium-sized powers will have considerably greater power and corporations and international institutions will be major constraints on state action.[13]

The authors of the report thus propose that on the way to 2035, EU countries will undergo a combination of two development scenarios: adaptation to challenges (or lack thereof), and managed evolution of the global system towards multipolarity, on which point it is posited that "a multipolar world will create strains on the existing system of global governance, as rising states wish for a greater share of control, while others will seek to maintain their existing position."[14] From the point of view of Western political sciences and the previous experience of Europeans countries, such a remark on tension is wholly justified. However, they will likely have to come to terms with this.

Overall, contemporary debates on a "post-American future" have clearly revealed there to be two camps: on the one hand are those who insist that the US should restore its global hegemony by one or another means, and on the other are those who take a more cautious and calculated position, at times even venturing to criticize American interventionism and the US' other deeds of past years.

Therefore, to begin with, it is necessary to analyze what unipolarity is, how American political scientists see this phenomenon, and what are the similarities and differences of opinion.

---

12 Global Trends to 2035. Geo-politics and international power. European Parliament Research Service, Global Trends Unit, September 2017. P. 6.

13 Ibid. P. 7-8.

14 Ibid. P. 74.

The Apologists of Unipolarity

For political scientists and scholars of international affairs, the late Charles Krauthammer went down in history not as the editor of *The Weekly Standard* or as the co-founder of the musical organization Pro Musica Hebraica, but rather as one of the most ardent apologists of unipolarity. Krauthammer's articles "The Unipolar Moment" and "The Unipolar Moment Revisited" have become classics of Atlanticist geopolitics in the post-modern era. Alongside the neoconservatives, Krauthammer embodied that wing of the American political elite which openly proclaims that the US needs to preserve its status as the hegemon and world policeman. We will examine Krauthammer's ideas in greater detail below through the prism of critical analysis and with regards to multipolarity. For now, there are a number of other American scholars of interest who have advanced their own theories and scenarios for the unipolar world model.

One contemporary supporter of unipolarity is Yale University Professor Nuno P. Monteiro, who in 2014 released the book *Theory of Unipolar Politics,* a work which can be called "good" insofar as, like Krauthammer, Monteiro openly calls things by their names and does not hide behind democratic rhetoric. Kenneth Waltz's argument on rationality, but - as Robert Keohane noted in his review of Monteiro's book: "like Watlz, he [Monteiro] deliberately ignores how domestic politics or ideas prompt states to take particular actions and downplays the role of multilateral institutions."[15] Monteiro's point of departure, which is shared by such scholarly advocates of US supremacy as Stephen Brooks and William Wohlforth, is that the current international system is unipolar. Monteiro argues that this order will remain in place in the future, even going so far as to introduce and constantly employ the new term "unipole" throughout his work. Monteiro's analysis of the dualism between unipolarity and multipolarity (in which we can also see the confrontation between Sea Power and Land Power) is based on

15 Robert O. Keohane, Theory of Unipolar Politics. By Nuno P. Monteiro. New York: Cambridge University Press, 2014. Perspectives on Politics, Volume 13, Issue 1 March 2015, pp. 256-257.
https://www.cambridge.org/core/journals/perspectives-on-politics/article/theory-of-unipolar-politics-by-nuno-p-monteiro-new-york-cambridge-university-press-2014-296p-8500-cloth-2899-paper/B25A7FB453F3DA8682CA94A56F639876

two main aspects: military power, particularly nuclear armaments, and economy - these are the geopolitical fundamentals which distinguish the role and status of any given state in the world system. It is important to note that Monteiro is thereby scientifically justifying none other than an aggressive, not peaceful natured unipolarity, as many of his predecessors did in their own times. In Monteiro's opinion, unipolarity encourages recalcitrant, minor powers to acquire or develop nuclear weapons, whereas the unipolar center, as a matter of course, seeks to prevent the proliferation of nuclear weapons. As follows, these two competing goals not only create conflicts of interests between the unipolar system and secondary states, but also undermine their ability to exert a calming affect on each other. Smaller powers cannot take on the commitment to not develop nuclear arms, while the unipolar center, for its part, cannot commit to not attacking secondary states. As a result, in Monteiro's words, "unipolarity will be prone to produce asymmetric and peripheral conflicts."[16] Why might unipolarity be prone to making this happen? Monteiro writes:

> if the unipole implements a strategy that threatens to contain the economic growth of rising powers, then these other states have greater incentives to invest in additional military capabilities beyond those that assure their immediate security and survival, thereby putting up a military challenge to the unipole...rising powers in a unipolar world may continue to convert their growing latent power into military power beyond the point at which their survival is guaranteed by a nuclear deterrent.

Further, Monteiro explains:

> Unipolarity will generate abundant opportunities for war between the unipole and recalcitrant minor powers that do not have the capabilities or allies necessary to deter it. It will also make ample room for conflict among minor powers, which are less likely to be disciplined by great-power allies, as would be the case when an overall balance of power is present. As a result, unipolarity will be prone to produce asymmetric and peripheral conflicts.[17]

16 Nuno P. Monteiro. Theory of Unipolar Politics. Cambridge University Press, 2014. P. 3.

17 Nuno P. Monteiro. Theory of Unipolar Politics. Cambridge University Press, 2014. P. 4-5.

Following this picture is an assertion which allows the reader to characterize the author as a great-power chauvinist, as Monteiro writes:

> ...a great power is a state that, in addition to having robust capabilities in all the relevant elements of power, is not significantly surpassed in two aspects of military power. The first aspect is the great power's capability to defend itself from aggression...a great power must have a plausible chance of avoiding defeat in an all-out defensive war against the most powerful state in the system. In addition, great powers must fulfill a military power-projection requirement. Specifically, a great power must possess the ability to engage unaided in sustained politico-military operations in at least one other relevant region of the globe beyond its own on a level similar to the most powerful state in the system.[18]

Without a doubt, we can see in this reasoning a justification for American power in its current form, e.g., in the likes of the military operations in Afghanistan, Iraq, Syria and the US' numerous military bases abroad. Monteiro rejects earlier critiques of unipolarity on the grounds that "Previous analyses of unipolarity have not adequately captured the fundamental difference between major and minor powers." Suggesting that the "distribution of military power" is "in principle independent from the distribution of economic power", Monteiro gradually arrives at his main thesis: "Unipolarity, then, highlights the concentration of military power in one state, the sole great power. It does not require economic power preponderance."[19]

Ultimately, Monteiro proposes a certain plan of action for the US: "The grand strategy of the unipole is therefore an important variable mediating between the structure of international politics - in this case, a unipolar structure - and the most important international outcomes in terms of conflict-producing and competition-inducing mechanisms."[20] In reality, equating international and unipolar structures implies that there is only one decision-making center, and that any audacity on the part of other countries, even if not of a conflictual nature, would be suppressed - and "audacity" or "competition" could mean anything

18 Ibidem. P. 44.

19 Ibidem. P. 25, 49.

20 Ibidem. P. 63.

from economic development to attempts to improve the prosperity of one's own people.

Furthermore, Monteiro distinguishes three key strategies for the "unipole": "defensive dominance", "offensive dominance", and "disengagement", each of which presupposes a special relationship between the superpower and one or more key components of the global status quo (existing territorial order and borders, international alliances, global distribution of power).[21] In Monteiro's next book from 2016: *Nuclear Politics: The Strategic Causes of Proliferation*, he continued to pursue this line of unipolarity. In his examination of Monteiro's notions, Michael Beckley has remarked:

> In bipolar or multipolar systems, there are no peripheries; anything that happens anywhere in the world has potential implications for great-power politics. Under such conditions, recalcitrant minor powers become logical targets because their insubordination threatens the prestige and credibility, if not the security, of their great power enemies.

Under unipolarity, by contrast, recalcitrant minor powers are minor players. They can threaten the unipole, but unipolarity prevents these threats from assuming great power proportions. Thus, a unipole may be able to credibly commit not to attack minor powers, despite the large power gap between them, because of its manifest lack of interest in going to war over minimal stakes.[22]

Such ingratiation before minor powers is strange, especially considering the fact that there was a periphery in the bipolar system in which the proxy agents of both superpowers repeatedly and directly clashed - for example, in Korea and Vietnam. We should also add that Monteiro calls those who criticize unipolarity and those who argue for the emergence of multipolarity - from the interpreters of Charles Krauthammer to Kenneth Waltz and Christopher Layne - none other than "Declinists."

---

21 Teoriya I praktika odnopolyarnoi politiki. Vestnik SPBGU. Ser. 6. 2016. Issue. 1. P. 154.

22 Michael Beckley, H-Diplo, ISSF, Roundtable, Volume VIII, No. 3 (2015) P. 7. https://issforum.org/ISSF/PDF/ISSF-Roundtable-8-3.pdf

William Wohlforth, like Charles Krauthammer, represents the wing of the supporters of unipolarity who believe that there is no other force in the world capable of somehow changing the existing balance that exists in favor of American hegemony.[23] Wohlforth belongs to the school of neorealism, closely collaborates with Stephen Brooks, and his research is most known in the form of the theory of "unipolar stability" - a notion which has been criticized by numerous scholars. While recently many American authors have been speaking about the challenges posed by China, Wohlforth and Brooks have responded to these discussions with the following thesis:

> Economic growth no longer translates as directly into military power as it did in the past, which means that it is now harder than ever for rising powers to rise and established ones to fall. And China—the only country with the raw potential to become a true global peer of the United States—also faces a more daunting challenge than previous rising states because of how far it lags behind technologically. Even though the United States' economic dominance has eroded from its peak, the country's military superiority is not going anywhere, nor is the globe-spanning alliance structure that constitutes the core of the existing liberal international order (unless Washington unwisely decides to throw it away). Rather than expecting a power transition in international politics, everyone should start getting used to a world in which the United States remains the sole superpower for decades to come. Lasting preeminence will help the United States ward off the greatest traditional international danger, war between the world's major powers. And it will give Washington options for dealing with nonstate threats such as terrorism and transnational challenges such as climate change.[24]

---

23 William Wohlforth, 'The Stability of a Unipolar World', International Security 24/2 (Summer 1999), 18; Stephen G. Brooks and William C. Wohlforth, World Out of Balance: International Relations and the Challenge of American Primacy (Princeton UP); Stephen G. Brooks and William C. Wohlforth, 'Hard Times for Soft Balancing', International Security 30/1 (Summer 2005), 72–108; Gerard Alexander and Keir Lieber, 'Waiting for Balancing: Why the World is Not Pushing Back', International Security 30/1 (Summer 2005), 109–39; Stephen G. Brooks & William C. Wohlforth (2016) America Abroad: The United States' Global Role in the 21st Century. Oxford: Oxford University Press.

24 Stephen G. Brooks and William C. Wohlforth, The Once and Future Superpower.

Yet throughout the history of its existence, the US has never prevented any wars but, on the contrary, has more often than not provoked and unleashed them. Moreover, accusing China of any "technological lag" seems clearly out of place, especially in the context of the US' heavy dependence on the import of Chinese products. Only relatively recently has Wohlforth begun to exhibit signs of uneasiness, most evidently disturbed by the changes in US' domestic and foreign policy course since the election of President Donald Trump, as well as by the growth of populist sentiments in Europe. In a joint article with Jennifer Lind published in February 2019, "The Future of the Liberal Order Is Conservative: A Strategy to Save the System", Wohlforth writes:

> for the past 25 years, the international order crafted by and for liberal states has itself been profoundly revisionist, aggressively exporting democracy and expanding in both depth and breadth. The scale of the current problems means that more of the same is not viable; the best response is to make the liberal order more conservative. Instead of expanding it to new places and new domains, the United States and its partners should consolidate the gains the order has reaped. The debate over U.S. grand strategy has traditionally been portrayed as a choice between retrenchment and ambitious expansionism. Conservatism offers a third way: it is a prudent option…[25]

It is altogether telling that Wohlforth does not recognize any systemic mistake to have arisen thanks to none other than the liberal order, not to mention the rising resistance to globalism not only in Europe, but also in the US itself. The crisis of the liberal system is first and foremost a crisis of values, and is not merely the result of a challenge posed by emergent and revisionist powers as American authors like to suggest. A conservative correction in one form or another would very well come in useful, since it weakens the positions of globalists both in the US and in recipient-countries hitherto subordinated to the ideological

---

Why China Won't Overtake the United States // April 13, 2016. https://www.foreignaffairs.com/articles/united-states/2016-04-13/once-and-future-superpower

25 Jennifer Lind and William C. Wohlforth, The Future of the Liberal Order Is Conservative. A Strategy to Save the System // February 12, 2019. https://www.foreignaffairs.com/articles/2019-02-12/future-liberal-order-conservative

imperatives of Washington. Yet Wohlforth, like Monteiro, dismisses the pathos of promoting human rights and democracy and insists on maintaining hegemony at any cost, even if such necessitates abandoning liberal rhetoric and launching military interventions. Overall, the notion of "illiberal hegemony" has been actively promoted ever since Donald Trump became President, just as Trump's campaign slogan "America First", so often cited by American authors, has been interpreted as a kind of marker of a new tendency in American foreign policy.

Yet another supporter of unipolarity among globally recognized political scientists and IR scholars is John Ikenberry, who argues that, in order to preserve its hegemonic role in the world, the US must share its power with "a broad coalition of liberal democratic states".[26] This alteration, of course, ought to be made under the leading role of the US. Unlike Wohlforth, Ikenberry recognizes a situation of crisis - but for him, this crisis is first and foremost a crisis of authority and "command." For a new liberal hegemonic system to function stably, Ikenberry proposes a combination of three elements: "balance", "command", and "conciliation." One review of Ikenberry's work has noted:

> The author is acutely aware that the current world order is in crisis - paradoxically because the United States' unipolar moment - with the «inside» Western system facing the Soviets turned into the «outside» order encompassing the globe - removed the U.S. of all constraints, leading it eventually to undermine the rules of the very order it had created. Yet Ikenberry remains optimistic. Thinking of the way forward, he argues that «power is most legitimate and durable when exercised within a system of rules,» noting that the best way to assert U.S. American power is to reaffirm the 'liberal hegemonic order'. Despite apparent flaws, the likelihood of the end of liberal order is small. Rather, the current state of affairs merely shows that the system has outgrown its American-led, hegemonic foundation, and the problems we see today are a symptom of the system's wild success, not its failure. Even in a system with few restraints to American unipolarity, no state engages in open balancing behavior against the United States.[27]

---

26 G. John Ikenberry. Liberal Leviathan: The Origins, Crisis, and Transformation of the American World Order. NJ: Princeton University Press, 2011. P. 10.

27 Oliver Stuenkel, Book review: "Liberal Leviathan" by G. John Ikenberry, 01

It is appropriate here to ask: Why should other countries or alliances necessarily be driven towards confrontation with the United States? When American strategies speak of rising threats posed by other powers, such is merely the fiction of these American strategies themselves. To this day, no hidden rivalries or hostile intentions have escalated into open conflict, and it is difficult to say unequivocally that actor A or actor B will necessarily strike actor C if the latter's economic power exceeds the measures of forecasted damage. Indeed, one can find rather paradoxical statements in Ikenberry's works. For instance, Ikenberry argues: "One step toward multipolarity is simply a diffusion of power away from the unipolar state. Unipolarity is, after all, a depiction of the distribution of power. So the distribution of power could simply and slowly evolve toward a system in which power is more widely shared."[28] On this note, it should be recalled that the US has already in the past distributed power among partners, such as through the establishment of alliances like NATO, SEATO, ANZUS, and through military and economic aid, and so on. Moreover, the US has a constant group of satellites in the United Nations, and whenever principal matters have arisen, such as those concerning "protecting national interests" or, indeed, in any cases of disagreements with "partners", as was the case with the aggression against Iraq in 2003, the US has repeatedly engaged in independent, unilateral decision making. It is highly doubtful that Washington will agree to hand over any authority to other countries in the future as Ikenberry suggests. It should also be noted that Ikenberry's work, *Liberal Leviathan: The Origins, Crisis, and Transformation of the American World Order* was published at the time when the US State Department pursued a multilateral strategy in foreign policy, which was Washington's act of global diversion, over the course of which a "reset" in relations with Russia and the Big Two project of the US and China were declared. Both initiatives proved unsuccessful for American policy.

The above-mentioned Michael Beckley is also a supporter of preserving unipolarity and American hegemony, his vision of which was presented in his book *Unrivaled: Why America Will Remain the*

Apr. 2012. https://www.postwesternworld.com/2012/04/01/book-review-liberal-leviathan-by-g-john-ikenberry/

28 G. John Ikenberry. Liberal Leviathan: The Origins, Crisis, and Transformation of the American World Order. NJ: Princeton University Press, 2011. P. 312.

World's Sole Superpower. As one review has noted, "Beckley's writing style pounds the reader with fact after fact to substantiate his central argument that even if America were in decline, which it is not, it will be some years, if ever, before its supremacy is challenged."[29] Beckley's *Unrivaled* also proposes a purist evaluation of the comparative positions of power, striving to calculate the power of a state on the basis of an audit of the costs it incurs over the course of maintaining this power. Three main forms of costs are accounted for: "production costs", or "the price a nation pays to generate wealth and military capabilities", "welfare costs", i.e., "the expenses a nation pays to keep its people alive" and to invest in social services, and "security costs", i.e., "the price a government pays to police and protect its citizens", i.e., on the maintenance of domestic administration and survival in the surrounding environment.[30]

In *Unrivaled*, Beckley attempts to prove that the United States is the most effective producer of power on the planet, that the EU is in need of unity, and that Russia is a country in decline, burdened with numerous problems ranging from alcoholism and corruption to other internal contradictions. Although China has experienced amazing economic expansion that has lifted tens of millions out of poverty and created a powerful armed forces, it is posited that democratic sentiments are repressed and China suffers from potential regional fragmentation and an aging population. It is altogether strange that Beckley assigns alcoholism and internal discord to Russia given that, according to official statistics, the share of the drinking population in Russia has decreased significantly, whereas in the US there are serious problems with narcotics, murder rates, and multiple levels of political contradictions - as the 2016 presidential elections showed. For now, let us note that Beckley sees the main challenge to US hegemony not in external threats, but in internal problems, hence the suspicion as to why Beckley avoids paying attention to such critical domestic issues as drug use and violence which, along with unemployment and political polarization, have attained epidemic proportions in the US.

29 Nick March. Review: 'Unrivaled - Why America Will Remain the World's Sole Superpower' // The National, Sep 27, 2018. https://www.thenational.ae/arts-culture/books/review-unrivaled-why-america-will-remain-the-world-s-sole-superpower-1.774702

30 Ali Wyne. Book Review: 'Unrivaled' by Michael Beckley, April 18, 2019. https://www.rand.org/blog/2019/04/book-review-unrivaled-by-michael-beckley.html

Nevertheless, Beckley believes that American dominance will persist, and that the main driving forces for economic growth - geography, institutions, and demography - supply sufficient, sustainable grounds for such. Although the US' indices are far from always in first place among relevant international ratings, they retain relatively high positions, and decades of big investments in defense technologies and training grant the US the unrivaled capability to generate and protect globally significant military power. There hardly exists any kind of balance to this force, insofar as the majority of countries prefer to take advantage of American "defense" and live at the cost of its economic contributions rather than becoming a US opponent. At the same time, the gap between the US' wealth and military forces and that of other countries remains unchanged. Beckley also rejects the theory of economic convergence as wishful thinking, not reality.

Some reviews of Beckley's work have drawn attention to comparisons between the US' and China's indices, concluding that both countries will need to find a certain consensus with regards to the future world order. One such review remarks "U.S. preeminence is safer than most contemporary commentary would have one believe" and that it is also "more resilient." In Beckley's words: "Unipolarity is not guaranteed to endure, but present trends strongly suggest that it will last for many decades."[31]

Others, on the contrary, suggest that China will overtake both the US and Russia together, and to this end suggest the need for a Russian-American geopolitical alliance, although for now issues such as Ukraine and Syria continue to hinder the development and improvement of bilateral relations between the two countries. Harry Kazianis has written on this matter: "While we might rightly see Moscow as a rogue nation today, tomorrow it could be a partner in containing a common foe."[32]

---

31 Ali Wyne. Book Review: 'Unrivaled' by Michael Beckley, April 18, 2019. https://www.rand.org/blog/2019/04/book-review-unrivaled-by-michael-beckley.html

32 Harry J. Kazianis. The Coming American-Russian Alliance Against China // The American Conservative, July 16, 2018. https://www.theamericanconservative.com/articles/the-coming-american-russian-alliance-against-china/comment-page-1/

Beckley's colleagues, nonetheless, have defended his positions. For instance, in his review of *Unrivaled*, Ikenberry writes: "He [Beckley] does not argue that the United States can—or should—try to preserve the unipolar era, but he does think that it will long remain the world's leading power."[33] Beckley has offered other attempts to analyze the balance of power between major geopolitical actors on previous occasions, for instance in his 2012 article, "China's Century? Why America's Edge Will Endure." In the latter, Beckley compared Chinese and US characteristics and concluded:

> It is impossible to say whether the current malaise is the beginning of the end of the unipolar era or simply an aberration. The best that can be done is to make plans for the future on the basis of long-term trends; and the trends suggest that the United States' economic, technological, and military lead over China will be an enduring feature of international relations, not a passing moment in time, but a deeply embedded condition that will persist well into this century.[34]

Further, Beckley writes:

> "In recent years, scholars' main message to policymakers has been to prepare for the rise of China and the end of unipolarity. This conclusion is probably wrong, but it is not necessarily bad for Americans to believe it is true. Fear can be harnessed in the service of virtuous policies. Fear of the Soviet Union spurred the construction of the interstate highway system. Perhaps unjustified fears about the decline of the United States and the rise of China can similarly be used in good cause."[35]

Another American scholar engaged in the study of unipolarity is Robert Jervis, who published the book *System Effects: Complexity*

---

33 G. John Ikenberry. Unrivaled: Why America Will Remain the World's Sole Superpower // Foreign Affairs, Oct. 16, 2018. https://www.foreignaffairs.com/reviews/capsule-review/2018-10-16/unrivaled-why-america-will-remain-worlds-sole-superpower

34 Michael Beckley. China's Century? Why America's Edge Will Endure // International Security, Vol. 36, No. 3 (Winter 2011/12), pp. 41–78. https://www.mitpressjournals.org/doi/pdf/10.1162/ISEC_a_00066

35 Ididem, P. 77.

in Political and Social Life[36] in 1997 and later, in 2009, authored a "structural analysis of unipolarity."[37] In the latter, Jervis argued

> To say that the world is now unipolar is neither to praise American power, let alone its leadership, nor to accuse the United States of having established a worldwide empire. It is to state a fact, but one whose meaning is far from clear, as we have neither a powerful theory nor much evidence about how unipolar systems operate. A central difficulty for sorting this out entails determining the extent to which behavior and outcomes we have seen stem from structure, rather than from other levels of analysis, such as idiosyncratic aspects of the international environment, the American domestic system, and the role of individual leaders.[38]

Credit should be given where due: this very approach aimed at directly studying the structures of unipolarity is altogether of interest, and can help in the deconstruction of unipolarity, in the discernment of its weak points and vulnerabilities, as well as in taking into account this whole experience over the course of developing multipolar strategies.

Another version holds that "the adjective 'unipolar' describes a system where one country excels in indicators of power such as population, resource endowment, economic capacity, military might, etc., while yet not necessarily conforming to a hegemony."[39] However, no such case

---

36 Jervis, Robert. System Effects: Complexity in Political and Social Life. Princeton University Press, 1997.

37 Jervis, Robert. 2009. "Unipolarity: A Structural Perspective." World Politics 61(1): pp 252-281. https://doi.org/10.1017/CBO9780511996337.008

38 Jervis, Robert. 2009. "Unipolarity: A Structural Perspective." World Politics 61(1): pp 252-281. https://doi.org/10.1017/CBO9780511996337.008 See also: Robert Jervis, "The Remaking of a Unipolar World," Washington Quarterly, Vol. 29, No. 3 (Summer 2006), pp. 7–19.

39 Luis L Schenoni, Subsystemic Unipolarities? Power Distribution and State Behaviour in South America and Southern Africa" in Strategic Analysis, 41(1):84-85. 2017. https://www.academia.edu/30528886/_Subsystemic_Unipolarities_Power_Distribution_and_State_Behaviour_in_South_America_and_Southern_Africa_in_Strategic_Analysis_41_1_74-86 , p. 74. ; G. John Ikenberry, Michael Mastanduno, William Wohlforth. Unipolarity, State Behavior, and Systemic Consequences', World Politics , 61(1), 2009, p. 5.

has been seen in practice. The neoconservative camp is represented in this case by Robert Kagan, one of whose latest books bears the title *The Jungle Grows Back: America and Our Imperiled World*, in which Kagan describes how the international system that the US has built is in danger:

> Now, however, that system is in jeopardy. The jungle — that place of chaos and disorder and war — 'is growing back. History is returning. Nations are reverting to old habits and traditions." Kagan does not lay all the blame on the United States, but he does see the country as responsible, through acts of omission and commission, for letting the system unravel. Trump is accelerating that, though he cannot be faulted for the rise of antidemocratic nationalism in Europe or the return of Asian rivalries. Kagan passionately believes that the only way to beat back the jungle and reverse these dangerous trends is for the United States to recommit itself to lead.'[40]

Nonpolarity, Chaos, and Interdependence

Another group of American scholars has been discussing whether or not we have arrived at a "post-American" world" or a "G-0" world, and there are increasingly few disagreements with the fact that the US is losing its power to influence the development of events across the world. The President of the Council on Foreign Relations and author of the theory of "nonpolarity"[41], Richard Haass, noted in his March 2018 article "Liberal World Order, R.I.P" that the liberal world order is now being threatened not by rogue states, totalitarian regimes, religious fanatics, or "backlash states" (special terms applied by liberals to peoples and countries which do not follow the Western capitalist path of development), but by its main architect itself: the United States of America.[42] Haass writes:

---

40 Zachary Karabell, The Jungle Grows Back: America and Our Imperiled World. By Robert Kagan // Nov. 16, 2018. https://www.nytimes.com/2018/11/16/books/review/robert-kagan-jungle-grows-back.html

41 Richard N. Haass, "The Age of Nonpolarity: What Will Follow U.S. Dominance," Foreign Affairs (May/June 2008).

42 Richard N. Haass, Liberal World Order, R.I.P. // March 21, 2018. https://www.cfr.org/article/liberal-world-order-rip

> Liberalism is in retreat. Democracies are feeling the effects of growing populism. Parties of the political extremes have gained ground in Europe. The vote in the United Kingdom in favor of leaving the EU attested to the loss of elite influence. Even the US is experiencing unprecedented attacks from its own president on the country's media, courts, and law-enforcement institutions. Authoritarian systems, including China, Russia, and Turkey, have become even more top-heavy. Countries such as Hungary and Poland seem uninterested in the fate of their young democracies.[43]

Further, Haass notes that "We are seeing the emergence of regional orders" and adds: "Attempts to build global frameworks are failing." The mention of "regional orders" here is especially important - for this is not "nonpolarity", as Haass proclaimed in 2008, but a sign of multipolarity. Haass' main skepticism is founded on the observation that Washington is indirectly changing the rules of the game without taking into account what its allies, partners, and clients in different corners of the world will do in turn. Haass writes:

> America's decision to abandon the role it has played for more than seven decades thus marks a turning point. The liberal world order cannot survive on its own, because others lack either the interest or the means to sustain it. The result will be a world that is less free, less prosperous, and less peaceful, for Americans and others alike.[44]

The latter statement, however, can be disputed. It is more than likely that the new world order may bring less prosperity to the US, insofar as hitherto this system has been built on the mechanism of patron-client relations, whereas now numerous countries are more independent in their choices of economics priorities and are not considering economic preferences for the US in exchange for security assurances.

In 2013, Haass noted: "The appeal of the American economic model took a major hit from the events of 2008; now we are doing the same to our political model." Further, Haass openly admits, the greatest threat to American national security is posed from within, by the

43 Ibidem.

44 Ibidem.

US' own political dysfunction. "The most important currency for a great power", Haass writes, "is to be reliable and predictable." Yet the US is no longer such and, Haass adds: "Americans are kidding themselves if they think they can insulate themselves from such a world. Globalization will visit us, whether we like it or not, whether we are ready or not."[45]

One of Haass' CFR colleagues, Stewart Patrick, completely agrees with the argument that the US itself is "burying" the international liberal order.[46] But now the US is not doing this alone, but alongside China. If the US had hoped that globalization processes would gradually transform China (and, perhaps, destroy it, as was the case with the USSR), then the result has been far from what America expected. China has undergone modernization without Westernization, as proclaimed earlier by the leader of the Islamic Revolution in Iran, Ayatollah Khomeini. And now China is expanding its influence in Eurasia in a particular manner which, in the majority of cases, is welcoming to countries as partners. These processes are undoubtedly painful for the US whose hegemony progressively, and irreversibly undermines. On this matter, Patrick writes:

> Its [China's] long-term ambition is to dismantle the U.S. alliance system in Asia, replacing it with a more benign (from Beijing's perspective) regional security order in which it enjoys pride of place, and ideally a sphere of influence commensurate with its power. China's Belt and Road initiative is part and parcel of this effort, offering not only (much-needed) infrastructure investments in neighboring countries but also the promise of greater political influence in Southeast, South, and Central Asia. More aggressively, China continues to advance outrageous jurisdictional claims over almost the entirety of the South China Sea, where it continues its island-building activities, as well as engaging in provocative actions against Japan in the East China Sea.

---

45 Richard Haass. The real threat to U.S. national security. 10/7/13. http://www.politico.com/story/2013/10/the-real-threat-to-us-national-security-97938.html

46 Stewart M. Patrick. China and Trump May Bury the Liberal International Order // Defense One, March 25, 2018 https://www.defenseone.com/ideas/2018/03/china-and-trump-threaten-bury-liberal-international-order/146937/?oref=defenseone_today_nl

As for the US:

> The United States, for its part, is a weary titan, no longer willing to bear the burdens of global leadership, either economically or geopolitically. Trump treats alliances as a protection racket, and the world economy as an arena of zero-sum competition. The result is a fraying liberal international order without a champion willing to invest in the system itself.[47]

In 2012, Robert Zoellick also pointed out:

> Because the United States has not faced up to its economic problems at home, its voice on international economics does not carry, its power has waned, and its strategic designs drift with the currents of the day's news. Without healthy economic growth, the United States will be unable to lead. Just as dangerously, it will lose its identity on the global stage if it loses its economic dynamism...[48]

On this point it is rather telling that the former President of the World Bank said precisely the same thing several months after he left his post. Such unpromising trends facing the US were also noted in a RAND Corporation study with the symbolic title "Fiscal Performance and U.S. International Influence", which stated:

> The Unites States today faces a dilemma. A persistently high level of government debt threatens future economic growth and constrains the ability of the government to pursue national interests, both international and domestic. Yet efforts to bring down the debt will further constrain government outlays and action—possibly for many years into the future.[49]

---

47 Stewart M. Patrick. China and Trump May Bury the Liberal International Order // Defense One, March 25, 2018 https://www.defenseone.com/ideas/2018/03/china-and-trump-threaten-bury-liberal-international-order/146937/?oref=defenseone_today_nl

48 Zoellick, Robert, "The Currency of Power," Foreign Policy, November 2012, pp. 67–73.

49 C. Richard Neu, Zhimin Mao, Ian P. Cook. Fiscal Performance and U.S. International Influence, RAND Corporation, 2013. P. 50.

Going through the history of public finance in the US, including the growth of government debt, the interdependence between trade and the dollar, and investments in the US' representation abroad, the authors argue: "Historically, the United States has used its economic strength and influence to play leading and constructive roles in creating, shaping, or sustaining numerous important international institutions, programs, and initiatives." Further, the RAND Corporation's senior economist Richard Neu writes: "The principal basis for U.S. economic power is the simple size of the U.S. economy." As follows, over the process of shrinking the American economy will immediately be rendered incapacitated, especially if we understand this "capacity" to mean the whole complex of administrative, social, political, diplomatic, and military measures which the US has implemented over the past 50 years and presented as the touchstone both within the country and to the outside world.

Immanuel Wallerstein has employed the allegory of the biblical Samson to describe the ongoing situation in the US. In his opinion, the US establishment does not even know what needs to be done, and therefore concludes: "That the temple is crumbling is a reality far beyond our efforts to hold it up, even if we wanted to."[50] In another article on the future collapse of the US, Wallerstein points towards several developments to be expected over the decade:

> Finally, there are two real consequences of which we can be fairly sure in the decade to come. The first is the end of the U.S. dollar as the currency of last resort. When this happens, the United States will have lost a major protection for its national budget and for the cost of its economic operations. The second is the decline, probably a serious decline, in the relative standard of living of U.S. citizens and residents. The political consequences of this latter development are hard to predict in detail but will not be insubstantial.[51]

In his book, *Nation of Devils: Democratic Leadership and the Problem of Obedience*, the Norwegian state functioner with experience in international organizations, Stein Ringer, confirms this outlook from another perspective, quoting: "American politics is no

50 Immanuel Wallerstein. The Samson Complex. 2013-10-20. http://alainet.org/active/68314

51 Immanuel Wallerstein. The World Consequences of US Decline, August 16, 2011. http://www.iwallerstein.com/consequences-decline/

longer characterized by the rule of the median *voter*, if it ever was. Instead, in contemporary America the median *capitalist* rules as both the Democratic and Republic parties adjust their policies to attract monied interests...American politicians are aware of having sunk into a murky bog of moral corruption but are trapped."[52] A summary of this development, similar to Richard Haass' is offered in the following words: "Today, American democratic exceptionalism is defined by a system that is dysfunctional in *all* the conditions that are needed for settlement and loyalty."[53] With regards to other countries who have followed the blueprints of liberalism, Ringer writes:

> Capitalism has collapsed into crisis in an orgy of deregulation. Money is transgressing into politics and undermining democracy itself. Economically destructive distributional injustice is rampant and increasing. Public poverty persists among private affluence. Global financial services exercise monopolistic power over national policies, unchecked by any semblance of global political power. Trust is haemorrhaging. The European Union, the greatest ever experiment in super-national democracy, is imploding. [54]

It is interesting to note that this panic and fear has gripped Western Europe and the US, i.e., the zone of Transatlanticism, while the recipes of liberalism have also been employed in other regions as well, such as in the experience of Singapore and other South-East Asian states. Yet in these places one does not encounter such panicking sentiments as in the West. Perhaps the reason behind this lies in the root differences between cultural types of societies, or in a different type of liberalism different from that of the West?

Another member of the Council on Foreign Relations and specialist on US strategy and foreign policy, Charles Kupchan, believes that the Western order will not be replaced by a new force or dominating political model. The 21st century will not be American, Chinese, Asian, or any other, because there will be no single world. For the first time in history, the world will be interdependent, without a center of gravity or global guardian. The strategy for the West towards the rest of the world that

52 Stein Ringer. Nation of Devils. Democratic Leadership and the Problem of Obedience. Yale University Press, 2013. P. 287, 290.

53 Ibid. P. 318.

54 Ibid. P. 338.

Kupchan proposes is forging a new consensus on legitimacy, sovereignty, and governance.[55] Kupchan's book *No One's World: The West, the Rising Rest, and the Coming Global Turn*, "calls on the American elite to reconsider their foreign policy and to structure in accordance with the changing world, and this in itself indicates some kind of rethinking of unipolarity, its results, and American responsibility for these results."[56]

A similar position is taken by the President of the New America think tank and former Director of Policy Planning of the US State Department from 2009-2011, Anne-Marie Slaughter. In her first major work, *A New World Order*, Slaughter attempted to demonstrate that the conventional nation-state system is no longer effective and that a network principle of interactions is more appropriate for current realities. In Slaughter's opinion, global governance must be exercised by means of a complex global web of "government networks."[57]. Another of Slaughter's works was co-authored with Ikenberry, and in a joint New America report from 2012 dedicated to formulating a new US "Grand Strategy", Slaughter argues that instead of being treated as poles (whether in a unipolar, bipolar, or multipolar system), states should be analyzed as the main knots of intersecting networks. In this view, the capacity of a state to position itself as close as possible to the center of critical networks, and its ability to mobilize, orchestrate, and create networks, is a vitally importance source of power.[58]

Meanwhile, a more skeptical point of view is adhered to by Ian Bremmer and David Gordon, who have forecasted the appearance of a "G-0" world in the wake of the inability of the G-8 and G-20 to lead the world any further.[59]

---

55 Charles A. Kupchan. No One's World. The West, the Rising Rest, and the Coming Global Turn. Oxford University Press, 2012.

56 Sergey Esin, gegemoniya ili mnogopolyarniy mir? Geopolitica.ru, 02.01.2013. https://www.geopolitica.ru/article/liberalnaya-gegemoniya-ili-mnogopolyarnyy-mir

57 Anne-Marie Slaughter, A New World Order, Princeton University Press, 2004.

58 Anne-Marie Slaughter, A Grand Strategy of Network Centrality // Art, Robert J, Peter Feaver, Richard Fontaine, Kristin M. Lord & Anne-Marie Slaughter, America's Path: Grand Strategy for the Next Administration, Center for a New American Security, 2012, P. 45, 46. https://web.archive.org/web/20150923205138/http://www.cnas.org/files/documents/publications/CNAS_AmericasPath_FontaineLord_0.pdf

59 Ian Bremmer and David Gordon, "G-Zero," Foreign Policy, January 7, 2011.

Exit Strategy

Insofar as there are alternative scenarios for the development of events, the current vacuum is gradually beginning to be filled with various political projects which differ in both form and content. At the same time, attention is being paid to appropriate mitigation strategies for handling the negative consequences to which the final collapse of Pax Americana might lead. If in Britain the main, most telling process of recent years has been the attempt to exit the EU, then in the US such attempts, while less noticeable, are underway. The US' European partners are worried that Washington will behave like a "bull in a china shop" or will attempt to use mechanisms which have long since been outmoded and taken out of practice. As Gerard Gallucci has noted in his article:

> But without a political and strategic vision for going beyond that to deal more comprehensively with the many challenges of the 21st Century, America falls back to its default setting relying on a panoply of military and intelligence approaches. This default setting includes direct military intervention on the ground (Afghanistan and Iraq), bombing from the air (Serbia, Libya and now Syria), drones and paramilitary operations (various places), overt and covert support (equipment and training to proxy actors) and massive electronic spying on everyone. When the US doesn't know what else to do but politics seems to require some form of action, the US defaults to its military and intelligence capabilities. This is really not a substitute for actual policy and without fitting into a comprehensive, sustained strategic framework usually makes things worse.[60]

This appraisal, of course, represents a certain extreme. Meanwhile, another perception of a more optimistic nature has been put forth, for example, by Ian Brodie of the Canadian Global Affairs Institute. Brodie believes that since 2008, partially thanks to the US' decline, Canada's role and capabilities have expanded; therefore, Canada should take advantage of the present moment to expand its influence. If before Canada followed the US' current (and such was understood by other countries and translated into a certain preferences - for example, for

---

60 Gerard M. Gallucci, America's default setting// Transconflict, 15 Oct, 2015. http://www.transconflict.com/2015/10/americas-default-setting-150/

the election of a European country to the UN Security Council instead of Canada), then now Canada is free to pursue a "democratic foreign policy."[61] Brodie presents three theses for a future strategy for Canada in these new circumstances:

1. Our privileged geography gives us freedom to choose where and when we engage beyond North America. We have economic and strategic opportunities across both the Atlantic and Pacific…

2. The United States is unlikely to return to the "sole superpower" status it had from 1991 until 2008." Brodie nevertheless recognizes that Canada's prospects are weak without US influence insofar as Canada desires the resolution of the US' internal economic problems. This might suit other countries as well, if Washington pursues an isolationist policy. Yet as far as one can see from here, this will not be the case; rather the US will attempt to continue its current foreign policy line.

3. With America's influence shrinking, new clubs of emerging markets and upper middle income countries are acquiring increasing influence. While Canada's international engagements are not hindered by a history as a colonial power, that fact alone does not make us part of the global south."

Here Brodie insightfully observes that the leaders of the global south are establishing international institutions to project their own possibilities. UNASUR, CELAC, and ALBA in Latin America as well as the Shanghai Cooperation Organization and the Eurasian Union, Brodie notes, "have been struck to blunt the influence of institutions from the world America made." Canada has not been invited to these projects even though these organizations have greater prospects and ambitions than the G-20. The BRICS Bank and the Asian Infrastructure Bank also represent serious players, and insofar as the US has not been up to reforming the IMF or World Bank, new organizations the likes of BRICS have "plenty of room" to "overtake the Bretton Woods institutions in innovation." "Canada", Brodie regrets, "once a dependable 'joiner' of international clubs, is finding itself shut out of the newer, more dynamic institutions."

61 Ian Brodie. After America, Canada's Moment? CDFAI, February 2015. http://www.cgai.ca/after_america_canadas_moment

It can be noted that the matter at hand here is the beginning of the restructuring of international organizations, especially as numerous contemporary structures are losing the trust of an increasing number of countries. Yet it is not only trust that is disappearing, but also competence, hence the situation of a vicious closed circle. It is interesting to note that liberals themselves predicted the decline of their structures responsible for international relations. For instance, in *Foreign Affairs* in 2015, Charles King observed that numerous programs devoted to diplomatic relations, transnational studies, political philosophy, and social disciplines have been closed in the US. It is only natural to expect that new generations of American diplomats will therefore be limited in their ability to perceive complex realities. Meanwhile, numerous "think tanks" have turned out to be mere covers for the implementation of political projects by certain lobbies and even completely alienated from decision making. As Professor Tom Nicholas points out:

> The bigger concern today is that Americans have reached a point where ignorance—at least regarding what is generally considered established knowledge in public policy—is seen as an actual virtue. To reject the advice of experts is to assert autonomy, a way for Americans to demonstrate their independence from nefarious elites—and insulate their increasingly fragile egos from ever being told they're wrong.[62]

Some have been willing to face the truth and admit that:

> the track record of American foreign policy is far from glorious and recent surveys thus reveal entirely sensible reactions to our failures. Instead of wringing its collective hands about the fragility of public support, Washington needs to wake up and start taking public opinion seriously. No one will confuse the average American with a foreign policy expert, but given America's

62 Tom Nichols, How America Lost Faith in Expertise. And Why That's a Giant Problem // Foreign Affairs, March/April 2017. https://www.foreignaffairs.com/articles/united-states/2017-02-13/how-america-lost-faith-expertise?cid=nlc-twofa-20170216&sp_mid=53441291&sp_rid=ZXZyYXppYUBnbWFpbC5jb20S1&spMailingID=53441291&spUserID=MjEwNDg3NDMyODk5S0&spJobID=1102802747&spReportId=MTEwMjgwMjc0NwS2

> history and current situation, public preferences are stable, clear, and prudent. The American public wants a less ambitious and less aggressive foreign policy than the United States has pursued since the end of the Cold War, and especially over the past 18 years. The task for Washington today is to embrace these attitudes and create a new foreign policy worthy of public support.[63]

Even fewer experts offer a solution to the problem. In his article "This Time It's Real: The End of Unipolarity and the Pax Americana", Christopher Layne has proposed a rational and logical conception for a unipolar "exit."[64] Layne sees the "external driver of American decline" to be the "rise of New Great Powers", pointing out:

> American decline is part of a broader trend in international politics: the shift of economic power away from the Euro-Atlantic core to rising great and regional powers (what economists sometimes refer to as the "emerging market" nations). Among the former are China, India, and Russia. The latter category includes Indonesia, Turkey, South Korea, Brazil, and South Africa. In a May 2011 report, the World Bank predicted that six countries - China, India, Brazil, Russia, Indonesia, and South Korea - will account for one-half of the world's economic growth between 2011 and 2025.

Layne also draws constant attention to China, arguing that China has "undercut the claims of unipolar stability theory" and emphasizing that "China is on course to overtake the United States as the world's largest economy...That China is poised to displace the United States as the world's largest economy has more than economic significance. It is significant geopolitically."[65] Recent statistics from the World Bank confirm Layne's forecast. In 2017 global GDP, PPP was constituted by:

---

63 A. Trevor Thrall. Mind the Gap: The Foreign Policy Disconnect between Washington and America, March 18, 2019. https://www.cato.org/blog/mind-gap-foreign-policy-disconnect-between-washington-america

64 Christopher Layne, This Time It's Real: The End of Unipolarity and the Pax Americana // International Studies Quarterly (2012), 3.

65 Ibid. P. 4.

China	23,300,782,88
EU	21,178,392,50
USA	19,390,604,00
India	9,448,658,81
Japan	5,562,821,81
Korea	1,969,105,86

In other words, China has already overtaken the United States. Further taking into consideration the number of other countries and associations currently demonstrating similar economic growth trends, it becomes clear that the US' indices are likely set to fall. Layne observes:

> The United States' mounting economic and fiscal problems - evidenced in summer 2011 by the debt ceiling debacle and Standard & Poors' downgrading of US Treasury bonds - are another [powerful indicator of America's relative decline]. There are two closely interconnected aspects of the United States' domestic difficulties that merit special attention: the spiraling US national debt and deepening doubts about the dollar's future role as the international economy's reserve currency. Between now and 2025, the looming debt and dollar crises almost certainly will compel the United States to retrench strategically, and to begin scaling back its overseas military commitments...America's geopolitical preeminence hinges on the dollar's reserve currency role. If the dollar loses that status, US hegemony will literally be unaffordable."[66] Layne's conclusion is unambiguous: "As the twenty-first century's second decade beings, history and multipolarity are staging a comeback."[67]

The Multipolar Moment

We began this chapter by mentioning Charles Krauthammer, and we shall conclude it with an analysis of his main works directly concerned with unipolarity and multipolarity.

66 Christopher Layne, This Time It's Real: The End of Unipolarity and the Pax Americana // International Studies Quarterly (2012), 3

67 Ibid. P. 6.

In his article, "The Unipolar Moment"[68], which was based on a series of lectures delivered in Washington, D.C. in September 1990, Charles Krauthammer wrote that a new world order was emerging in which the United States would be the only superpower. In the second paragraph of the article, Krauthammer introduced three main theses being discussed in the US political science community at the time: (1) the rise of multipolarity (interestingly enough, he suggests a "diminished Soviet Union/Russia" as one future pole, thus anticipating the collapse of the Soviet Union), (2) weakened consensus on foreign policy within the US, and (3) a diminishing of the threat of war in the post-Soviet era. Krauthammer promptly dismissed these arguments as erroneous, and instead spoke of the coming triumph of a unipolar world under the undisputed dominance of the US and its Western allies. Krauthammer did, however, immediately make one reservation: "No doubt, multipolarity will come in time. In perhaps another generation or so there will be great powers coequal with the United States and the world will, in structure, resemble the pre-World War I era."

Has this moment arrived? For now, let us refrain from making hasty statements, and first analyze on what grounds Krauthammer based his conclusions, where he was right, and where he was mistaken. Such an excursion into the history of geopolitical thought will refresh our memory as to the methods by which Washington operates.

Krauthammer presents the Persian Gulf crisis and Washington's reaction as an example of unwavering US might: "In the gulf, without the United States leading and prodding, bribing and blackmailing, no one would have stirred. Nothing would have been done: no embargo, no 'Desert Shield,' no threat of force." In other words, this was not a multilateral action as it might have seemed, but the exclusive concoction of the US. As Krauthammer writes further on: "It is largely for domestic reasons, therefore, that American political leaders make sure to dress unilateral action in multilateral clothing." This is done, evidently, because American citizens need legitimacy for the sake of their faith in democracy.

Yet here Krauthammer immediately follows up with a question: How long can America maintain its unipolar preeminence? To this end,

68 Charles Krauthammer// Foreign Affairs, Vol. 70, No. 1, America and the World 1990/91 (1990/1991), pp. 23-33. http://www.jstor.org/stable/20044692

light must be shed on theories of decline and imperial overstrain. Here Krauthammer introduces some figures - the United States was then spending 5.4% of GDP on defense, whereas earlier it spent nearly twice as much, and was now planning a reduction to 4% by 1995. However, Krauthammer adds that "American collapse to second-rank status will be not for foreign but for domestic reasons." Let us take note of this.

Considering the balance between US domestic and foreign policy, Krauthammer suggests that it is "a mistake to view America's exertions abroad as nothing but a drain on its economy…America's involvement abroad is in many ways an essential pillar of the American economy. The United States is, like Britain before it, a commercial, maritime, trading nation that needs an open, stable world environment in which to thrive." Later on, he adds that America is interested in maintaining its unipolar status, but questions whether Americans support such.

Here we can see mention of a dichotomy between the interests of the political elite and ordinary American taxpayers. Krauthammer himself notes that American isolationism "seems the logical, God-given foreign policy for the United States" by virtue of geography and the history of America's founding, which is said to be have been motivated by the desire to distance itself from the intrigues and conflicts of the Old World.

Krauthammer also mentions another option, which he calls a far more "sophisticated" and "serious" school of international relations which insists on national interests - realism. In this context, he argues: "International stability is never a given. It is never the norm. When achieved, it is the product of self-conscious action by the great powers, and most particularly of the greatest power, which now and for the foreseeable future is the United States. If America wants stability, it will have to create it. Communism…is quite dead. But there will constantly be new threats disturbing our peace." First and foremost among these threats is posited to be the proliferation of weapons of mass destruction. Also notable are such concepts as "rogue states" and "failed states," although Krauthammer speaks of only one type - "The Weapon State," under which he mentions Iraq, North Korea, and Libya. In his opinion, in order to become a Weapon State, a country only needs to develop its own industry, and then additional interests will arise which might conflict with the interests of other countries. This point is not discussed directly, but it is clear based on the context. Krauthammer writes:

> With the rise of the Weapon State, there is no alternative to confronting, deterring and, if necessary, disarming states that brandish and use weapons of mass destruction. And there is no one to do that but the United States, backed by as many allies as will join the endeavor. The alternative to such robust and difficult interventionism - the alternative to unipolarity - is not a stable, static multipolar world. It is not an eighteenth-century world in which mature powers like Europe, Russia, China, America, and Japan jockey for position in the game of nations. The alternative to unipolarity is chaos.

Thus, Krauthammer recognizes that multipolarity is not only possible, but has historical precedent and, moreover, can help establish static stability (although the role of Japan in the 18th century, and indeed that of America, is up for debate).

Krauthammer's next article on the same topic appeared twelve years later under the title "The Unipolar Moment Revisited."[69] He begins with the same thesis as earlier, asking whether the US will face decline. Krauthammer argues that the third episode of American unipolarity has arrived with the threat of war posed by rogue states acquiring weapons of mass destruction. It is worth noting that this article happened to be released a year after the terrorist attack in New York and just before the invasion of Iraq (which was launched without UN sanction or the support of the US' European partners). Krauthammer writes: "American dominance has not gone unnoticed. During the 1990s, it was mainly China and Russia that denounced unipolarity in their occasional joint communiqués. As the new century dawned it was on everyone's lips. A French foreign minister dubbed the United States not a superpower but a hyperpower." In other words, many countries did not take a liking to American dominance, and this was manifested against the backdrop of the bombing of Serbia and the occupation of Afghanistan, which were something like demonstrative wars at a distance that showed the whole world the new forms of US power.

69 Charles Krauthammer. The Unipolar Moment Revisited// The National Interest—Winter 2002/03. pp. 5-17.

If before the 9/11 terrorist attack many were pondering the possibility of an anti-hegemonic alliance, then afterwards many began offering the US their support, which "accentuated" the "historical anomaly of American unipolarity." This happened by virtue of the "American anti-terrorism ultimatum", which was essentially a mandate for the widespread use of military force by the US. Preventative operations violated traditional doctrines of just war, which led to a crisis of unipolarity. According to Krauthammer, this unipolarity found definitive formulation in the words of Pentagon chief Donald Rumsfeld on Afghanistan and the "War on Terror": "the mission determines the coalition." The mission is determined by the US.

Important here is Krauthammer's admission that so-called multilateralism was merely a means of "liberal internationalism" to keep the US from falling into embarrassing situations in which other countries in disagreement with Washington's position could "isolate" the US and make decisions themselves. If we soberly analyze both the "multilateral" approach of Madeleine Albright during the Bill Clinton administration, as well as the same rhetoric employed by Barack Obama and Hillary Clinton with her "reset", then it is obvious that the "openness" and "interestedness" of the US has been but a cover for imposing its agenda. All of this was pursued, in Krauthammer's words "in service to a larger vision: remaking the international system in the image of domestic civil society", i.e., the American model.

From this standpoint, the nation-state is seen as an anarchic legacy of the past. Thus, Krauthammer explains, it is important for liberals to accelerate the erosion of sovereignty by means of new technologies and the unhindered movement of capital across borders. But America, as the great sovereign, must be "domesticated" by and for liberals who feel "discomfort" with US dominance. This in turn becomes a challenge to unipolarity, as the dominant pole inevitably comes to be diluted through international agreements, interdependences, and new norms.

At this point, Krauthammer briefly summarizes the contention between two schools of international relations - liberalism and realism - with regards to "paper or power", i.e., agreements or threats and the use of force. In passing, Krauthammer reminds the reader of the question of multipolarity and actually contradicts himself. If in his previous article he spoke rather positively of multipolarity as once incarnated and possibly on the rise again, then this time his tone has changed dramatically. He writes: "Multipolarity is inherently fluid and unpredictable. Europe practiced multipolarity for centuries and found it so unstable and bloody, culminating in 1914 in the catastrophic collapse of delicately balanced alliance systems, that Europe sought its permanent abolition in political and economic union. Having abjured multipolarity for the region, it is odd in the extreme to then prefer multipolarity for the world."

Prototypes of multipolarity actually existed in more places than just Europe by the 20th century. Before the arrival of European colonizers in Asia, Africa, and both Americas, similar systems existed which used special mechanisms of checks and balances that differed from European norms. Moreover, European countries developed within the paradigm of rationalism and the Enlightenment, which leaves Krauthammer's argument unconvincing. Krauthammer can be understood, however, if we recognize the author's Western-centric mindset and American political scientists' propensity to justify double standards. Moreover, the nature of this shift can be explained as being in the interests of many countries to develop multipolarity during this period (including not only China and Russia, but also the "left pivot" in Latin America, and the founding of the African Union in July 2002).

Further on, Krauthammer unveils his message: "[the] principal aim is to maintain the stability and relative tranquility of the current international system by enforcing, maintaining and extending the current peace. The form of realism that I am arguing for—call it the new unilateralism—is clear in its determination to self-consciously and confidently deploy American power in pursuit of those global ends." Thus, in contrast to isolationist realism, this approach proposes that the US pursue none other than global objectives in Europe, Asia, Africa, South America, and the world ocean.

But let us recall what actually happened in 2002-2003. NATO officially invited Bulgaria, Latvia, Lithuania, Romania, Slovakia, and Slovenia to join its alliance; the state of Yugoslavia ceased to exist with its partition into Serbia and Montenegro; American troops occupied Afghanistan and Iraq; Israel carried out punitive operations against Palestinians; numerous terrorist attacks took place on Russian and Turkish soil; and a series of color revolutions began in the post-Soviet space following the effective testing of this new type of coup d'etat in Yugoslavia. For Krauthammer, this must all be "stability and relative tranquility." Ironically, this actually might be the case for the US, since all of these events took place with direct or disguised encouragement from Washington and outside of the borders of the United States (except for the terrorist attack of September 11th, 2001, which to this day remains the subject of serious debates). The maintenance of this unipolarity also means the preservation of the post-colonial legacy with its artificial division of the globe into first, second, and third worlds, entailing the merciless exploitation of the natural resources of countries incapable of effectively defending their sovereignty from transnational corporations, predatory policies of the IMF and World Bank and, of course, the US' right to military intervention in other countries under false pretexts. As is well known, the concept of "Responsibility to Protect" was tested in Haiti in 1994 and in Yugoslavia in the early 1990's and in 1999 to detach Kosovo and Metohija.

According to Krauthammer, the US should be "advancing democracy and preserving the peace by acting as balancer of last resort", and "countries will cooperate with us, first, out of their own self-interest and, second, out of the need and desire to cultivate good relations with the world's superpower." In other words, other countries are presented with no real choice.

Although Washington uses both unilateral and multilateral approaches in similar fashion to advance its interests, there is one principal difference between the two which Krauthammer discerns in the form of a question: "What do you do if, at the end of the day, the Security Council refuses to back you?" As we very well know, even after the UN Security Council blocked its resolution on Iraq, the US acted as it saw fit. Even before this entered into force (let us recall that Krauthammer's second article was released several months before the invasion of Iraq in 2003), Krauthammer believed that the unipolar moment had already become the unipolar era.

Thus, the article concludes with the following:

> The new unilateralism argues explicitly and unashamedly for maintaining unipolarity, for sustaining America's unrivaled dominance for the foreseeable future. The future of the unipolar

> era hinges on whether America is governed by those who wish to retain, augment and use unipolarity to advance not just American but global ends, or whether America is governed by those who wish to give it up—either by allowing unipolarity to decay as they retreat to Fortress America, or by passing on the burden by gradually transferring power to multilateral institutions as heirs to American hegemony.

Krauthammer therefore reiterates that unipolarity will be challenged not from without, but from within.

Krauthammer is partially correct that the unipolar regime depended on the US political elite. The lack of clear consensus therein and the ever-increasing gap between the aspirations of the American people and the corporate interests of the establishment which incessantly leans towards globalism, all yielded to the phenomenon of populism and helped Donald Trump win elections with partially isolationist slogans. Krauthammer was incorrect in his panicking over the proliferation of weapons of mass destruction. In the nearly 20 years since, the real balance in this sphere has remained virtually unchanged. Only the DPRK has increased its military-technological capabilities to a level causing panic reactions among US military and political circles. Without a doubt, another important landmark to be distinguished on this note is the decision by Russia's leadership to deploy troops to Syria to help in the fight against terrorism.

The unipolar era never arrived. The unipolar moment unfortunately lasted for nearly two decades, but it was not an era. Krauthammer was right in his first article when he argued that multipolarity would arrive after one generation. Indeed, if we follow the criteria set for challenges facing the US, then according to such documents as the US

National Security Strategy[70] and National Defense Strategy[71], the US now faces competitors in the face of certain powers familiar to us in the

70 National Security Strategy of the United States of America, December 2017. https://www.whitehouse.gov/wp-content/uploads/2017/12/NSS-Final-12-18-2017-0905-1.pdf

71 Summary of the National Defense Strategy. Sharpening the American Military's Competitive Edge. https://www.defense.gov/Portals/1/Documents/pubs/2018-National-Defense-Strategy-Summary.pdf

multipolar declarations of Russia and China. Iran and the DPRK have also openly challenged unipolarity and been assigned by Washington to the club of "rogue states." Over the past few years, additional studies have increasingly suggested that America is losing its status as the global center of power in the face of emerging multipolarity.[72]

Therefore, we can say that Krauthammer was mistaken in saying that unipolarity would be threatened from within the United States. Threats have always come from the outside and, in different conditions, whether embryonic or frozen, have anticipated appropriate opportunities to change national strategies. As a matter of course, a number of countries have seized the first opportunity to escape Washington's control. These cases can be called different things - whether "opportunism", "transitioning to an active anti-colonial stage", "searching for new solutions", or "reactions to the US' actions" - depending on the ideological framework and school of international relations employed.

Now the multipolar moment is happening. In other words, it has been proposed that "America's unipolar moment is over. It began with the breakup of the Soviet Union in December 1991 and ended with the collapse of Lehman Brothers on September 15, 2008."[73] The main task consists in seeing to it that this multipolar moment does not end as quickly American unipolarity, but is transformed into stable multipolarity.

72 See C. Richard Neu, Zhimin Mao, Ian P. Cook. Fiscal Performance and U.S. International Influence, RAND Corporation, 2013; Global Trends 2030: Alternative Worlds, a publication of the National Intelligence Council, December 2012. http://worldview.unc.edu/files/2013/10/Global-Trends-2030-Executive-Summary.pdf; Global Trends to 2035 Geo-politics and international power. European Parliament, September 2017. http://www.europarl.europa.eu/RegData/etudes/STUD/2017/603263/EPRS_STU(2017)603263_EN.pdf; https://www.dni.gov/index.php/global-trends-home

73 Robert J. Art, Selective Engagement in the Era of Austerity // Art, Robert J, Peter Feaver, Richard Fontaine, Kristin
M. Lord & Anne-Marie Slaughter, America's Path: Grand Strategy for the Next Administration, Center for a New American Security, 2012, P. 19. https://web.archive.org/web/20150923205138/http://www.cnas.org/files/documents/publications/CNAS_AmericasPath_FontaineLord_0.pdf

2

Multipolarity in the Context of International Standards

A number of scholars and experts have recognized current geopolitical processes as amounting to none other than the formation of a multipolar model of world order in the political, economic, and social spheres of life-activities. This model itself is multi-layered and interconnected. The emergence of new alliances as well as international platforms and clubs for coordination has served as a catalyst for these processes. It has been noted that integration projects and cooperation between states foreshadow the emergence of a new multipolar system whose foundations are being built in Eurasia and South America.[1] Moreover, it has been emphasized that the new world order will arise out of a counter-positive era between the tendency of unipolarity and the globalization of the West (under the leadership of America) on the one hand, and the Eurasian, multipolar trend on the other.[2]

Perhaps the most difficult aspect of this process is identifying to what extent multipolarity has already become the *modus vivendi* of some countries and regions, and distinguishing just when a multipolar world order will be finally formed. In other words, there are still no clear criteria for multipolarity.

In one of their works, John Arquilla and David Rondfeldt, who are better known among conflict specialists as the theorists of network wars, assert that the contemporary world has already become

1 Pereyra Mele, Carlos Alberto. De la Unipolaridad a la Multipolaridad. 12 de agosto de 2010. http://licpereyramele.blogspot.com/2010/08/de-la-unipolaridad-la-multipolaridad.html

2 Graziani, Tiberio. Geopolitika I mejdunarodnoe pravo v epohu ekspansii zapadnoi civilizatsii na planete. March 2008. http://www.eurasia-rivista.org/cogit_content/editoriali/EkpVuEuVpuuHixNIdd.shtml

multipolar, in which soft power is being evermore applied to manage political processes[3], a notion which they compare to a lighthouse on a rock. Herein the question begs itself: when did multipolarity begin to emerge? Perhaps by distinguishing certain historical points, it will be easier to predict the coming future? Before endeavoring to determine a timeframe for the appearance of multipolarity, however, it is necessary to appeal to the very theory of geopolitical poles.

Poles in the International System

The theory of poles and polarity was first developed by the Western school in political science and is associated with the realist school of international relations. Goedele de Keersmaeker of the Ghent Institute for International Studies argues that the term "multipolar" and multipolarity" begin to appear in "The New York Times" toward the end of the 1960s and the early 1970s. Its introduction is closely related to the foreign policy of the tandem Nixon-Kissinger that started from the view that the world remained militarily bipolar for the time being, but was quickly moving to multipolarity in economic and other fields.[4]

Keersmaeker notes "the poles as a central structuring element of the physical or social reality. When it comes to international relations this suggests the presence of great powers that have a defining role in the structuring of the international systems, in contrast to other states."[5] The briefest characterization of poles in the international political system was offered by the American political scientist Richard Rosecrance in 1963: "Multipolar, bipolar, and unipolar international systems may be distinguished as follows: multipolarity is a multi-bloc or actor system; bipolarity is a two-bloc or actor system; unipolarity requires in addition a single directorate of the preponderant bloc."[6]

Indicatively, Rosecrance speaks not about one state or two states, but

3 Arquilla, John; Ronfeldt, David. Networks and Netwars: The Future of Terror, Crime, and Militancy. Santa Monica: RAND, 2001.

4 Goedele De Keersmaeker, Polarity, Balance of Power and International Relations Theory: Post-Cold War and the 19th Century Compared. Springer, 2017, P. 14.

5 Ibid, P. 16.

6 Richard Rosecrance. Action and Reaction in World Politics: International Systems in Perspective. Praeger: 1963, P. 234.

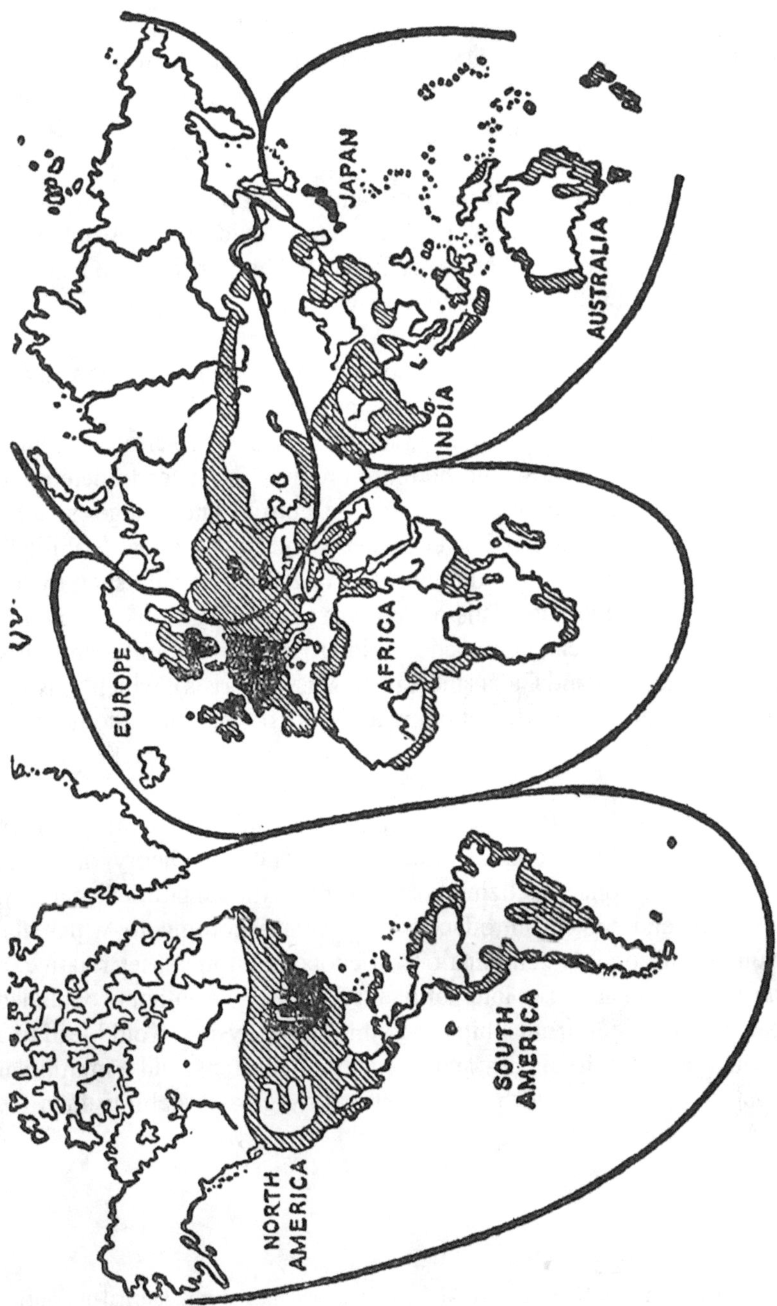

Pan-regions of Karl Haushofer: Pan-America, EuroAfrica, Pan-Russia and the Asian zone of prosperity.

uses the term "bloc" or "actor", which expands the category of a pole. In this regard, his theory is seen as close to the ideas of the German geopolitical school, such as those of Carl Schmitt and Karl Haushofer, who spoke of geopolitical "great spaces."

Rosecrance also believed that any future multipolar moment would be a window of opportunity in which states would finally abandon the struggle for power, would be satisfied with their positions, and engage in more meaningful international governance.[7]

Karl Deutsch and David Singer also examined multipolarity as a means for encouraging major players to engage in greater cooperation.[8] The argument in this case is that, given an absence of serious disputes between states, there would be more grounds for states to determine their respective common interests. Deutsch and Singer's joint publication, "Multipolar Power Systems and International Stability", was published in 1964 in the journal *World Politics* published by the John Hopkins Institute. This period was marked by crisis in both the Soviet and American approaches to international relations, especially concerning Asia and Cuba (the Cuban Missile Crisis), which thus led a number of scholars to attempt to forecast potential international situations.

On the basis of L. Richardson's concept of political stability, which analyzes the likelihood of war, R. Dahrendorf's theory of social conflict, and conceptualizing potential international political stability, Deutsch and Singer introduced a formula according to which the number of possible combinations of cooperation increases relative to an increase in actors in international relations. The authors concluded that the transition from a bipolar to multipolar system would lead to a reduction in the frequency and intensity of conflicts, and a multipolar system in itself would be characterized by greater stability than the bipolar model.

---

7 Rosecrance, R.N. Bipolarity, Multipolarity, and the Future// Journal of Conflict Resolution, 1966. 10/3, pp. 314-327.

8 Deutsch, K.W. & Singer, D. Multipolar Power Systems and International Stability// World Politics, 1964, 16/3, pp. 390-406.

Nuclear, Cluster and (Un)Balanced Multipolarity

Furthermore, the notion of poles and balance of forces evolved in the context of nuclear deterrence. Kenneth Waltz proceeded from the fact that states are rational actors predisposed to minimize risks. Nuclear states at odds with each other will behave extremely cautiously insofar as they understand that the cost of conflict might be too great. In Waltz's opinion, states with small nuclear capacities can successfully apply a strategy of deterrence in regards to much more powerful nuclear powers. In this regard, Waltz sees no point in excessive and costly build-ups of nuclear arsenals, instead advocating minimally sufficient deterrent potential: "More is not better if it is enough to have fewer." The pacifying effect of nuclear weapons lies in that the strategic importance of territory dramatically decreases with the appearance of nuclear potential. Before, conquering territory was considered to be an important measure in creating a "security buffer" around a state. Now, when missiles with nuclear warheads have become the main guarantor of security, the incentives to expand territorial boundaries have been weakened, thus removing one of the main historical causes of war.[9]

The idea of rational choice was expanded upon by the international relations theorists Bruce Bueno de Mesquita and David Lalman, who noted that if foreign policy decisions are conceptualized from the perspective of realist or domestic policy, then this influences how we understand choosing foreign policy goals and the role of state politicians. These two perspectives differ from one another in their supporters' assumptions and proposals regarding the role of the unitary actor. The realists presume the existence of a strong unitary actor who makes decisions on the basis of the balance of forces and other strategic interests established by virtue of the state's position in the international order. From the standpoint of domestic policy, it is assumed that the unitary actor will be weaker. Bueno de Mesquita and Lalman explain that similar to the unitary actor in realism, the domestic unitary actor is responsible for choosing strategic actions necessary for realizing society's goals to the extent of its abilities. Unlike the realist unitary actor, the domestic unitary actor does not purport to define the goals of foreign policy. These goals arise from internal political processes.[10]

---

9 Lukin A. Yadernoe rasprostranenie: zlo ili blago?//Geopolitika №4, 2010.

10 Bruce Bueno de Mesquita and David Lalman, War and Reason: Domestic and International Imperatives (New Haven, CT: Yale University Press, 1992. P. 17.

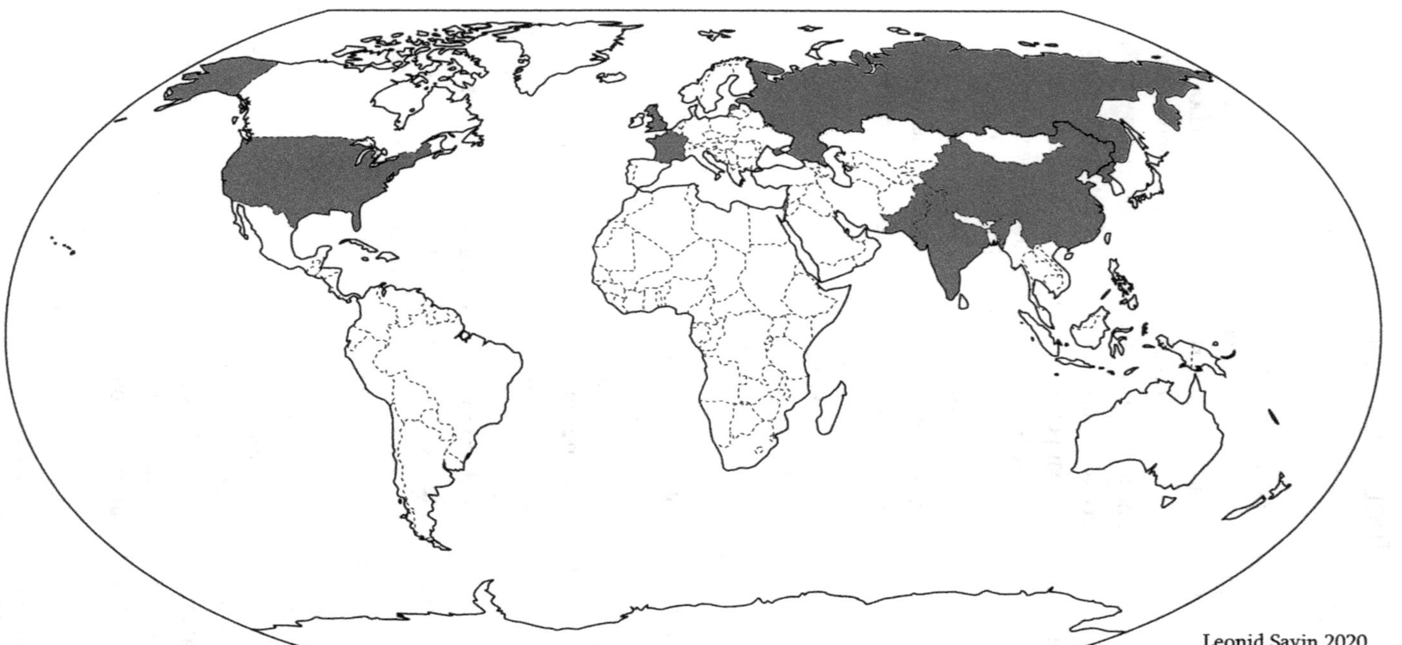

Nuclear multipolarity: the club includes the USA, Russia, Great Britain, France, Israel, China, India, Pakistan and North Korea. All states possessing nuclear weapons, with the exception of the United States, are located in Eurasia.

In the opinion of the above-mentioned authors, the logic of the theory of rational deterrence lends preference to waiting as opposed to attacking as long as the defending side boasts endurance for a second strike, an adequate warning system, and a command center for its nuclear forces which can function after a strike and ensure a rapid, retaliatory strike against the attacker. Under these conditions, in which the instigator cannot devise a war plan guaranteeing an unpunished first strike, the defending side has the advantage, with deterrence presuming it can withstand the tension during crisis.

The professor of political science and author of numerous works on security issues, control over nuclear weapons and missile defense, Stephen Cimbala, has expressed certain concerns over nuclear multipolarity. Cimbala suggests that unlike during the Cold War, a multipolar world of competing regional nuclear powers could create an unmanageable stress-test testing the hypotheses built on realism or rational deterrence.[11] This statement proposes to reassess theories of political realism, although Cimbala himself figures among the supporters of a rigid hierarchy of power. He remarks: "International politics is a game of oligopoly, in which the few rule the many."[12]

In addition to nuclear multipolarity, a number of scholars are of the opinion that the emergence of a multipolar political world order is inevitable after a certain period of time. Brian Healy and Arthur Stein of the Center for International Studies at Cornell University stated in 1973 that "the emergence of China has already been hailed as creating a "triangular" or "tripolar" relationship. Japan, Western Europe, and India will soon extend that tripolarity to quintipolarity or sextipolarity. Oddly enough, therefore, the future may be not unlike the nineteenth-century past."[13]

---

11 Stephen J. Cimbala, Nuclear Weapons in a Multipolar World, New York: Routledge, 2016, P. 129.

12 Stephen J. Cimbala, Nuclear Proliferation in the Twenty-First Century: Realism, Rationality, or Uncertainty? Strategic Studies Quarterly, Spring 2017, P. 132.

13 Healy B., Stein A. The Balance of Power in International History// Journal of Conflict Resolution, Vol. 17 No. 1, March 1973, P. 34. http://www.grandstrategy.net/Articles-pdf/The_Balance_of_Power_in_Intl_History.pdf

In the mid 1980's, Frank Wayman introduced the concept of "cluster multipolarity." Wayman pointed out: "A system is power multipolar when capabilities are more evenly distributed than in the power bipolar condition, and when hostility is still high….A system is cluster multipolar when the states are more evenly distributed throughout the space, with many opportunities for intermediaries and many crosscutting loyalties to moderate hostility…Power bipolarity and power multipolarity are mutually exclusive categories."[14]

It should be noted, however, that Wayman considered bipolarity and multipolarity in the context of European politics and the possibility of a military conflict repeating in the future. Thus, this polarization is consciously understood as something negative, where power poles are inevitably predisposed towards fierce competition with one another. The possibility of conflict in one form or another between two neighboring states can therefore never be ruled out, as was particularly true following the coup d'etat in Ukraine in 2014 and the developments that subsequently engulfed the Middle East and North Africa starting in 2011. Insofar as a shift in the geopolitical balance inevitably entails the emergence of a power vacuum, it is better to anticipate potential scenarios and plan for strategic decisions beforehand.

John Mearsheimer has proposed two models of multipolarity. "The configuration of power that generates the most fear," Mearsheimer writes, "is a multipolar system that contains a potential hegemony - what I call 'unbalanced multipolarity."[15] Multipolar systems without a potential hegemony, i.e., "balanced multipolarity" according to Mearsheimer, is "likely to have power asymmetries among their members, although these asymmetries will not be as pronounced as the gaps created by the presence of an aspiring hegemon. Therefore, balanced multipolarity is likely to generate less fear than unbalanced multipolarity, but more fear than bipolarity."[16]

---

14 Wayman, Frank. Bipolarity and War: The Role of Capability Concentration and Alliance Patterns among Major Powers, 1816-1965 // Journal of Peace Research, Vol. 21, No, 1. 1984, P. 62.

15 Mearsheimer J. J. The Tragedy of Great Power Politics. New York: W.W. Norton & Company, Inc., 2014. P. 44.

16 Ibid. 45.

In this very context in 2012, Amitai Etzioni wrote that "there are few signs of significant contributions to the international order from the "new powers,"[17] This automatically means increased potential for conflict. Even though a certain inertia will continue for some time, "one might conclude that all major world players agree that the international system is becoming multipolar or is already, if it were not for some American academics who continue to claim that the world is unipolar and will remain so for some time."[18]

Indeed, a number of foreign authors have undertaken attempts to develop the notion of an overlap between bipolar and multipolar systems.[19] The Russian geopolitician Alexander Dugin has suggested that "a pole in a multipolar world, like this world itself, should be stable, i.e., it must represent a result of strategic integration."[20] In other words, this means a military, political, economic, geographical, and civilizational entity encompassing regional states with their own interests unified under a single umbrella pole. Such an approach is close to the ideas of Carl Schmitt and Richard Rosecrance. In tandem with this, however, one also needs to consider Alexander Dugin's proposal for a Fourth Political Theory which rejects not only the principles of liberal political theory, but also the two opposing ideologies of the 20th century, Marxism and Fascism (National-Socialism).

On the other hand, some countries, by virtue of their particular national cultures and geographical positions, have already claimed for themselves the role of an independent pole, albeit light in geopolitical weight, relevant position, and potential. For example, Professor Terumasa Nakanishi of Kyoto University believes that the only option for Japan in the course of the overarching transition from a world

17 Etzioni A. The Myth of Multipolarity.// The National Interest, October 5, 2012. http://nationalinterest.org/commentary/the-myth-multipolarity-7500

18 Goedele De Keersmaeker. Multipolar Myths and Unipolar Fantasies// Security Policy Brief, No. 60, February 2015. P. 1.

19 Burns, A.L. From Balance to Deterrence: A theoretical Anaysis.// World Politics, vol. IX, 1957, pp. 494-529; Zoppo, C. E. Nuclear Technology, Multipolarity, and International Stability. // World Politics, vol. XVIII, 1957, pp. 579-606; Rosecrance R. Bipolarity, Multipolarity, and Future. // Journal of Conflict Resolution, vol. X, 1966.

20 Dugin A.G. Teoriya mnolopolyarnogo mira. Pluriversum. Moscow: Academic project, 2015. P. 262.

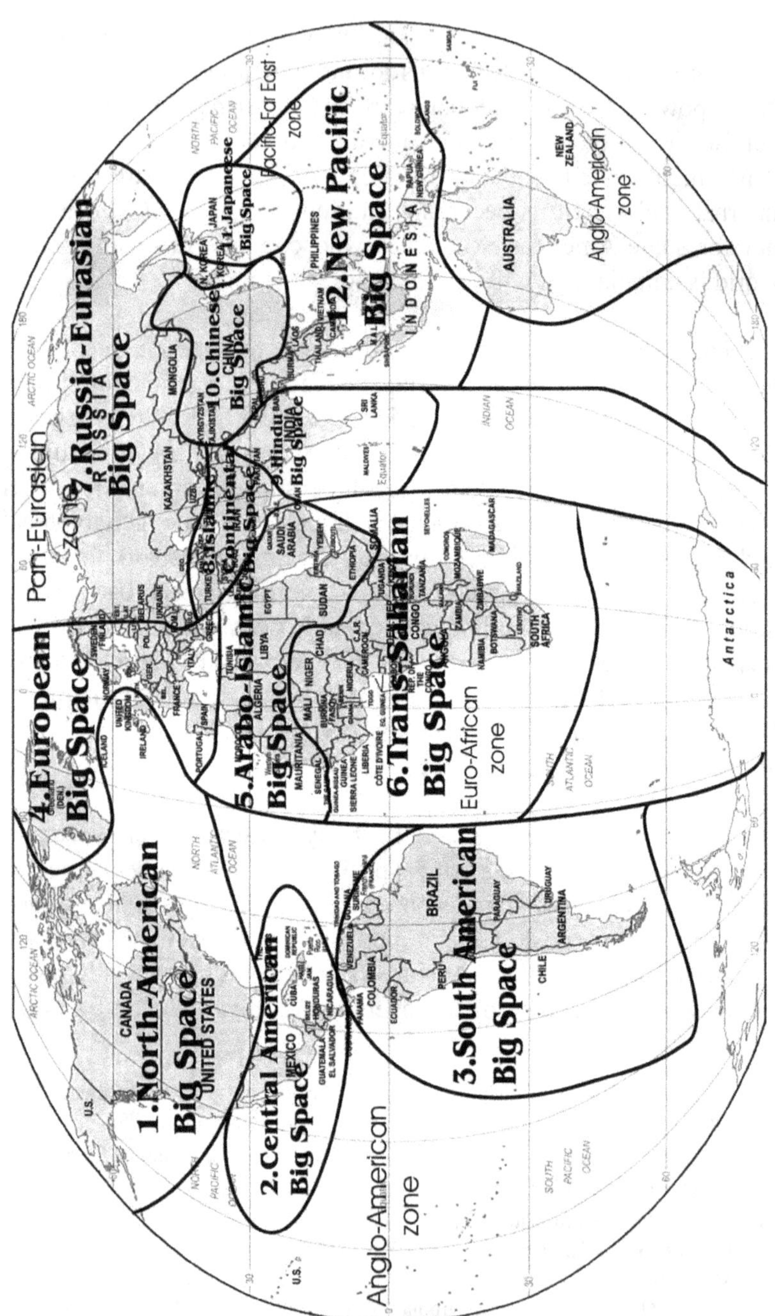

A model of a multipolar world with four zones and twelve big spaces, proposed by Alexander Dugin (2002). As can be seen in the map, some "big spaces" are conditional and coincide with the borders of states (India and Japan).

order dominated by the US towards multipolarity is "becoming a pole."[21] Although this claim might seem to be a bit naive given Japan's own limited sovereignty, Nakanishi's opinion should be heard out precisely because of the particular quality of the Japanese people's national mentality. The term "national" does not quite explain complex phenomenon insofar as it is associated with the Western European philosophical school of Modernity, and it would be more correct to speak of different countries' "strategic culture", but we shall discuss this below.

Finally, there could also exist a pole consisting of a mosaic of spaces lacking common borders.[22] For example only Russia and China, and China and India have common borders in BRICS, while in the Eurasian Economic Union, Armenia does not share a border with the union's other participants.

Hegemony, Balance of Power, and Transition Theory

As we can see, many neo-realists in the paradigm of international relations consider multipolarity to be a source of potential instability and danger that will ultimately lead other subjects to attempt to balance the power of the hegemon through the use of hard or soft power. At the same time, some scholars argue that well-structured hierarchy guarantees peace and stability. Moreover, most of them concur that in the final count, the transfer of power to competitors and weakened policy will undermine the superiority of the hegemon and trigger the growth of other powers in opposition to it. These arguments refer us to several more concepts directly related to multipolarity.

First of all, the question begs itself: how will the transition from one actor (or group) to another be realized? In the broadest sense, power transition theory - once again - is related to the realist approach in international

21 Aurelia George Mulgan. Japan's choices in a multipolar world// East Asia Forum, 6 February 2009. http://www.egmontinstitute.be/wp-content/uploads/2015/02/SPB60-.pdf

22 Savin L.V. Eksterritorialnost i dinamika geopoliticheskih polyusov // Leviathan, № 4, 2012. P. 67.

relations.[23] It is believed that this theory was developed at the beginning of the Cold War by the Professor of Political Science at the University of Michigan, Abramo Organski (an immigrant from Italy).

This theory is predicated on the conviction that the power of a state (which Organski originally defined as the rate of state GDP per capita) defines the role of a given state in the global arena.[24] The result is a hierarchic international system with an uneven balance of power. Those who have the greatest might are distinguished as dominant powers and exercise enormous influence on the international system as a whole. During the Cold War, there were two such dominant forces - the USSR and USA. It is important to note that, according to Organski, there exists a difference between a "Great Power" and dominant powers. Power transition theory denotes great powers as those countries experiencing rapid growth rates even despite the fact that their absolute power might remain less than that of a dominant state. When a great power, based on its rapid growth, is dissatisfied with the existing balance of power established by the dominant power, then it will search for a new outlet in the international system.[25]

Interestingly enough in this vein, in the 1960's Organski proposed that the USA ally itself with the Soviet Union in order to contain China. In his opinion, the fact that both the USSR and the People's Republic of China adhered to Communist ideology at the time would not hinder this move. However, the Nixon-Kissinger duo bet on China.

Power transition theory has been used in the West as a framework for evaluating democratic reforms and liberalization in different countries. It is no coincidence that after the collapse of the Soviet Union, the states of the Warsaw Pact were called "transitional democracies." Some of them were successfully drawn into the Western system via EU and NATO integration, while others (the post-Soviet space) continued to be targets of the West's synergetic foreign policy strategy. Balance of power theory, on the other hand, is related to classical

---

23 Amee Patel, Davidson College. The End of the Unipolar International Order? Implications of the Recent Thaw in
Sino-Indian Relations // Greater China, Winter 2006, P. 14.

24 Organski, AFK. World Politics. New York, 1958.

25 Douglas Lemke,"The Continuation of History: Power Transition Theory and the End of the Cold War," Journal of Peace Research, vol. 34, no. 1 (1997), 24.

international relations and was originally put forth by Kenneth Waltz, who advocated nuclear multipolarity. This theory's main thesis is that alliances are considered by great powers to be a means for deterring the expansionism of a dominant power.

Waltz advocated the establishment of a multipolar system in which great powers, sometimes in the form of coalitions, would counter-balance a dominant power. Both theories - power transition theory and balance of power theory - are recognized as offering valuable insights into the dynamic and static characteristics of nation-states.[26] But there are some differences. Power transition theory focuses on the dynamic nature of power shifts and asserts that alliances cannot withstand constant fluctuations of power, whereas balance of power theory concentrates on static analysis which assumes that alliances serve some kind of constant which aids great powers in counter-balancing the power of a hegemon.[27] Dicocco and Levi wrote: "Organski rejected balance of power theory, according to which equality of opportunity between opponents aids peace, and instead asserted that such a condition most likely leads to war."[28]

Hegemony is the next term directly associated with both balance of power and theories of political polarity. The term "hegemony" is often used as a synonym for "empire" or "leadership," and therefore is in need of clarification. We find the first mention of hegemony in the works of the Ancient Greek historian and Peloponnesian War veteran Thucydides, who described the regional rivalry between Athens and Sparta who both drew their allies and neighboring peoples into the war.[29] However, the most famous definition comes from the works of the Italian Marxist Antonio Gramsci, as expressed in his *Prison Notebooks*.[30]

---

26 Michael Mastanduno,"Preserving the Unipolar Moment: Realist theories and U.S. Grand Strategy after the Cold War," International Security, vol. 21, no. 4 (Spring 1997), 54.

27 Michael Mastanduno,"Preserving the Unipolar Moment: Realist theories and U.S. Grand Strategy after the Cold War," International Security, vol. 21, no. 4 (Spring 1997), 56.

28 Jonathan DiCocco and Jack Levy,"Power Shifts and Problem Shifts: e Evolution of the Power Transition Research Program," e Journal of Conflict Resolution, vol. 43, no. 6 (December 1999), 681.

29 Thucydidus. Hystory. Moscow: Academic project, 2012.

30 Gramsci, Antonio. Quaderni del carcere. 4 vols. Torino: Einaudi, 1975.

A social class, Gramsci claimed, acts hegemonically when it attempts to create a new order and forms a universal ideology which subordinates the interests of subjugated classes to its interests, or when it presents and affirms its interests as the interests of all of society. Hegemony is understood as the capacity of a hegemon to make subordinated classes believe that power is based on the consensus of the majority. Hegemony, therefore, is a form of dominance which refrains from the use of force.

Another, albeit less famous but similar concept of hegemony was proposed by the German jurist and philosopher Heinrich Triepel, who devoted one of his works to the subject of hegemony. Triepel believed hegemony to be a form of power situated on the mezzanine level of the continuum between simple influence and dominance.[31] Unlike dominance, hegemony does not resort to coercion, but is rather a form of power constructed on tameness characterizing the high degree of self-restraint on the part of a hegemon. Triepel believed hegemony to be a particular kind of leadership, but he emphasized that, in international relations, allegiance to a hegemon is not based on "joyous devotion", as in the field of social relations, but rather on the calculations of weaker states and their recognition of their own weakness.

Also of interest are Triepel's reflections on types of hegemony, which he distinguishes as "allogenic", "endogenous", and "heterogenous." Heterogenous hegemony is always more difficult than endogenous hegemony, especially if heterogeneity is matched with national and religious allogenesis. Austrian hegemony in Italy was perceived as foreign domination, and when Italian national feelings had developed, its fate was sealed. Meanwhile, Austrian hegemony in Germany was extremely adversely affected by the fact that the German element in the Habsburg Empire increasingly took a back-seat to other ethnic groups to the point that Austria was considered to be only a semi-German state. In addition, Triepel spoke of "egoistic" and "altruistic" hegemony, and pointed out that both motives are usually mixed, thus rendering cases in which one is completely absent rare. Thus, the only question is which comes to the fore. In blocs consisting of two states under pluralistic hegemony, egoistic or "egocentric" motives are predominant. In federated hegemons, egoism and altruism are approximately balanced so that the community can work not only on itself, but on everyone.

31 Triepel, Heinrich. Die Hegemonie. Ein Buch von führenden Staaten. Stuttgart: Kohlhammer, 1938. P. 140.

However, the altruism of a hegemon never reaches the point of sacrificing itself. Under no circumstances does a state commit to such.

Overall, Gramsci and Triepel are united by the fact that both authors emphasized values, methods of persuasion, and cultural influence in the broadest sense of the word, not corcive decisions on the part of a hegemonic actor.

William Robinson has pointed to four types of hegemony in the context of historical evolution and the global capitalist system: (1) hegemony as international domination, which is tied to the realist school; (2) state hegemony which relates to inter-state relations and the power of core states; (3) hegemony as rivalry between historical blocs in a given political order (particularity of the social structure of accumulation); and (4) consensual domination or ideological hegemony.[32] A state capable of combining all four positions can achieve the status of undisputed hegemon.[33] In an historical context, Giovanni Arrighi in his work *The Long Twentieth Century: Money, Power, and the Origins of Our Times*, points to three hegemons which replaced each other: the Dutch hegemon (from 1588 to 1713), the British hegemon (from 1713 to 1921), and the American hegemon (from 1921 to the present). Here we should remark that Eugene Wittkopf, in his research related to power transition theory discussed above, relied on George Modelski's Seapower Concentration Index.[34] Modelski, for his part, based his ideas on those of the founder of world-systems analysis, Fernand Braudel, and Braudel's notion of *longue durée* ("long time") was developed to show the integrity of large socio-cultural formations, i.e., civilizations. Cyclical time was used to show the rises and drops in significant processes bearing economic and political consequences.

According to Mearsheimer, "a hegemon is a state that is so powerful that it dominates all the other states in the system."[35] Marsheimer also notes that "states that achieve regional hegemony seek to

32 Robinson, William I. Gramsci and Globalisation: From Nation-State to Transnational Hegemony// Critical Review of International Social and Political Philosophy 8, no. 4, 2005, P. 1–16.

33 Savin L.V. O nekotorih aspektah kontrgegemonii // Leviathan № 5, 2013. P. 81.

34 Wittkopf, Eugene R. (1997). World Politics: Trend and Transformation. New York: St. Martin's Press.

35 Ibid. 40.

prevent great powers in other regions from duplicating their feat... Thus the United States, for example, played a key role in preventing imperial Japan, Wilhelmine Germany, Nazi Germany, and the Soviet Union from gaining regional supremacy."[36] A review of the relevant literature suggests that hegemony is characterized by six fundamental dimensions:

[Hegemony] is a situation of (1) great material asymmetry in favour of one state —the hegemon—who has (2) enough military power to systematically defeat any potential contester in the system, (3) controls the access to rough materials, natural resources, capital and markets, (4) has competitive advantages in the production of value-added goods, (5) generates an accepted ideology reflecting this status quo, and (6) is functionally differentiated from other states in the system, being expected to provide certain public goods—such as security or commercial and financial stability. This definition is consistent amongst renowned authors from different subfields and backgrounds that directly theorized about hegemonic relations and is also used by most IR scholars that employ the concept.[37]

Based on these provisions, we see that: (1) multipolarity and balance of power (and power transfer) are correlated; (2) hegemony reflects the idea of power being transferred from one global pole to another; and (3) the hegemony of one pole can be challenged by another pole (or poles).

Indicatively enough, in the 20th century, American hegemony was opposed by two attempts - that of Nazi Germany and the Soviet Union. Both counter-projects turned out to be unsuccessful. This competition is consistent with Alexander Dugin's concept of the Fourth Political Theory. Liberalism as the First Political Theory shifts the hegemonic pole from Britain to the USA, while the Second Political Theory based on Marxism establishes a pole with the Russian Empire, transformed into the Soviet Union, as its base.

---

36 Ibid. 41.

37 Luis L Schenoni, Subsystemic Unipolarities? Power Distribution and State Behaviour in South America and Southern Africa" in Strategic Analysis, 41(1):84-85. 2017. https://www.academia.edu/30528886/_Subsystemic_Unipolarities_Power_Distribution_and_State_Behaviour_in_South_America_and_Southern_Africa_in_Strategic_Analysis_41_1_74-86

The US did not recognize the USSR for a long time[38] precisely because of the ideological threat such posed to its leadership. The Soviet project, which also appealed to freedom and the struggle against oppression, posed real competition to the liberal type of rights and freedoms. The Third Political Theory in the face of National-Socialism and fascism arose as a reaction to Marxism and Liberalism. Both the second and third hegemonies, however, arose and ceased to exist in the 20th century even though their ideas and techniques are partially kept alive in various countries.

According to the Argentine geopolitician Carlos Alberto Pereira Mele, hegemony was realized in the 20th century thanks to the Trilateral Commission, which insisted on a neo-liberal order and marginalized Europe. These actions were also fairly harshly felt in Latin America, leading to resistance on the part of certain states (the most vivid representatives of whom were the leaders of national movements, such as Castro, Torres, Vargas, Velasco, Alvadaro, Peron), and later incited reaction and the transformation of the continent expressed in the creation of regional blocs - UNASUR, MERCOSUR, CELAC, ALBA.[39]

It is obvious that the US is presently losing its hegemony, having ceased to be the only pole, the lonely superpower.[40] However, the question arises as to what will replace the existing order. If we follow Western theories of international relations, then it can be assumed on the basis of GDP, defense spending growth, and other factors taken into account in the index of geopolitical might, that China will be the next global hegemon. Indeed, this state's economic growth, especially its financial-credit policies towards other countries and infrastructural projects in Eurasia, Africa, and Latin America, have demonstrated significant successes over the past decade. China is forecasted to have increased influence by virtue of its unobtrusive expansion and economic instruments which, unlike the IMF and World Bank, do not entail political strings attached for client countries. However, such a

38 Diplomatic recognition came in 1933 largely due to the Great Depression in the US and Japanese expansion in the Far East. Washington's about-face in regards to Moscow was therefore stipulated first and foremost by domestic problems and the US national and geopolitical interests.

39 Savin L.V. O nekotorih aspektah kontrgegemonii // Leviathan № 5, 2013. P. 82.

40 Samuel P. Huntington, "The Lonely Superpower," Foreign Affairs 78, no. 2 (March/April 1999)

theory reflects an exclusively Western approach entailing numerous theories of international relations and their surrogates. The Chinese leadership, meanwhile, adheres to its own doctrine of peaceful coexistence.

Amitav Acharya argues that the liberal international order is de facto tied to hegemonic order, both being the products of the US or the West under the leadership of the US. At the same time, the constant aspiration for both diversity and hegemony creates a fundamental tension within the liberal international order, thereby leading to the loss of hegemonic positions.[41] Robert Keohane's model of "liberal economic arrangements"[42] thus turns out to be insolvent, as regional integration projects based in neo-functionalism gradually collapse the dictatorship of liberal hegemony.

Those who challenge the US are called "anti-hegemonists" and are divided into "substantialists" and "accidentalists." The first group calls into question the very existence of the hegemonic system and proposes different models for cooperation between nations. The second group consists of those players which, although having experienced difficulties in cooperating with various elements of the hegemonic system, do not call this system into doubt.[43] According to this principle, the scale of anti-hegemonic forces can be composed by pointing to the interrelations between countries.

Together with this, additional, alternative scenarios are possible with regards to newly emerging countries.

Interestingly enough in this vein, the political-economy professor Mick Moore from the Institute of Development Research (UK) believes that political power is different in different places and includes something

41 Amitav Acharya, Hegemony and Diversity in the 'Liberal International Order': Theory and Reality // Jan 14, 2020, https://www.e-ir.info/2020/01/14/hegemony-and-diversity-in-the-liberal-international-order-theory-and-reality/

42 Robert Keohane, After Hegemony: Cooperation and Discord in the World Political Economy, Princeton: Princeton University Press, 1984.

43 Sanaei M. O strategii I taktike vneshnei politiki IRI (v regionalnom kontekste)/ Iran v usloviyah novih geopoliticheskih realiy (к 40-letiyu Islamskoi revolyutsii). Moscow: Sadra, 2019. p. 135.

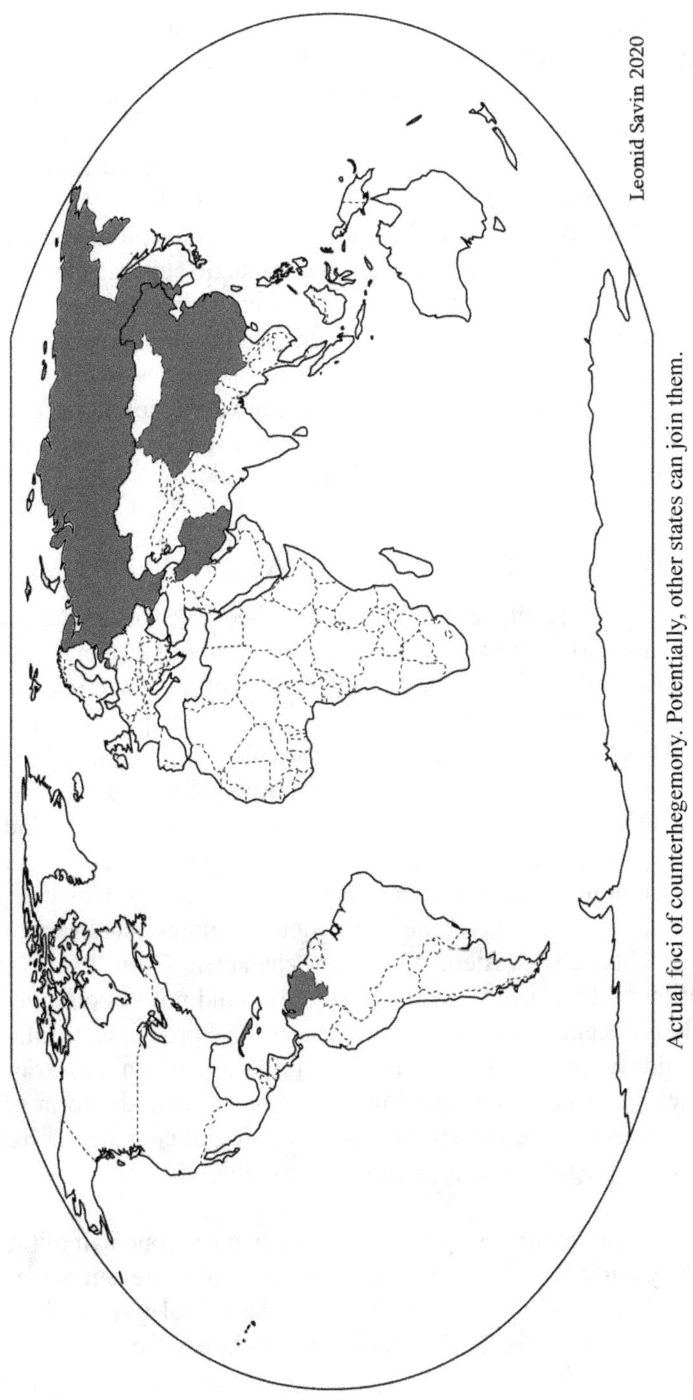

Actual foci of counterhegemony. Potentially, other states can join them.

more than simply the state, with patterns of political power being more complex and differentiated. This heterodox notion, along with others, undermines the monopoly of the classical Western school of international relations in its most familiar formats. Taking into account individual regional processes (such as the implementation of integration projects - UNASUR, MERCOSUR, CELAC, ALBA - underway in Latin America, and ASEAN in the Pacific region) and the religious aspects and attitudes of countries' strategic cultures directly influencing political decisions, we can see that emerging multipolarity is much broader, deeper, and interconnected than the mere presence of potential poles and balance of power in Western theories of political realism. This opens up opportunities for innovative solutions and authentic methodologies which can be applied in certain regions with complete disregard for liberal political ideology.

The Historical Inception of Multipolarity

Despite the debates of recent years, the theories and strategies of transitioning to a multipolar world order possess a number of objective preconditions and have boasted periods of increased interest from the international community of politicians and experts. Before the First World War, there existed a certain balance of power which is sometimes considered to have been a prototype of multipolarity. A number of authors refer to an experience of multipolarity in the period between the First and Second World Wars when the political regimes of liberalism, communism, and fascism existed simultaneously. However, it is necessary to mention that the international regimes existing then bore an exclusively Western European character. Even Russia's participation in the concert of European powers did not smooth over the clearly Eurocentric approach to resolving global problems. Insofar as the majority of Asian, African, and Latin American countries were directly dependent on their European hegemons in the form of various empires or were former colonies, speaking of genuine, global multipolarity in regards to this period is impossible.

Precursors to real multipolarity appeared only in the second half of the 20th century. First and foremost, it is necessary to note the emergence of the Non-Aligned Movement within the bipolar global system which was officially established by 25 states at the Belgrade Conference in September 1961. The movement's establishment was preceded by the

Bandung Conference in 1955 and the trilateral consultations between Josip Broz Tito, Gamal Abdel Nasser, and Jawaharlal Nehru in 1956. The founding principle of this organization was non-participation in military blocs, primarily NATO and the Warsaw Pact but also the Baghdad Pact, CEATO, and ANZUS. At the present moment, this international organization consists of 119 states and holds conferences every three to four years.[44] Today, this movement could also afford powerful support for the international strategy of multipolarity, as was noted in the Russian-Chinese Joint Declaration on a Multipolar World on April 23rd, 1997[45] and has been pointed out in various studies.[46]

In addition to this movement, it is also necessary to mention the Organization of Solidarity with the People of Asia, Africa and Latin America (Organización de Solidaridad con los Pueblos de Asia, Africa y América Latina, OSPAAAL[47]), which was founded in January 1966 in Havana following a conference between the three continents and meetings between politicians from Guinea, Congo, South Africa, Vietnam, Syria, the DPRK, the PLO, Cuba, Puerto Rico, Chile, and the Dominican Republic. Given the political orientation of the organizers, OSPAAAL has a certain ideological commitment and can rightfully be called an international left movement prone to revisionism and a lack of rigid dogmatism. In recent times, the movement has internally attached great importance to various international projects in the likes of ALBA and UNASUR as well as to analyzing various mechanisms initiated by Washington ranging from ALCA to USAID projects.[48] In the context of attempts by the US and a number of Western European countries to reformat their presence in Asian, African, and Latin American countries - which have been condemned as neo-colonial

44 Perhaps the fact that the Arab Spring and numerous conflicts have affected states involved in the Non-Aligned Movement, such as Egypt, Tunisia, Libya, Syria, Bahrain, Ivory Coast, Sudan, and Iran, is indirectly related to attempts to reduce this organization's weight in the global arena. The last conference was held in July 2019 in Azerbajan.

45 Russian-Chinese Joint Declaration about multipolar world and new emerging order// Diplomatic Vestnil. 1997. № 5. P. 19-21.

46 Caragea, Anton. The Non-Aligned Movement: A Chance for a Multipolar World. September 28,2009. http://inthesenewtimes.com/2009/09/30/the-non-aligned-movement-a-chance-for-a-multipolar-world/

47 http://www.ospaaal.com/

48 Calloni S. Guerra preventiva sin fronteras y terrorismo de Estado Mundial.// Tricontinental Magazine №170/2011. P. 11.

ambitions - OSPAAAL could also play a significant role in developing new rules for international relations.

South-East Asian countries prefer to speak not of national associations, but regional groups. In this perspective, the Association of Southeast Asian Nations (ASEAN) might act as an independent center of power. This alliance was founded in 1967 and includes ten states in the region. In turn, ASEAN was preceded by the Association of Southeast Asia (ASA) established in 1961 consisting of the Philippines, Malaysia, and Thailand. ASEAN's goals are:

- To accelerate the economic growth, social progress and cultural development in the region through joint endeavours in the spirit of equality and partnership in order to strengthen the foundation for a prosperous and peaceful community of Southeast Asian Nations;
- To promote regional peace and stability through abiding respect for justice and the rule of law in the relationship among countries of the region and adherence to the principles of the United Nations Charter;
- To maintain close and beneficial cooperation with existing international and regional organisations with similar aims and purposes, and explore all avenues for even closer cooperation among themselves.[49]

It is significant that ASEAN's representatives actively employ the concept of multipolarity in their discursive practice. ASEAN's strategy for work with partners, known as the ASEAN Plus Three Process including Asia-Pacific Economic Cooperation (APEC), the Asia-Europe Meeting (ASEM) and Asia Cooperation Dialogue (ACD), was released in November 2003 and says: "ASEAN admitted India, China and Russia as dialogue partners in a strategic move to secure the peace and security of the region in the Post Cold War era whether multi-polarity became the new reality of politics."[50] Thailand's Minister of Foreign Affairs noted in 2012: "As the world will increasingly become more multipolar

49 http://asean.org/asean/about-asean/

50 ASEAN's Strategy Towards Its Dialogue Partners and ASEAN Plus Three Process, by S. Pushpanathan
http://asean.org/?static_post=asean-s-strategy-towards-its-dialogue-partners-and-asean-plus-three-process-by-s-pushpanathan

in nature, ASEAN must remain in the driving seat of the ARF process so as to ensure its effectiveness and relevance to our region."[51]

On May 23rd, 2014, the Secretary General of ASEAN said during his speech in Tokyo: "The growing strength and multi-polarity of the globalized world also suggests ASEAN's engagement should widen beyond its current engagement with its dialogue partners. This new environment may favor an expanded economic engagement with other regions of the world, besides a deepening and broadening of the current arrangements with China, India and other East Asian countries."[52] What's more, at the ASEAN + India summit in 1998, the Indian side stated that "ASEAN and India also share the belief that multipolarity and democratisation, regionally and globally, are the best guarantees for peace, security and stability."[53]

China for its part has repeatedly expressed its conviction that it is on board with the course towards multipolarity.[54] What's more, the Sochi Declaration of May 20th, 2016 dedicated to the 20th anniversary of partnership between ASEAN and Russia identified "a growing trend towards multipolarity."[55]

---

51 Opening Statement of His Excellency Mr. Prachuab Chaiyasan Minister of Foreign Affairs of Thailand, July 3rd, 2012
http://asean.org/?static_post=opening-statement-of-his-excellency-mr-prachuab-chaiyasan-minister-of-foreign-affairs-of-thailand

52 Speech by H.E. Le Luong Minh Secretary-General of ASEAN at the Nikkei - 20th International Conference on the Future of Asia 23 May 2014, Tokyo "ASEAN in the Next 20 Years".
http://www.asean.org/storage/images/resources/Speech/SG/2014/23%20May%202014_Speech_%20Nikkei%20%2020th%20International%20Conference%20on%20the%20Future%20of%20Asia_ASEAN%20in%20the%20Next%2020%20Years.pdf

53 Statement by Deputy Chairman Planning Commission of India Jaswant Singh on the Occasion of the ASEAN 31st Post Ministerial Conferences PMC 9+1) Plenary Session July 29, 1998 Manila
http://asean.org/?static_post=statement-by-deputy-chairman-planning-commission-of-india-jaswant-singh-on-the-occasion-of-the-asean-31st-post-ministerial-conferences-pmc-91-plenary-session-july-29-1998-manila-2

54 Opening Statement By H.E. Mr. Qian Qichen Vice Premier and Minister of Foreign Affairs of China
http://asean.org/?static_post=opening-statement-by-he-mr-qian-qichen-vice-premier-and-minister-of-foreign-affairs-of-china

55 Sochi Declaration of the ASEAN-Russian Federation Commemorative Summit

The potential of Africa and Latin America should also be remembered. The African Union established in 2002 is the successor of the Union of African States created in the 1960's on the initiative of the President of Ghana, Kwame Nkrumah, the Organization of African Unity founded on May 25th, 1964, as well as the African Economic Community which started working in 1991. For Africa, however, the "search for an original, unique path is fraught with difficulties: breaking with the West threatens economic collapse, while the maintaining of ties with Western capital leads to new rounds of dependency. However, the majority of people in Tropical Africa understand the need to turn to the heritage of their own culture and to the rebirth of 'suppressed identities.'"[56] As has already been noted, several continental integration projects are also ongoing in parallel in Latin America.

Crises as a Catalyst for Multipolarity

Many Western scholars have noted that the US' unilateral aggression against Iraq largely contributed to a rethinking of international processes as well as the legitimization and institutionalization of ideas of multipolarity. There exist differing analyses of these events ranging from the use of force to ideology. For example, an Asian Times columnist criticizing the US' actions in the Middle East remarked:"The real enemy is neo-liberalism. The war on Iraq is part of a push to make the world safe for neo-liberalism. This war is a self-destructive cancer growing inside US neo-imperialism."[57] Immanual Wallerstein, for instance, although he does see the Iraq campaign as a serious mistake on the part of the Bush Administration, sees more serious reasons behind the decline of American might linked to the shifting structure of the world-system.[58] On the other hand, Clifford

to Mark the 20th Anniversary of ASEAN-Russian Federation Dialogue Partnership "Moving Towards a Strategic Partnership for Mutual Benefit". http://www.asean.org/storage/2016/05/Sochi-Declaration-of-the-ASEAN-Russia-Commemorative-Summit-Final.pdf

56 Moseiko A.N. Rol' traditsionnogo substrata civilizatsii Tropicheskoy Afriki i formirovanie samobitnoi paradigmi razvitiya regiona // Afrika v usloviyah smeni paradigmi mirovogo razvitiya. Moscow.: Institut Afriki RAN, 2011. p. 77.

57 Liu H. The war that may end the age of superpower. Asian Times. April 5, 2003. http://www.atimes.com/atimes/Middle_East/ED05Ak01.html

58 Wallerstein I. Precipitate Decline: The Advent of Multipolarity.//Harvard International Review. Spring 2007. pp. 54-59.

Kiracofe Jr., a former member of the US Senate Committee on Foreign Relations, shifts the blame for the US' distorted foreign policy course on to George Bush and his entourage.[59] In his opinion, the Bush Administration's mistake was that American superiority in leading international affairs was violated. Moreover, one of the most famous authorities in the field of international relations and diplomacy, John Bassett Moore, says that "American statesmen sought to regulate the relations of nations by law, not only as a measure for the protection of the weak against the strong, but also as the only means of assuring the peace of the world."[60] Bush employed the Nazi German concept of Machtpolitik which led to an imbalance of forces on a global scale.

In Kiracofe's opinion, it is necessary to restore earlier American perspectives in the spirit of the constructive, non-imperialist foreign policy tradition best embodied by President John Quincy Adams. Such a restoration would include a study of the positive relations that were developed with India, China, Russia, Japan, and the Middle East over the course of the 18th and 19th centuries, when the United States rather comfortably acted in a multipolar and multicultural international community.

Paul van Hooft associates multipolarity with the implementation of the US' Grand Strategy, including the interventions in Iraq and Afghanistan, pointing out that:

> The cumulative effect of these developments suggests that American grand strategy can now be best characterised as selective engagement or partial primacy, underlining that the US has definitely moved away from collective security / liberal internationalism...The consequences for Europe of multipolarity and the resulting shift towards a US grand strategy of selective engagement are varied, and in turn will impact the fundaments of the multilateral order. A unifying Europe has clearly not become a challenger to American unipolarity, nor have the intra-European rivalries reignited as realism predicted.. The

59 Kiracofe, Clifford A. Jr. The U.S.A. Confronts a Multipolar World. EIR-sponsored seminar in Berlin, Germany, Jan. 12, 2005. https://larouchepub.com/other/2005/site_packages/jan12-13_berlin/050112_berlin_kiracofe.html

60 Moore, John Bassett. American Diplomacy. NY: Harper and Brothers, 1905, pp. 251-252.

> pressures of multipolarity, together with the significant trend of re-nationalisation, is likely to push the global order towards an unstable hybrid of multi-tiered and region-centric arrangements.[61]

Thus, it turns out that the US itself initiated the establishment of multipolarity through the implementation of its Grand Strategy, perhaps without suspecting or desiring such.

In an interview with a French TV channel in February 2003, Vladimir Putin commented on the Iraq crisis, stating: "If we want the world to be more predictable, more forecastable, and this means more safe, then the world should be multipolar and all participants of the international community should adhere to certain laws, particularly the norms of international law."[62] By the time of the second invasion of Iraq, however, two more events had taken place which gave significant impetus to reassessing the view of global convergence and mondialism, i.e., the doctrine of a unipolar world in one form or another. These were the crisis in East Asia, which in 1998 came to affect Russia and the CIS countries as well, and NATO's aggression against Yugoslavia in the spring of 1999. Parallel to this, Washington imposed its financial policies on Third World countries through the World Bank and IMF, which allowed many state leaders to see a glimpse of the future, in rather gloomy terms, if the world moved in the direction of neoliberalism. What's more, the global financial crisis of 2007 once again underscored the dead-end nature of the global neoliberal model. On the eve of the Big Twenty summit in Seoul, an article in *The Guardian* noted that the crisis had shattered the West's ideological dominance.[63] Meanwhile, the US had retained certain influence based on military might while other countries were still far from establishing parity. According to the article's author, Pierre Baler, only one way out is left for the US:

---

61 Paul van Hooft. Multipolarity, Multilateralism, and Strategic Competition. Conference: 08/12 Annual GREEN-GEM Doctoral Summer School, At Shanghai, China. August 2012. https://www.researchgate.net/publication/266260303_Multipolarity_Multilateralism_and_Strategic_Competition

62 Interview TF-1, 11 Feb. 2003. http://kremlin.ru/events/president/transcripts/21869

63 Pierre Buhler. The weary US titan and a new multipolar order. guardian.co.uk. 2 November 2010. http://www.guardian.co.uk/commentisfree/cifamerica/2010/nov/02/us-america-economic-leadership

summoning new creative resources capable of coping with systemic failure. This systemic breakdown, as was noted, is largely linked to financial speculation and the US' parasitic economy which threatens the whole world and "keeps globalization afloat."[64]

Although the US is trying to "reset" its relations with both longtime partners such as the EU and countries such as Russia, China, India, and others, Washington's program of promoting liberal democracy no longer works as effectively as before; access to cheap natural resources is becoming more difficult; and new, rising centers of power are increasingly strongly asserting their political positions tied to their cultural identity. Thus, the question is one of civilizational identity, which cannot be uniform nor universal.

Undoubtedly, globalization itself represents a kind of challenge which has compelled both industrial, developed countries, and states earlier belonging to the Second and Third Worlds to reassess their state development and foreign policy strategies. It is no coincidence that a study conducted under the auspices of the Carnegie Foundation on the EU and India noted the following:

> As the tectonic drifts of the twenty-first century shift global power from West to East, from North to South, from the Atlantic to the Pacific region, as so-called nontraditional security threats ranging from terrorism to climate change and energy dependency increasingly dominate risk assessments, and as globalization and technological progress stress the growing importance of soft power vis-à-vis exclusive reliance on hard power, both the EU and India are trying to define their roles in an emerging multipolar world.[65]

This genuine sign of equality between the Old World and a former colony displays a shift in ideological paradigm involving the familiarization of a new type of thinking. As Thierry de Montbrial has remarked in linking the concept of multipolarity with diversity and globality, recognizing the world as multipolar entails a number of

64 Jalife-Rahme, Alfredo. Bajo la Lupa. La parasitaria economía de EU amenaza a la humanidad.//La Jornada. 7 de agosto de 2011. http://www.jornada.unam.mx/2011/08/07/opinion/018o1pol

65 Bernd von Muenchow-Pohl, India and Europe in a Multipolar World. Carnegie Endowment for International Peace, 2012. P. 10.

serious conceptual consequences.[66] The elements of this new doctrine for international cooperation still demand serious development in a number of venues - in diplomacy, science, and culture - and harmonization by means of broad discussion among the international expert community.

The West's Reaction to Multipolarity

Without a doubt, the overwhelming majority of the liberal-capitalist camp remain skeptical towards any possibility of multipolarity insofar as it rejects (in theory and practice) the US' indisputable reign. In his article, "The Emergence of a Multipolar World"[67], David Kampf points out how American intellectuals and politicians have forecasted certain trends and reacted to changing circumstances:

> 1987: In *The Rise and Fall of the Great Powers*[68], Yale University historian Paul Kennedy predicts the balance of military power will shift over the coming 20 to 30 years, creating a truly multipolar world by around 2009. 'If the patterns of history are any guide, the multipolar economic balance will begin to shift the military balances,' he later tells the New York Times.
>
> December 25, 1991: The Soviet Union ceases to exist, eliminating the second Cold War 'pole' and launching a debate about the new world order. 'Global politics,' Samuel Huntington argues later in *Foreign Affairs,* 'is now passing through one or two uni-multipolar decades before it enters a truly multipolar 21st century.'
>
> April 23, 1997: Fear of U.S. unipolarity inspires China and Russia to sign a 'Joint Declaration on a Multipolar World and the Establishment of a New International Order' in Moscow.

66 Monbrial de, Thiery. Mir stal mnogopolyarnim, raznorodnim, globalnim// Mejdunarodnie processi. Issue 7. N. 3 (21), 2009. http://www.intertrends.ru/twenty-first/006.htm

67 Kampf, David. The Emergence of a Multipolar World.// Foreign Policy. Oct. 20, 2009. http://foreignpolicyblogs.com/2009/10/20/the-emergence-of-a-multipolar-world/

68 Kennedy, Paul. The Rise and Fall of the Great Powers: Economic Change and Military Conflict From 1500 to 2000. New York: Vintage Books, 1987.

February 2, 2000: Secretary of State Madeleine Albright, who earlier dubbed the United States the 'indispensable nation,' claims the U.S. is not looking to 'establish and enforce' a unipolar world. Economic integration, she says, has already created 'the kind of world that might even be called 'multipolar.'[69]'

January 26, 2007: A New York Times editorial describes the 'emergence of a multipolar world,' with China taking 'a parallel place at the table along with other centers of power, like Brussels or Tokyo.'

November 20, 2008: In its 'Global Trends 2025' report, the U.S. National Intelligence Council declares the advent of a 'global multipolar system' as one of the world's 'relative certainties' within two decades.

2009: U.S. President Barack Obama takes office with what many deem a multipolar worldview, prioritizing rising powers such as Brazil, China, India, and Russia. 'We will lead by inducing greater cooperation among a greater number of actors and reducing competition, tilting the balance away from a multipolar world and toward a multipartner world,' Secretary of State Hillary Clinton says in a July address.

July 22, 2009: 'We are trying to build a multipolar world,' U.S. Vice President Joseph Biden declares in a speech in Ukraine."

In *Foreign Affairs* in 1999, Samuel Huntington also pointed out that after one or two decades the world would enter "a truly multipolar 21st century."[70] We might also add that in 2007, when the world heard Vladimir Putin's famous Munich speech, the Western press was flooded with publications on multipolarity. The estimates and forecasts were different, but all of them noted the trend of the US' decline in the role of global hegemon. For instance, an article in *The Guardian* remarked:

---

69 Savin L.V. Predposilki mnogopolyarnogo mirovogo poryadka // Geopolitika №12, 2011. P.41-51.

70 Huntington, Samuel. The Lonely Superpower //Foreign Affairs, March/April 1999.

> Around these three poles - Europe, India and South America - it would be possible to galvanise a new global democratic sentiment that rejects unipolarist assumptions without being antagonistic towards the US. The end of American primacy is coming, whether Washington likes it or not. The choice is between a bipolar system in which it faces an authoritarian and increasingly confident China, or a multipolar order in which it can share the challenges of global leadership with other centres of democratic power. The shift from unipolarity to a democratic multipolarity should be our common project of the 21st century.[71]

In addition, various studies have been conducted on the structure of the new world order, a number of which have been authored by European think tanks.[72] For example, in 2007 the London-based Centre for European Reform developed seven recommendations for further action in the context of emerging multipolarity: (1) In the economic sphere, reforms must be introduced aimed at increasing competition and developing new schemes for working with migrants, and the energy and service markets should be liberalized; (2) The EU should lead the international community on the issue of climate change by implementing environmental technologies in developing countries, and convince the US to join this global system, a new model for which might be established in 2012; (3) The EU should continue to expand, incorporate Muslim countries, first and foremost Turkey, which would allow the EU to be more influential; (4) Common programs on security policy and international affairs should be strengthened; (5) Cooperation should be improved in the field of law and internal affairs to fight terrorism and organized crime by combining existing services into a single agency; (6) The EU should support international law and update the organization of global governance, a priority of which should be creating a uranium bank under the supervision of the IAEA to be processed into fuel and eliminating enrichment cycles in other countries; and (7) The EU should engage in constructive cooperation with other global forces, including non-democratic regimes, while giving clear preference to relations with the US.[73] As history has

71 Clark, David. Like it or not, the US will have to accept a multipolar world. The Guardian, 16 February 2007. http://www.guardian.co.uk/commentisfree/2007/feb/16/comment.usa

72 See two publications in the Geopolitika №12, 2011.

73 Grant, Charles. Preparing for the multipolar world: European foreign and

shown, not a single one of these points was successfully implemented. Only some of them have been partially implemented.

In purporting an increased role played by non-state actors, the famous political scientist James Rosenau characterized this era of geopolitical turbulence as a collapse of the global system into state-centric and multi-centric components.

Close to this model is Dale Walton's concept of Revolution in Strategic Perspective, which holds that the present situation in international relations is a transition period tied to a changing geopolitical map of the world with a degree of unpredictability surrounding actors' behavior. Revolution in strategic perspective is concerned with the radical change of views on politics, the last such revolution being that of the great geographical discoveries of the 16th century, after which began the post-Colombian era that ended in the 20th century.[74]

NATO Allied Command Transformation's strategic analyst, Maurizio Geri, has put forth the hypothesis that "in the longer view [this] could also open space for the world actors to build new alliances independently and alternative to the US hegemony, for a global balance of power like during the Cold War, this time with China and his allies." Furthermore: "So what we are witnessing with the new populism, nationalism and 'conflictism' of Trump, it is not only a political, economic and cultural shift, it is also an ideological and paradigmatic one: from cooperation we are passing to conflict as a legitimate tool of international relations, similar to the economic-materialist concept of Marx and Schumpeter of 'creative destruction'. The creators are destroying what they created in order to be reborn as new leaders in the future chaos."[75]

The joyful notes on multipolarity sometimes sounded by American politicians of a liberal persuasion can be somewhat misleading. It is

---

security policy in 2020. Centre for European Reform. London. 2007. P. 5-8. http://www.cer.org.uk/pdf/e783_18dec07.pdf

74 Dale Walton. Geopolitics and the Great Powers in the Twenty-first Century: Multipolarity and Revolution in Strategic Perspective. Routledge, 2009.

75 Maurizio Geri, The End of Pax Americana or a New Realignment? Feb 26, 2017. http://www.e-ir.info/2017/02/26/the-end-of-pax-americana-or-a-new-realignment/

necessary to clearly distinguish what is borne in mind. For instance, it has been noted that "optimists see a smooth evolutionary transition from unipolarity to multipolarity, as the great powers, old and new, find ways to build and jointly manage a new global architecture that preserves the essential features of the existing liberal order. For them, multipolarity implies multilateralism."[76]

Other alternative theories also possess a clearly Western-centric character and essentially represent yet another edition of neo-colonialism. The model ascribed to Oran Young, who proposes his own description of the simultaneous influence of global and regional power processes imbued with elements of continuity and discontinuity[77], is consistent with the ideas of the military strategist Thomas Barnett on the "the Functioning Core" and "Non-integrating gap" from which, in his opinion, spring threats to the homogenized and interconnected Western world. Immanuel Wallerstein's world-system idea is analogous in this regard, as is the critical school of geopolitics which appeals to democratic values and collective decision-making and which, upon more detailed analysis, represents a reduction of liberalism with the values of the Enlightenment epoch at its core - secularism, individualism, and epistemological racism.

Of course, the main schools and theories of international relations - realism, constructivism, liberalism, and Marxism - are all rooted in the Western-centric scientific paradigm and, as follows, if we begin to deconstruct them, then we find many inappropriate motives with respect to international relations. For example, how can the formula of the "democratic majority" be considered in international voting? Is India identical to the tiny state of Luxembourg? How does this explain a number of nations in which the vast majority of people are followers of this or that religion, while the Westphalian system with its secular foundation is a necessary element of international relations? It is quite clear that questions of relations between states or alliances do not fit into existing bourgeois theories of international relations, something which sends the Western community, if not into panic, then into skepticism regarding the future world order.

---

76 Randall Schweller, Emerging Powers in an Age of Disorder, Global Governance 17 (2011), 285.

77 Young Oran R. Political Discontinuities in the International System. // World Politics, vol. XX, 1968, pp. 369-392.

On this note, modern integration processes in Latin American countries, the inter-continental model in the likes of BRICS, the Eurasian Economic Union, the operations of the Shanghai Cooperation Organization, the Chinese One Belt One Road project, and other similar initiatives have been harshly criticized by the Western community. Meanwhile, they harmoniously fit into strategies of establishing a new world order on the basis of the geopolitics of Great Spaces as proposed by Carl Schmitt, and also lend to the development of an alternative political theory. In parallel to this, blame is put on developing countries for putting state power over international rules and sovereignty above the principle of multilateralism. By virtue of this, it has been claimed that the transition to a new order is more likely to be characterized by hostility and competition rather than cooperation.[78] In this context, we would like to point out certain modern Western political scientists' deliberate distortions or misunderstanding of the teachings of classical liberalism.

As Noam Chomsky has aptly noted, current apologists for this ideology merely quote the beginning of Adam Smith's book, *The Wealth of Nations*, where it speaks of the benefits of competition and free markets. Practically no liberal apologists reach the point which discusses the necessity of uniform starting conditions.[79] If we look at those consistent theorists and practitioners of the free market, then we see a recognition on their part of coming multipolarity. The article "Managing in a Multipolar World"[80] published in 2012 and written by several authors who are partners of Booz & Company analyzes the unprecedented disruption of the functioning of markets over the past 10 years as traditionally successful and iconic American and European companies have begun to give way to the rapidly growing markets of developing countries. The authors point out that these events have created a multipolar world which is moving at different speeds and represents a wider spectrum of requirements for success than the global markets' norms of past years, when there was one or several

78 See article in The Financial Times: http://www.ft.com/cms/s/0daca7cc-0955-11e0-ada6-00144feabdc0,Authorised=false.html?_i_location=http%3A%2F%2Fwww.ft.com%2Fcms%2Fs%2F0%2F0daca7cc-0955-11e0-ada6-00144feabdc0.html&_i_referer=http%3A%2F%2Finosmi.ru%2Fworld%2F20101217%2F165002339.html#axzz18MWoPzPb

79 Chomsky N. Class Warfare. Monroe: Common, Courage Press, 1996.

80 Paolo Pigorini, Ashok Divakaran, and Ariel Fleichman. Managing in a Multipolar World. May 7, 2012. http://www.strategy-business.com/article/00112?pg=all

centers of power and influence. No universal answer exists to the question of how to manage markets and lead global business, although there are three interrelated imperatives. These are the necessity of balancing organizational structure and operating models, more dispersed decision-making mechanisms, and personnel management emphasizing diversity and local talent.

Indeed, some economists consider multipolarity to be an alternative financial system. For example, amidst discussion on financial, credit, and monetary management, former French President Nicolas Sarkozy asserted: "We must then consider the suitability of an international monetary system dominated by a single currency in a now-multipolar world."[81] Multipolarity is thus considered to be a process of redressing injustice as well as simply a process of global economic transition.[82]

However, the most commonly-held belief among opponents of multipolarity is that multipolarity will be more conducive to war than bipolarity or unipolarity.

Mearsheimer in turn argues:

> War is more likely in multipolarity than bipolarity for three reasons. First, there are more opportunities for war, because there are more potential conflict dyads in a multipolar system. Second, imbalances of power are more commonplace in a multipolar world, and thus great powers are more likely to have the capability to win a war, making deterrence more difficult and war more likely. Third, the potential for miscalculation is greater in multipolarity: states might think they have the capability to coerce or conquer another state when, in fact, they do not.[83]

This rationale is primarily based on citing several historical examples. Let us look at just what precisely such a perception is tied to. One opponent of multipolarity writes:

---

81 Sarkozy, N. 18th Ambassador's Conference. 25 August, 2010. www.franceonu.org/spip.php?article5123.

82 Daniel Fiott. The EU's Normative Power in a Multipolar World// EUSA Biennial Conference 2011, Boston, United States P. 4.

83 Mearsheimer J. J. The Tragedy of Great Power Politics. New York: W.W. Norton & Company, Inc., 2014. P. 338.

At the beginning of the 17th century, the multi-polar European order was swept away by the Thirty Years War, a conflict that lasted from 1618 to 1648 and was triggered by religious, territorial and dynastic disputes over the internal politics and balance of power among various Christian groups and principalities. The conflict involved the Holy Roman Empire of the Hapsburgs, German Protestant princes, the foreign powers of France, Sweden, Denmark, England and the United Provinces and was ended by the Peace of Westphalia, which introduced the concept of state sovereignty and gave rise to the modern international system of states. This system of states was challenged by the expansion of the Napoleonic Empire at the beginning of the 19th century. After the defeat of the Emperor, in 1815 the great powers held the Congress of Vienna to re-establish the previous state order and formulated the Concert of Europe as a mechanism to enforce their decisions. The Concert of Europe was composed by the Quadruple Alliance of Russia, Prussia, Austria and Great Britain and was aimed to achieve a balance of power in Europe, preserving the territorial status quo, protecting legitimate governments and containing France after decades of war. The Concert of Europe was one of the few historical examples of stable multi-polarity: the regular meetings of the great powers assured decades of peace and stability in the continent. The Concert of Europe suppressed uprisings for constitutional governments in Italy and Spain, secured the independence of Greece and Belgium but did not prevent the Crimean War in 1853 and a return to great power rivalry.

During the 20th century multi-polar international systems resulted in instability and led to two world wars in less than 50 years. The balance of power and the system of alliances of the early 20th century was swept away by the assassination of Franz Ferdinand of Austria in 1914. That event triggered World War I, a global conflict that caused the death of more than 15 million people in less than five years. After a few decades, the multi-polar world had emerged after World War I with a new system of alliances and the multilateral body of the League of Nations was not able to tame the totalitarian aspirations of Hitler. The German invasion of Poland in 1939 triggered World War II, the deadliest conflict in history which resulted in millions of deaths and in the holocaust. Since the end of the World War II the world has never

> been multi-polar again, nevertheless these historical accounts seem to indicate how multi-polarity often created an unstable and unpredictable world, characterized by shifting alliances and by the aspiration of the rising powers to change the balance of power and create a new order.[84]

Here we can see several misconceptions regarding multipolarity. First of all, in terms of historical analysis, the subject at hand is the European theater. Yet many actors had their own colonies outside of Europe. Accordingly, this was but a limited multipolarity, and the players in this system controlled the majority of territory beyond Europe, as a result of which conflicts of interests frequently arose. After the second half of the 20th century, the situation changed dramatically and the world now features a much greater number of independent and nominally sovereign states.

A similar mistake was committed by Mearsheimer in his attempt to equate a multipolar system to the actions of states or coalitions in Europe in the Modern era. In his opinion, the 18th to 20th centuries saw a succession of seven periods:

1. Napoleonic era I, 1792-93 (1 year), balanced multipolarity;
2. Napoleonic era II, 1793-1815 (22 years), unbalanced multipolarity;
3. Nineteenth century, 1815-1902 (88 years), balanced multipolarity;
4. Kaiserreich era, 1903-18 (16 years), unbalanced multipolarity;
5. Interwar years, 1919-38 (20 years), balanced multipolarity;
6. Nazi era, 1939-45 (6 years), unbalanced multipolarity; and
7. Cold War, 1945-90 (46 years), bipolarity.[85]

But this point of view is rather narrow in its approach and cannot be taken as a reliable account, especially since China, India, and Pakistan have developed nuclear arms.

Secondly, the above-mentioned "concert" coincided with nationalism's

---

84 Andrea Edoardo Varisco. Towards a Multi-Polar International System: Which Prospects for Global Peace? Jun 3, 2013. http://www.e-ir.info/2013/06/03/towards-a-multi-polar-international-system-which-prospects-for-global-peace/

85 Mearsheimer J. J. The Tragedy of Great Power Politics. New York: W.W. Norton & Company, Inc., 2014. P. 348.

appearance on the stage, which was used as an affirmation of a new type of identity tied to the loyalty of citizens to a state system as well as for subversive separatist activities in those powers with clearly multi-ethnic structures and did not present themselves as capable of reformatting into monolithic communities (for example, the national liberation movement in the Balkan territories of the Ottoman Empire and the attempts at self-determination by Slavs and Hungarians in Austria-Hungary).

Thirdly, perhaps intentionally or perhaps out of ignorance, in this case the author fails to mention Russia's role in the Congress of Vienna. Such was convened precisely on the initiative of the Russian Empire. Perhaps this event would not have taken place without Russia's participation, and the European balance of power would not be so stable as during the 40 years after the Congress of Vienna and before the outbreak of the Crimean War.

In these three cases, we can clearly see the role of Eurocentrism as a complex linked to politics, culture, and religion in provoking conflicts at a time when the Russian element for some time aided in balancing the European system of forces and interests. Consequentially, non-European or non-Western influence on the system of international relations will play a positive role in the current stage.

Fourthly, nuclear multipolarity has already existed for many years, and has not led to serious conflicts between countries possessing nuclear arms. On the contrary, such has led to a more balanced policy since decision-making entities understand the great responsibility and risk entailed by using weapons of mass destruction. There is also the view that believes in a balance between the conflictual point of view and the development of the new global architecture. For example, Priva Chetty believes:

> With the continuous development of countries in their various sectors of hard and soft power leads to a multi polar world order. In such a system, each country thrives to exert dominance in its neighborhood with checking the advancement of its hostile partners. Observing the recent trends, vast human cataclysms of the past century is likely to repeat, owing to development of nuclear power working as deterrents to each other. Rather, as Fareed Zakaria asserts, co-existence of multi-polar world with

> the combination of both East and West is what the 21st century world order is heading to.[86]

If we disengage from these harsh critiques of multipolarity and instead translate ongoing discussions into a global political paradigm, we have the need for a new ideological foundation that differs from the dogma of neoliberalism and capitalism.

Extending this to the global political paradigm, we discover the necessity of a new ideological foundation differing from the dogmas of neoliberalism and capitalism. Secondly, there is the need to reject the model of global governance or mondialism that has been adopted as a rule by the political elites of a number of countries (this also means rejecting the WTO's standards, the decisions of the Davos forum, the Bilderberg Club, and other structures representing neo-imperialist cartels). Thirdly, this means pluralism in political and economic cultures, an emphasis on identity or, as is said in Latin America, indigenism, in contrast to the homogenous, universal agenda called for by the US. New ideas and more detailed studies of the existing traditions of different regions which have hitherto been excluded from global discourse for various reasons will offer crucial help in the intellectual process of establishing multipolarity. In line with the thought of the Eurasianist geopolitical school, emerging multipolarity should overcome the positivist approach of existing theories of international relations built on the model of interactions between nation-states.[87]

In accordance with the vision of the Eurasianist geopolitical school, impending multipolarity must overcome the positivist approach in existing theories of international relations built on the interactions of nation-states.[88] Other schools and theories might also help in the construction of a non-contradictory, logical system that can be competently and adequately applied in practice with adjustments for regional specificities and differences.

---

86 Priya Chetty. Unipolar, bipolar and multipolar World order. July 25, 2015. https://www.projectguru.in/publications/unipolar-bipolar-or-multipolar-world-order/

87 Dugin A.G. Teoriya mnogopolyarnogo mira. Moscow: Evraziyskoe dvizhenie, 2012.

88 Ibidem.

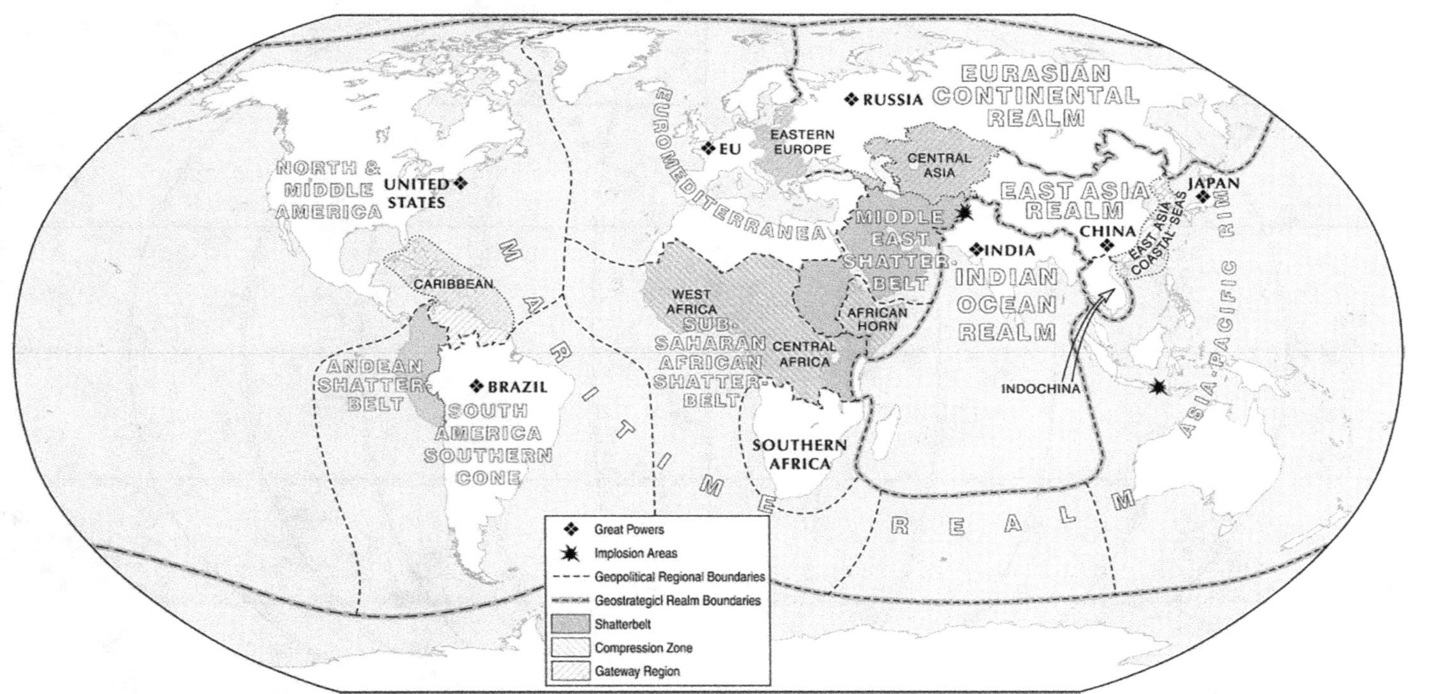

Model of the geopolitical zones at the beginning of the 21st century proposed by American author Saul Bernard Cohen. Brazil, the EU, India, China, Russia, the United States and Japan labeled as Great powers. Source: Saul Bernard Cohen, Geopolitics. The Geography of International Relations. London: Rowman & Littlefield, 2015. P. 451.

3

Non-Western Approaches to Multipolarity

In the previous chapter we reviewed the foundational elements on which a multipolar system is built. We recognized that multipolarity was initially a Western theory associated with the political school of (neo)realism. We also showed that the possibility of multipolarity began to be discussed even back during the time of the bipolar system. After the onset of temporary unipolarity which provoked dysfunction in the international system, various crises contributed to the evolution of the concept of multipolarity in both East and West. In this chapter, we will examine the key theoretical constructs being elaborated by the main actors (states) that are shaping the multipolar world order, including discussions on this topic ongoing within certain countries and polemics with multipolarity's opponents.

The Chinese Contribution to the Theory and Practice of Multipolarity

Modern Chinese politicians derive their doctrine of multipolarity from the Cold War era, and in particular the five principles of peaceful coexistence which formed the basis of the 1954 treaty with India. These five principles are:

1. Mutual respect for territorial integrity and sovereignty
2. Non-aggression
3. Non-interference in internal affairs
4. Equality and mutual benefit
5. Peaceful coexistence

China began actively participating in the development of the multipolar strategy under discussion today more than 30 years ago, for which there exists a specific Chinese term, *duojihua*, (多极化) meaning multipolarity or "multipolarism."[1]

1 Lee, John. An Exceptional Obsession // The American Interest. May/June 2010. http://www.the-american-interest.com/article.cfm?piece=80

In an article from early 1986 entitled "Prospects for the international situation"[2], Deng Xiaoping's national security advisor, Huan Xiang, who also boasted experience in diplomatic service abroad and cooperation with Shanghai academic circles, indicated that insofar as the Cold War conflict had become relatively stable, the world's superpowers were effectively losing the ability to control their own camps, hence the beginning of political multipolarity. The first step in this direction was the emergence of the strategic USSR-USA-China triangle following which, in the author's opinion, a quintipolar world would appear including Japan and Europe.

Two years before this article's publication, Huan Xiang noted in 1984 that: "The old world order has already disintegrated and the new world order is now taking shape, but up to now it still has not yet completely formed…The US' domination in the Asia-Pacific region will end… Japan knows what role it should play, but it still hesitates…China must go through a long period of hard work . . . 30 to 50 years will make it truly powerful."[3] Huan also pointed to what the confrontation between the USSR and USA was leading to: "The two largest military powers are weakening and entering into decline…In military terms, they are evolving in the direction of multipolarity…if the Star Wars plan develops, multipolarization could develop toward bipolarization, and could again return to bipolarization. If secondary ranked countries want to carry out a Star Wars plan, it will be very difficult. The position of those countries will immediately decline."[4]

In January 1986, however, any uncertainty regarding the future structure of the world evaporated[5] and its transformation and

---

2 Huan Xiang, "Zhanwang 1986 nian guoji xingshi" (Prospects for the 1986 international situation), in Huan Xiang wenji, Beijing: Shijie zhishi chubanshe, 1994, 1291. Originally published in Liaowang, no. 1 (1986).

3 Huan Xiang, "Yatai diqu xingshi he Mei-Su de zhengduo zhanlue" (The situation in the Asia-Pacific region and U.S.-Soviet rivalry strategy), in Huan Xiang wenji, 1115. This article originally appeared in Guoji zhanwang (International Outlook), no. 14 (1984).

4 Huan Xiang, "Xin jishu geming dui junshi de yingxiang" (The influence of the new technological revolution on military affairs), in Huan Xiang wenji (The collected works of Huan Xiang)(Beijing: Shijie zhishi chubanshe, 1994), 2: 1263. This article was originally published in Liberation Army Daily, June 7 and June 14, 1985.

5 It cannot be ruled out that this Chinese author's opinion was influenced by the

transition acquired clear traits and stages. In Huan Xiang's words: "The future international politics and economics are facing a new period."[6] By 1986, Huan Xiang was no longer alone in his forecasts. Another author published an article in China's National Defense University's journal entitled "The development of global strategic multipolarity."[7] After some time, multipolarity was already regarded as the trend of the 21st century.[8]

It bears noting, however, that this concept of multipolarity eventually came to be met with opponents, albeit not immediately. In 1997, senior analyst for the Institute of American Studies of the Chinese Academy of Social Sciences, Yang Dazhou, published an article entitled "My opinion on the global structure after the Cold War" which subjected the traditional Chinese view on multipolarity to thorough, detailed criticism.[9] The article's main arguments consisted of the following theses:

- The United States will maintain its superpower status for at least three decades.
- The United States will maintain its alliances with Japan and Germany.
- In the next two to three decades, there will be no period of "uncertainty."
- There will be no extended transition period from this trend towards multipolarity.
- There already exists a "pluralist" global structure of "one superpower and four powers."

---

shift in the USSR's political course. In 1985, Mikhail Gorbachev assumed the post of General Secretary of CPSU and subsequently launched Perestroika.

6 Huan Xiang, "Wo guo 'qiwu' qijian mianlin guoji zhengzhi jingji huanjing de fenxi" (An analysis of the international political and economic environment that China is facing during its seventh five-year plan), in Huan Xiang wenji, Beijing: Shijie zhishi chubanshe, 1994, 1300.

7 Gao Heng, "Shijie zhanlue geju zhengxiang duojihua fazhan" (Development of global strategic multipolarity), Guofang daxue xuebao (National Defense University Journal), no. 2 (1986): 32-33.

8 Luo Renshi, "Strategic Structure, Contradictions and the New World Order," International Strategic Studies 19, no.1 (March 1991): 1-6.

9 Yang Dazhou, "Dui lengzhan hou shijie geju zhi wo jian", Heping yu Fazhan (Peace and Development) 60, no. 2 (June 1997): 41-45.

- Only the United States is a genuine "pole" capable of resolving key issues in any region, as exemplified in the case of the Dayton Accords. "The United States plays a leading role which no other nation can replace…it is the only country which is a 'pole.'"
- China "does not possess sufficient qualification to be a 'pole.'"
- For more than 20 years, no other nations, including Third World countries, will become major powers capable of challenging the five strongest. Thus, the phrase which many analysts adhere to of "one super, the rest strong" is actually inappropriate.
- It is unlikely that large local wars will break out between nations.

Of course, these theses drew criticism first and foremost from conservative Chinese circles, such as the military. The editor of the National Defense University's journal, *International Strategic Studies*, subsequently decided that an article by General Huang Zhenji would be suitable as a response despite the fact that it was rather sharp in tone and "unusual" in style.[10] General Huang mentioned excerpts of Yang's article without directly quoting it and confirmed the original point of view on each of these points:

- The US' decline is inevitable and underway.
- The US' global influence is already severely restricted.
- Quintipolar multipolarity is inevitable, especially in terms of the growing tensions between the United States, Japan, and Germany (as was evidenced by fresh meetings of the highest level between the European Union and Asia which excluded the declining United States).
- The emergence of the "Third World" has changed global politics and will contain the United States.
- Local wars are certain even though "peace and development" will be the main trend in the "uncertain" transitional period of coming decades.

---

10 Huang Zhengji, "Shijie duojihua qushi buke kangju" (The inevitable trend toward multipolarity), Guoji zhanlue yanjiu (International Strategic Studies) 46, no. 4 (October 1997): 1-3.

Here it is also necessary to note how the Chinese have understood the global political order of the past two centuries while taking into account the fact that the country was effectively a colony and under occupation until only the second half of the 20th century. China's authorities believe that global politics is a system or "strategic pattern", among which they distinguish five different pattern periods:

1. The Vienna System: 1815-1870
2. The Transitional System marked by Germany and Italy's unification and the Meiji reforms
3. The Versailles System: 1920-1945
4. The Yalta System: 1945-1989
5. Transition period...

As can be seen, such an approach shares common elements with Braudel and other authors' concepts. However, there are some differences, namely, minor differentiations which allow us to draw conclusions on the different criteria for evaluating the global system that are peculiar to the Asian (non-Western) type of thinking.

By the end of the 1990's, three approaches to future multipolarity had been developed in China. Xi Runchang from China's Academy of Social Sciences who, like Yang Dazhou, said that there will be "one superpower and four strong powers", suggested that this pattern represents the new global structure: "Currently there has already basically formed a new embryonic structure supported by the five powers . . . in the 21st century, this new structure will further form and be perfected."[11]

Yan Xuetong from the Chinese Institute of Contemporary International Studies presented a second scenario known as the "theory of the completion of the main project of multipolarity." Yan argues that the "The basic establishment of the great nations' strategic relations in 1996 caused the post-Cold War transition from a bipolar structure to a one super many strong structure to be completed."[12]

---

11 Xi Runchang, "Shijie zhengzhi xin geju de chuxing ji qi qianjing" (The embryonic form of the world's new political structure and its prospects), Heping yu fazhan (Peace and Development), no. 1 (1997), cited in Li Zhongcheng, Kua shiji de shijie zhengzhi (Trans century world politics)(Beijing: Shishi chubanshe, 1997), 29.

12 Yan Xuetong, "1996-1997 nian guoji xingshi yu Zhonguo duiwai guanxi

Song Baoxian and Yu Xiaoqiu's works from the same institute suppose a third scenario closer to that envisioned by Huang Zhenji and the conservative camp in which "multipolarity is formed" and other countries besides the five strongest only become stronger. They argue that "the development of trends of multipolarity is accelerating" and "a new group of powers is arising" which will play "the role of restricting the five main powers" thus making the trend of multipolarity as the global structure more attractive and diverse.[13]

In 1997, another senior analyst at the Chinese Institute of Contemporary International Studies, Li Zhongcheng, summated these three differing views on the future global structure put forth by the institute and Academy of Social Science's analysts. Li does not criticize any of the authors, whose ideas he merely presents, but his own expressed views are evidently closer to the third purported scenario.[14]

Yan Xuetong from the Chinese Institute of Contemporary International Studies became the one who genuinely attempted to develop an alternative approach to questions of multipolarity, as when he wrote: "The new international structure has some special characteristics, the most important of which is the replacement of 'poles'(*ji*) by 'units' (*yuan*). The nature of 'poles' is long-term stable confrontation, but the nature of 'units' is that the dominant position of key countries is determined by the nature of specific affairs."[15]

These distinctions deviated from the conservative line. For example, a large part of Yang Dazhou's article centered on challenging this point of view by means of the tactic of establishing and clarifying definitions for such key words and phrases as "pole", "transition era",

---

baogao" (A report on the 1996-1997 international situation and China's foreign relations), Zhanlue yu guanli (Strategy and Management), supplementary issue (1996-1997), cited in Li Zhongcheng, Kua shiji de shijie zhengzhi, 31.

13 Song Baoxian and Yu Xiaoqiu, "Shijie duojihua qushi jishu fazhan" (The world's multipolarity trend continues to develop), Renmin ribao (People's Daily), December 28, 1994, cited in Li Zhongcheng, Kua shiji de shijie zhengzhi , 32.

14 Wu Hua, Shen Weili, and Zhen Hongtao, Nan Ya zhi shi--Indu (The lion of South Asia--India)(Beijing: Shishi chubanshe, 1997), 2.

15 Yan Xuetong, Zhongguo guojia liyi fenxi (Analysis of China's national interests) (Tianjin: Tianjin renmin chubanshe, 1996), 55.

"pluralization" (duoyuanhua), "multipolarization" (duojihua), "large nation" (daguo), and "power" (qiangguo). Dazhou defined a "pole" as something founded on the standards of the Cold War era when the only poles were the United States and Soviet Union. Accordingly, the "four strong powers" are not poles because "when compared to the Soviet Union, there still is a great distance."[16]

In a similar vein, in his argument against those who claimed that the world is in a transition era set to continue for an indefinite period of time, Yang argues that any transition is by definition not uncertain: "Some people believe that the post-Cold War transition period could continue for 20, even 30 years. This type of argument is not appropriate; a 'transition period' always has an ending time. Suppose the 'transition period' goes on for 20 or 30 years, then this itself already constitutes a new structure different from that of the Cold War period."[17]

Overall, Chinese analysts have argued that China should not be purely passive, but can and even should aid the inauguration of the multipolar trend and accelerate its tempo. For example, China is purported to be in a position to help Europe become a pole. One Chinese author has claimed that the EU wants to play a more important international role as a "powerful, independent pole" in the unfolding multipolar world, and thus is "seeking to at the same time strengthen its ties with the world's major powers", hence the release of the important political document, "Building a Comprehensive Partnership with China" in March 1997. The Chinese Institute of Contemporary International Studies' Feng Zhongping calls this a "strategic partnership." In Feng's opinion, these new relations with China will "help the EU in its long quest to establish itself on the world stage and become an independent 'pole' in global affairs." The basis for the EU possibly becoming such a "pole" is explained by "China's status in the unfolding global balance of power."[18]

A similar argument was advanced by Shen Yihui, who claimed that the "EU should count on China's support" because "the establishment

16 Yang Dazhoug, "Dui lengzhan hou shijie geju zhi wo jian," 43.

17 Ibid, 42.

18 Feng Zhongping, "An Analysis of the China Policy of the European Union," Contemporary International Relations 8, no. 4 (April 1988): 1-6. Feng is Deputy Director of the Division for Western European Studies at CICIR.

of closer ties with China will allow Western Europe to play a greater role in international affairs." Shen adds that China can not only help the EU gain authority in world affairs, but also that improved relations between China and the EU could help the latter in other problems." In economic terms, he argues, "the Chinese market is needed to catalyze economic growth in Europe." Even in the sphere of security, "China can be used to create a security zone around the EU."[19]

Subsequent years have shown that Beijing has been met with certain resistance despite the fact that China has partially penetrated Europe's market. It should also be noted that current Chinese leader Xi Jinping's predecessor, Jiang Zemin, highlighted the concept of multipolarity, economic globalization, and the development of science and technology as the fundamental global trends of the era.[20]

Russia's Response

Many ascribe the first steps in developing a strategy for multipolarity in international relations to Russia as well. Indeed, this claim has some merit. In Moscow on April 23rd, 1997, Russia and China signed the "Joint Declaration on a Multipolar World and the Establishment of a New International Order", and on May 15th the declaration was registered in the UN.[21] The document asserted that the Russian Federation and People's Republic of China will strive to promote the development of a multipolar world and new international order. The text also remarked that international relations had undergone

19 Shen Yihui, "Cross-Century European-Chinese Relations," Liaowang, no. 14 (April 6, 1998): 40-41, in FBIS-CHI-98-114, April 24, 1998. For an additional article discussing improving Sino-EU relations see Wang Xingqiao, "A Positive Step Taken by the European Union to Promote Relations with China," Beijing Xinhua Domestic Service, July 1, 1998, in FBIS-CHI-98-191, July 10, 1998.

20 General Secretary of the Communist Party of China from 1989 to 2002 as Chairman of the Central Military Commission of the Communist Party of China from 1989 to 2004 and as President of the People's Republic of China from 1993 to 2003. Jiang has been described as the «core of the third generation» of Communist Party leaders since 1989.

21 Russian-Chinese Joint Declaration on a Multipolar World and the Establishment of a New International Order, adopted in Moscow on 23 April 1997. Letter dated 15 May 1997 from the Permanent Representatives of China and the Russian Federation to the United Nations addressed to the Secretary-General, Distr. GENERAL A/52/153, S/1997/384, 20 May 1997.

profound changes at the end of the 20th century and affirmed a diversity of political, economic, and cultural paths of development for all countries and an increasing role for forces advocating peace and broad international cooperation. Furthermore, the document reads: "A growing number of countries are beginning to recognize the need for mutual respect, equality and mutual advantage - but not for hegemony and power politics - and for dialogue and cooperation - but not for confrontation and conflict. The establishment of a peaceful, stable, just and rational new international political and economic order is becoming a pressing need of the times and an imperative of historical development." In addition, the declaration voiced the notion that every state has a right to, proceeding on the basis of its unique circumstances, independently and autonomously choose its own path of development without interference from other states. In the words of the statement: "Differences in their social systems, ideologies and value systems must not become an obstacle to the development of normal relations between States." At the same time, it was emphasized that China and Russia are switching to a new form of mutual relations and that such is not directed against any other countries.

Hopes then arose that the UN would play an important role in establishing a new international order, and developing countries and the Non-Aligned Movement were named as important forces contributing to the formation of a multipolar world. The Joint Statement of the People's Republic of China and the Russian Federation on the International Order of the 21st Century, which was signed in Moscow on July 1st, 2005 by Russian President Vladimir Putin and PRC President Xu Jintao, logically continued this line.[22] This declaration was a response to the US invasion of Iraq, a reaction to this challenge which was intended to strengthen efforts to organize a new international order. One part in the new declaration read:

> The main trend of the world today is not towards a "clash of civilizations"; rather, it underscores the imperative of engaging in global cooperation. The diversity of civilizations in the world and the diversification of development models should be respected and safeguarded. Differences in the historical backgrounds, cultural traditions, social and political systems, value concepts,

22 http://archive.kremlin.ru/events/articles/2005/06/90767/153816.shtml

> and development paths of countries should not become an excuse for interfering in the internal affairs of other countries. Different civilizations should conduct dialogue, exchange experiences, draw on each other's experiences, learn from each other's strong points to make up for their own shortcomings, and seek common progress on the basis of mutual respect and tolerance. Cultural exchanges should be increased in order to establish relations of friendship and trust among countries.

Russia and China drew attention to the establishment of the Shanghai Cooperation Organization and the intensification of cooperation between BRIC countries and later BRICS, which is seen as an attempt at establishing individual rules for the game at least in each country's zone of strategic interests. In the sphere of its own strategic interests, as proclaimed by President Medvedev following Georgia's attack on South Ossetia in August 2008, Russia uses the Eurasian Economic Community as an economic integration instrument and military cooperation within the CSTO. Directly introduced into Russia's foreign policy doctrine in 2000 was the provision that "Russia will seek the creation of a multipolar system of international relations which genuinely reflects the diversity of the modern world with its diversity of interests."[23]

In the concept document of 2008, multipolarity was associated first and foremost with global security. The document said that Russia "considers that the present fundamental development trends, including the emerging multipolarity, and diversification of risks and threats lead to the conclusion that the strategic stability issue cannot anymore be addressed exclusively within the framework of Russia / US relations." In addition, it was noted that "economic growth in those countries and regions converts into their political influence, the trend to a polycentric world order growing further."[24]

In turn, the foreign policy concept of the Russian Federation passed in February 2013 posited:

23 The Foreign Policy Concept of the Russian Federation. 28 June 2000.

24 The Foreign Policy Concept of the Russian Federation, 12 January 2008. http://en.kremlin.ru/supplement/4116

> International relations are in the process of transition, the essence of which is the creation of a polycentric system of international relations. That process is not an easy one. It is accompanied by increased economic and political turbulence at the global and regional levels. International relations become increasingly complex and unpredictable. With tendency for decentralization of the global system of governance, regional governance emerges as a basis for the polycentric model of the world (with the UN being another foundation), reflecting the world's diversity and variety. New centers of economic growth and political power increasingly take responsibility for their respective regions. Regional integration becomes an effective means to increase competitiveness of the participating states. Networks and associations, trade pacts and other economic agreements, as well as regional reserve currencies serve as instruments to enhance security and financial and economic stability.[25]

The following foreign policy concept which entered into force in November 2016 left out the terms "polycentricity" and "multipolarity", but the course towards multipolarity was indirectly confirmed in the affirmation of "facilitating the development of constructive dialogue and partnership with a view to promoting harmony and mutual enrichment among various cultures and civilizations." The document also took note of an "eroding" of the "global economic and political dominance of the traditional western powers", affirming that "the cultural and civilizational diversity of the world and the existence of multiple development models have been clearer than ever."[26]

Meanwhile, polycentricity and multipolarity have regularly been reflected in the national security strategies of the Russian Federation. The course towards multipolarity was proclaimed back in 2000 in the Presidential Decree of the National Security Concept of the Russian Federation, which stated: "Russia will help shape the ideology behind

25 The Foreign Policy Concept of the Russian Federation, 12 February 2013. https://www.mid.ru/en/foreign_policy/official_documents/-/asset_publisher/CptICkB6BZ29/content/id/122186

26 Foreign Policy Concept of the Russian Federation, approved by President of the Russian Federation Vladimir Putin on November 30, 2016. https://www.mid.ru/en/foreign_policy/official_documents/-/asset_publisher/CptICkB6BZ29/content/id/2542248

the rise of a multipolar world...Russia's national interests in the international sphere lie in upholding its sovereignty and strengthening its positions as a great power and as one of the influential centers of a multipolar world, in development of equal and mutually advantageous relations with all countries and integrative associations..." The concept document also formulated: "Internationally, threats to Russian national security are manifested in attempts by other states to counteract its strengthening as one of the centers of influence in a multipolar world, to hinder realization of its national interests and to weaken its positions in Europe, the Middle East, Transcaucasia, Central Asia and the Asia-Pacific Region."[27]

The strategy document approved in 2009 indicates that "Russia has... restored the country's potential to enhance its competitiveness and defend its national interests as a key subject within evolving multipolar international relations. According to the document, the long-term national interests of the Russian Federation lie in "transforming the Russian Federation into a world power, whose activity is directed at supporting the strategic stability and mutually beneficial partner relationships within the multipolar world." The section on national and strategic priorities says that Russia will "concentrate its efforts and resources on...strategic stability and equitable strategic partnership, on the basis of Russia's active participation in the development of the multipolar model of the international system.[28]

The subsequent document, signed into law on 31 December 2015 to replace the latter, re-featured and de facto affirmed the term polycentricity, stating: "A solid basis has been created at this time for further increasing the Russian Federation's economic, political, military, and spiritual potentials and for enhancing its role in shaping a polycentric world." However, the document also noted that "the process of shaping a new polycentric model of the world order is being accompanied by an increase in global and regional instability." One of the national security tasks formulated therein is "consolidating the

---

27 National Security Concept of the Russian Federation, Presidential Decree No. 24, 10 January 2000.
https://www.mid.ru/en/foreign_policy/official_documents/-/asset_publisher/CptICkB6BZ29/content/id/589768

28 National Security Strategy of the Russian Federation to 2020, 12 May 2009.
http://thailand.mid.ru/en/national-security-strategy-of-the-russian-federation

Russian Federation's status as a leading world power, whose actions are aimed at maintaining strategic stability and mutually beneficial partnerships in a polycentric world."[29]

Russian President Vladimir Putin's speech at the Munich Security Conference on 10 February 2007, which subsequently became famously known as the "Munich Speech", also went down in history as an important stage in the promotion of multipolarity. Vladimir Putin noted in his speech:

> The unipolar world that had been proposed after the Cold War did not take place either. The history of humanity certainly has gone through unipolar periods and seen aspirations to world supremacy…However, what is a unipolar world? However one might embellish this term, at the end of the day it refers to one type of situation, namely one centre of authority, one centre of force, one centre of decision-making. It is a world in which there is one master, one sovereign. And at the end of the day this is pernicious not only for all those within this system, but also for the sovereign itself because it destroys itself from within. And this certainly has nothing in common with democracy. Because, as you know, democracy is the power of the majority in light of the interests and opinions of the minority…I consider that the unipolar model is not only unacceptable but also impossible in today's world… There is no reason to doubt that the economic potential of the new centres of global economic growth will inevitably be converted into political influence and will strengthen multipolarity.[30]

In addition, Putin's speech called into doubt the legitimacy of a number of country's military operations. Although the countries in mind were not directly named, it was clear that this meant first and foremost the US and NATO countries. Putin also emphasized that the use of force can only be considered legitimate when a corresponding

---

29 National Security Strategy of the Russian Federation, Presidential Decree 683, 31 December 2015.
http://www.ieee.es/Galerias/fichero/OtrasPublicaciones/Internacional/2016/Russian-National-Security-Strategy-31Dec2015.pdf

30 Speech and the Following Discussion at the Munich Conference on Security Policy, 10 February 2007. http://en.kremlin.ru/events/president/transcripts/24034

resolution has been adopted on the basis of the regulations of and within the framework of the UN. Thus, the emphasis fell on continuing the system that took shape in the conditions of the conclusion of the Second World War and the establishment of the UN as a platform for resolving disputes between states. The Munich speech also touched upon disarmament, the militarization of space, the upsetting of the balance within the OSCE, and economic security, on which points the emphasis was again on upholding and adhering to the same, common, established principles. Further, Vladimir Putin commented on the practice of developed countries allocating resources for the "struggle against poverty" in "the world's poorest countries" only for such to be sold to their own companies, thereby de facto constituting occupation and in turn only strengthening economic depression and provoking the escalation of radicalism and extremism in reaction. At the end of his speech, Putin spoke of the need to "interact with responsible and independent partners with whom we could work together in constructing a fair and democratic world order that would ensure security and prosperity not only for a select few, but for all." The latter statement could be called the Russian formula of multipolarity.

It should be noted, however, that Russian politicians, diplomats, and scholars' understanding of the need to develop a theory of multipolarity has its roots in a crisis situation. First, there was the collapse of the Soviet Union which was accompanied by ethnic conflicts. A similar collapse occurred in Yugoslavia and led to several foreign interventions and the transformation of the regional political map. NATO's bombing of Yugoslavia and the Albanian proclamation of Kosovo were a painful blow not only to the Federal Republic of Yugoslavia which at the time consisted of Serbia and Montenegro, but to the European geopolitical system as a whole. In addition, the collapse of Marxist doctrine and the negative experience of IMF and World Bank reforms in Russia led to an understanding of the need to develop a distinct foreign and domestic policy. Although the inertia of the Soviet era made itself felt, certain attempts were made at rethinking Russia's role and place in the global political system.

September 11th, 2001 also affected perceptions of the global system in a new vein. It is no coincidence that in an article from September 2003, a Russian advocate of multipolarity and political heavyweight who served as prime minister in 1999, Yevgeny Primakov, noted that "what followed the events of September 11 showed more clearly than ever the confrontation between two trends. On the one hand, there was the preservation of the world order, save for some modernization, founded on such a mechanism for multilateral actions as the United Nations. On the other, there was 'unilateralism', or the bet that decisions that are vitally important for humanity can be taken by one country, the United States, on the grounds of Washington's subjective perception of international reality."[31] Primakov pointed out that the EU was becoming a center of power comparable in its capacity to the US, while China, Russia, India, and Japan were also in no hurry to trail behind the wake of events set by Washington. Also highlighted in this regard is the UN's role in the formation of multipolarity. Previously, Primakov had observed that "the uneven development of states will manifest itself primarily in antagonistic forms…historically, no dominant power can establish a unipolar world order."[32]

Here it is important to note that Yevgeny Primakov had at the time already condemned the US leadership, pointing instead to rapidly expanding opportunities for other countries and alliances. "The fall of the USSR as a counterbalance to America does not give reason to believe that the US is an undisputed winner and, accordingly, that the world should be unipolar with only one center in Washington. This contradicts the very course of global development. For instance, China and India's respective GDP's are larger than that of the US. US leadership in scientific and technological progress as one of the main conditions of the unipolar world is also being actively contested today."[33] This is confirmed by statistical data: "By 2011 four major centers of scientific progress had formed - the USA (31% of global spending on scientific research in terms of purchasing power parity), the European Union (24%), China (14%), and Japan (11%)."[34]

---

31 Primakov E. Mr bez sverhderzhav. 02.09.2003. http://www.globalaffairs.ru/number/n_1560

32 Primakov E. Mir posle 11 sentyabrya. Moscow, 2002. P. 155.

33 Bondar A. Evgeniy Primakov: «Mir budet mnogopolyarnim». Stoletie, 28.03.2008. http://www.stoletie.ru/ekskliuziv/evgeni_primakov_mir_budet_mnogopolyarnim.htm

34 Nikonov Y. Komparativniy analiz podhodov k organizatsii finansirovaniya strategii innovatsionnogo razvitiya natsionalnih ekonomik za rubezhom // Vestnik Tomskogo gosudarstvennogo universiteta. № 392, 2015. P. 145.

Primakov argued against liberals and globalists, affirming that:

> The transition to a multipolar system is a process, not a single change with a finished character. Therefore, great importance is attached to various trends, sometimes contradictory ones, manifesting themselves over the course of this transition. Some of them have their source in the unequal development of states and the successes or failures of integration associations. The fluctuating ratio between, relatively speaking, the course towards restarting relations and the inertial line of states' conduct inherited from the Cold War and ingrained during the period of outright confrontation, is directly impacted. This relation between two tendencies manifests itself in the political, military, and economic fields as well. Therefore, the correct conclusion that a multipolar world order does not in itself in the conditions of globalization lead to conflict situations, or military clashes, does not exclude the altogether complex environment in which the process of the transition to such a system takes place.[35]

Being a supporter of the creation of the Russia-India-China triangle that could balance out the aggressive behavior of the US and other challenges, Primakov is rightfully considered to be one of the first Russian practicians of multipolarity. Thanks to his official position and numerous foreign contacts, Russia's position vis-a-vis the future world order was successfully conveyed to the widest range of decision-makers possible and consolidated in the foreign policy of the Russian Federation.[36]

Alexander Dugin's doctrine of neo-Eurasianism was another ideological and intellectual platform which gave impetus to the development of multipolarity. The program of Eurasianist ideology asserts:

> At the level of a planetary trend, Eurasianism is a global, revolutionary, civilizational concept which, in gradually refining itself, is to become a new ideological platform for mutual understanding and cooperation for a wide conglomerate of

35 Primakov E. Misli vskuh. Moscow.: Rossijskaya gazeta, 2011. P. 159–160.

36 Primakov E. Vizovi i alternativi mnogopolyarnogo mira: rol Rossii. Moscow, 2014.

> different forces, states, peoples, cultures, and confessions which reject Atlanticist globalization...Eurasianism is the sum of all the natural and artificial, objective and subjective obstacles along the path to unipolar globalization, at once elevated from the level of simple negation to being a positive project, a creative alternative.[37]

Although classical Eurasianism was concerned solely with the destiny of Russia which it characterized as "Eurasia" by virtue of its uniqueness, vast territory, and central situation between "classical" Europe and Asia, Alexander Dugin's concept has supplemented this ideology with new methodologies and scholarly concepts. Thus, Eurasianism has acquired a global dimension and moved beyond the borders of the Eurasian continent. In this new understanding, "Eurasianism is a philosophy of multipolar globalization designed to unite all the societies and peoples of the earth in the construction of a unique and authentic world, every component of which would be organically derived from historical traditions and local cultures."[38]

Rather close to this formula is the opinion of another Russian scholar, Boris Martynov, who noted that newly emergent multipolarity cannot be of any other dimension than civilizational. Martynov emphasizes:

> Inter-civilizational communication is already a reality of the modern world in which different economic and financial institutions, non-state structures, and religious, business, and public associations and, finally, individuals as representatives of their civilizational archetypes are increasingly active apart from states and alongside their lasting multi-profile and multilevel international contacts of various kinds...In addition, the advantage of a system of multipolar world order in view of the unipolar and bipolar ones lies in that it must be based on law to function. The correctness of this observation is obvious in the case of the unipolar world which operates on the basis of the 'understandings' of the main player in the global system. This is true for bipolarity as well, where each of the two 'equally-responsible' subjects strive to ensure themselves a 'free hand' in their zones of influence regardless of international

37 Dugin A. Evraziyskaya missiya. Moscow: Mezhdunarodnoe evraziyskoe dvizhenie, 2005. P. 11.

38 Ibid, 33.

> law. However, law is needed for interaction between several major players wielding approximately comparable might and influence in order to guarantee a reasonable modus vivendi between them. This is especially true for such a complex system as civilizational multipolarity.[39]

The deterioration of relations with the West has pushed Russia towards more actively developing a strategy for multipolarity, especially as: "The multilateralism promoted by the EU and the United States presupposes that Russia joins the established international institutions whose agenda is set mostly by the West. However, these approaches are criticized by Russia as, in fact, being a form of collective unilateralism, and this critical attitude gives rise to a number of alternative visions of a multipolar world."[40]

More recently, some authors have categorically stated that a "multi-pole world order" is, without a doubt, no longer merely a concept but an objective historical reality whose formation is already underway and will continue to take shape over the course of a lengthy transition period. The preconditions of this transition arose back still "under the tent" of bipolarity.[41] It has also been proclaimed that "the establishment of a multipolar world corresponds to Russia's aspirations"[42] and that "our country wields all that is necessary to take a leading position in both the economic and cultural spheres in the new multipolar world."[43]

However, far from all Russian scholars and diplomats have assigned a positive nature to emerging multipolarity. For example, the director of the Russian Academy of Science's Institute for US and Canadian Studies, Sergey Rogov, has claimed that "the new polycentric system

---

39 Martynov B. Mnogopolyarniy ili mnogocivilizatsionniy mir?// Mezhdunarodnie processi. Number 7. Issue 3 (21). Sent.-Dec. 2009. http://www.intertrends.ru/twenty-first.htm

40 Andrey Makarychev, Viatcheslav Morozov.. Global Governance 17 (2011), 369.

41 Simoniya N., Torkunov A. Noviy mirovoy poryadok: ot bipolyarnosti k mnogoplyarnosti // Polis. Politicheskie issledovaniya. 2015. № 3. p. 27-37. https://www.politstudies.ru/files/File/2015/3/2015-3-SIMONIA-TORKUNOV.pdf

42 Kurilev K. Ukrainskiy krizis I mezhdunarodnaya bezopasnost. Moscow: LENAND, 2018. P. 186.

43 Baykov S. Rossiya I noviy miroporyadok XXI veka // Post-Soviet materik. No 1 (13), 2017. p. 11.

lacks common 'rules of the game', norms, and institutions which could effectively regulate interaction between centers of power, including both cooperation and rivalry." Thus, in this view, the trend towards multipolarity generates "instability and unpredictability as to the evolution of the modern system of international relations and threatens to send the situation spinning out of control."[44] This claim is clearly based on the mondialist paradigm which insists on a strictly limited ideological standard. We have already reviewed the criticism of this approach in the second chapter.

A similar opinion is maintained by Andrey Kortunov of the Russian International Affairs Council, who believes that "the future of the world order - if we are speaking about order, and not a 'game without rules' or 'war of all against all' - should be sought not in multipolarity, but in multilaterialism. These two terms sound similar, but their content is different. Multipolarity presumes the construction of a new world order on the basis of force, while multilateralism proposes the basis of interests."[45] If we take into consideration that the organization which Kortunov heads is a kind of analogue of the American Council on Foreign Affairs and is primarily oriented towards cooperation with the West, as well as the fact that Kortunov worked in the United States for a long time and is immersed in Western liberal ideology[46], then his statement can be seen as quite logical and reflective of the position of Russian Westernist-liberals, who merely reproduce Western patterns even when, at times, they are compelled to lend such a flare of patriotism.

44 Rogov S, Rossiya I SSHA: Uroki istorii I vivodi na budushee // Rossiya I Amerika v XXI veke, № 1, 2006. http://www.rusus.ru/?act=read&id=15

45 Kortunov A. Pochemu mir ne stanovitsya mnogopolyarnim. RSMD, 27 June 2018. http://russiancouncil.ru/analytics-and-comments/analytics/pochemu-mir-ne-stanovitsya-mnogopolyarnym/

46 Kortunov is also the president of the "New Eurasia Foundation", founded in 2004 as a daughter division of the American Eurasia Foundation, which is financed by USAID, George Soros' Open Society Institute, and other Western organizations. The foundation belongs to the fifth column within Russia and has been suspected of carrying out "soft power" operations aimed at the undermining of Russian statehood. For more details, see: Sivkova A. Fond «Novaya Evraziya» prosyat priznat inostrannim agentom // Izvestia, 16 June 2015. https://iz.ru/news/587729; SSHA sozdayut v Rossii novuyu pioneriyu // Ivan-chay, 19.05.2015. https://ivan4.ru/news/semeynye_tsennosti/ssha_sozdayut_v_rossii_novuyu_pioneriyu/

A more cautious assessment has been offered by Fedor Lukyanov, who notes: "Multipolarity may now be understood as a way of structuring the global international system where the basic constituent parts are no longer individual states but instead conglomerations of economic interests, united around the most powerful centers of attraction and economic growth."[47] Lukyanov also suggests that: "The future arrangement of poles in a multipolar world is unclear and any attempt to base strategy on an assessment of the future character of the international system may very soon prove to be a miscalculation. The major objective which still preoccupies Russian minds is how to restore the country's ability to be an independent center of influence."[48]

Without a doubt, even if we cast aside the influence of the liberal cartel on foreign policy decision-making, Russia's assumption of its natural role as leader of the construction of a multipolar world is a necessary (but far from sufficient) condition for the existence of multipolarity.[49] Adequate cooperation with other centers of power on both the Eurasian continent and beyond is necessary.

India And Multipolarity

India has not unreasonably expanded the Chinese vision of five poles to include six actors. Thus, Indian theories of multipolarity also deserve attentive study. The Indian political scientist Suryanarayana believes that multipolarity is conceivable as a stable principle of international relations only between states that have developed organically as "power houses."[50] Implicit in this notion is a criticism of colonialism, neocolonialism as well as the chimerical political culture vividly exemplified in the US which, with its strategic notion of the "Frontier" and historical statehood, cannot represent such an organic power house.

"By engaging in economic reform," it is assumed, "India will have the

47 Fyodor Lukyanov, Russian Dilemmas in a Muitipolar World, Journal of International Affairs, Spring/Summer 2010, Vol. 63, No. 2. 24

48 Ibidem. P. 31.

49 Ambrosio, Thomas. Challenging America's Global Preeminence: Russia's Quest for Multipolarity. London/New York: Routledge, 2017.

50 Suryanarayana P.S. Multipolarity: vision and reality.// The Hindu. October 13, 2000. http://www.hindu.com/2000/10/13/stories/05132523.htm

opportunity to develop and exploit its large population and economic opportunity to become a global power in an increasingly multi-polar system, thereby allowing for an ambitious foreign policy permitting India to protect its interests in South Asia and act as the preeminent power in the region."[51] It has also been noted that India has earned "high political credibility in most parts of the world on top of its growing economic stature, it seems reluctant to capitalize on this. Unwilling to break with the creeds that have guided its foreign policy since independence but, rather, trying to conserve them by adapting them to the emerging new multipolar order."[52] Upon attaining a new economic level, moreover, India will inevitably strengthen its military and political presence in the Indian Ocean.

University of Colorado Professor Peter Harris believes that multipolarity will be directly linked to a shift in the balance of forces in the Indian Ocean. Harris writes:

> Today, centuries of relative unipolarity are giving way to noticeable multipolarity. India's announcement of a base in the Seychelles is another important step in this direction—a sign that New Delhi is doubling down on its blue water navy and attendant power-projection capabilities. From the Seychellois island of Assumption, which is already equipped with an airstrip, the Indian military—even if it is limited by geography to maintaining only a tiny military presence—will boast a central position in the Western Indian Ocean, close to the East African coastline and astride the important maritime trade route that runs from the Mozambique Channel to the Arabian Sea.
>
> It is not just India that is beefing up its presence in the region, of course. Late last year, China announced the creation of its first permanent overseas base in Djibouti at the mouth of the Red Sea, and Beijing continues to expand its naval capabilities (most recently by announcing the construction of its first Chinese-made aircraft carrier). With the United States also present in Djibouti—

51 Corey Bolyard, Rising in the Storm: India's Bid for Global Power in a Multi-Polar System During Development, CIMSEC, April 19, 2017. http://cimsec.org/32185-2/32185

52 Bernd von Muenchow-Pohl, India and Europe in a Multipolar World. Carnegie Endowment for International Peace, 2012. P. 39.

as well as Bahrain, Diego Garcia and elsewhere—this means that at least three of the great powers are demonstrably seeking to expand their military reach in the Indian Ocean. And middle powers such as Britain and France also boast considerable military assets in the wider region…

International Relations theory helps to delineate three scenarios that might play out. First, the great powers could cooperate to combat piracy, maintain geopolitical stability, and keep sea lanes open. This is the hope of liberal academicians, who see few conflicts of interest between the various powers in terms of their vision for the ocean's future; on the contrary, a common stake in policing the commons should provide great impetus to maintaining regional stability. Second, however, the Indian Ocean could become the focus of great power competition and even outright conflict, as distrust and divergent interests push states to shun collaboration. This is the pessimistic prediction of most realist scholars.

But third, the Indian Ocean could become the scene of a new sort of world order—or, to put it more accurately, world orders—as rival great powers go about organizing their own spheres of influence that exist discretely and distinctly with one another's. Such a world was outlined by Charles Kupchan in his book, No One's World, in which the author argued that the coming international system will be characterized by decentralization, pluralism, and co-existence…

Whatever the form of international governance that emerges in the Indian Ocean, then, it will have to accommodate the reality that several great powers have vital interests in the region. Come conflict or cooperation, political order in the Indian Ocean will have to be multipolar in character—if, indeed, it is not already. The prospects for peace and harmonious cooperation under such circumstances are not altogether bleak, but they are not endlessly auspicious either. In many ways, twenty-first century geopolitics begins here.[53]

In their joint article, "The multipolar Asian century: Contestation

53 Peter Harris, How to Live in a Multipolar World // National Interest, January 3, 2016. http://nationalinterest.org/feature/how-live-multipolar-world-14787

or competition?", Samir Saran, a senior research fellow and vice president of the Observer Research Foundation (India) and Ashok Malik, a senior research fellow at the Australian Lowy Institute for International Policy, also assign India an important place in the future world order and focus on the Asia-Pacific region as a possible source for the formation of a multipolar world. Saran and Malik suggest three possible scenarios:

Should the US choose to bequeath the liberal, international order to Asian forces, India will be the heir-apparent. India would not, under this circumstance, play the role of a great power — because Asia is too fractious and politically vibrant to be managed by one entity — but simply that of a 'bridge power'. India is in a unique and catalytic position, with its ability to singularly span the geographic and ideological length of the continent. But two variables will need to be determined. Can the US find it within itself to incubate an order that may not afford it the pride of place like the trans-Atlantic system? And, can India get its act together and be alive to the opportunity it has to become the inheritor of a liberal Asia?

The second possibility for an Asian order is that it resembles the 19th century Concert of Europe, an unstable but necessary political coalition of major powers on the continent. The 'big eight' in Asia (China, India Japan, Saudi Arabia, Iran, Australia, Russia and America) would all be locked in a marriage of convenience, bringing their disparate interests to heel for the greater cause of shared governance. Difficult as it would be to predict the contours of this system, it would likely be focused on preventing shocks to 'core' governance functions in Asia, such as the preservation of the financial system, territorial and political sovereignties and inter-dependent security arrangements. Given that each major player in this system would see this as an ad hoc mechanism, its chances of devolving into a debilitating bilateral or multi-front conflict for superiority would be high — very much like the Concert that gave way to the First World War.

A third possibility could see the emergence of an Asian political architecture that does not involve the US. This system — or more precisely, a universe of subsystems — would see the regional economic and security alliances take a prominent role in managing their areas of interest. As a consequence, institutions like ASEAN, the

Shanghai Cooperation Organisation, the AIIB, the Gulf Cooperation Council and the South Asian Association of Regional Cooperation will become the 'hubs' of governance. The US would remain distantly engaged with these sub-systems, but would be neither invested in their continuity, or affiliated to its membership.

There also exists the point of view that India will represent the third pole of a multipolar world (besides the US and China) by 2050.[54] Given that the author of this model is Hindu, such a theory is of a clearly prejudiced character. On the other hand, a tripolar system a priori cannot be multipolar. What's more, India's leadership considers Russia to be one pole of the multipolar world, as was stated by Indian Prime Minister Narendra Modi during his visit to Moscow in December 2015, who said that he sees in Russia a "significant partner in the economic transformation of India and the creation of a balanced, stable, inclusive, multipolar world."[55]

However, the Indian view of multipolarity implicitly harbors negative perceptions of China due to territorial disputes and, in a broader context, due to the civilizational competition between these two countries. Russia is also an often subject of criticism. For example, the retired Indian diplomat M. Bhadrakumar has remarked: "Russia and China give lip-service to their shared interests with developing countries and they profess ardor for a polycentric world order, ultimately they remain self-centered, comfortable in the knowledge of their assured veto power in the UN and their sequestered place within the discriminatory nuclear Non-Proliferation Treaty (NPT) regime. Unsurprisingly, they are paramountly focused on perpetuating their privileged position as arbiters of regional problems."[56]

Nevertheless, the understanding that the window of opportunities could expand considerably under none other than multipolarity continues to push India in this direction. As Amee Patel has pointed

---

54 Gupta, Amit. "US-India-China: Assessing Tripolarity". China Report 42.1 (2006): 69-83

55 Press statement after Russian-Indian negotiations, 24 Dec. 2015. http://www.kremlin.ru/events/president/news/51011

56 M. K. Bhadrakumar, India's Course Correction on Iran, Iran Review, May 23, 2010. http://www.iranreview.org/content/Documents/India_s_Course_Correction_on_Iran.htm

out in the context of India-China dialogue: "While improved relations could alleviate each nation's challenges, a further motivation is given by India's shared resentment toward the international system."[57]

Iran Joins the Game

At the turn of the millennium, Irani's President from 1997-2005, Mohammad Khatami, proposed the concept of dialogue of civilizations. Initially being a counter-thesis to Samuel Huntington's work, *The Clash of Civilizations*, Khatami insisted on and argued for the need for discussion between different religions and cultures, especially during his address to the 53rd session of the UN General Assembly (1998-1999) when he officially declared 2001 to be the Year of Dialogue Among Civilizations. The peculiarity of Mohammad Khatami's theory of "dialogue of civilizations" rests in that it offers a systematic, scholarly, and practically feasible and purposeful use of exchange between civilizations to overcome barriers of alienation between different players on the global political scene to prevent crisis situations in the world taking into account the modern level of technological and communication development and with an eye towards global problems which threaten the very existence of mankind.[58] Khatami said:

We should not forget that cultures and civilizations always have interaction and mutual influence. New abilities were formed due to their interaction. Non-dialogue paradigm leads to a deadlock, to overcome which we inevitably appeal to the dialogue approaches. Constructive indicators of dialogue certainly must not be limited only to the spheres of politics and culture. Not all constructive indicators of culture are only cultural ones; since economic, social, cultural and educational aspects participate in this formation. Therefore, promotion of dialogue of civilizations should be recognized as a multi-sided necessity.[59]

---

57 Amee Patel, The End of the Unipolar International Order? Implications of the Recent Thaw in Sino-Indian Relations // Greater China, Winter 2006, P. 18

58 Melikhov I. S.M. Khatami: mezhcivilizatsionniy dialog I musulmanskoe soobshestvo // Diplomaticheskiy vestnik, № 9. 2001.

59 Seyyed Mohammad Khatami. Dialogue among Civilizations. High-Level Conference. Eurasia in the XXIst Century: Dialogue of Cultures, or Conflict of Civilizations? Issyk-Kul, Kyrgyzstan, 10 and 11 June 2004. Paris, 2005. http://unesdoc.unesco.org/images/0014/001465/146593E.pdf

In 2001, however, a terrorist attack struck New York and the American neoconservatives subsequently triumphed in their insisting on the necessity of military intervention in Iraq and Afghanistan under the pretext of fighting terrorism and finding (non-existent) weapons of mass destruction. The harsh dualism put forth as an ultimatum by the George W. Bush Administration to the tune of "those who aren't with us, are with the terrorists" buried any efforts at establishing such a dialogue of civilizations.

During the presidency of Khatami's successor, Mahmoud Ahmadinejad, Iran became yet another pretext for the West's contrived "concerns." Meanwhile, on the other hand, Iran became an object of interest for all those forces resisting Washington-led unipolar globalization. High prices and demand for oil contributed to Iran's economic development, although sanctions imposed by Western countries and later the UN hampered the Iranian economy. Despite this, Iran demonstrated political resilience to outside influence, remained loyal to its ideological principles, and affirmed its right to be an influential player in the region. In addition, Iran under Ahmadinejad began actively cooperating with those Latin American countries which adopted an anti-imperialist foreign policy course. The fact that these countries' leaderships, and first and foremost Venezuela, Ecuador, Nicaragua, and Bolivia adhered to socialist views did not hinder the establishment of an alliance which set for itself the goal of political multipolarity based on respect for the sovereignty of states and their peoples' cultural traditions. Cooperation with Russia, China, and African countries was also amplified.

Moreover, similar views came to be shared by other senior politicians of the Islamic Republic of Iran. In May 2006, the Commander-in-Chief of the Islamic Revolutionary Guard Corps, General Yahya Rahim Safavi, stressed that "Today, taking into account countries such as Russia, China, India, and Iran, the world is moving in the direction of multipolarity contrary to the desire of the USA."[60] Ahmadinejad continued Iran's course towards multipolarity during his second presidential term as well. At the 65th session of the UN General Assembly in October 2010, Ahmadinejad said:

60 Iran I Rossiyskaya Federatsiya: Rossiya, Kitai, India i Iran – liniya moshnoy sili, 10 May 2006. http://www.iran.ru/news/politics/39484/Iran_i_Rossiyskaya_Federaciya_Rossiya_Kitay_Indiya_i_Iran_liniya_moshchnoy_sily

> The inefficiency of capitalism and existing global governance and its structures has manifested itself for many years, and the majority of countries and peoples are in search of fundamental changes for the sake of justice in international relations…The world is in need of the logic of compassion, justice, and universal cooperation, not the logic of force, domination, unipolarity, war, and intimidation…The Iranian people and the majority of peoples and governments of the world are against the current, discriminatory global governance. The inhumane nature of this governance has brought it to a standstill and requires radical revision. Universal cooperation, pure thoughts, and divine and humane governance are needed to remedy the situation in the world and to transition to peace and prosperity.[61]

The Supreme Leader of Iran, Ayatollah Khamenei, also stressed the pursuit of multipolarity. During his speech at the 16th summit of the Non-Aligned Movement in Tehran in August 2012, Khamenei pointed out the need to reform the UN, drew attention to the West's unilateral imposition of its programs undermining the principles of democracy, the destructive work of monopolized mass media, and problems of weapons of mass destruction. Khamenei proposed the doctrine of a "Middle East without nuclear weapons" by which, of course, he meant Israel as an outcast in this issue, and highlighted the need to improve "political productivity in global governance."[62] Without a doubt, such a venue as the Non-Aligned Movement's summit is not only for political reports advising the need for high morality and justice, but is a platform for criticizing neo-imperialism. It is a powerful pooling of leaders and senior officials of states from all continents to meet and take advantage of a decent opportunity to reach agreements, discuss the prospects of joint projects, and reduce possible friction in diplomatic relations.[63] Iran's role in this regard is very indicative.

---

61 Выступление президента Ирана на 65-й сессии Генеральной Ассамблеи ООН, 04 октября 2010 http://www.iran.ru/news/interview/68545/Vystuplenie_prezidenta_Irana_na_65_y_sessii_Generalnoy_Assamblei_OON

62 Vistuplenie ayatolli Khamenei na sammite Dvizheniya neprisoedineniya.// Geopolitica.ru, 31.08.12 http://www.geopolitica.ru/Articles/1483/

63 Savin L. Iran, Dvizheniye neprisoedineniya I mnogopolyarnost. Geopolitica.ru, 17.09.2012 https://www.geopolitica.ru/article/dvizhenie-neprisoedineniya-iran-i-mnogopolyarnost

If Iran de facto is and has been before a geopolitical center, then the changing international situation has opened the possibility for it to transform its status and rise to the level of a geopolitical pole. If Iran is approached not only as a sovereign nation-state, but as a center of Shiite Islam, then we undoubtedly see that Iran's influence in a number of countries with Shiite populations makes it a geopolitical subject of a different level and significance. Lebanon, Syria, Iraq, Yemen, and Palestine are states which depend on support from Iran through various mechanisms.

The Iranian international relations expert Behzad Khoshandam posits that 2016 was a turning point for Iran in regards to choosing its international course, which was finally confirmed to be that of multipolarity. This is due to several interconnected factors: (1) the signing of the nuclear deal with six countries (a manifestation of the logic of Iran's strategic patience in political, trade, economic, and other interests); (2) rapprochement with Russia; (3) Trump's victory in the US presidential elections; (4) understanding the hostile intentions of the numerous countries conducting proxy wars against Iran (Qatar, Saudi Arabia, Israel); (5) and the overall serious turn towards Eurasia.[64] To this we can add the strategic agreement with China announced in January 2016 which includes Beijing actively supporting Iran in acquiring full membership in the SCO.[65]

Indeed, in the opinion of Iranian scholars, the country's national interests are best protected in none other than the multipolar paradigm of global politics. Mohammad Mehdi Mazaheri from Tehran University believes that only in a multipolar international system can regional cooperation and balanced relations with all powerful states help countries achieve their national interests.[66] The Iranian political scientist Massoud Mousavi Shafaei from Tarbiat Modares University

---

64 Behzad Khoshandam, Iran's Foreign Policy in 2016, Iran Review, December 28, 2016.
http://www.iranreview.org/content/Documents/Iran-s-Foreign-Policy-in-2016.htm

65 Iran, China Announce Roadmap for Strategic Partnership, Farsnews, Jan 23, 2016. http://en.farsnews.com/newstext.aspx?nn=13941103001266

66 Mohammad Mehdi Mazaheri, Russia Bracing for Multipolar International System, Iran Review, September 21, 2015.
http://www.iranreview.org/content/Documents/Russia-Bracing-for-Multipolar-International-System.htm

has proposed that Iran take advantage of the fluidity of the international system and the emergence of new conditions for active operations in different regional environments. Insofar as Iran is located between the Middle East and Central Asia, it indeed does have a choice. The Middle East is submerged in chaos, ethnic conflicts, wars, and terror, and this crisis will likely continue for an indefinite period of time. In these circumstances, the restoration of order in the region under the leadership of a single hegemonic power or even under the pressure of large powers is seen as practically impossible.[67] Given that the US instrumentalizes most Arab countries to contain Iran's geopolitical ambitions, this thesis is justified. Washington simply will not allow Iran to be more actively engaged in the region even if Iranian intentions are altogether benevolent and noble. Therefore, in Massoud Mousavi Shafaei's opinion, Iran must reorient itself and its geo-economic logic towards Central Asia and Southeast Asia. However, this does not mean an end to Iranian presence in the Middle East necessary to defend its vital national security interests.

The opinion has also been expressed that Russia, Iran, and China "all feel that [a] multipolar world is the only condition for future development of our planet and its inhabitants. They have experienced again and again that unilateral dictates emanating from US, instead of solving problems, generates more and more of them. So it is obviously in their interests, to get united on the issue of multi-polarity, and insist – through various institutions like US, or press, or even new military alliances – that the business as usual – is not going to be accepted."[68]

Iran understands that joining the multipolar club inevitably means pressure from the West. Thus, Tehran can expect new challenges, as can the other architects of the multipolar world order. In this vein

---

67 Massoud Mousavi Shafaei, Iran's Foreign Policy Needs Paradigm Change: Transition from Middle Eastern Terror to Geo-economics of Asian Hope, Iran Review, January 31, 2017. http://www.iranreview.org/content/Documents/Iran-s-Foreign-Policy-Needs-Paradigm-Change-Transition-from-Middle-Eastern-Terror-to-Geo-economics-of-Asian-Hope.htm

68 Prof. Golstein: 'Russia, Iran, China Feel Multi-Polar World is Only Condition for Future Development', Jul 17, 2016. http://en.farsnews.com/newstext.aspx?nn=13950421000941

Tehran University Professor Jahangir Karami has noted that although Russia can effectively restrict the US' unilateral approach through the UN, NATO expansion challenges Russia's efforts, as was the case with the crises provoked in Ukraine and Syria aimed directly against Moscow.[69]

Nevertheless, Iran has a long history of withstanding Western hegemony and other forces from the first contacts with the Portuguese in the early 16th century to the seizure of the US Embassy during the Islamic Revolution of 1979. Indeed, opposing US sanctions and working to develop their own economic approaches and conduct in international affairs are characteristic of Iran's course towards multipolarity.

The Latin American Pivot

It should also be noted that turbulent geopolitical processes tied to anti-colonial movements and the restructuring of the Americas have been underway in the Western hemisphere since the 19th century. When many eminent South American natives dreamed of creating states of a new type[70], their northern neighbors who had already gained independence were planning to deprive Spain of its colonies as soon as the opportunity arose.[71] This largely explains the emergence of the US' Monroe Doctrine, its intervention in South American states' domestic affairs, and Washington's labelling of this part of the world as the "US' backyard."

Since the 1990's, partially thanks to the emergence of new communication technologies, Latin America has been home to a rise in social movements mainly of a left orientation. In addition to radical groups ranging from the Peruvian Sendero Luminoso to the Revolutionary Armed Forces of Colombia (FARC) and National Liberal Army (ELN) which operate in the underground, significant successes and support from the local population have also been

---

69 Jahangir Karami, Russia, Crises in Syria and Ukraine, and the Future of the International System, Iran Review, Appril 15, 2014. http://www.iranreview.org/content/Documents/Russia-Crises-in-Syria-and-Ukraine-and-the-Future-of-the-International-System.htm

70 For example, Francisco de Miranda's project for Greater Colombia

71 Rydjord J. Foreign Interest in the Independence of New Spain. Durham, 1935, pp.99,104.

achieved in Mexico by the Zapatista Army of National Liberation (EZLN) whose leader, Subcomandante Marcos, has become a symbol of anti-globalism. The Salvadoran guerrillas of the Farabundo Marti National Liberation Front have been practically legalized and have acted as one of the main political parties. In Nicaragua, the Sandinista National Liberation Front (FSLN) has for quite some time held the largest number of seats in parliament.

The failure of economic reforms aimed at structural readjustment and initiated by the World Bank in the 1990's finally dispelled the myth of the neo-liberal miracle and led to the so-called "left turn" in South and Central America. The failure of right-wing regimes to cope with systemic crises allowed left populists to come to power in the likes of Hugo Chavez, Manuel Zelaya, Rafael Correa, and Evo Morales. These leaders' actions do not fit into the logic of classical socialism associated with the teachings of Marx and the Soviet system. It is thus no coincidence that the writer Heinz Dietrich has called Venezuelan leader Hugo Chavez's course "21st century socialism." These new Latin American leaders not only reject capitalist principles and are fighting neo-imperialism, but are also engaged in rethinking political dogma, reviving local customs and culture (indigenism), and advocating environmental consciousness and a multipolar world order.[72]

Nationalizing resources and the various companies which earlier extracted excessive profits from these territories has been a characteristic move of such left-wing governments of the past several decades. This has drawn criticism from liberal-oriented regimes and transnational cooperations since policies such as those most consistently pursued by Hugo Chavez in Venezuela have infringed on their economic interests.[73] Hugo Chavez himself is well known as the author of the term "axis of good" which he counterposed in 2006 to the American concept of the "axis of evil."[74] According to the Venezuelan ideologists of Chavismo, "a multipolar world is an invention of men of revolution. It is the establishment of a just, balanced world without

72 Savin L. Vek Latinskoy Ameriki. Sbudetsya li mechta Simona Bolivara? // Odnako, 11 March 2013. pp. 40 — 44.

73 Savin L. Paradigmalnie sdvigi v Zapadnom polusharii // Geopolitika № 5, 2011. pp. 4 - 11.

74 This phrase was used by George Bush Jr. during speech to Congress Jan. 29, 2002.

empires, domination, and exploitation. It is a world in which the realm of human prosperity will rise above selfish ambitions, a world where mutual benefit will govern relations and global destruction will be cast into the dustbin of history."[75]

Cultural identity is of great importance to the peoples of this region's countries. In this sense, it is very telling that Latin American political scientists are increasingly using the expression "Nuestra America" ("Our America") instead of the usual "Latin America."[76] In the early 2000's, the theory of "eco-regionalism" also became popular throughout Latin America. Bolivia, for instance, sharply criticized the Western scheme to introduce taxes on emissions, claiming that they, Western countries, themselves once mercilessly exploited natural resources whereas now, upon acquiring more advanced and high-tech types of production, they want to shift the burden of responsibility onto Third World states. Rejecting capitalism (the Bolivian concept of Sumak kawsay, or "bio-pluralism"), relying on traditional values, recognizing diversity (multinational states and autonomy), counter-hegemonic rhetoric, and self-determination and de-colonization - all of these make up the distinct features of the Latin American integration project whose ideologues are also undertaking studies of the experience of European peoples. It bears recognition that Ibero-Americans possess significant advantages such as a common language (Portuguese is spoken in Brazil but is a close relative of Spanish), a common religion, and history of national-liberation struggles against European metropolises.

Latin American integration has several levels and is associated with various initiatives, first and foremost Unasur, Mercosur, CELAC, and ALBA. The Bolivarian Alliance for the Peoples of Our America is a kind of ideological bloc founded in 2004 on the initiative of Fidel Castro and Hugo Chavez. As can be presumed, the alliance includes socialist-oriented states, but its main goal remains cooperation and intensifying trade relations. ALBA, meanwhile, includes eight countries: Bolivia, Venezuela, Cuba, Ecuador, Nicaragua, the Dominican Republic, Antigua and Barbuda, Saint Vincent, and the Grenadines.

---

75 Eva Golinger. Venezuela: ot zadnego dvora k mnogopolyarnomu miru / Geopolitika № 5, 2011. p. 83.

76 This term was first employed by the Cuban poet and revolutionary Jose Marti in 1891.

As for Paraguay, in the summer of 2012, the placeman of left forces, Paraguayan President Fernando Lugo, was ousted. "Impeaching him was not difficult," the Argentine geopolitician Carlos Pereira de Melo remarks. "After all, this decision was backed in Washington. Moreover, right-wing traditions are extremely strong in Paraguay (for over forty years the country was ruled by the dictator Alfredo Stroessner who made no effort to hide his sympathy for the German Nazis). The Paraguayan oligarchy will now most likely prevent this country, which is considered the heart of South America, from joining integration processes on the continent." Moreover, Paraguay could become the US' main foothold in the region, especially considering the fact that it is home to the large American base in Mariscal Estigarribia. For Bolivia, which is part of the ALBA bloc, this means geo-strategic encirclement in the likes of Operation Anaconda. The US has military bases in neighboring Peru as well, and a powerful network of oligarchs with ties to Washington remains in Chile.

However, despite all the obstacles created by the US, the states making up the ALBA bloc have achieved certain successes. It is worth noting among their large joint projects the general bank dealing with finances, common education programs, the development of transport infrastructure, and the establishment of the ALBA Cultural Fund and the University of Tourism. The ALBA countries have distributed amongst themselves responsibilities for various sectors, and large national projects have been connected with integration mechanisms, creating preconditions which would guarantee that control by transnational corporations is impossible.

If Cuba and Venezuela are considered to be the leaders of the ALBA bloc, then the key role in Mercosur (the Southern Common Market) is played by Argentina and Brazil. It is these states who in 1985 signed off on a program of economic integration and cooperation which laid the foundations for a regional association focusing on trade. Mercosur also includes Venezuela, Uruguay, and Paraguay (whose membership was suspended from June 2012 to April 2013). At the present moment, Mercosur encompasses a huge space stretching from the Tierra del Fuego to the Caribbean Basin with an area of 12.8 million kilometers squared and a population numbering 275 million people. The potential of this union can be judged on the basis that its territory encompasses two-thirds of the world's fresh water reserves and 20% of the world's oil.

In 2004, Mercosur and the Andean Community, originally counting Bolivia, Columbia, Peru, Chile (which left in 1976), Ecuador, and Venezuela (who was in the organization from 1973 to 2011), held negotiations on the creation of a new union, Unasur, or Union of South American Nations. The organization was established on December 9th, 2004 at a summit of 12 Latin American states in the Peruvian city of Cusco. The ideas engrained in the Andean group, such as developing a common economic policy, coordinating projects, and harmonizing legislation, have since spread to the whole of South America. In May 2012, at the 3rd Unasur Energy Council in Caracas, an agreement was signed guaranteeing the protection of regional resources and envisioning integration in the energy sector. A plan was adopted to construct 30 infrastructural projects including three transport corridors running across South America and connecting the Pacific and Atlantic oceans.

As for fiscal policy, Unasur countries have agreed on a common currency, the SUCRE, which is usually associated with the Bolivarian Alliance, an example which demonstrates the interdependence of the integration projects under examination. The Union of South American Nations is trying to pursue a common foreign policy as well, with Unasur states jointly defending the interests of the organization's members as in the case of Argentina in its dispute with Great Britain over sovereignty over the Malvinas Islands. In 2012, Chile, Venezuela, Bolivia, and other countries in the union brought the question of "returning the islands to Buenos Aires" to the UN Committee on Decolonization. In another recent example, Ecuador was able to enlist Unasur's support in the Julian Assange case.

Unasur's leaders are aiming to establish collective defense mechanisms as well. At an extraordinary summit of the organization held in Brazil in 2008, the South American Defense Council was founded as an advisory and coordinating body whose task is analyzing and eliminating possible threats in the region. Not only are unresolved territorial problems persistent in Latin America, but enormous resources are concentrated here, such as tropical forests which are distinguished by the greatest biodiversity in the world. In addition, by 2025 the region will produce 40% of all food on Earth. Given the dim predications on access to food and water in the future, a common defense policy is a vital issue for Latin American countries.

Yet another integration project is CELAC (Community of Latin American and Caribbean States), a regional political and economic organization founded on April 17th, 2007 during the first meeting on energy integration held between the leaders of Argentina, Bolivia, Brazil, Venezuela, Guyana, Colombia, Paraguay, Peru, Suriname, Uruguay, Chile, and Ecuador, on the Venezuelan island of Margarita. Without a doubt, CELAC is a counterweight to Washington's project, the Organization of American States. Moreover, one of the union's main goals is opposing the US' regional policy. It is no coincidence that the late Venezuelan President Hugo Chavez became a kind of symbolic figure for the community's leaders.

On the other hand, unlike ALBA, CELAC intentionally avoids ideologization in attempting to work out a consolidated position on most issues. Speaking in Caracas in December 2011, Uruguayan President Pepe Mujica urged his colleagues to refrain from dogmatism, stating: "You can hold any views - right, left, centrist, or whatever you please." The community encompasses a whole spectrum of tendencies ranging from Argentine syndicalists to Brazilian supporters of federalization and 21st century socialism. CELAC has even come to include Mexico, which has always been sidelined from integration processes in Latin America given its membership in NAFTA (the North American Free Trade Agreement). This points to the umbrella nature of the organization which is nonetheless presently considered to be the most powerful instrument for integration in the region.

Although in recent years neoliberals have launched successful counter-revolutionary offensives in Brazil and Argentina, successfully carried out a coup in Bolivia that ousted Evo Morales, and left Venezuela on the verge of collapse, it is to be expected that the seeds of multipolarity will still bear fruit. The 2019 Argentinian presidential elections saw the victory of Alberto Fernández, who has begun to return to the country's old course before the neoliberal revanche of the pro-American oligarch Mauricio Macri. The 2018 election of Andrés Manuel López Obrador as President of Mexico in 2018 also symbolized Mexico's tiredness of years of US interference and Washington's imposition of rules along its own game-scenarios. As the Argentine geopolitician Professor Carlos Alberto Pereira Mele has noted:

> In any case, the new unipolar system had a short life and came to an end in the beginning of the 21st century once Russia once again put up a challenge in world affairs and the two Asian giants, China and India, are turning into an economic and strategic force. In global terms, the significance of some Latin American countries is growing, such as Brazil, Argentina, and Venezuela. Relations between these countries and China, Russia, and Iran are important, and seem to be acquiring strategic importance, foreshadowing the emergence of a new multipolar system whose foundations are being built in Eurasia and South America.[77]

The Argentine political scientist and philosopher Alberto Buela has also pointed out:

> Brazil and Argentina form an axis around which the geopolitics of South America revolve. This axis should strive to form a 'floating' rhombus with power lines running through the capital of Brazil, Buenos Aires, Lima, and Caracas in order to defend the Heartland of South America. The principle of integration should be the following. Given that Brazil's economy is five times larger than Argentina's, contributions should be made according to this proportion. Integration is proportional, not equal. In this case, equality would be the first source of injustice. Brazil and Argentina should first and foremost establish a common currency (el austral) in order to strengthen their economies against the dollar and the euro. At the same time, they should create a single grain export company in order to avoid the diktats of the Chicago stock market. Next, it is necessary to form joint naval forces to control the sea territories of the Atlantic Ocean lying off of the wide coast to avert the robberies that occur in the South Atlantic by dividing the total sovereign space. This is not a stumbling block, but a point of unification.[78]

Indeed, if Martin Heidegger called Russia the land of the future in saying that "the history of the earth of the future lies in the not yet-liberated essence of Russianness," then in regards to Latin America there is the prescient statement of the no less eminent German

77 Pereyra Mele, Carlos Alberto. De la Unipolaridad a la Multipolaridad. 12 de agosto de 2010. http://licpereyramele.blogspot.com/2010/08/de-la-unipolaridad-la-multipolaridad.html

78 Buela A. Geopolitika Yuzhnoy Ameriki // Geopolitika № 5, 2011. P. 20.

philosopher, Hegel, who in his lectures on the philosophy of history said that "America is therefore the land of the future, where, in the ages that lie before us, the burden of the World's History shall reveal itself – perhaps in a contest between North and South America."[79]

New Actors, New Norms

Ethical and normative aspects are also essential criteria in the development of geopolitical multipolarity. First and foremost, we can see a certain dichotomy in evaluations of multipolarity. If for the Eastern point of view of multipolarity coexistence and cooperation are salient, as is particularly the case for the Chinese author Zhang Yulin who points out that there exist different centers of power with considerable influence on regional and international affairs, then Western perspectives on multipolarity are largely critical in their positions. Those authors who have formulated theories of multipolarity on the basis of political (neo)realism, such as Kenneth Waltz and John Mearsheimer, although they talk about the desirability of multiple poles of power, nevertheless suggest that a single pole can challenge another. In the context of the hyperrealist school, such challenges are virtually inevitable. Famous theorists of the cycles of war and hegemony in the likes of Thompson and Modelski also prefer the classical balance of power in which the political structure of a multipolar world will consist of autonomous centers housing distinctively expressed cultures and their own nuclear arsenals and space systems. In their view, it is assumed that each center will have its own sphere of influence.

Secondly, international law is clearly dominated by normativism even though numerous provisions of international law are regularly violated and ignored by the weakening pole that is the United States of America. Normativism, with its roots in the Vienna school of law whose founder is considered to be Hans Kelsen and according to which law is viewed solely as an objective logical form abstracted from social, psychological, and historical content, cannot be used as an axiom in the study and practice of international multipolarity. Indeed, the classical methods of political science - the historical,

79 Hegel translation from https://www.marxists.org/reference/archive/hegel/help/quotes.htm; Hegel, G.W.F. Vorlesung uber die Philosophie der Weltgeschichte. In: Die Vernunft in der Geschichte. Hamburg: F. Meiner Verlag, 1994. Band 1, p. 209.

value-normative, and institutional - indicate that there is no one single approach. Historical development has been uneven across all regions, and different cultures and peoples have their own values that have influenced the formation of their political institutions. Even while being pressured by Western theoretical concepts and practices (whether imposed or accepted voluntarily under the influence of the West), many countries of the world have still preserved vestiges of their local and regional institutions rooted in local identity (culture, religion, traditions). As follows, new laws should be formulated for international relations which will be effective and recognized by the majority of actors as adequate new conditions for global world order. Without a doubt, a normative theory of multipolarity is a priori built on cooperative ethics and goes far beyond the egoistic solipsism of unipolarity in which all ethical questions are turned into the domestic affairs of the leading state and all other are supposed to follow and submit to the latter. From the viewpoint of multipolarity, on the contrary, the point is not even whether a superpower can effectively act alone or not, but that cooperation is in itself necessary and good.[80]

Another important aspect of multipolar theory is that it allows for defying the US and the historical West as a whole and these countries' use of force against weaker states. This criticism, even in rhetoric, is appropriate for a number of countries since the matter at hand is first and foremost the value of respecting sovereignty, cooperation, and peacefully resolving conflicts.

Nevertheless, questions remain which do not yet have clear answers. How many poles there will be is one such quantitive question. If we operate with the modernist paradigm, then we see that there are several levels of multipolarity. Firstly, there is the existing number of states in the world. Secondly, there is the criteria of these states' respective sovereignty, since the difference between real and nominal sovereignty can be enormous, and all countries are built on a certain scale of sovereignty. Thirdly, there is the presence of states in certain alliances, the implications of which are in need of clarification. For example, while Turkey is a NATO member, it is nonetheless pursuing a foreign policy which radically differs from that of the Western bloc

80 Savin L. Empiricheskie I normativnie aspekti mnogopolyarnosti // Geopolitica.ru. http://www.geopolitica.ru/article/empiricheskie-i-normativnye-aspekty-mnogopolyarnosti

of the North Atlantic alliance. We can presume that even given clear criteria, there will be no certain number of poles, i.e., the international structure will be in a constant state of flux and outgoing poles will come to be replaced by emerging ones.

There is also the sub-level of multipolarity within states in the ethnic, religious, and administrative dimensions. The director of the Center for Geopolitical Studies at the Russian Academy of Science's Institute of Europe, Konstantin Sorokin, who was one of the pioneers of Russian multipolar theory, has also pointed out that, due to the fact that ethno-civilizational or cultural communities overlap with global economic zones and given that the totality of historical traditions, views, and varying evaluations all influence the evolution of the geopolitical map of the world, the geopolitical map of the modern world is therein multi-layered and polycentric.[81]

In the next chapter, we will turn to discuss the various nuances and subtleties of such terms crucial to the institutionalization of multipolarity.

81 Sorokin K. Geopolitika sovremennogo mira i Rossiya //Polis, 1995. №1-2.

4

Polycentricity and Pluriversality

In the second chapter we showed how the very term "multipolarity" is of American (Anglo-Saxon) origin, and in the third chapter we examined similar concepts that have been developed in other countries. As various scholars have indicated, varying interpretations of multipolarity have provoked certain conceptual dilemmas. For instance, a report on long-term global trends prepared by the Zurich Center for Security Studies in 2012 noted that:

> The advantage of 'multipolarity' is that it accounts for the ongoing diffusion of power that extends beyond uni-, bi-, or-tripolarity. But the problem with the term is that it suggests a degree of autonomy and separateness of each 'pole' that fails to do justice to the interconnections and complexities of a globalised world. The term also conceals that rising powers are still willing to work within the Western shaped world economic system, at least to some extent. This is why the current state of play may be better described as 'polycentric'. Unlike 'multipolarity', the notion of 'polycentricism' says nothing about how the different centres of power relate to each other. Just as importantly, it does not elicit connotations with the famous but ill-fated multipolar system in Europe prior to 1914 that initially provided for regular great power consultation, but eventually ended in all-out war. The prospects for stable order and effective global governance are not good today. Yet, military confrontation between the great powers is not a likely scenario either, as the emerging polycentric system is tied together in ways that render a degree of international cooperation all but indispensable.[1]

1 Daniel Mockli (ed.), Strategic Trends 2012. Key Developments in Global Affairs, Center for Security Studies, ETH Zurich, March 2012. P. 12.

The Swiss scholars involved in this summation approached the issue from the standpoint of reviewing security issues in a globalized world and tried to find an adequate expression for contemporary trends. However, there also exist purely technical approaches and ideological theories which employ the term "polycentric".

The concept of "polycentricity" had been used before to describe the functioning of complex economic subjects. Accordingly, if management theories are springboards for geopolitical practice, then this model's basic elaborations already exist. In a literal sense, the term "polycentric" suggests some kind of spatial unit with several centers. However, the term does not specify what kind of centers are in question, hence the obvious need to review various concepts and starting points before discussing polycentrism.

Four levels of this concept can be discussed in the context of political-administrative approaches. The analytical-descriptive level is needed for describing, measuring, and characterizing the current state of a spatial object by means of precisely determining how long a country or capital can be "polycentric." Secondly, this concept can be understood in a normative sense which might help, for example, in reorganizing the spatial configuration of an object, i.e., either to promote/create polycentrism or support/utilize an existing polycentric structure. Thirdly, when it comes to spatial entities, it is necessary to specify their spatial scale, i.e., at the city level, city-region, mega-regional level, or even on the national or transnational levels. Upon closer examination, the concept of polycentrism concept thus challenges our understanding of centers in urban areas, since this can concern either their roles and functional ties (relations) or their concrete morphological forms (the structure of urban fabric). This differentiation between the functional and morphological understandings of polycentrism constitutes the fourth dimension.[2]

In the contemporary situation which features the presence of city-states and megalopoli that can easily compete with some states in the

2 Peter Schmitt, Polycentricity and metropolitan planning, Journal of Nordregio, No 3, 2010. http://www.nordregio.se/Metameny/About-Nordregio/Journal-of-Nordregio/Journal-of-Nordregio-2010/Journal-of-Nordregio-no-3-2010/Polycentricity-and-metropolitan-planning/

classical understanding in the most varied criteria (number of residents and their ethnic identity, length of external borders, domestic GDP, taxes, industry, transport hubs, etc.), such an approach seems wholly appropriate for more articulated geopolitical analysis.[3] Moreover, in the framework of federal models of state governance, polycentrism serves as a marker of complex relations between all administrative centers. Regional cooperation also fits into this model since it allows subjects to "escape" mandatory compliance with a single regulator, such as in the face of a political capital, and cooperate with other subjects (including foreign ones) within a certain space.

To some extent, the idea of polycentrism is reflected in offshore zones as well. While offshores can act as "black holes" for the economies of sovereign states, on the other hand, they can also be free economic zones removing various trade barriers clearly within the framework of the operator's economic sovereignty.

It should also be noted that the theory of polycentrism is also well known in the form of the ideological contribution of the Italian community Palmiro Togliatti as an understanding of the relative characteristics of the working conditions facing communist parties in different countries following the de-Stalinization process in the Soviet Union in 1956. What if one were to apply such an analysis to other parties and movements? For example, in comparing Eurosceptics in the EU and the conglomerate of movements in African and Asian countries associated with Islam? Another fruitful endeavor from this perspective could be evaluating illiberal democracies and populist regimes in various parties of the world as well as monarchical regimes, a great variety of which still exist ranging from the United Kingdom's constitutional monarchy to the hereditary autocracy of Saudi Arabia which appeared relatively recently compared to other dynastic forms of rule. Let us also note that since Togliatti the term "polycentrism" has become popular in political science, urban planning, logistics, sociology, and as an expression for unity in diversity.

In 1969, international relations and globalization expert Howard V. Perlmutter proposed the conceptual model of EPG, or Ethnocentrism-

3 For example, Moscow has more inhabitants than Portugal, and the economy of the city-state of Singapore is many times greater than that of many Central European countries.

Polycentrism-Geocentrism, which he subsequently expanded with his colleague David A Heenan to include Regionalism. This model, famously known by the acronym EPRG, remains essential in international management and human resources.[4] This theory posits that polycentrism, unlike ethnocentrism, regionalism, and geocentrism, is based on political orientation, albeit through the prism of controlling commodity-monetary flows, human resources, and labor. In this case, polycentrism can be defined as a host country's orientation reflecting goals and objectives in relation to various management strategies and planning procedures in international operations. In this approach, polycentrism is in one way or another connected to issues of management and control.[5]

However, insofar as forms of political control can differ, this inevitably leads to the understanding of a multiplicity of political systems and automatically rejects the monopoly of liberal parliamentarism imposed by the West as the only acceptable political system. Extending this approach, we can see that the notion of polycentrism, in addition to connoting management, is contiguous to theories of law, state governance, and administration. Canada for instance has included polycentricity in its administrative law and specifically refers to a "polycentric issue" as "one which involves a large number of interlocking and interacting interests and considerations." For example, one of Canada's official documents reads: "While judicial procedure is premised on a bipolar opposition of parties, interests, and factual discovery, some problems require the consideration of numerous interests simultaneously, and the promulgation of solutions which concurrently balance benefits and costs for many different parties. Where an administrative structure more closely resembles this model, courts will exercise restraint."[6]

Polycentric law became world-famous thanks to Professor Tom Bell who, as a student at the University of Chicago's law faculty, wrote a book

4 Perlmutter, H. V., The Tortuous Evolution of Multinational Enterprises, in: Columbia Journal of World Business, 1/1969, pp. 9–18. Perlmutter, H. V., Heenan, D. A. (1974), How Multinational Should Your Top Managers Be?, in: Harvard Business Review, 52. Jg., Heft 6/1974, S. 121–132.

5 Calof, L. J., Beamish, W. P. "The right attitude for international success." Business Quarterly, 1994: 105–110.

6 Pushpanathan v. Canada (Minister of Citizenship and Immigration), [1998] 1 S.C.R. 982, para. 36.

entitled *Polycentric Law* in which he noted that other authors use phrases such as "de-monopolized law" to describe polycentric alternatives. Bell outlined traditional customary law (also known as consolamentum law) before the establishment of states and in accordance with the works of Friedrich A. Hayek, Bruce L. Benson, and David D. Friedman. Bell mentioned the customary law of the Anglo-Saxons, ecclesiastical law, guild law, and trade law as examples of polycentric law. On this note, he suggests that customary and statutory law have co-existed throughout history, an example being Roman law being applied to Romans throughout the Roman Empire at the same time as indigenous peoples' legal systems remained permitted for non-Romans.[7]

Polycentric theory has also attracted the interest of market researchers, especially public economists.[8] Rather paradoxically, it is from none other than ideas of a polycentric market that a number of Western scholars came to the conclusion that "Polycentricity can be utilized as a conceptual framework for drawing inspiration not only from the market but also from democracy or any other complex system incorporating the simultaneous functioning of multiple centers of governance and decision making with different interests, perspectives, and values."[9] In our opinion, it is very important that namely these three categories - interests, perspectives, and values - were distinguished. "Interests" as a concept is related to the realist school and paradigm in international relations, while "perspectives" suggests some kind of teleology, i.e., a goal-setting actor, and "values" are associated with the core of strategic culture or what has commonly been called the "national idea," "cultural-historical traditions", or irrational motives in the collective behavior of a people. For a complex society inhabited by several ethnic groups and where citizens identify with several religious confessions, or where social class differences have been preserved (to some extent they continue to exist in all types of societies, including in both the US and North Korea, but are often portrayed as between professional specialization or peculiarities of local stratification), a polycentric system appears to be a natural necessity for genuinely democratic

7 Tom W. Bell, Polycentric Law, Institute for Humane Studies Review, Volume 7, Number 1 Winter 1991/92.

8 Lindblom, C. E. (1979). Still Muddling, Not Yet Through. Public Administration Review, 39(6), 517-526.

9 Aligica, P. D., & Tarko, V. (2012). Polycentricity: From Polanyi to Ostrom, and Beyond. Governance, 25(2), 237-262.

procedures. In this context, the ability of groups to resolve their own problems on the basis of options institutionally included in the mode of self-government is fundamental to the notion of polycentrism.[10]

Only relatively recently has polycentrism come to be used as an anti-liberal or anti-capitalist platform. In 2006, following the summit of the World Social Forum in Caracas, Michael Blanding from *The Nation* illustrated a confrontation between "unicentrism" characterized by imperial, neo-liberal, and neo-conservative economic and political theories and institutions, and people searching for an alternative, or adherents of "polycentrism."[11] As a point of interest, the World Social Forum itself was held in a genuinely polycentric format as it was held not only in Venezuela, but in parallel also in Mali and Pakistan. Although the forum mainly involved left socialists, including a large Trotskyist lobby (which is characteristic of the anti-globalist movement as a whole), the overall critique of neoliberalism and transnational corporations voiced at the forum also relied on rhetoric on the rights of peoples, social responsibility, and the search for a political alternative. At the time, this was manifested in Latin America in the Bolivarian Revolution with its emphasis on indigenism, solidarity, and anti-Americanism.

It should be noted that Russia's political establishment also not uncommonly uses the word "polycentricity" - sometimes as a synonym for multipolarity, but also as a special, more "peace-loving" trend in global politics insofar as "polarity presumes the confrontation of poles and their binary opposition."[12] Meanwhile, Russian scholars recognize that comparing the emerging polycentric world order to historical examples of polycentricity is difficult. Besides the aspect of deep interdependence, the polycentricity of the early 21st century possesses a number of different, important peculiarities. These differences include global asymmetry insofar as the US still boasts overwhelming

10 McGinnis, M. Polycentricity and Local Public Economies: Readings from the Workshop in Political Theory and Policy Analysis. Ann Arbor: University of Michigan Press, 1999.

11 Michael Blanding, The World Social Forum: Protest or Celebration? The Nation, February 16, 2006. https://www.thenation.com/article/world-social-forum-protest-or-celebration/

12 Dynkin A., Ivanova N. (ed.) Rossiya v politsentrichnom mire. Moscow: Ves mir, 2011. P. 157.

superiority in a number of fields, and a multi-level character in which there exist: (1) a military-diplomatic dimension of global politics with the evolution of quickly developing giant states; (2) an economic dimension with the growing role of transnational actors; (3) global demographic shifts; (4) a specific space representing a domain of symbols, ideals, and cultural codes and their deconstructions; and (5) a geopolitical and geo-economic level.[13]

Here it is necessary to note that the very term "polycentricity" in itself harbors some interesting connotations. Despite being translated to mean "many", the first part ("poly-") etymologically refers to both "pole" and "polis" (all three words are of Ancient Greek origin), and the second part presupposes the existence of centers in the context of international politics, i.e., states or a group of states which can influence the dynamic of international relations. In his *Parmenides*, Martin Heidegger contributed an interesting remark in regards to the Greek term "polis", which once again confirms the importance and necessity of serious etymological analysis. By virtue of its profundity, we shall reproduce this quote in full:

> Πόλις is the πόλος, the pole, the place around which everything appearing to the Greeks as a being turns in a peculiar way. The pole is the place around which all beings turn and precisely in such a way that in the domain of this place beings show their turning and their conditions. The pole, as this place, lets beings appear in their Being and show the totality of their condition. The pole does not produce and does not create beings in their Being, but as pole it is the abode of the unconsciousness of beings as a whole. The πόλις is the essence of the place [*Ort*], or, as we say, it is the settlement (*Ort-schaft*) of the historical dwelling of Greek humanity. Because the πόλις lets the totality of beings come in this or that way into the unconcealedness of its condition, the πόλις is therefore essentially related to the Being of beings. Between πόλις and "Being" there is a primordial relation.[14]

Heidegger thus concludes that "polis" is not a city, state, nor a combination of the two, but the place of the history of the Greeks, the

13 Ibid, pp. 158 — 159.

14 Heidegger M., Parmenides, Indiana University Press (1992), 89-90.

focus of their essence, and that there is a direct link between πόλις and ἀλήθεια (this Greek word is usually translated into Russian as "truth") Thus, in order to capture polycentricity, one needs to search for the foci and distribution areas of the essence of the numerous peoples of our planet. Here we can once again mention strategic cultures and their cores.

Pluriversum

In addition to multipolarity and polycentricity, there is yet another concept which challenges the totalitarianism of liberal universality. This is the notion of "pluriversum."

In 2011, the world-renowned sociologist Bruno Latour remarked that "We all - both people and things - live in a pluriversum and there exist different, sometimes conflicting ways to bring this world to some kind of form, or forms, of unity." In Latour's opinion, "using this word [pluriversum] allows us to leave open the question of by what means we will or will not bring unity to the diversity of worlds."[15] Latour admits that he borrowed the term "pluriversum" from the famous American philosopher and psychologist William James in order to counterpose it to the notion of the "universe." In an essay written in 1895, William James wrote: "Truly all we know of good and beauty proceeds from nature, but none the less so all we know of evil. Visible nature is all plasticity and indifference, a multiverse, as one might call it, and not a universe."[16] In his later book, *A Pluralistic Universe*, published in 1909, James defended the mystical and anti-pragmatic point of view that doctrines distort rather than reveal reality. This work of James' was, along with his *The Varieties of Religious Experience*, dedicated to philosophical theories. In the former, James concludes: "For pluralism, all that we are required to admit as the constitution of reality is what we ourselves find empirically realized in every minimum of finite life…Pluralism lets things really exist in the each-form or distributively."[17]

---

15 Latur B, Mozhem li mi vernutsya na Zemlyu? // Vokrug Sveta, 01 Dec. 2011. http://www.vokrugsveta.ru/vs/article/7547/

16 James, William (October 1895), "Is Life Worth Living?", International Journal of Ethics, 1896, 6: 10.

17 James, William. A Pluralistic Universe. Cambridge, MA: Harvard University Press, 1977.

Scholars have distinguished Jamesian pluralism and "democratic temperament" as tied to James' own anti-imperialist convictions and the suspicions he harbored towards monism. Attempts have also been made to "reconstruct" a pluralistic universe through questioning pluralism and social unity and striving to associate James with a radical democratic view which avoids simplicity.[18]

Another American philosopher of a mystical-metaphysical orientation, Benjamin Paul Blood, published a book entitled *Pluriversum* in 1920.[19] Blood's approach has been compared to the ideas of Swedenborg, Plato, and Burns, and he is considered to be one of the founding fathers of pluralist philosophy. William James was familiar with Blood's works and the two maintained correspondence.

Despite such an interesting start to American philosophy, in practice other ideas unfortunately won out in the late 19th-early 20th century. In the 20th century, however, the topics of "multiverse" and "pluralism" did come into demand largely among physicists and philosophers and unrelated to political ideologies.[20] The famous philosopher David Kellogg Lewis also appealed to "pluriversality" and developed the theory of "modal realism", according to which all "possible worlds" and just as real as the "real world."[21] Lewis put forth six theses in defense of his argument:

- Possible worlds exist and are just as real as our world;
- Possible worlds as the same things as our world - they differ in content, not kind;
- Possible worlds cannot be reduced to something more basic - they are irreducible entities in themselves;

18 Jonathan McKenzie. Pragmatism, Pluralism, Politics: William James's Tragic Sense of Life// Theory & Event Volume 12, Issue 1, 2009.

19 Benjamin Paul Blood. Pluriverse (Routledge Revivals): An Essay in the Philosophy of Pluralism. https://archive.org/details/pluriverseaness00bloogoog

20 Tim Wilkinson, The Multiverse Conundrum, 2012. https://philosophynow.org/issues/89/The_Multiverse_Conundrum

21 Lewis, David K: On the Plurality of Worlds; Blackwell, Oxford 1986.

- Relevance is a barometer. When we distinguish our world from other possible worlds in saying that it is the only real one, we have in mind only that it is ours;
- Possible worlds are unified by the spatial-temporal interrelation of their parts. Every world is spatially isolated from the world;
- Possible worlds are causally isolated from each other.

Although Lewis' ideas are more controversial than anything, his very posing of such a question stimulated thinking on the actualization of political action, which earlier was believed to be unthinkable or, at the very least, undesirable for various reasons.

With the first signs of crisis of the capitalist model - no matter according to what scheme, whether the liberal one with the domination of private capital or the Marxist with state intervention and coercion - different activists, especially in post-colonial countries, increasingly appealed to original ideals, religious doctrines, environmental consciousness, and art as possible answers to the 20th century's economy-centric dogma. One example of such is Ernesto Cardenal (1925 - 2020), a Catholic priest and one of the main ideologists of liberation theology. Later, from 1979-1988, Cardenal occupied the post of Minister of Culture in the Sandinista government in Nicaragua and was also the co-founder of the cultural organization Casas de las Tres Mundos. Cardena believed that art and poetry are intimately connected to politics, and one of his later books bore the title *Pluriverse*.[22] Cardenal's poetry is often compared to the works of Pablo Neruda and Ezra Pound, both of which were directly related to politics. The world-renowned Nicaraguan poet Cardenal constantly referred to the mythological constructs, culture, and history of Central America.[23] In the opinion of *Pluriverse*'s reviewers, the book has a "mystical-cosmic-scientific" dimension in which one finds "wildlife, geology, weather, stars, people; there is always a strain of natural history running parallel with the history of imperialism, revolution, or daily life."[24]

22 Ernesto Cardenal, Pluriverse: New and Selected Poems. Edited by Jonathan Cohen. Various Translators. New York: New Directions, 2009.

23 Ernesto Cardenal, Quetzalcoatal, Editorial Nueva Nicaragua-Ediciones Monimbo, 1985; Homenaje a los indios americanos (poems), Universidad Nacional Autonoma de Nicaragua, 1969.

24 Brent Aldrich. The Revolution that Started in the Stars, A Review of Pluriverse:

The idea of pluriverse was also picked up by an anthropology professor of Ibero-American heritage at the University of North Carolina, Arturo Escobar, who argued that "the profound relationality of all life, these newer tendencies show that there are indeed relational worldviews or ontologies for which the world is always multiple – a pluriverse."[25] According to Escobar:

> Arguments about the need for an epochal transition are a sign of the times; they reflect the depth of the contemporary crises. Transition discourses (TDs) are emerging today with particular richness and intensity from a multiplicity of sites, principally social movements, some civil society NGOs, and from intellectuals with significant connections to environmental and cultural struggles. TDs are prominent in several fields, including those of culture, ecology, religion and spirituality, and alternative science (e.g., living systems and complexity).

Further, Escobar writes

> A hallmark of contemporary TDs is the fact that they posit radical cultural and institutional transformations – indeed, a transition to an altogether different world. This is variously conceptualized in terms of a paradigm shift, a change of civilizational model, or even the coming of an entirely new era beyond the modern dualist, reductionist, and economic age. This change is often seen as already happening, although most TDs warn that the results are by no means guaranteed. Thomas Berry's, notion of The Great Work – a transition 'from the period when humans were a disruptive force on the planet Earth to the period when humans become present to the planet in a manner that is mutually enhancing' – captures well this spirit. Berry calls the new era Ecozoic. The radical discontinuity between the human and the non-human domains is at the basis of many of the critiques. Along with the ideas of a separate self and of an economic domain disembedded from social life, this discontinuity is seen as the most central feature of modern ontology, or worldview.

New and Selected Poems by Ernesto Cardenal. February 20, 2009. http://englewoodreview.org/featured-pluriverse-new-and-selected-poems-by-ernesto-cardenal-vol-2-8/

25 Arturo Escobar, Challenges to Sustainability // Development, 2011. Vol. 54.2.

> The bridging of these divides is posited as crucial to healing society and the planet by secular and religious visions alike – whether it is through the notions of inter-connectedness and interdependencies of ecology…or frameworks based on self-organization and complexity focused on co-emergent systems of relations.

On this note, Escobar mentions the fact that the constitutions of Bolivia and Ecuador include such doctrines as *sumak kawsay* (Quechua), *suma qamaña* (Aymara), and *buen vivir* (which in Spanish means "to live well"). Buen-vivir presents a different philosophy of life and vision of society which subordinates economic criteria to human dignity and social justice. Escobar writes:

> Globalization discourses of all kinds assume that the world is some sort of 'global space' that will progressively and inevitably be fully occupied by capitalist modernity. There is something terribly wrong with this imaginary if we are to take the pluriverse seriously, let alone if we are to confront the ever worsening ecological and social crises. This view of globalization as universal, fully economized, and de-localized is made possible by the immense power of corporations and maintained within manageable levels of order / disorder by military might.
>
> Rather than in terms of globalization, the evolving pluriverse might be described as a process of planetarization articulated around a vision of the Earth as a living whole that is always emerging out of the manifold biophysical, human, and spiritual elements and relations that make it up. Many of the features envisioned in the TDs – from strategies of re-localization to the rise of an ecological civilization – will find a more auspicious home in this notion. We need to stop burdening the Earth with the dualisms of the past centuries, and acknowledge the radical interrelatedness, openness, and plurality that inhabit it. To accomplish this goal, we need to start thinking about human practice in terms of ontological design, or the design of other worlds and knowledges. Design would no longer involve the instrumental taming of the world for human purposes, but building worlds in which humans and the Earth can coexist and flourish.

> Pluriversal studies cannot be defined in opposition to globalization studies, nor as its complement, but needs to be outlined as an altogether different intellectual and political project. No single notion of the world, the human, civilization, the future, or even the natural can fully occupy the space of pluriversal studies. Even if partly building on the critical traditions of the modern natural, human and social sciences, pluriversal studies will travel its own path as it discovers worlds and knowledges that the sciences have effaced or only gleaned obliquely. This, it seems to me, might constitute the basis for conceptions of sustainability that go beyond the business as usual understanding of sustainable development. This notion of sustainability would be one capable of inspiring the popular and scientific imaginations alike to take steps that are at once pragmatic and transformative in the path towards more ethical and ecological words.

In another one of his works, Escobar speaks of the necessity of affirming a new, holistic cultural in place of the dualism, reductionism, and economism of modernity.[26]

Appeals to the South American tradition are not accidental. The region's pre-Columbus civilization constitutes a rich bed of worldviews and philosophical thought that for several centuries was tightly shut out by European modernity. The idea of pluriversality has thus been met with wide acclaim by scholars of South American heritage.

Amaya Querejazu of Colombia's University of Los Andes posits:

> Taking the pluriverse as an ontological starting point, implies not simply tolerating difference, but actually understanding that reality is constituted not only by many worlds, but by many kinds of worlds, many ontologies, many ways of being in the world, many ways of knowing reality…[T]he pluriverse implies the existence of many worlds somehow interconnected, in other words the human world is connected to the natural world and also to the spiritual world. This means these three kinds of worlds coexist in time and space. It entails a vision where the earth is a whole living being always emerging, encouraging the discovery

26 Escobar, Arturo. Más Allá Del Desarrollo: Postdesarrollo Y Transiciones Hacia El Pluriverso. Revista de Antropologia Social, 21, 2012. P. 40.

> and the imagination of different forms of planetarization in which human beings, along with other beings can coexist enriching each other.[27]

In this sense, the pluriverse is where the natural, religious, spiritual, political, and social are not separated.[28]

In this model, the notion of the pluriverse is understood as entailing multiple ontologies, or multiple worlds, which are supposed to be known, not simply seen as multiple perspectives on one world. Universalist discourses and globalist projects, on the other hand, are based on a unitary ontology and imperialist epistemology which presume that there is one world known on a global scale within one way of thinking and, consequently, governed and controlled in these terms.

Querejazu agrees that the notion of the universe is significantly strong and has been imposed as reality by means of various processes, some more violent than others. This idea has become so strong and so "natural" that it seems indisputable. But if we think about reality and what it covers (space, time, truth, subjectivity/objectivity, etc.), then we can see that everything is a social construct created by our consciousness in connection to our environment and in accordance with our knowledge or ontologies. "Ontologies and epistemologies of other worlds show other ways of experimenting and knowing the global and allow us to overcome some of the already restraining categories and traditional concepts of international politics such as state, sovereignty, territory, personhood." Of course, in attempting to overcome barriers and access these new frontiers, these concepts must be approached very carefully in order to not destroy the very foundations of society or, as they say, throw the baby out with the bathwater.

Querejazu suggests a valid trajectory: "The pluriverse covered and silenced by the modern myth needs to be fully disclosed, allowing the coexistence of other narratives and world views that are not necessarily encompassed by Western ontology." In Querejazu's

27 Amaya Querejazu, Encountering the Pluriverse: Looking for Alternatives in Other Worlds Revista Brasileira de Política Internacional, 59(2): e007, 2016, P. 3-4.

28 Blaser, Mario. Un Relato de La Globalización Desde El Chaco. Al-Qantara. Vol. XIX. Popayán: Editorial Universidad del Cauca, 2013.

opinion: "By embarking ourselves in the recovery and the encounter of the pluriverse, we can see that the political is much more than what has been accepted by Western mainstream thought. Just by considering that non-humans can have political agency."

University of California Professor Marisol de la Cadena defends such a seemingly extravagant notion, having begun studying Andean identity after meeting with representatives of the Quechua people in Peru. Her sources of information and inspiration were political activists who practiced traditional Indian rituals. In the Quechua language, such experts are called "Pampamisayoq" (literally translated: "the one with the desk") and are capable of communicating with the surrounding environment. It was from then that Marisol de la Cadena learned of the relationship between people and earthly entities, which subsequently inspired her to study the possibility of different, inclusive political alternatives.

In one of her works, de la Cadena writes:

> The current appearance of Andean indigeneity—the presence of earth-beings demanding a place in politics—may imply the insurgence of those proscribed practices disputing the monopoly of science to define "Nature" and, thus, provincializing its alleged universal ontology as specific to the West: one world (even if perhaps the most powerful one) in a pluriverse. This appearance of indigeneities may inaugurate a different politics, plural not because they are enacted by bodies marked by gender, race, ethnicity, or sexuality demanding rights, or by environmentalists representing nature, but because they bring earth-beings to the political, and force into visibility the antagonism that proscribed their worlds.[29]

De la Cadena thus perfectly understands the problems which the praxis of such pluriversal politics can elicit, hence subsequent references to the works of Carl Schmitt and Jacques Ranciere's notion of disagreement.[30] Moreover, she attributes particular signs

29 de la Cadena, Marisol . "Indigenous Cosmopolitics in the Andes: Conceptual Reflections Beyond 'Politics.'" Cultural Anthropology 25, no. 2 (2010), P. 346. https://doi.org/10.14506/

30 Ranciere, Jacques. Disagreement: Politics and Philosophy. Minneapolis:

to the pluriverse: "The idea of a pluriverse is utopian indeed: not because other socionatural formations and their earth-practices do not take place, but because we have learned to ignore their occurrence, considering it a thing of the past or, what is the same, a matter of ignorance and superstition."[31]

However, is such an approach really utopian? Invisible spirits are recognized not only by all the Abrahamic religions, but also in Buddhism and Hinduism. Any Asian shaman can confirm the existence of three worlds - the upper, middle, and lower - which is something characteristic for the Indo-European tradition as a whole as well, whose signs we can see in the myths of different European peoples. For instance, historical wars frequently featured cases which later became legends, tales, and teachings about aid from a heavenly army, protection afforded by the virgin, angels, or saints from enemy attacks and subsequent victory. The custom of praying before battle was widespread all the way up until the 20th century. In this context, such is but more intensive communication with entities from another world as discussed by Querejazu and de la Cadena, all the while amidst war as a continuation of politics by other means (Clausewitz). What's more, a number of countries' constitutions mention God (and as follows there are also those invisible forces which Christianity calls angels or demons depending on their ontology) and even the most liberal states' politicians commonly appeal to such notions. In one famous instance, US President George W. Bush justified the invasion of Iraq with a phrase to the tune of "God told me to go fight Al-Qaeda and I did, then he instructed me to go after Saddam, and I did." Yet another such revelation received by Bush from the spirit world was "George, go and fight the terrorists in Afghanistan."[32]

Speaking of the complexity of the task at hand, de la Cadena believes that two steps must be taken forward:

University of Minnesota Press, 1999.

31 de la Cadena, Marisol . "Indigenous Cosmopolitics in the Andes: Conceptual Reflections Beyond 'Politics.'" Cultural Anthropology 25, no. 2 (2010), P. 360. https://doi.org/10.14506/

32 We, of course, are inclined to believe that if George W. Bush was honest and did not simply use such as a rhetorical method, then it was not God, but some kind of wicked demon which gave him such advice.

> This would require two steps in the reconceptualization of (what Mouffe calls[33]) the political before pluriversal politics could start. The first step is to recognize that the world is more than one socionatural formation; the second is to interconnect such plurality without making the diverse worlds commensurable. The utopian process is, thus, the redefinition of the baseline of the political, from one where politics started with a hegemonic definition that housed the superiority of the socionatural formation of the West and its practices, to one that starts with a symmetric understanding of plural worlds, their socionatural formations and their practices. From the prior baseline (or, rather, the one we are used to) politics appeared as an affair among humans after denying the ontological copresence of other socionatural formations and its practices and translating the denial, with the use of universal history, from an antagonistic maneuver—a declaration of war against worlds deemed inferior—into a necessary condition for one good, livable world order. The new baseline is precisely the breaking of the silence, making the antagonism public to enable its transformation into agonism. At this point, rather than the biopolitical war that both liberalism and socialism waged against its alleged "others," a new pluriversal political configuration—perhaps a cosmopolitics, in Stengers's[34] terms—would connect different worlds with its socionatural formations—all with the possibility of becoming legitimate adversaries not only within nation-states but also across the world.[35]

Similarly spirited ideas can be traced in the works of Walter Mignolo, an Argentine literary theorist, semioticist, and professor at Duke University's Center for Latin America and Caribbean Studies, who has developed the idea of the pluriversum in the context of the

33 Mouffe, Chantal. On the Political. New York: Routledge, 2000.

34 Isabelle Stengers, known for her joint book with Ilia Prigozhin on chaos theory, proposes to slow down the construction of this common world and create a space for doubt in regards to what is "good." The "cosmos" and its "cosmopolitics" refers to "the unknown constituted by these multiple divergent worlds and to the articulation of which they could eventually be capable." See Stengers, Isabelle. The Cosmopolitical Proposal. In Making Things Public: Atmospheres of Democracy. Bruno Latour and Peter Weibel, eds. Pp. 994–1004. Cambridge, MA: MIT Press, 2005.

35 de la Cadena, Marisol. "Indigenous Cosmopolitics in the Andes: Conceptual Reflections Beyond 'Politics.'" Cultural Anthropology 25, no. 2 (2010): 334–370. https://doi.org/10.14506/

"epistemology of (de)colonialism." Many of Mignolo's works are devoted to problems of racial inequality in the context of historical geopolitical struggles. For example, Mignolo writes:

> [G]eo-historical and bio-graphic loci of enunciation have been located by and through the making and transformation of the colonial matrix of power: a racial system of social classification that invented Occidentalism (e.g. Indias Occidentales), that created the conditions for Orientalism; distinguished the South of Europe from its center (Hegel) and, on that long history, remapped the world as first, second and third during the Cold War. Places of nonthought (of myth, non-western religions, folklore, underdevelopment involving regions and people) today have been waking up from the long process of westernization.[36]

Mignolo also draws attention to linguistic theory and the creation of "discursive frames." He writes that comprehensive and regular frames known as scientific disciplines developed out of the classical "trivium" and "cuadrivium" adapted by Christian theology. During the era of secularization, a radical shift occurred in thinking and the organization of knowledge. Kant and Humboldt's university model along with the ideas of secularism (from Galileo to Newton) led to the establishment of a new philosophical school of thought. By the end of the 19th and beginning of the 20th century, this led to a division between the natural sciences and the humanities. On this note, Mignolo draws attention to the fact that the six modern languages of Italian, Spanish, Portuguese, German, French, and English are, in addition to being based on Greek and Latin, tied to the dominant powers from the time of the Renaissance through the Enlightenment to the present day. These six languages forged a "tool" for constructing a concept of knowledge which spread to all regions of the world. Naturally, the question arises: where is the place of Arabic, Chinese, Hindi, Urdu, Aymara, Swahili, and many other languages? Mignolo explains:

> Suppose that you belong to the category of the anthropos – the anthropos stands for the concept of the "other" in most contemporary debates about alterity – the "other," however,

36 Walter Mignolo, Epistemic Disobedience, Independent Thought and De-Colonial Freedom, Theory, Culture, and Society, Vol. 26(7-8), 2009. P. 2-3. http://waltermignolo.com/wp-content/uploads/2013/03/epistemicdisobedience-2.pdf

> doesn't exist ontologically. It is a discursive invention. Who invented "the other" if not the same in the process of constructing the same? Such an invention is the outcome of an enunciation. The enunciation doesn't name an existing entity, but invents it. The enunciation needs an enunciator (agent), an institution (not everyone can invent the anthropos), but to impose the anthropos as "the other" in the collective imaginary, it is necessary to be in a position of managing the discourse (verbal, visual, audial) by which you name and describe an entity (the anthropos or "the other") and succeed in making believe that it exists. Today, the anthropos ("the other") impinges on the lives of men and women of color, gays and lesbians, people and languages of the non-European/US world from China to the Middle East and from Bolivia to Ghana.[37]

Mignolo concludes that today we can see three scenarios along the lines of which the global future will develop:

1. Re-westernization and the unfinished project of Western modernity;

2. De-westernization and the limits of Western modernity;

3. De-coloniality and the emergence of a global political society decoupled from re-westernization and de-westernization.

The Indian thinker Partha Chatterjee gravitates in the same direction and proposes to reorient "Eurocentric modernism" towards the future where an "our modernism" (meaning of and for all regions of the world) will arise. The future of "our modernity", according to Chatterjee, does not depend on "their modernity", for the West's expansion is a fact, but is unabashedly unrepentant and "ours." Chatterjee writes: "Somehow, from the very beginning, we had a shrewd guess that given the close complicity between modern knowledges and modern regimes of power, we would for ever remain consumers of universal modernity; never would be taken seriously as its producers. It is for this reason that we have tried, for over a hundred years, to take our

37 Walter Mignolo, Geopolitics of Sensing and Knowing On (De)Coloniality, Border Thinking, and Epistemic Disobedience, 09. 2011. http://eipcp.net/transversal/0112/mignolo/en

eyes away from this chimera of universal modernity and clear up a space where we might become the creators of our own modernity."[38]

Such self-criticism is commendable. However, it can be addressed not only towards India or those countries which were someone's colonies during one historical period, but also to those states that have voluntarily imitated the West by copying its model of organizing knowledge, society, political system, etc. Russia is also no exception even though it has never officially been anyone's colony - since the Petrine reforms up to the present moment a number of social and state institutions remain afflicted with Western-centrism.

In terms of pluralistic studies, it is necessary to mention two more authors. Of particular interest are the works of the political science professor at John Hopkins University, William Connolly, an adherent to the continental school of political philosophy who has continued to develop James' ideas. In his work *Pluralism*, Connolly attempts to summarize his extensive work on ensuring a political theory of "bicameral orientation." This positions essentially contends that the individual (1) has a "creed" which he accepts and (2) recognizes that this creed is disputable. This "bicameral orientation" exists in both the socio-political sphere, the sphere of knowledge and within the universe itself, lending it ethical, gnoseological, and metaphysical flavor. Connolly employs James' notion of "rubbish" as movement in the direction of an ecological interpretation of pluralism, thus asserting that the quasi-chaos of the world imposes constraints on individual factors and sovereignty.[39] For Connolly, James' significance lies in this diminished sovereignty and the reduced political opportunities existing in this sphere. James' pluralism allows a broad faith to coexist which by nature reduces suffering. This type of pluralism and degree of acceptability and appraisal among numerous worldviews, in Connolly's opinion, is a recipe for a genuine democratic society. In one of his later works from 2013, *The Fragility of Things*, Connolly indicatively criticizes neoliberalism for its bizarre attention to only one self-organizing system - the market.[40]

---

38 Chaterjee, Partha (1998) 'Talking about Our Modernity in Two Languages', in A Possible India: Essays in Political Criticism. Calcutta: Oxford University Press. P. 275.

39 Connolly, William. Pluralism. Durham, North Carolina: Duke University Press, 2005: 72-73.

40 Connolly, William. The Fragility of Things: Self-Organizing Processes,

Finally, when it comes to geopolitics, it is impossible to avoid paying attention to Carl Schmitt, who said that "there is always a Pluriversum of different peoples and states."[41] Schmitt deconstructed the false promise of those heralds of globalization in the interwar period with the utmost clarity, illustrating how it is impossible to establish a completely global political project:

> The political entity presupposes the real existence of an enemy and therefore coexistence with another political entity. As long as a state exists, there will thus always be in the world more than just one state. A world state which embraces the entire globe and all of humanity cannot exist. The political world is a pluriverse, not a universe...The political entity cannot by its very nature be universal in the sense of embracing all of humanity and the entire world. If the different states, religions, classes, and other human groupings on earth should be so unified that a conflict among them is impossible and even inconceivable and if civil war should forever be foreclosed in a realm which embraces the globe, then the distinction of friend and enemy would also cease. What remains is neither politics nor state, but culture, civilization, economic, morality, law, art, entertainment, etc. If and when this condition will appear, I do not know. At the moment, this is not the case. And it is self-deluding to believe that the termination of a modern war would lead to world peace - thus setting forth the idyllic goal of complete and final depoliticalization - simply because a war between the great powers today may easily turn into a world war.
>
> Humanity as such cannot wage war because it has no enemy, at least not on this planet. The concept of humanity excludes the concept of the enemy, because the enemy does not cease to be a human being - and hence there is no specific differentiation in that concept. That wars are waged in the name of humanity is not a contradiction of this simple truth; quite the contrary, it has an especially intensive political meaning. When a state fights its political enemy in the name of humanity, it is not a war for the

Neoliberal Fantasies, and Democratic Activism. Durham, North Carolina: Duke University Press, 2013.

41 Schmitt C.: Der Begriff des Politischen. In: Archiv für Sozialwissenschaften und Sozialpolitik. 58 (1927), S. 1–33.

> sake of humanity, but a war wherein a particular state seeks to usurp a universal concept against its military opponent. At the expense of its opponent, it tries to identify itself with humanity in the same way as one can misuse peace, justice, progress, and civilization in order to claim these as one's own and to deny the same to the enemy.
>
> The concept of humanity is an especially useful ideological instrument of imperialist expansion, and in its ethical-humanitarian form it is a specific vehicle of economic imperialism.[42]

It is significant that attempts by renowned liberal thinkers to refute Carl Schmitt's theory have provenly failed. Jurgen Habermas tried to construct an "absent dialogue" between Kant - updated and reinterpreted in light of what separates us from the 18th century institutionally and legally - and Schmitt "updated" as the representative of strong objections to the cosmopolitan projects.[43] In the end, Habermas could not profoundly study Schmitt's alternative to cosmopolitanism which consists not simply of "returning" to the sovereign nation-state, but also imagining the political Pluriversum based on the concept of Großraum.[44]

Having examined the theories put forth by European, North American, South American, and other thinkers from over the past century and especially the past two decades, we have arrived at the conclusion that "the world is a pluriversum of diverse peoples, cultures, and civilizations whose differences need defending from the leveling, homogenizing forces of liberalism's global market."[45] We can also

42 Citing Schmitt C. Ponyatie Politicheskogo // Voprosi Sotsiologii. 1992. № 1. pp. 37-67. / English translation from https://books.google.com/books?id=JFqV-VtjlLoC&printsec=frontcover&hl=pl&source=gbs_ge_summary_r&cad=0#v=onepage&q=imperialism&f=false

43 Habermas J. "Kant's Idea of Perpetual Peace, with the Benefit of Two Hundred Years' Hindsight (1995)," in: James Bohman and Matthias Lutz-Bachmann (eds.), Perpetual Peace. Essays on Kant's Cosmopolitan Ideal, The MIT Press, 1997.

44 Monod J.-C., Ron Estes. Toward Perpetual War? The Stakes and Limits of Schmitt's Critique of Kant's Cosmopolitanism. The New Centennial Review, Volume 13, Number 1, Spring 2013, pp. 137-160

45 O'Meara M. Benoist's Pluriversum. An Ethnonationalist Critique, The Occidental Quarterly, Vol. 5, No. 3. P. 30 http://www.toqonline.com/archives/v5n3/53-mo-pluriversum.pdf

draw certain related conclusions on multipolarity, polycentricity, and pluriversality.

Multipolarity is a well-established term that is a product of Western thought. For the West's political elite, which is inclined to expand its hegemony on a planetary scale, this concept is a frightening ideology that might not only destroy unipolarity through competition posed by other centers of power, but also threatens to generate regional and global conflicts. More moderate views suggest a calm perception of the onset of multipolarity, whether in terms of political alliances or the dismantling of the Bretton-Woods dollar system as the global economy's lifeline. This is good insofar as multipolarity presents a clear and rational argument within Western political science and can be used in polemics with liberals.

At the same time, a different interpretation of multipolarity is possible, including a different understanding of the pole, which was demonstrated by the example of Heidegger.

Polycentricity has a broader interpretation. Administrative governance, economic management, comparative political science, and jurisprudence all use it as an effective instrument for realizing public interests and channeling potential conflicts in a constructive direction. Polycentricity can also be used widely in the political sciences for critically analyzing unipolarity. As we have seen, more interesting etymological interpretations can also be turned to when necessary.

The Pluriverse (or pluriversality) concerns the field of political philosophy and is associated with the deepest level of political ideas, hence the difficulty of expressing it in a language familiar to science and avoiding metaphysics, religion, mythology, and anthropology. This concept, nevertheless, is already widely employed by various scholars, thus lending it academic weight.

All three of these terms can be used to refer to the new global geopolitical reality, but it would be desirable to specify the context and concrete situation so as to not introduce confusion into this working taxonomy. In order to clear a space to - at least theoretically - build pluriversal poles, it is necessary to proceed with deconstructing

Western epistemology and analyze not only the political coercion manifested in colonialism and racism, but also the notions of space and time, which are two very important characteristics or, as we will see, often exclusive attributes, of any society. We must also consider the issues of security and freedom from an altogether different angle, which are core concepts for human activity and statehood, and transition further to collective politics and its foundations which have also already been assigned various definitions and interpretations.

5

Deconstructing the West

As we have seen, the critique of unipolar hegemony and the search for political instruments conducive to establishing a multipolar, pluriversal world system are closely connected to conceptualizations of the West and its various synonyms or manifestations, such as imperialism, liberalism, capitalism, cosmopolitanism, globalism, etc. Europe, the United States, and Euro-Atlanticism as a kind of common geopolitical space and strategy fulfill the role of the main agents of the "West." If we proceed from the necessity of rethinking the West as a political concept to "resetting" it and relieving it of its attachment to such negative attributes as racism, supremacy, exceptionalism, slavery, wars of conquest, political manipulation, etc., then we arrive at the formulation of a number of alternatives, such as:

- a non-West
- an Anti-West
- a New West
- the East (and North and South) as a spatial, ideological concept.

The matter is complicated, however, by the fact that the historical West encompasses a variety of contradictions. First of all, the "external" designation of the West cannot be regarded as 100% established. For example, Chinese definitions of the "West" have changed over time. Before the Ming dynasty (1386-1644) the term "West" meant anything west of China's border. Following Zheng He's seven voyages between 1405 and 1433, this concept was expanded to include such regions as India and Arabia. Only under the Qing dynasty (1644-1911) did the "West" come to comprise Europe and America.[1]

1 Zheng He xia xiyang yanjiu wenxuan (1905–2005) [A Collection of Research Papers on Zheng He's Sail to the West (1905–2005)], comp. the Committee to Celebrate the 600th Anniversary of Zheng He's Voyage to the West, Beijing: Haiyang chubanshe, 2005. P. 73–74.

Secondly, the method of deconstruction employable as an analytical tool itself originated in the West and is associated with post-modern models. On the one hand, this is good because it demonstrates the self-criticism of some Western schools of thought. On the other hand, it can hinder the revelation of the potential of non-Western thinking through its imposition of the general trend of Western style post-colonial studies, which continue to operate with European rationality, or through applying post-modernist deconstruction to traditional societies (including through the use of new technologies and media). Therefore, even the most brilliant critiques of the West produced from within must be considered with extreme caution. For example, the Frankfurt School theorists could be neo-Marxist critics of the capitalist system, as they were indeed perceived for many years, but the discovery of ties between several of this movement's figures and questionable organizations allows one to suspect that they were simply Cold War tools.[2] Besides, neo-Marxist offshoots are doubtful anyways - as a "rethinking of Marxism" in new political conditions, these trends may touch on all possible issues, but are much less radical in regards to the posing of questions. Such creates more illusions and problems than solutions. Given that Marxism was a reworking of the ideas of Adam Smith, putting class struggle and changes in political-economic systems at the forefront, and taking into consideration how Leon Trotsky's ideas of permanent revolution undermined the ideological purity of this doctrine, its new versions can hardly be considered a global alternative.

Something similar can be said of the French school of post-structuralism/post-modernism, especially the ideas of Michel Foucault. Of course, tribute must be paid to such Foucaultian concepts as the "archaeology of knowledge", the "disciplinary society," etc., as well as his interdisciplinary research methodology. Realizing that the origin of forms of knowledge must be analyzed not in terms of consciousness, perception and ideology, but in terms of the tactics and strategies of power, Foucault came close to geography, which he highlighted as at the center of his interests. Foucault writes: "Tactics and strategies deployed through implantations, distributions, demarcations, control of territories and organisations of domains which could well make up a sort of geopolitics where my preoccupations would link up with your methods."[3]

2 Sonders F.S. CRU I mir iskusstv. Moscow: Kuchkovo pole, 2013.

3 Foucalt M. *Power/Knowledge: Selected Interviews and Other Writings*, 1972-77. – Brighton: Harvester Press, 1980. p. 77.

In his work *Space, Knowledge, and Power* (1981), Foucault raises the question of "spatializing" knowledge and the link between this aspect and the new form of relations between space and power made possible thanks to the appearance of new communication forms, such as railways which in turn have led to the emergence of various social phenomena.[4] The very "knowledge-power" pair which troubled Foucault throughout his life leads through the prism of the works of classical geopolitics to the conceptualization of the formation of a people's character depending on geographical conditions and the influence of the ethos (the synthesis of ideas and moral complexes) on international politics, and the adoption of this or that model strategy for state development therein.[5]

Foucault also considers issues of topology from a historical perspective, tracing how approaches to space have changed.[6] Ultimately, Foucault argues that "the West is but a small piece of the world whose strange and turbulent fate ultimately imposed Western manners of thinking, speaking, and doing on the whole world." He adds that "almost all means and mechanisms used across the world to reduce the West's influence and relieve its yoke...these tools were forged by the West itself."[7] However, we must also take into consideration the fact that "Foucault introduced a normalization of perversion into the French university system, proclaiming a psychopathy which is fatal for the human race to be but one of many healthy lifestyles. Introducing the image of 'acceptable' sodomites and lesbians as a social group into the French humanities, Foucault initiated its spread throughout society."[8] As follows, even anti-colonial and anti-racist theories

4 Michel Foucault not without irony pointed out that a theory appeared in France after the introduction of railways which posited that railways were supposed to foster communication between peoples and contribute to universalization, thanks to which war would become impossible, but that the German military command, being more cunning and farsighted, had rightly thought otherwise and used railways to facilitate the waging of war.

5 Savin L. Fuko: diskurs znaniya I geografiya vlasti. http://www.geoflex.ru/library/publications/geography/michel-foucault

6 Foucault M. "Des espaces autres" (conference au Cercle d'etudes architecturales, 14 mars 1967), Architecture, Mouvement, Continuite, № 5, octobre 1984, pp. 46-49.

7 Foucault M. Intellektuali I vlast, chast 3. Stati o interview 1970-1984. Moscow: Praxis, 2006. P. 9.

8 Livry A. Kto ukral Evropu?// Literaturnaya gazeta, №10-11 (6545), 17.03.2016. http://www.lgz.ru/article/-10-6545-17-03-2016/kto-ukral-evropu-1/

and their authors should be analyzed in accordance with criteria of different value categories, just as they should be approached while keeping state sovereignty in mind.

The misled borrowing of any Western ideas can have long term effects, as can be seen in the case of justifications for the uprising in Haiti against the French Empire on the part of some intellectuals of African descent who mixed Hegel and racial liberation ("black slaves against white oppressors"), which led to the misappropriation of the banner of freedom and equality for anti-white sentiments.[9] Nalini Bhushan and Jay Garfield make a similar argument in noting how neo-Hegelianism penetrated India along with British missionaries. On the other hand, the main places where the most famous Indian philosophers could immigrate during the occupation period were Cambridge and Germany, where their students also actively absorbed Western ideas. British neo-Hegelian idealism thus had a significant impact on both the Hindus and Muslims of India, a fact which bore certain consequences for the development of socio-political ideas in the country during British occupation.[10]

Independently of political ideologies and academic schools of thought, one can approximately conclude that the very idea of the West has three key characteristics. The West is a particular understanding of society, time, and space which led to (1) the emergence of racism in various forms, (2) ideas of linear time separated from space, as well as (3) the exaggeration of Europe's position (and later the US') as a special place in which a special community had formed that claimed global governance and assigned labels to other peoples. It is only natural that other versions of society, time, and space were thereby marginalized and relegated to the periphery of the "civilized world."

As an example we can cite the terms of political geography, which are considered to be well-established but not reflective of objective reality.

---

9 George Ciccariello-Maher, 'So Much the Worse for the Whites': Dialectics of the Haitian Revolution // Journal of French and Francophone Philosophy, Vol XXII, No 1, 2014. https://thecharnelhouse.org/wp-content/uploads/2017/05/george-ciccariello-maher-so-much-the-worse-for-the-whites-dialectics-of-the-haitian-revolution.pdf

10 Nalini Bhushan and Jay L . Garfield. Minds Without Fear. Philosophy in the Indian Renaissance. Oxford University Press, 2017.

Let us take, for instance, the notion of the "Middle" or "Near East." For whom is this region "middle" or "near" and what are the criteria employed to define such a distance? For Europe, the Middle East is not the East. For Russia as well as the countries of Asia and Africa, even more so. It is believed that the term "Middle East" or "Near East" arose in the 1850s in the British India Office. Nevertheless, the term has been widespread in circulation ever since the American naval strategist Alfred Thayer Mahan employed it to designate the territory stretching between Arabia and India in his article "The Persian Gulf and International Relations" published in 1902 in the British journal *The National Review*. From the viewpoint of the Atlantic, this really is East, but if we take into account that Japan is also in the East, then it would make sense to deem such the "Near" or "Middle" East.

It is important to note in this regard that the very notion of the "Old World" and the emergence of the "New World" (and after it the Second and Third Worlds) can be traced back to Eurocentrism (as if the Middle East, China, India, the peoples of Central Asia and Siberia, and the civilizations of South and North America did not exist earlier). "For perhaps the major lesson of postcolonial scholarship over the last thirty-five years has been that the developmentalist, progressive reading of history – in which Europe or 'the West' is viewed as the outcome of a progressive, historical development – and the so-called civilizing mission of the West, both of which have served historically to justify colonialism and imperialism and continue to underwrite the informal imperialism of the current world economic, legal, and political order, are deeply intertwined."[11]

Racism and Colonialism

One explanation for the West's aggressive expansionist approach can be found in Professor John Hobson's *The Eurocentric Conception Of World Politics: Western International Theory, 1760-2010*[12], in which Hobson convincingly demonstrates that virtually all fundamental Western

11 Amy Allen, Penn State. Adorno, Foucault, and the End of Progress: Critical Theory in Postcolonial Times P. 4. https://www.law.berkeley.edu/wp-content/uploads/2015/04/Adorno-Foucault-and-the-End-of-Progress-Critical-Theory-in-Post-colonial-times.pdf

12 John M. Hobson, The Eurocentric Conception Of World Politics: Western International Theory, 1760-2010, Cambridge: Cambridge University Press, 2012.

ideas, be they imperialist or, on the contrary, socialist and Marxist, have their roots in racial prejudice. Not only scientific racism, which accentuates skin color and skull and eye shape, but also race-culture realism, according to which the world is divided into three societies, civilized, savage, and barbaric - both of these forms developed out of Western society. The "authors" of the latter notion designate the Euro-Atlantic community as "civilized", while the "savages" are represented by the countries of Africa, and Asians, including China and Russia, are "barbarians."[13] Hence the logic of the West in which "barbarians" are seen as potentially dangerous - after all, they once destroyed Rome, the ancient citadel of civilization. Therein follows the necessity of presenting the "barbarian" countries in an unfavorable light to both civilization's own citizens, on whom it depends for electoral and political support and taxes for armed forces, as well as to partner countries which can be used in future conflicts as proxies against the "barbarians."

The Chicago University professor of Indian origin, Dipesh Chakrabarty, known for his significant contribution to post-colonial theory and subaltern studies, criticizes the historicism closely tied to the West's notion of linear time. In his book, *Provincializing Europe*, he argues that Western historiography's historicism universalizes liberalism, projecting it to all corners of the map. Chakrabarty suggests that the ultimate goal of every society according to this historicist framework is the development of nationalism[14], which he understands in only general terms. The main thrust of Chakrabarty's work is to overthrow Western-Eurocentric globalism. Indeed, Chakrabarty's critique of European thought is quite intriguing. In his treatise, *The Climate of History: Four Theses*[15], he attempts to rethink the labels previously assigned to such widely employed categories as nature and humanity, including previous discussions on the topic.

---

13 The term "barbarians" was used by the father of history, Herodotus, as a contrast to the Hellenic peoples. These "barbarians" could even be natives whom the Hellenes drove away from their own ancestral lands. Later Europeans used this approach towards indigenous peoples in Africa who were given the exonym "Berbers."

14 Chakrabarty D. Provincializing Europe: Postcolonial Thought and Historical Difference. Princeton University Press, 2007.

15 Chakrabarty D. The Climate of History: Four Theses // Critical Inquiry 35, Winter 2009.
http://www.law.uvic.ca/demcon/2013%20readings/Chakrabarty%20-%20Climate%20of%20History.pdf

In discussing Benedetto Croce's 1893 essay, "History Brought Under the General Concept of Art", Collingwood writes: "Croce, altogether rejecting the [German idea] that history is a science, cut himself off at one blow from naturalism and turned towards the idea of history as something radically different from nature."[16] David Roberts offers a fuller account of Croce's more mature ideas, such as how Croce drew attention to the ideas of Ernst Mach and Henri Poincare to argue that "the notions of the natural sciences are human constructs designed for human purposes…When we look at nature, we find only ourselves." We do not "understand ourselves best as part of the natural world." Thus, Roberts argues, "Croce proclaimed that there is no human world other than the human world, and thus accepted Vico's central doctrine that we can know the human world because we ourselves created it. For Croce, all material objects are included in human thought, and the very "existence" of something is a human concept that means something only in the context of human problems and goals.[17] Thus, Croce and Collingwood embrace history and the nature of humanity to the extent that the latter can have history in purposeful human action. What exists beyond actually does not exist because it does not exist for people in any meaningful sense. It is telling that such a specific approach based on the solipsism of Western European consciousness is projected onto all of humanity by many European authors.

Characterizing the current situation of international relations and assessing attempts at developing a common consensus, Chakrabarty writes that such is "more like a universal that arises from a shared sense of a catastrophe. It calls for a global approach to politics without the myth of a global identity, for, unlike a Hegelian universal, it cannot subsume particularities. We may provisionally call it a 'negative universal history.'"[18] The notion of "negative universal history" has also been developed in detail by another post-colonial scholar, Antonio Vazquez-Arroyo.[19] For example, Adorno suggests that "we must think

16 Collingwood, The Idea of History. New York, 1976, p 294.

17 David D. Roberts, Benedetto Croce and the Uses of Historicism. Berkeley and Los Angeles: University of California Press, 1987. pp. 59, 60, 62.

18 Chakrabarty D. The Climate of History: Four Theses // Critical Inquiry 35, Winter 2009. P. 222.

19 Vázquez-Arroyo, Antonio Y., Universal History Disavowed: On Critical Theory and Postcolonialism // Postcolonial Studies 11: 4,IO December 2008. pp. 451-473.

of the concept of universality as negativity."[20] It is indicative that many important concepts and criteria in the West have been developed from precisely such a negative approach. John Stuart Mills, for instance, speaks of negative freedom as institutionalized in Western society as a template for determining the functions and roles of individuals within the state.

Martin Heidegger tried to overcome this approach: "Freedom from . . . is independence from nature. By this we mean that human action as such is not primarily caused by natural processes; it is not bound by the lawfulness of natural processes...According to this, freedom means independence from God, autonomy in relation to God... So the full concept of negative freedom amounts to independence of man from the world and God."[21] "Non-negative" freedom, according to Heidegger, can thus mean (1) positive freedom opposed to negative freedom, or (2) freedom which is neither negative nor positive. In this vein Heidegger appeals to Kant's reflections and presents a model according to which practical freedom is based on negative freedom (independence from susceptibility) as well as positive freedom (self-regulation) and, in turn, is associated with transcendental freedom.

No less interesting reflections on the formation of Western European identity can be found in the work by Lucien Goldman, *Le Dieu Cache*. Goldman's work describes the process of European rationalization as (1) initially diminishing people and things to the level of objects; (2) removing the idea of community from economic and social life; and (3) leading to the emergence of a tragic worldview which has but one temporal dimension - the present - in terms of maintaining the deepest values contrary to the new emerging mentality.[22] This tragic perception of the world subsequently yielded rather gloomy effects in world history.

John Hobson also exposes the discourse associated with the two key figures of classical liberalism: Adam Smith and Immanuel Kant. Insofar as they are considered to be the first liberal internationalists whose works

20 Karen Ng, Hegel and Adorno on Negative Universal History. The Dialectics of Species-Life. in Michael Monahan, Creolizing Hegel. NY: Rowman & Littlefield International Ltd., 2017. P. 114.

21 Heidegger M. The Essence of Human Freedom. An Intoduction to Philosopy. London: Continuum, 2002. P. 4-5.

22 Lucien Goldman. Le Dieu Cache. Ed. Gallimard. Paris, 1959.

mark the beginning of anti-imperialist politics while including liberal cosmopolitanism and cultural pluralism in relation to non-European societies, Hobson goes to the trouble of proving the fallacy of such reasoning and identifies implicit racism in both philosophers' ideas. In his opinion, "both Smith and Kant were Eurocentric and exhibited various degrees of intolerance of non-European societies" while supposedly standing on the side of anti-imperialism. The paradox lies in that "the claim that a Eurocentric stance need not imply an imperialist politics is one that is confounding for postcolonial scholars" and that the Enlightenment is "far more heterogeneous than is generally recognized by postcolonial critics."[23]

Adam Smith's racial supremacism can be detected in his fundamental work, *An Inquiry into the Nature and Causes of the Wealth of Nations*, which despite the title is based virtually only on the experience of Great Britain and its colonies. Book III, entitled "Of the Different Progress of Opulence in Different Nations", is most insignificant and small in volume and its area of study is restricted to Europe after the fall of the Roman Empire. Smith nonetheless draws definitive conclusions on the interrelationship between the price of certain goods and the size of arable land. If the greater part of a country is uncultivated, then such "clearly demonstrates that the stock and population of the country did not bear the same proportion to the extent of its territory, which they commonly do in civilized countries, and that society was at that time, and in that country, but in its infancy." According to this logic, nomadic peoples, the inhabitants of tropical regions, mountain ranges, forests, polar zones, and even river and sea costs automatically fall into the register of "uncivilized" due to a lack of arable land. For Smith, it is only natural that everything that is best be implicitly associated with Britain. "King John of England, for example, appears to have been a most munificent benefactor to his towns," he writes in the chapter on the antagonism between supreme rulers and feudal lords.[24]

As Hobson writes, anti-imperialists and paternalist Eurocentrics, in one way or another by virtue of their views of world order,

23 John M. Hobson. The Eurocentric Conception Of World Politics: Western International Theory, 1760-2010, Cambridge: Cambridge University Press, 2012. P. 59, 60.

24 Smith translations from http://oll.libertyfund.org/titles/smith-an-inquiry-into-the-nature-and-causes-of-the-wealth-of-nations-cannan-ed-vol-1

distinguish between Western civilization and an Eastern world of barbarism and savagery. It is this endowment of capacity for independent development that mainly distinguishes Kant and Smith from their paternalistic liberal brethren. As follows, Eastern peoples capable of self-development do not require catalytic impetus from the Western civilizing mission. It is important to note that Smith and Kant said Eastern societies not only should, but are obliged to develop. Thus, while not supporting cultural pluralism, they stood on the side of Eurocentric cultural monism and believed to be irrational and unacceptable the existence of pre-modern, barbaric and savage non-European societies in the conditions of emerging global interdependence (although Kant's intolerance of non-European societies was more explicit than Smith's). This led both to argue for the "necessity of development" of non-European societies and therein the creation of an informal, hierarchical conception of global politics and related scale of degrees of sovereignty in European states boast full sovereignty while non-European polities are essentially granted "limited sovereignty." In addition, the latter are faced with abandoning their cultural identities and becoming European nations. Thus, both Kant and Smith forged the idealized European conceptualization of world politics.[25]

Furthermore, Hobson blames Kant for being at the forefront of the racial approach in geography and anthropology at the same time that he produced his cosmopolitan political manuscripts, various fragments of which fundamentally contradict each other. For example, his "Physical Geography", published in the early 20th century, reads: "In hot countries men mature more quickly in every respect but they do not attain the perfection of the temperate zones. Humanity achieves its greatest perfection with the White race. The yellow Indians have somewhat less talent. The Negroes are much inferior and some of the peoples of the Americas are well below them."[26]

---

25 John M. Hobson, The Eurocentric Conception of World Politics: Western International Theory, 1760-2010, Cambridge: Cambridge University Press, 2012. P. 61-62.

26 translation from https://books.google.pl/books?id=die3eja9ZPYC&pg=PA275&lpg=PA275&dq=kant+in+warm+countries+physical+geography&source=bl&ots=XJIS2X7EZ7&sig=F41E0HmTNmPWDc2ZOPNZjuazs-k&hl=pl&sa=X&ved=0ahUKEwiY7qPPvMXVAhVGZVAKHV0BDvgQ6AEIMTAB#v=onepage&q=kant%20in%20warm%20countries%20physical%20geography&f=false

However, even if the philosophical ideas of European thinkers have not always been obviously racist or predatory in nature, then in applied politics colonialism has always been a common tool of European powers. Each colonizing power could have different justifications, but the means were always the same. For Italy, expansion into North Africa was the creation of a "New Roman Empire", while Germany spoke of Weltpolitik, but both countries projected military force into their spheres of interest. Nor did France, where the principles of "liberty, equality, and fraternity" were developed and the rights of man proclaimed, refrain from subsequently colonizing its own neighbors. In 1881, the Secretary General of the Valenciennes Society declared: "If a nation wants to remain or become great, it must colonize."[27]

In his 1877 *Études sur les colonies et la colonisation au regard de la France*, Abbe Ravaisson wrote: "There has never been a great power without great colonies. The greatness of empires has always come at the height of the moment when their colonial expansion is maximal and their fall always coincides with the loss of their colonies."[28] If we stand on the side of objectivity, however, including when it comes to archaeological artifacts, then it is apparent that the West's suppression of all manifestations of other cultures (social, philosophical, political, and economic) is based on attempting to avoid open and honest competition, instead opting to use the knowledge and technology of others to strengthen their own power. In his earlier work, *The Eastern Origins of Western Civilisation*, Hobson noted: "This marginalisation of the East constitutes a highly significant silence because it conceals three major points. First, the East actively pioneered its own substantial economic development after about 500. Second, the East actively created and maintained the global economy after 500. Third, and above all, the East has significantly and actively contributed to the rise of the West by pioneering and delivering many advanced 'resource portfolios' [e.g. technologies, institutions and ideas] to Europe."[29]

27 H. Brunschwig, French Colonialism, 1871–1914: Myths and Realities (rev. edn, London, 1966), pp. 28 – 29.

28 Robert S. G. Fletcher. British Imperialism and 'The Tribal Question'. Desert Administration and Nomadic Societies in the Middle East, 1919–1936, Oxford University Press, 2015. P. 6.

29 John M. Hobson, The Eastern Origins of Western Civilisation, Cambridge University Press, 2004. P. 5.

From the Mercator maps, in which the European part is shown as excessively enlarged from its real size, to scientific falsifications in texts, such an approach by Western scholars has been aimed at glorifying the West and suppressing the East.

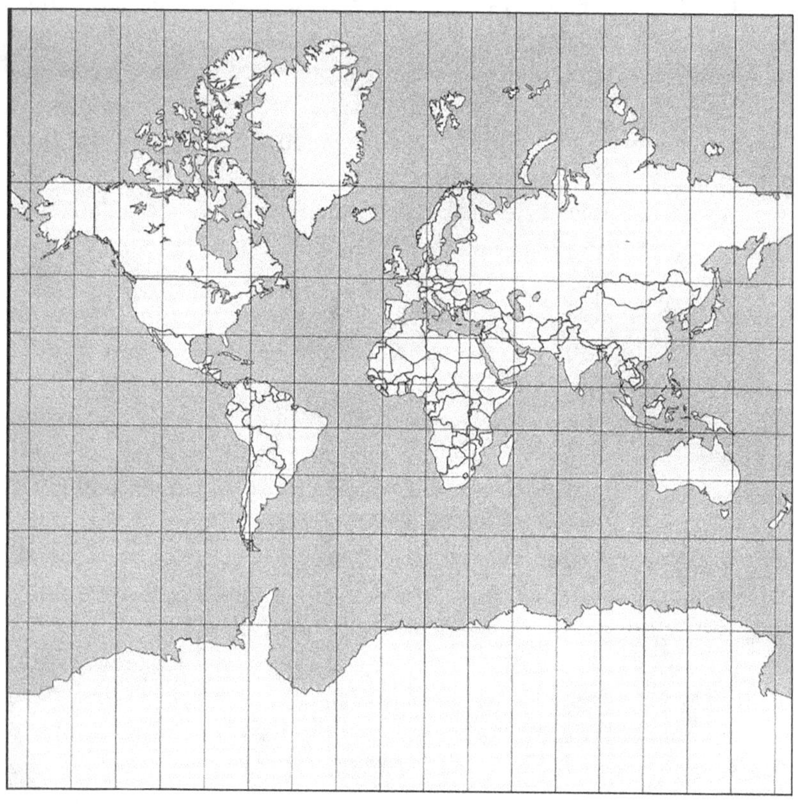

The projection of the world of the Flemish cartographer and geographer Gerard Mercator from the XVI century. commonly used as a pattern.

As a result, according to Hobson, a kind of orientalist and patriarchal construct of "West vs. East" has developed and expressed itself in the following purported points of contrast:

The dynamic West:

- Inventive, ingenious, proactive
- Rational
- Scientific

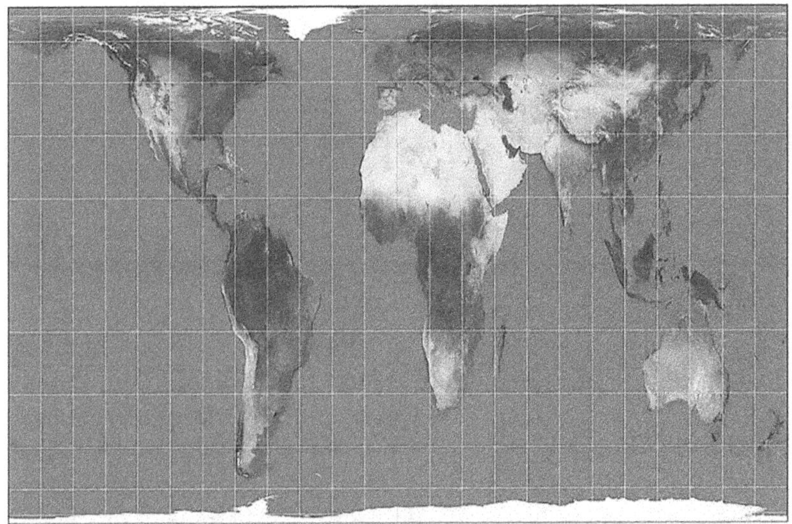

The Gall-Peters projection is less familiar, but it shows the real dimensions of the land and, accordingly, the countries. Here you can see that Western Europe is much smaller than on the map of Mercator.

- Disciplined, ordered, self-controlled, sane, sensible
- Mind-oriented
- Paternal, independent, functional
- Free, democratic, tolerant, honest
- Civilised
- Morally and economically progressive

The unchanging East:

- Imitative, ignorant, passive
- Irrational
- Superstitious, ritualistic
- Lazy, chaotic/erratic, spontaneous, insane, emotional
- Body-oriented, exotic and alluring
- Childlike, dependent, dysfunctional
- Enslaved, despotic, intolerant, corrupt
- Savage/barbaric
- Morally regressive and economically stagnant

By the 20th century, under the dominant role of Britain, a complete vision had taken shape which included five different conceptual trends:

- The theory of Eastern despotism
- The theory of the East of Peter Pan
- Classification by climate and temperament
- The emergence of Protestant evangelism
- The emergence of social Darwinism and scientific racism[30]

Great Britain's interest in the East led to the emergence of Orientalism, or the special technique of combining the "philosophical" doctrines of classic Anglo-Saxon authors, racial theory, and justifications for colonial exploitation.[31] The scholar of Palestinian origin Edward Said presents as a telling case of Orientalism the speech of Lord Balfour in the House of Commons in 1910 on the justification of continued English presence in Egypt. In his speech marked by clear moralizing tones, Balfour noted the Egyptian nation's great contribution to history "despite" the fact that a despotic form of government has always prevailed in Eastern countries, and claimed that the English knew Egyptian civilization better than anyone else. As a Western nation, England had from the very beginning possessed the "beginnings of those capacities for self-government" and "merits" hence the necessity of England continuing the "dirty work, the inferior work, of carrying on the necessary labour." Pointing to other similar instances, Edward Said observed that Western political consciousness believes that there exist peoples who simply cannot represent themselves, and who must be represented by others. Thus, despite different achievements in various fields, unequal discourse is imposed on these peoples. Said calls this the "distribution of geopolitical awareness into aesthetic, scholarly, economic, sociological, historical, and philological texts."[32] At first the issue is a figurative space in which the concept of the "East" arises, a kind of intellectual project which is then projected onto reality. Basing himself on Antonio Gramsci's theory of hegemony (the domination of cultural forms over others as opposed to hard power politics[33]), Said considers the cultural concept of the "East" to be

30 Ibid. P. 224.

31 Bracken, Harry. Essence, Accident and Race, Hermathena 116. Winter 1973. p. 81-96.

32 Orientalism translations from https://books.google.pl/books?id=66sIHa2VTmoC&printsec=frontcover&hl=pl&source=gbs_ge_summary_r&cad=0#v=onepage&q=Balfour&f=false

33 Gramsci, Antonio. The Prison Notebooks: Selections. N.Y.: International Publishers, 1971

an instrument of political manipulation, a kind of intellectual terror against indigenous populations.[34]

But this terror has not only been intellectual. Under King James in the 16th century, ethnic cleansing of the Irish by the English was metaphorically called "planting", thus comparing the natives to weeds and portraying settlers from England and Scotland as "good seeds."[35] The English subsequently spread such "seeds" (literally and figuratively) to Native American lands, which were simply incorporated into the British Empire. The rationale or justification for such was fairly simple - the land belonged to he who fenced the land and put his work into it. Since the local Native Americans were hunters and gatherers, it did not occur to them to build fences, and in the end they were simply deprived of their heritage. Those who did not agree with the law of Terra Nullius (which has at times been taken out of the old chests of Anglo-Saxon political philosophers and applied to different aspects of the contemporary situation, such as cyberspace or the "World Ocean"[36]) were simply eliminated.

English settlers, the backbone of which was made up by evangelical sects and missionary societies, almost immediately felt themselves to be the masters of these new lands and created a new type of man who would later become known as the Yankee, not particularly caring about their guilt in the direct or indirect (more were killed by disease than armed conflicts) murder of the indigenous population. They believed and propagated the idea that such pleased God. The Governor of Carolina in the late 16th century, John Archdale, proclaimed: "The Hand of God has been eminently seen in thinning the Indians, to make room for the English." The echoes of the seizure of American lands by English sects remain prominent in the names of many cities and states of the US, such as Virginia, Philadelphia, and Salem, whose names are directly related to biblical motifs. The name of the state of Pennsylvania is derived from the name of its governor and owner, the Quaker William Penn, who declared independence from the British

34 Savin L. Ot sherifa do terrorista. Ocherki o geopolitike SSHA. Moscow: Evraziyskoe dvizhenie, 2012. P. 12.

35 Ferguson, Niall. Empire. How Britain made the modern world. Penguin Group, 2004.

36 It bears noting that the US has not ratified the International Law of the Sea yet wields the largest navy in the world.

Crown, using private law for the land. "Puritanism plus profit" - Nile Ferguson thus dubs the success formula of New England.

The most extreme manifestations of racial complexes in the 20th century were social Darwinism and eugenics.[37] Although these reached their apogee in Nazi Germany, the roots of this ideology lie in Great Britain and the United States.

The famous Anglo-Saxon geopoliticians Alfred Thayer Mahan and Halford Mackinder called the global interdependence that had become a fait accompli by the end of the 19th century the "closing of the world." This was perceived or presented as a threat in which Eastern peoples, as a result of this new global confluence, were purported to be at the West's doorstep. In 1897, Mahan called such closeness a potential source of political freedom. He associated this not only with the possible growth of other countries' military might, but suggested that conflict could be produced by civilizations with different spiritual ideas and strongly differing political capacities rapidly coming together. Special institutions were subsequently established to study other peoples with the aim of further "homogenizing them" in accordance with the Western model. In 1901, Great Britain established the Royal Central Asian Society which "resolved to consider 'Central Asian questions…in all their bearings - political as well as economic or scientific."[38] If the Royal Geographical Society was an organization that strengthened Britain's political presence through scientific narratives, and the Royal Asiatic Society fulfilled the function of managing British intelligence in its respective region, then the Royal Central Asian Society was supposed, as Lord Curzon who served as the organization's president[39] from 1918 to 1925, said: "not only to read papers [but to] train men and inspire men…to support the interests of our Empire."[40] Without a doubt, this "inspiration" was meant not

37 The term "eugenics" was coined by Francis Galton and derived from two roots - "good" and "genes."

38 RSAA: Minute Book 1: C. Tupp, 'Inception and Progress of the Central Asian Society', 10 Mar. 1908.

39 The list of the organization's presidents includes: George Curzon (1918–1925), William Robert Wellesley Peel (1925–1930), Edmund Allenby (1930–1936), George Lloyd (1936–1941), William Malcolm Hailey (1941–1947) и Archibald Wavell (1947–1950).

40 Robert S. G. Fletcher. British Imperialism and 'The Tribal Question'. Desert

only for British subjects, but also the peoples under direct or indirect British control. This was called "managing mentality", be it applied to Arabs, Kurds, Africans, Tibetans, or other peoples, and this policy was not limited to the interests of Great Britain which at the turn of the 19th and 20th centuries was still considered to a global superpower possessing colonies in all parts of the world.

Such scholars as Charles Dilke (*Greater Britain, a record of a travel in English-speaking countries during 1866-67,* issued in 1868), John Robert Seeley (*The Expansion of England*, 1883), Josiah Strong[41], John Fiske[42], David Ritchie[43] and Walter Bagehot had by the start of the 20th century already founded a vision of world politics "that entailed the natural spread of the English or Anglo-Saxon race and which projected the piercing light of civilization into the dark places beyond Europe and the United States."

American Exceptionalism

The American philosopher and historian John Fiske became famous for his thesis that "it was the English race's 'manifest destiny' to conquer the barbarous regions so as to eventually create a world 'covered with cheerful homesteads, blessed with a Sabbath of perpetual peace.'" In Hobson's classification, Fiske was a "liberal-racist" who "very much echoed the conception of the 'benign' civilizing mission."[44]Additionally, there were the racist-realists, i.e., those politicians who combined national exceptionalism with the necessity of defending their country's national interests on the international arena, such as Whitelaw Reid (1900), Henry Cabot Lodge (1899), and US President Theodore Roosevelt.

Administration and Nomadic Societies in the Middle East, 1919–1936, Oxford University Press, 2015. P. 23

41 Strong, Josiah. Expansion Under the New World-Conditions. New York: Baker & Taylor, 1900.

42 Fiske, John. The critical period of American history, 1783-1789. Boston, N. Y., 1898.

43 https://archive.org/details/cu31924030242618/page/n7

44 John M. Hobson, The Eurocentric Conception Of World Politics: Western International Theory, 1760-2010, Cambridge: Cambridge University Press, 2012. P. 107.

Even earlier, in 1839, the editor of *The United States Magazine and Democratic Review*, John Louis O'Sullivan, formulated the principle of Manifest Destiny in one of his articles. Within two years, he had begun a political career and in 1851 participated in the attempted conquest of Cuba. Three years later, he became a diplomat and served as US Ambassador to Portugal. O'Sullivan's ideas received wide acclaim and support. Even some foreign authors "found" connections between divine predestination and the destiny of the American people. For example, the French politician and foreign minister Alexis de Tocqueville wrote in his book *Democracy in America*: "God himself who, by giving them a boundless continent, granted them the means to remain equal and free for a long time to come."[45]

In the opinion of the American neoconservative Irving Kristoll, the idea of democracy was subject to rethinking after the publication of Frederick Jackson Turner and Charles A. Byrd's writings on the Frontier.[46] Their call to rewrite American history in a new spirit and formulate future policy was heeded by their contemporaries who began to more actively employ methods of expansion. Even earlier, the Frontier scholar E. Godkin, polemicizing in his 1865 article "Aristocratic Opinions on Democracy", recognized the aggressive, egotistical individualism, disregard for public order, and philistine materialism of the Frontier as preventing American democracy from achieving a more exalted state.

The American historian Brooks Adams, who is believed to be one of the ideological founding fathers of Atlanticism and expansionism, spoke of the US as the "New Empire." The very titles of his books - *American Economic Supremacy* (1900), *The New Industrial Revolution* (1901), *The New Empire* (1902) - speak for themselves. Alongside promoting Anglo-Saxon racism, he called for turning the Pacific Ocean into an inland sea for America and foretold the impending showdown with Russia. According to Adams, Europe's role had receded into the

45 Translation from https://books.google.pl/books?id=tRowXQtXrgAC&pg=PA322&lpg=PA322&dq=de+tocqueville+boundless+continent&source=bl&ots=m257MIieTb&sig=ykzVFcqLccomJBlzyJAutZsagP8&hl=pl&sa=X&ved=0ahUKEwjVzIrc-cbVAhVCJ1AKHZF6BYoQ6AEIPzAD#v=onepage&q=de%20tocqueville%20boundless%20continent&f=false

46 Kristol I. American historians and the democraticc idea// American Scholar, N.Y., 1969-1970.

background insofar as the wars of the future would be waged not against individual nations but against an entire continent. In his *The New Empire*, Adams indulges in rather candid remarks: "We have expanded into Asia, we have attracted the fragments of the Spanish dominions, and reaching out into China we have checked the advance of Russia and Germany, in territory which, until yesterday, had been supposed to be beyond our sphere. We are penetrating into Europe, and Great Britain especially is gradually assuming the position of a dependency, which must rely on us as the base from which she draws her food in peace, and without which she could not stand in war."[47] These words were written more than ten years before the First World War when, under US President William McKinley, the Americans conquered Spain's colonies, occupying Cuba, Puerto Rico, and the Philippines, annexed Hawaii, and proclaimed the end of Monroe Doctrine isolationism.

Adams led a group of historians at George Hopkins University who argued for US exceptionalism as for God's chosen people and developed political mechanisms for further aggressive policies. The historian John Burgess, in his book *Political Science and Comparative Constitutional Law* (1890), asserted that the US is a political nation and therefore has the right to and should expand its system to the rest of the world, using any means if necessary. This and similar concepts were upheld by a number of scholars, politicians, economists, and financiers, and found practical expression after some time. Even the notion of democracy was altered to fit the pattern of interests of political and oligarchical groups in the US. The big American businessman Henry James Sr., the father of the writer Henry James and the founder of the doctrine of pragmatism, William James, said in 1852 that "democracy is not so much a new form of political life as a relaxation and disorganization of old forms...It is the abolition of everything that came before it." It is from this standpoint, of course, that the US has "brought democracy" to Iraq, Syria, and Ukraine, destroying old forms of government often by means of carpet bombing and, when possible, together with their agents, as was done with Saddam Hussein.

Currently, any forms of Nazism or racial discrimination are officially condemned in nearly all states, with a corresponding declaration having

47 Adams, Brooks. The New Empire, N.Y., Macmillan & Co, 1902. P. 208-209.

been made by the UN. The situation with neo-colonialism is more complicated since the dependence of many countries has a multilevel character (political, economic, historical, contractual, or constitutional as in Japan, etc.). But even the disappearance of scientific racism in its evolutionary-biological form does not mean that racist thinking in scientific discourse has ended altogether. The new, post-biological form of racism is now widely prevalent in Western social sciences.[48]

Critical Race Theory (CRT) arose as a response to such guerrilla tactics of liberal racism. Interestingly enough, this initiative received impetus and developed directly within the United States, where hidden racism has been studied on the social and political levels by both the colored population and those scholars who do not wish to shut their eyes to objective reality.[49] CRT recognizes that racism is engrained in the very fabric and system of American society. Thus, there might not be racist individuals, but institutional racism remains pervasive in the dominant culture. This is the main analytical lens that CRT uses in studying existing power structures. CRT asserts that these power structures are built on white privilege and white supremacy, thus perpetuating the marginalization of people of color. Overall, the CRT trend freely combines two common themes. Firstly, CRT argues that white supremacy and racial power persist over long periods of time and that law can play a certain role in this process. Secondly, CRT works have investigated the possibility of transforming relations between law and racial power and, more broadly, attempts at realizing racial emancipation.

Here it is important to note that CRT goes beyond the standard approach of "protecting human rights." It breaks with the original liberal values which became the cornerstone of human rights activists starting with the French Revolution. In addition, CRT addresses the question of the normativity of "whiteness." For example, according to this theory, alienation occurs even within the white race, such as when the Irish belonged to the category of "other" before they began to be identified as white.

A revisionist interpretation of human rights in the US and progress is fundamental to CRT. For example, Mary Dudziak conducted a study

48 Thomas MacCarthy. Race, Empire and the Idea of Human Development. 2009.

49 Savin L. Critical Racial Theory. Seminar in the MSU, 14.01.2013. https://www.youtube.com/watch?v=lYrMuL13TnM

of US government agency archives, including the correspondences of diplomatic departments, and showed that rather than for the sake of improving the rights of colored people in America, practically all anti-discrimination laws in the US have been adopted by virtue of considerations of improving the US' image in Third World countries.[50] On a related note, one of the founders of CRT, Derrick Bell, has argued that the black civil rights movement was tied to the personal interests of white elites. Jeffrey Pyle has noted that scholars in the CRT field attack the very foundations of (classical) liberal order, including theories of equality and legality, Enlightenment rationalism, and the neutral principles of constitutional law. These liberal values, according to CRT scholars' arguments, do not have a solid foundation in principle, but are merely social constructs designed to justify white supremacy. The rule of law, according to Critical Race Theory, is a false promise of government rule, and patience for listening to false promises has already run out.[51]

CRT's critique of liberalism does not end there. CRT scholars have advocated a more aggressive approach to social reconstitution unlike liberalism, which claims a more cautious approach. To a great extent, CRT has relied on political organizing in contrast to liberalism's reliance on legal means. This approach harbors the possibility of revolutionary transformations. Over the past 10 years, CRT's main interests have been in:

- Material analysis of race and racism, especially the ways in which the globalization process has acquired a racial tinge and intersects with ethnicity and religion;
- Power structures, especially in regards to nation-states and nationalist ideologies. If at its initial stage CRT focused on issues of social welfare and the law enforcement system in the US, then now it is dealing with questions of democracy, empire, transnationalism, and imperialism;
- Cultural studies and discourse analysis synthesizing the work of different spheres such as ideology, mass media, and popular culture.

50 Dudziak, Mary (1993-11). "Desegregation as a Cold War Imperative". Stanford Law Review 41 (1): 61-120. JSTOR http://www.jstor.org/stable/1228836

51 Race, Equality and the Rule of Law: Critical Race Theory's Attack on the Promises of Liberalism author. Boston College Law Review. 11 March 2012.

CRT is an open theory which challenges the established order, an attribute which is typical of political multipolarity. Will Oremus has written that CRT is radical "in the sense that it questions fundamental assumptions. Critical race theorists argue that what many Americans think of as the "white race" does not describe a distinct group of people but rather a social construct that serves to benefit some groups and marginalize others. And unlike some strands of academic and legal thought, critical race theory has an open and activist agenda, with an emphasis on storytelling and personal experience." However, Oremus qualifies, CRT is not radical "in the sense of being outside the mainstream: Critical race theory is widely taught and studied."[52]

While CRT is often not immediately recognizable as a theory insofar as it is tied to the interests of not only scholars, but also the wider public, many famous scholars have prepared multiple versions of their works on this theory for different audiences. CRT theory is interdisciplinary and makes use of multiple different research methodologies, relying on the paradigm of interdependence, recognizing that race and racism are connected to sex, ethnicity, class, gender, or nations as systems of power. Contemporary Critical Race Theory often engages and explores these intersections.

Time, Temporality, and History

The emergence of the Western-centric worldview and science is also tied to a particular understanding of time. Time concerns the calendar system, techniques of synchronization, perceptions of the past, present, and future, and approaches to history.

It is a universally obvious fact that the temporal system and calendar time which now dominate are those which arose alongside European imperialism and have been disseminated through colonialism and global trade.[53] Anthropologists have long been interested in how concepts of time are linked to the exercise of power and the structuring of political and social activities.[54] From the standpoint of the pluriversum,

52 http://www.slate.com/articles/news_and_politics/explainer/2012/03/derrick_bell_controversy_what_s_critical_race_theory_and_is_it_radical_.html

53 Bartky, I. One Time Fits All. Stanford: Stanford University Press, 2007; Birth, K. K. Objects of Time. New York: Palgrave Macmillan, 2012.

54 Greenhouse, Carol. A Moment's Notice: Time Politics Across Cultures. Ithaca:

time cannot be perceived as something abstract, as a single measure providing merely a chronological arrangement of events. Instead, there exists a close relationship between cultural ideas of time and political preferences. Historical examples demonstrate that the concept of timekeeping is directly tied to power. Calendars, for instance, were historically introduced in political entities, such as China, Ancient Rome, the Mayan Empire, etc. Even in Europe, definitions of time were associated with institutions of rule (monarchies) up until the 17th century.[55] The current systems of law in Western democracies are also directly tied to time, a point which we will examine in depth in a later chapter on legal systems.

Western capitalism took shape with the help of a certain logic of basic terms, synchronized operations, and wages which were defined by units of time and not directly from the perspective of an ideal system of time for the most productive work for the majority of the population of a given land. These units of time are now used as a means of control and discipline and include timezones which are subordinated to a conditional zero - the geographical meridian passing through the axis of the Greenwich Observatory. Hence the notion of Greenwich Mean Time (GMT) or Greenwich time as the mean solar time of the meridian passing through the former location of the Royal Greenwich Observatory in London. It is obvious, however, that Great Britain is not the center of temporal reference from the point of view of geographical location nor from the standpoint of astronomical feasibility (the equator line is deemed more convenient for reporting in certain circumstances). As the British astronomer W.H.M. Christie said in 1886: "The advantage of making the world day coincide with the Greenwich civil day is that the change of date at the commencement of a new day falls in the hours of the night throughout Europe, Africa, and Asia, and that it does not occur in the ordinary office-hours (10 am to 4 pm) in any important country except New Zealand."[56]

Cornell University Press, 1996;

Rutz, H. J. 'Introduction: The Idea of a Politics of Time.' In: Rutz, H. J. (ed.) The Politics of Time. American Ethnological Society Monograph Series, Number 4, 1992. Washington, D. C.: American Anthropological Association.

55 Wilcox, D. J. The Measure of Time Past. Chicago: University of Chicago Press, 1987.

56 Christie, W. H. M. Universal or World Time. Nature, 1886. April 1: 521-523.

Later the Greenwich Meridian-based time system was integrated into the structure and design of computer systems. Henceforth, all computer operations received a timestamp and commands are often fulfilled in a certain time sequence on the basis of these timestamps. Timestamps are globally synchronized with the Coordinated Universal Time (UTC) by a time scale supported by the International Bureau of Weights and Measures (BIPM). The BIPM defines the UTC by using measurements obtained from atomic clocks distributed around the globe. As a result, the definition and allocation of time has reached an unprecedented level of clarity and precision - yet another cultural trait of Eurocentrism.[57]

It is only natural that other cultures would be based on a different logic. Jewish Zmanim and Christian canonical time were defined in terms of seasons which served as points of time, not measures of duration. During the Edo period, Japanese clocks divided day into six daytime hours and six nighttime hours and a device was created to capture seasonal variations. The Chinese system of time and Hindu Jyotish (astrology) are linked to the interaction of celestial cycles. To this day, the Gregorian and Julian calendars are different, Passover being celebrated on different days even among Orthodox peoples - only Russians and Serbs use the Julian calendar for worship whereas the rest rely on the Gregorian, i.e., the universal secular calendar. Furthermore, Muslims and some Asian peoples base their time on a lunar, not solar calendar.

On Barak shows how the current use of Western time standards around the globe is not the result of a conscious debate or signing of agreement between the leaders of different countries. Instead, it is solely a Western scientific preference and, despite bearing some traces of the Egyptian sense of time, is largely a consequence of colonialism.[58] Thus, while clear, fixed, and uniform character of time may create the illusion that it is apolitical, decisions on where to place the meridian are hotly contested to this day.[59] Debates are also ongoing on other issues related to time, such as the problem of leap seconds. The European minority oversleeps whatever disruptions might be

57 Dohrn Van Rossum, G. History of the Hour. Chicago: University of Chicago Press, 1996.

58 Barak, On. On Time. Berkeley: University of California Press, 2013.

59 Barrows, A. The Cosmic Time of Empire. Berkeley: University of California Press, 2011.

caused by leap seconds, but Asians have to deal with the problem insofar as these fall on the morning business cycle.[60]

The International Telecommunication Union began dealing with this question within the UN in 2001, but the US, the UK, and China clung to their own differing positions and arguments. The Americans were concerned that computer systems would crash, thus potentially causing deaths (such as in airplane crashes[61]), while the British were worried over Greenwich losing its status[62] and possible consequences for banks. The Chinese appealed to continuing to tie time to the rotation of the Earth insofar as the solar day is of great importance to the Chinese people.[63]

As for national calendar holidays, here we can see a symbiosis of cultural (religious) traditions and political events. These are different for all countries, although some dates are recognized globally and celebrated everywhere (such as the New Year on January 1st). The politicization of national holidays, moreover, is obvious when we consider independence days, historical battles, or victory days. It is no coincidence that some states have abolished some holidays over the course of reforms after considering them inappropriate, or simply introduced new ones. Nevertheless, many countries hold festivals which clearly reflect agro-astronomical connections (such as the Duanwu Dragon Boat Festival and Mid-Autumn Festival in China, the Holi or Festival or Colors in India, or St. Patrick's Day in Ireland, etc.). All of this testifies to cultural-political diversity which, despite globalization, manifests itself even in calendar traditions.

---

60 Software patches are used to coordinate leap seconds in order to guarantee that a computer successfully processes such. But malfunctions do happen, as was the case in 2012 when the Qantas AIRWAY reservation system crashed after attempting to process a leap second.

61 Allan, S. L. 'Planes Will Crash! Things that Leap Seconds Didn't, and Did, Cause.' In: Seago, J. H., Seaman, R. L., Seidelmann, P. K., and Allen, S. L. (eds) Requirements for UTC and Civil Timekeeping on Earth. American Astronautical Society, Science and Technology Series vol. 115. San Diego: Univelt, 2013.

62 Swinford, S. 'Greenwich Mean Time could drift to the US, minister warns.' Daily Telegraph. May 14, 2014. http://www.telegraph.co.uk/news/politics/10831974/Greenwich-Mean-Time-could-drift-to-the-US-minister-warns.html

63 Han Chunhao. 'Space Odyssey: Time-scales and Global Navigation Satellite Systems.' ITU News. Number 7, September, 2013.

There is yet another aspect of no little importance in regards to perceptions of time. Modern society is dominated by the point of view that time exists separately from space. This idea became widespread after Issac Newton's theory was recognized as a universal model. Friedrich Georg Jünger evaluated such a situation as extremely depressing: "Now no one possesses a picture of the world in the sense of a world understood as a picture, and our visual representations of the world are very scarce. Time appears to us to be more important than space, and the notion of time according to which a person experiences a lack of time, suppresses all spatial representations."[64]

In many traditional societies both before the Enlightenment era and still today, one finds the belief that there can be multiple times. What's more, for these cultures time, or times, are inextricably linked with space, hence the mythological tales of special places where one day is equal to an earthly year or where time stops or passes quicker. Today such "magical time" is projected onto various cultural-historical attractions and special places such as large metropolitan areas (in which a different feeling of time prevails) and so-called anomalous zones.

All in all, "time is an objectively given social category of thought produced within societies and, is consequently differently defined in each of them. Social time is detached from and opposed to natural time."[65] Based on similar observations, the American anthropologist and cross cultural scholar Edward Hall proposed a division of society into two types of cultures with different approaches to time. A "monochronic culture" experiences a period of time as a linear progression of events in which the past is understood not as the category of "here" but as "how we got here." Unlike monochronic culture, "polychronic culture" experiences a number of time frames and "the past is tied to the understanding of 'here' which is expressed in different ways for different things."[66] These two types of cultures behave fundamentally differently. As a rule monochromes usually perform one task for a certain period of time, while polychromes usually engage in several matters simultaneously.

64 Friedrich Georg Junger. Sprache und Denken. Verlag Vittorio Klostermann, 1962. p. 50.

65 Urry, John. Sociology beyond societies. Mobilities for the twenty-first century. London: Routledge, 2000. p. 158.

66 Hall E. The Dance of Life: The Other Dimension of Time. New York: Anchor Press / Doubleday, 1983. P. 218.

This is not to say that one of these types fulfills a set task better or faster, but simply that man's relation to demands and attitudes is different. While one type of culture might be predominant in a country, polychromes can exist in a monochronic society and vice versa. For instance, it is well known that the Chinese build their plans on the basis of a long-term approach; thus China's state strategy or private business initiatives may require decades to achieve some objectives. In India, a similar culture of time perception exists which is also associated with the Hindu worldview, according to which man is imprisoned in the cycle of rebirths. Foreigners visiting India might note that despite technological advances in logistics (with the highest railway density in the world), it is very difficult to estimate the time of arrival at a destination in advance. While inheriting the outer shell from British colonizers, the Indians have remained loyal to their culture in which minutes and hours mean little. The proverb "time is money" obviously does not relate to this people. Other peoples focus on attaining speedy results, hence why confusion over future prospects can arise when representatives of opposing views (short term vs. long term) meet. The example of Russians and Belarusians also demonstrates how two related ethnic communities can differ significantly from one another in terms of their criteria of time. "In some sense, the Russian people live feeling time as eternity in which it will 'always' be...Belarusians do not live in a guaranteed 'eternity' and are forced to live by spurts and calculation."[67]

History as fixed time is also important to the resolution of political issues which might have far-sighted strategies. Numerous facts suggest that a number of states deliberately distort historical events for political purposes. The mechanisms of such falsification have been quite sophisticated and effective. For example, three scholars - James Hardy (the former dean of Louisiana State University and Professor of History), Leonard Hochberg (a professor at the same university who together with George Friedman founded the Center for Geopolitical Studies based at the university and later the notorious Stratfor center, and Geoffrey Sloan from the University of Reading, UK) - wrote in their "Winning the War, Losing the Peace: When Victory is Tantamount to Defeat" on the geopolitical turmoil facing Europe and the US that "victory in the Cold War was undoubtedly

67 Shevtsov Y. Obiedinyonnaya natsiya. Phenomen Belarusi. Moscow: Evropa, 2005. p. 70.

a triumph of the (classical) liberal and civilized way of life over fascism."[68] Under discussion here is not only Germany, Italy, and their allies including Japan, but also the Soviet Union, as the collapse of the USSR is characterized as the defeat of "Soviet-style fascism that led to Marxist ideology temporarily losing its reputation." In addition to such an interpretation of history, the authors raise present-day issues. For example, they attribute two main features to the Shanghai Cooperation Organization: (1) all states included in this organization, besides India, are fascist or authoritarian; and (2) these states do not like Western policy in trade, finance, intellectual property, and human rights. It turns out that, according to the theories of these biased professors, the USSR and its peoples had been fascist since 1917, and now Russia is. These Anglo-Saxon professors shamefully pass over in silence the fact that fascism excludes a multi-party system (as for SCO states only China has a one-party system) and free press, whereas such exists in Russia, is even often financed by London and Washington, and does not hesitate in its selection of epithets for state figures and Russian history.[69] Not coincidentally, in 2014 Russia adopted a federal law aimed at countering attempted assaults on the historical memory of events that took place during the Second World War.

This is also a matter of principal importance for the future. Liberalism is based on the idea of constant progress, evolution, and a better future. This notion unites both capitalism and Marxism insofar as both see the past as marked by insufficiently developed societies, ideas, and technologies. This is the paradigm of linear time which has been constantly recycled in critiques of the past. Meanwhile, it is on the present that virtually all attention is concentrated.

There exists another point of view on this matter most clearly expressed by the German thinker Arthur Moeller van den Bruck, who wrote: "A conservative is a person who refuses to believe that the purpose of our life lies in a brief lapse of time...He sees that people are born in certain epochs and that we only continue what others have started and

---

68 James D. Hardy, Jr, Leonard Hochberg, Geoffrey Sloan. Winning the war, Losing the peace: When Victory is Tantamount to Defeat.Mackinder Forum. July 6, 2010. http://www.mackinderforum.org/commentaries/Winning%20the%20War%2C%20Losing%20the%20Peace

69 Savin L. Institutsionalniy racism Zapada // Geopolitica.ru, 17.10.2014. https://www.geopolitica.ru/article/institucionalnyy-rasizm-zapada

that those who will come after will continue what we have begun. He sees that individuals disappear in time while the Whole remains…He recognizes the power that links the past to the future."[70] This passage reflects an idea of continuity, the principle of social holism, and a sense of eternity. This passage is quite relevant a hundred years later. Are environmentalists not speaking of the urgent need to preserve the environment for future generations? Numerous scholars are also calling for justice, pointing to limited natural resources and the need to limit the greed of individuals, groups, and institutions. Otfried Haffe writes of compensatory or "corrective" justice: "Whether the individual, group, or generation - anyone who takes anything out of common property is obliged to return something of equal value. Like any parents seeking to leave their children the greatest inheritance possible, so will a more generous population leave their corresponding per saldo as possible to a richer Earth."[71]

However, the practice of political liberalism does not draw lessons from the past and does not project the future from the standpoint of eternity. This can be seen in the ruthless exploitation of natural resources, the activities of economic institutions, and the destructive tax, social, and educational policies of most Western countries. Paradoxically, the possibility of an improved future lies in conservative policy, since such shows real concern for future generations. Arthur Moeller van den Bruck's prominent thesis that eternity is on the conservative's side can be supplemented with no less of an important idea, namely, that the conservative not only conserves, but creates value.[72] Therefore, the development of a new political theory on the basis of conservative ideas is the answer which many politicians and intellectuals have sought, having sensed the hopelessness of further pursuing the liberal agenda.

Space

The third point which has already been partially considered is space. As already established, the projection of the Mercator is distorted and the Ortelius map also has considerable errors. But the point is

70 Arthur Moeller van den Bruck. Konservator // Russkoe Vremya, №1, 2009. h. 66.

71 Otfrid Hoeffe. Spravedlivost: Philosophskoe vvedenie. Moscow: Praxis, 2007. pp. 132 – 133.

72 Savin L. Arthur Moeller van den Bruck I mladokonservativnaya revolutsiya v Germanii // Russkoe Vremya, №1, 2009. p. 63.

that Western European cartography emerged fairly late as a utilitarian science needed for geographical discoveries, i.e., conquests.

The maps of the ancient world - both symbolic ones and those based on accurate measurement systems - belong to the Middle East (Babylon, Egypt), China, Korea, and India.

Yet Western science puts particular emphasis on Ancient Greece (as the source of Europe and the West). While admitting that the Greeks did start systematically working with maps (Ptolemy laid the foundations of mathematical geography), it is necessary to take note of this intentional accent of Hellenic exclusivity. For example, Hecataeus of Miletus' map puts Greece at the center of the Earth, and this method of positioning one's state or region is used in many countries to this day.

Rather tellingly, despite its military and political power and proximity to Hellenic cultural traditions, Rome only used the itinerario, a special table which calculated the time to a destination based on available

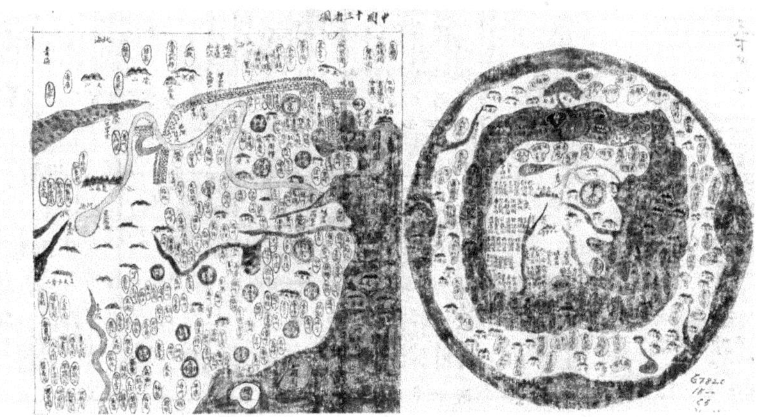

Images of maps from Babylon (previous page) and Ancient China (above).

data. Only later were simple diagrams of roads added to city lists. Traditional maps were still far off. The fact that Muslim peoples - the Arabs and Turks - contributed greatly to the development of cartography is a point which Western historiography prefers to pass over in silence. The *Book of Roger* (*Tabula Rogeriana* in Latin or

Reconstruction of the map of Hecateus of Miletus.

Nuzhat al-mushtāq fi'khtirāq al-āfāq in Arabic, which is translated as "The Book of Pleasant Journeys into Faraway Lands"), which presents the Moroccan geographer al-Sharif al-Idrisi's commentary on the map of the known world (mid 12th century) in the form of a silver planisphere on paper which he worked on for 18 years in the court of Sicilian King Roger II, is a stunning masterpiece portraying numerous countries, peoples, and climate zones. As for sources, al-Idrisi mentions not only ancient authors, but also 10 Arab scholars.

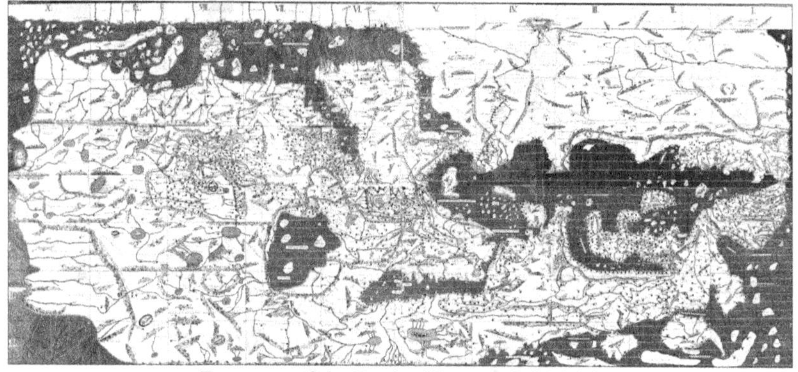

Fragment of the Book of Roger of al-Idrisi.

Even earlier, in 833, Muhammad Ibn Musa al-Khwarizmi's *Kitāb Ṣūrat al-arḍ* (*The Image of the Earth*) established the Prime Meridian east of Alexandria. The British put the Prime Meridian as passing through Greenwich in 1851 despite the fact that different delineations still existed in the mid 19th century. The first International Geographical Congress was held in Antwerp in 1871, one of the resolutions of which recommended adopting the Greenwich Meridian as the Prime Meridian for all sea maps and all countries. This was finally introduced into geography in 1884 under the guise of an "international agreement." Meanwhile, the most systematic map of the world showing navigation routes was produced by the Turkish Admiral Haji Muhiddin Piri Ibn Haji, also known as Piri Reis, in Constantinople. The *Book of Navigation* (Kitab-i-Bahrie) was written in the early 16th century on the basis of available accounts but is rightfully considered to be the first modern map.

If European sources are nevertheless sometimes compelled to appeal to the Turko-Persian-Arab and Muslim legacies (the corpus of ancient authors arrived back in Europe via Muslims and in Arabic translations), then the cartographical work of Indians, the Chinese, Koreans, Moguls, Russians, and pre-Columbian peoples of the Americas remain virtually untouched. If maps allow a bridge to be built between the present and the past (including an artificially constructed one), then modern spacial theories show how space, spacial practice, and interaction with other spaces and practices is co-constitutive. Space is thus neither innocent nor a given. It reflects power relations, normative pressures, past histories, and forward trajectories.[73] The Russian scholar Dmitry Zamyatin has pointed out:

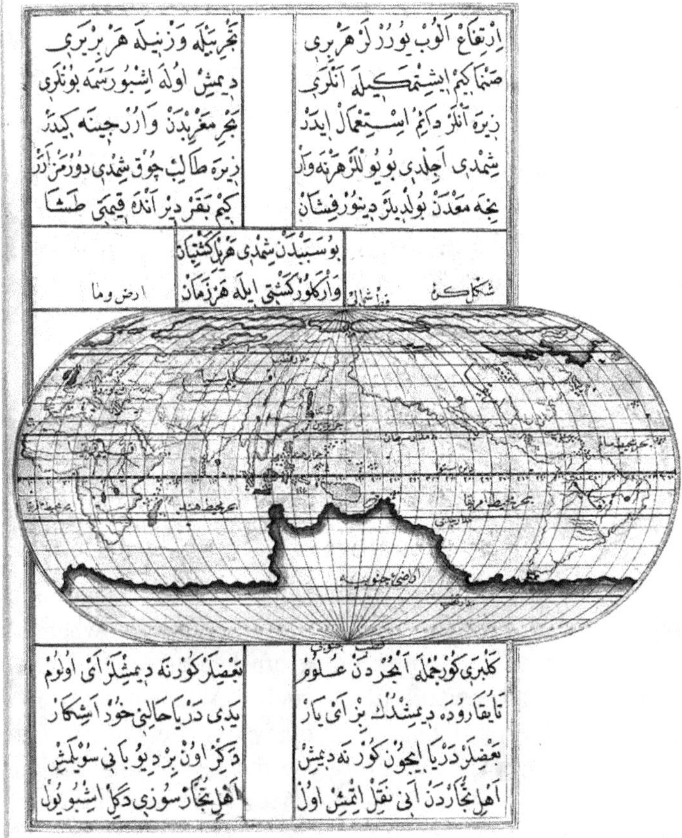

One of the pages of the atlas Kitab-i-Bahrie, which was made before the Mercator map.

73 Jan Shaw. Space, Gender, and Memory in Middle English Romance Architectures of Wonder in Melusine. NY: Palgrave Macmillan, 2016. P. 9.

> Geographical images of this or that historical era are a mental or cultural 'product' composed of two main 'ingredients': first, the individual-group imagination of space oriented towards specific views of concrete personalities in their immediate socio-cultural circumstances and communication, and, secondly, the era's dominant, mass, public imagination of space which nonetheless has its roots in what are at first pioneer visions of this or that intellectual spokesman of the era - whether a scientist, theologian, philosopher, artist, or writer.[74]

Thus, ancient thinking and artistic products of the era, like those of the medieval world, are bound together with the processing of a particular view of other regions (and peoples), and they produce relevant concepts (for example, the image of the City of God surrounded by the chaotic outside space; the Promised Land, etc.). The appearance of three-dimensional space not only undermined classical iconography, but also established new relationships with the environment. Of course, after Galileo Galilei, Blaise Pascal, René Descartes, and Isaac Newton, the world could not remain the same as it was before them.

Halford Mackinder reflects this perception in his book Democratic Ideals and Reality.[75]

> If for Plato space (*Khôra*) was the place of the transition from the speculative to the material where the idea could materialize, and for Aristotle space is a place filled with different bodies, then Newton's space is dead, forever the same and motionless, a repository of different items in the middle of nowhere that must be infused with something or brushed aside. Perhaps the subconscious pull towards filling such Newtonian space is the apogee of the West's global expansion, where after the era of great geographical discoveries there arose the need to continuously work with this "void", to fill the *Terra Nullius* with Western ideas, doctrines, and constructs (both mental and physical).

---

74 Dmitriy Zamyatin. Hunnu v Parise. K metageografii russkoi istorii. SPb.: Aleteya, 2016. pp. 43 — 44.

75 Mackinder H. Democratic Ideals and Reality. A Study in the Politics of Reconstruction. Washington, D.C.:National Defense University Press, 1942. P. 66.

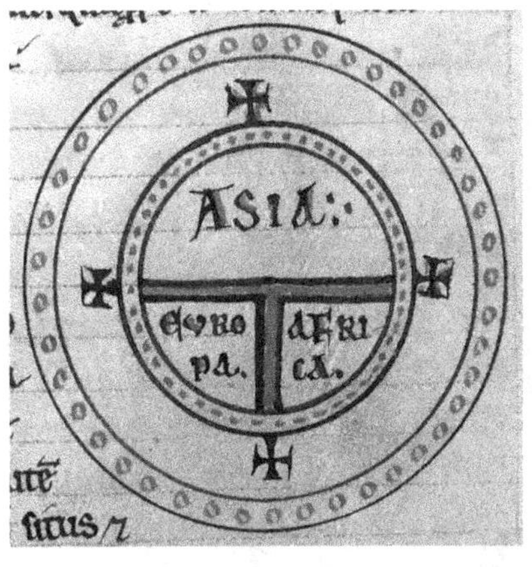

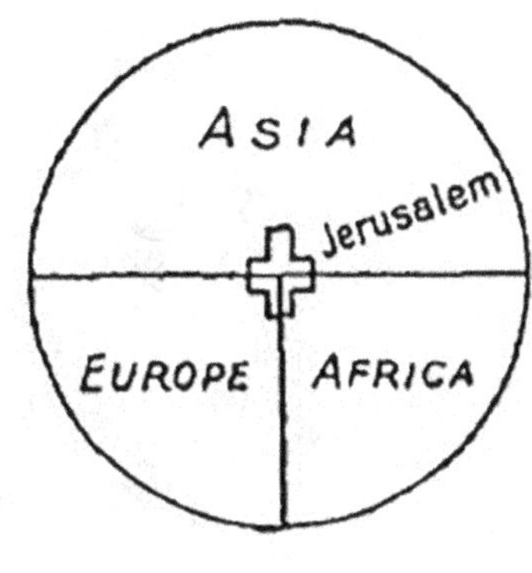

Above Left: Schematic representation of the world of the Middle Ages. This picture, called the T and O map (or T-O map), was published in the work of Isidore of Seville "Etymology" (VII century) and was subsequently repeatedly reproduced. The influence of Christian ideas is evident here. However, it is assumed that a similar image was previously used by the ancient Greek philosopher Anaximander (VI century BC), where the center was the Aegean Sea. At Eratosthenes of Cyrene (III century BC), who was the first to calculate the size of the Earth, Asia Minor was located in the center.

Above Right: Halford Mackinder reflects this perception in his book Democratic Ideals and Reality. Source: Mackinder H. Democratic Ideals and Reality. A Study in the Politics of Reconstruction. Washington, D.C.:National Defense University Press, 1942. P. 66.

If the Western approach to space since the Enlightenment has been utilitarian and aimed at conquering nature, arranging logistics routes, setting up communication nodes, and forging bases of support (of a military, economic, or intellectual nature - such as universitics and religious organizations), then the traditional approach is clearly different altogether insofar as the surrounding environment as a whole is attributed to a primordial concept, and because the landscape encapsulating an ethnos originally influences the psychological attitudes of a people. Forest, steppe, mountains, desert, islands, sea coast - these types of habitats shaped not only economic culture and anthropological features, but also behavior. It can be said that certain particular mental codes formed over the course of centuries, each one different whether for seafaring peoples, nomads, and forest or mountain dwellers. Such stereotypes as "proud highlanders", "sleepy marsh inhabitants," "plain steppe folk", etc. reflect the differences in the worldviews of the people of different geographical spaces. There are cases of binary

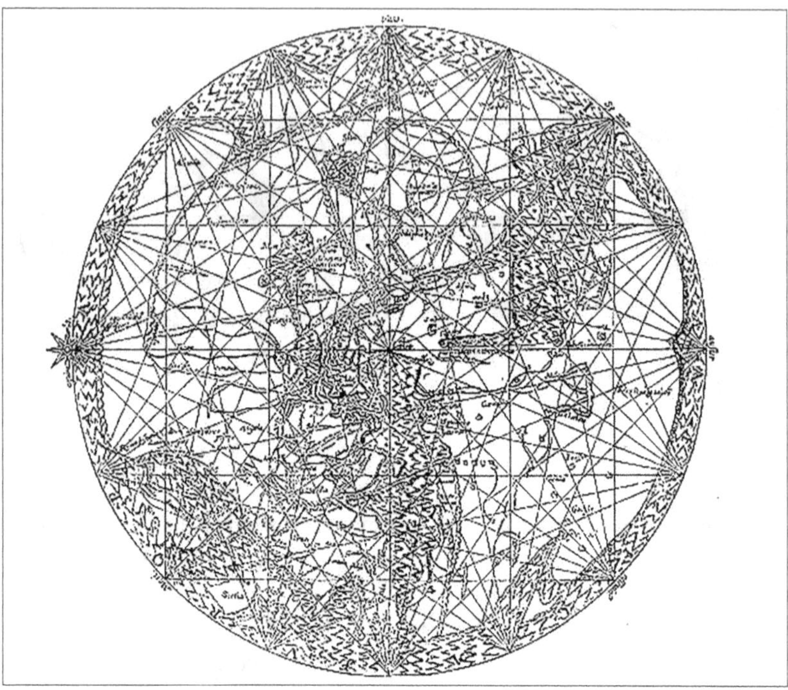

World map of the Genoese cartographer Petro Vesconte at the beginning of the XIV century reflects the idea of Sea Power. It is made on the principle of portulan - navigation routes on the sea. The circular approach was applied first time. This technique influenced European cartography for the next two centuries.

(consisting of two elements) division of these types of peoples in which it is common to juxtapose settled and nomadic cultures, land vs. sea peoples, or mountain and steppe dwellers. One can also assess a people based on how it approaches its surrounding natural environment - does it believe such to be an organic part of itself or something hostile or alien? The Slavs developed their understanding of something whole and inextricably tied to the substance of the people itself. "A genus has [*pri rode* in Russian - Tr.] some kind of livestock and is surrounded by vegetation, and taken together this ensures the existence of the genus, and this is called nature [*priroda* in Russian - Tr.]."[76]

Since the time of Ancient Greece, relationships with land and sea have been expressed in terms of Sparta vs. Athens, as the former state valued its land-based lifestyle, although without denying the

76 Kolesov V. Drevnyaya Rus. Nasledie v slove. Mir cheloveka. SPb, 2000. p. 31.

importance of a fleet, while the latter from the beginning hedged its existence on sea routes, a value that was reflected in the political decisions of the *poleis*. As Thucydides wrote: "The policy of Lacedaemon was not to exact tribute from her allies, but merely to secure their subservience to her interests by establishing oligarchies among them; Athens, on the contrary, had by degrees deprived hers of their ships, and imposed instead contributions in money..."[77] This dichotomy (division into two parts) later became known in terms of Rome vs. Carthage, and in geopolitics received the categorization of Land Power vs. Sea Power.

We can also mention the principles of the sacred division of space which include not only land and water elements, but also hypothetical worlds such as the underworld and the heavenly realm. In traditional culture space was never homogenous. In addition to the binary top-bottom antithesis, "right" vs. "left", etc., there have also been notions of a tripartite world (upper, middle, and lower), notions of a greater number of sides than four, and sacred places which serve as landmarks and markers of good or bad. The Russian philologist and historian Alexander Podosinov has proposed an interesting thesis in regards to the peoples of Eurasia whose orientation towards the mountain belt bore "a sacred importance for all the peoples surrounding it north or south."[78] It is therefore quite natural that the ethnoi living south of the mountain peaks sacralized the North whereas the peoples of the North, conversely, "deified" the southern side. For example, for the Buryats the South-East *(urda zug)* is the world of their ancestors in contrast to the world of the dead in the North.[79]

---

77 Translation from https://www.gutenberg.org/files/7142/7142-h/7142-h.htm#link2HCH0001

78 Podosinov A.V. Orientatsiya po storonam sveta v arkhaicheskikh kulturakh Evrazii. Moscow: Yaziki russkoi kulturi, 1999. p. 545.

79 An attraction towards mountain peaks can be seen in many other peoples as well. The Armenians believe Ararat in Turkey to be their sacred mount; Elbrus serves as a landmark in the North Caucasus; the Altai peoples' sacred mountain is Belukha, etc. The negative attitude towards a given direction, which is prevalent in a number of peoples, is the result of threats which originated from that direction. For China, this was the North against nomads from where they built the Great Wall of China. Rus, however, did not develop a negative attitude towards the East despite the fact that numerous Turkic nomads often came from the East, sometimes destroying everything in their path. The West, on the other hand, has become an expression for something negative or something

Thus, if we take as our starting point the current situation, in which the fading pockets of numerous traditions are still resisting the lethal tide of globalization, then it is clear that a multipolar and pluriversal political geography must be devoted to the cause of returning the numerous spaces of our planet to their true ontological status.

---

associated with deception and destruction, even though attempts at conquering Rus from this geographical direction began relatively late. For many peoples, the East is the sacred direction, as the sun rises from there. The Ancient Indians, for instance, had eight directions with their own patron deities.

6

Law and Justice

The problem of neo-colonialism and one-sided interpretations of law (to the detriment of other legal schools) became more relevant than ever following the collapse of the Soviet Union, when the world became unipolar and the US began imposing its rules, norms, and values upon the rest of the world. Parallel to this, transnational corporations, most of whose headquarters were in the West, began aggressively expanding into other countries, a move which almost always yielded negative consequences for these countries' populations.

International Governance in the Interests of the West

At the time, more often than not one could detect the trend that transnational corporations worked in tandem with the US State Department, with Washington affording legal protection to the interests of trade, financial, consulting, and industrial companies abroad. If we add to this list other puppet supranational institutions such as the World Trade Organization, Hague Tribunal, and thc London Court of International Arbitration, etc., then, in the end, we are dealing with a well-organized network, a neo-liberal cartel which overwhelms and crushes nation-states, not to mention individual countries' private businesses. It remains a paradox that this cartel's actions are at odds with most national legislations and international law, the latter of which was historically established in the interests of Western political elites and continues to be used solely for the profit of this small group.

In general, the concept of the nation-state and the unification of public structures into a single country with a common territory is an exclusively Western phenomenon.[1] Instead of international law extending to all states in equal measure, the marked colonial legacy of Eurocentric states remains. Given that the pursuit of universal sovereignty and international law is in itself a colonial mission, the very degree to which international law reflects the interests of Western superpowers is obvious. Based on this historical argument, one can conclude that from a legal standpoint, the national judicial systems of post-colonial states still remain within the overall colonial judicial system from the era of imperialism. Thus, even if non-Western states contribute significantly to international legislation, this still benefits their former colonial masters. Taken as a whole, international law to a large extent merely reflects the sovereign will of Western states and inhibits legal pluralism on the part of post-colonial states.[2]

When international law (*jus inter gentium*) was first introduced as a scientific category by the Catholic theologian Francisco de Vittorio in the 16th century, it was assumed that all states were equal regardless of their size and economic weight. Moreover, Vittorio argued that there is not and cannot be any universal civil jurisdiction which covers all peoples and, thus, there are no universal civil rights. Even if we consider Western countries themselves, one can find serious legal conflicts. For instance, within the US, citizens are alienated from those rights and freedoms which were taken to form the basis of the American state by the founding fathers. As is well known, America lives "on the basis of three main types of legal norms: (1) the Constitution (Common Law); (2) laws enacted by Congress (Statutory Law); and (3) court rulings which interpret federal laws (Case Law). Court rulings are essentially the main source of legal norms. This is called 'precedential law'. However, America is a country of 'legislative law', not precedential. In the US Constitution (Article 1) it is written that Congress is the only legislative authority. Moreover, laws are supposed to be written in accessible English understandable to the ordinary person of average intellect. If a law is formulated insufficiently clearly, it is considered to be void (void for vagueness). This is why laws are not subject to

1 K. J. Holsti. The State, War and the State of War, Cambridge, Cambridge University Press, 1996. p. 203.

2 Snekha Dauda. Naskolko mejdunarodnoe pravo virazhaet suverennuyu volyu gosudarstv // Geopolitica.ru, 18.04.2016 https://www.geopolitica.ru/article/naskolko-mezhdunarodnoe-pravo-vyrazhaet-suverennuyu-volyu-gosudarstv

interpretation; they mean what they say, nothing more and nothing less. The only task of the court is to determine whether this or that new law has been violated in a particular case, and under no circumstances does it interpret this law."[3]

Thus, although the United States appears to be upholding the Law and various rights, an allegation which is often used as a pretext for the country to interfere in the affairs of other states, including through the use of military intervention, the very criteria of legality in the US are in fact blurred. On the other hand, given the US' imperial and hegemonic ambitions, it is obvious why Washington can so easily cling to one position in one case and hold an altogether different one in another case under the very same legal circumstances insofar as it suits US interests. For example, the US recognized Kosovo's independence despite the fact that it violated the Helsinki Accords, yet refused to recognize the referendum in Crimea on reunification with Russia.

As Andrew Ross believes, this is "offensive realism and hegemonic stability theory gone wild." In his opinion, "maintaining world order means maintaining the American empire. For the new imperialists, the new world order is an American order. What is good for America cannot but be good for everyone else. There is no real distinction between U.S. interests and the interests of the rest of the world." Furthermore: "Globalization is revealed to be Americanization. Its management is the management of imperial order. Its broadening and deepening is the broadening and deepening of imperial rule." In this view, America should be free to do what it deems necessary, including acting alone, since everything that happened post-9/11, such as the declaration of the War on Terror and the invasion of Iraq were done for the sake of peace. In other words: "Small wars and imperial policing are what empires do—and they don't need anyone's permission."[4]

Thus, we can see that according to this view the US is an exceptional nation which establishes the rules of the game for the rest of the world on the grounds of its own beliefs as to what is good and what is bad,

---

3 Fridman V. Socialist States of America. Deja Vu, ili novie pesni o starom. Moscow: NC ENAS, 2006. p. 44.

4 Ross, Andrew L. What is to be Done with U.S. Predominance? Grand Strategy Choices and Challenges.//William B. Ruger. A Nation at War: Reconciling Ends and Means. Naval War College. Newport, Rhode Island. 2005 P. 38.

what is permissible and what actions are to be immediately suppressed and their initiators punished.

Another, more "soft" view of future world order from within the US can be found among some Democrats and libertarians, who prefer that globalization be realized not unilaterally by Washington, but that the US have as many helpers and allies as possible, thus lending a veneer of legality to future political processes in the international arena. One most vivid representative of such a globalist trend is Francis Fukuyama, who in one of his works on the future of the US, noted that the most meaningful way to use American might at the present stage is not using military force, but the capacity of the United States to shape international institutions.[5] Fukuyama proposes that the UN be replaced by a new structure which, in his vision, should be some kind of network of global organizations that can provide power and legitimacy to actions against various attempts at violating the world order. Let us add that this order would still be an American one, and these global organizations would largely be based out of the United States and uphold Washington's interests. This, however, is already happening within the UN, which has been penetrated by various transnational corporations under the guise of their "concerns" and desire to "assume responsibility." This is in fact a distribution of spheres of influence and authority among various political and financial groups that have their own consensus on the main issues of visions for world order.

A similar vision is shared by the influential American sociologist Amitai Etzioni, who is famous for his theory of global communitarianism. Etzioni writes: "There are, however, some reasons to hold that these bodies may well serve as elements of a global architecture that strains under the burden of having to process new policies and institutional arrangements with scores of nations, if not with 200 of them. The new global authorities are a very different kind of building block, on which the evolving global architecture draws. The most developed one, the Global Antiterrorism Authority, is a sort of worldwide police department, run by the United States and its allies."[6]

5 Fukuyama F. America at the Crossroads: Democracy, Power, and the Neoconservative Legacy. Yale University Press, 2006. p. 251.

6 Amitai Etzioni, From Empire to Community: A New Approach to International Relations, Macmillan Publishers, 2015, pp. 349, https://www.scribd.com/

The UN, however, still remains a conduit for US interests, and it should be recalled that the very idea of the League of Nations, later reformatted into the UN, also has mondialist roots. In order to garner support in the UN Security Council, the US secretly negotiates with countries in need of loans or softened conditions presented for economic policies. For example, when the first Gulf War began and Ecuador was a member of the UN Security Council, Ecuador voted together with the US on 12 resolutions and abstained from only two. In 1991, Ecuador received $20 million from the IMF in Special Drawing Rights. Yemen, on the other hand, did not vote in favor of the invasion of Iraq for a number of reasons. The US Secretary of State handed a note to Yemen's Ambassador in Washington, which read: "This vote will cost you more than ever."[7] Immediately afterwards, the US ceased all aid to Yemen, thus provoking a currency shortage in the country. The IMF did not sign another agreement with Yemen until 1996. Zimbabwe, meanwhile, which also belonged to the UN Security Council, voted in 1992, unlike Yemen, in support of 11 resolutions against Iraq. As a result, it gained new preferential terms for IMF loans.[8] According to Dreher and Jensen's study, if countries vote in accordance with the US position at the UN General Assembly, then the IMF presents them with fewer stipulations for cooperation.[9]

Even if viewed in terms of equal rights and duties for all players, "the international legal order continues to lack universal, centralized, legislative and adjudicatory bodies that could definitively delineate the sources of law and judge their content."[10] What, then, can be said of a pluriversal approach which would be inherently more valued, complex, and often contradictory? Sooner or later, a pluriversal platform will be inevitable, insofar as "all existing legal systems in the world (and their corresponding senses of legal justice) are deeply

---

book/250170258/From-Empire-to-Community-A-New-Approach-to-International-Relations

7 Bandow D. Avoiding War/ JSTOR// Foreign Policy Magazine, 1992, 89. P. 161.

8 Rous K.B. Mehanizmi I predeli vlityanoya SSHA v MVF. Moscow: RAN, 2013. p. 55.

9 Dreher A., Jensen N.M. Independent Actor or Agent? An Empirical Analysis of the Impact of US Interests on IMF Conditions// KOF Working Papers, 2005.

10 D. Hollis, Why State Consent Still Matters – Non-state Actors, Treatise, and the Changing Sources of International Law, Berkeley Journal of International Law, Vol. 23, 2005. p. 144.

rooted in national soils and, as follows, adapt to respond to existing reality in different ways."[11]

Law in the Crucible of History

Although in the present period legal norms are developed by politicians, laws originally predated politicians or were adopted only during the formation of political associations. In ancient times, many laws were attributed either to deities or cultural heroes, often those first kings who asserted order on the territory subject to them. The founding father of historical science, Herodotus, recalls that for Athens, the laws which were at the time called "prescriptions", or Θεσμοί[12], were compiled by one of their wise citizens, Solon (7th-6th centuries BC), who immediately afterwards retired to traveling for ten years so that Athenians could not force him to change anything. As Carl Schmitt pointed out, Solon's decrees were later transformed into the nomos, or νόμος, which can be translated not only as "law", but "the spirit of the law." It is no accident that in Ancient Greece this term was subject to various interpretations. Although Schmitt calls the nomos to be a foundational process combining order and localization, it was in fact the original seizure of land which represented a first form of demarcation and classification of space, its initial division and distribution.[13]

Besides the nomos, Ancient Greece was also home to the resolution, or ψήφισμα, which is a specific decree by a popular assembly comparable to the decisions of modern-day parliaments. Referring to Aristotle, Schmitt points out the difference between the resolution and the nomos, the latter being that which defines a measure. In Ancient Greece one can also find the Themis, or Θέμις, which literally means "rule" or "rule over."[14] Such was distinguished by divine origin and established a set of unwritten rights, maxims, and prohibitions handed down by the oracles which "perpetuated in the consciousness of the court a behavior which should be maintained whenever the matter at hand is

11 Martynov B. Zapad i ne-Zapad: proshloe, nastoyashee… budushee? Moscow: ILA RAN, 2015. p. 32.

12 This name is associated with the goddess Demeter who was called the "Law-Bringer" (Θεσμοφόρος), hence the celebration of Thesmophoria.

13 Schmitt C. Nomos Zemli v mezhdunarodnom prave Jus Publicum Europaeum. SPb: Vladimir Dal, 2008. p. 46.

14 This word is also the origin of "themis" as an appellation for justice.

order in the genus."[15] According to Benveniste, Θέμις supplemented δίκη, which is often translated as "justice", "judgement", or "sentence", while δικασπόλος was the judge (originally the king) who monitors compliance with formulary regulations and has the right to pronounce the corresponding rule. The Latin word dico, or "to say", is directly related to the Greek δίκη, and the Latin ius, which is translated as "law", is directly associated with the utterance of the oath (ius iurandum).

Morality, customs, and traditions are all in one way or another tied to legal codes and laws. But they can differ. The German teacher and anthropologist Eugen Fink warned against following the "commanding" or forbidding functions of morality since "in moral systems, often opposite ones, we find views that contain different evaluations albeit related to the same phenomenon."[16]

Even earlier than the Greeks, there is written evidence of laws in the Code of Hammurabi (18th century BC) written in the Akkadian cuneiform language. It is believed that, at this time, the system of law was so complete in terms of normative content and the use of legal constructs that it was superior to later Roman law from which European legal science originates, particularly the Justinian digests from the 6th century which laid the basis for modern civil law. However, many Western scholars are deliberately silent about the fact that Justinian was the Emperor of the Eastern Roman Empire, i.e., Byzantium, and they attach no importance to the development of legal aspects in Eastern Christianity, i.e. Orthodoxy, therein reducing the further development of the commentators (first the glossators and after them the post-glossators, who interpreted law in accordance with contemporary conditions) to the Bologna school of law, Germanic law, and the Code of Napoleon. It is only natural that, upon undergoing several stages of distortion, Roman law lost its original meaning, acquiring the scholastic deductions of copyists and commentators. Although they have been treated as supplements to the "national" laws in European countries, fragments of the digests based on the earlier Roman "law of peoples" (ius gentium) - in particular the declaration of war and concluding of peace, the division of peoples and the formation of new states, the status of ambassadors and the

15 Benvenist E. Slovar indoevropeyskih sotsialnikh terminov. Moscow: Progress, 1995. p. 301.

16 Fink E. Osnovnie phenomeni chelovecheskogo bitiya. Moscow: Kanon+, 2017. p. 43.

order of embassies, the protection of foreigners' rights, and the status of prisoners - lie at the heart of international law, only distorted to meet the needs of Western countries.

Even if we take the earliest periods of the birth of law in Ancient Greece and Ancient Rome, we can already detect important differences. As is well known, portions of communities were compelled to migrate to other places due to overpopulation and a lack of sufficient land to meet needs. "A Roman colony, therefore, whether we consider the nature of the establishment itself, or the motives for making it, was altogether different from a Greek one. The words accordingly, which in the original languages denote those different establishments, have very different meanings. The Latin word (Colonia) signifies simply a plantation. The Greek word (αποικα), on the contrary, signifies a separation of dwelling, a departure from home, a going out of the house."[17] Over time, Rome developed a special institution which distributed land amongst the younger generation. The Curiate Assemblies in city-states decided, on the proposal of the father, which son should inherit the land and what part of the proles (offspring) should be landless, or "proletarians" (proletarii).[18]

It is Jean-Jacques Rousseau's idea of the social contract and John Hobbes' vision of a system of control and balance in society as proposed in his work, *Leviathan*, that lie at the heart of the modern notion of a legal system and which are to this day considered to be important milestones in the history of global jurisprudence. But what about the legal schools of other regions, such as India, China, sub-Saharan Africa, and North and South America? After all, their teachings and conceptualizations of justice, accountability, duty, etc. each have their own distinct features. Over the course of its evolution, the Western legal school often simply ignored the already developed legal codes of other regions, many of which were nevertheless at one point or another adopted in the West. For example, three centuries before the first Western declaration of human rights, the League of the Iroquois in North America had declared all members of the Iroquois tribes to be free and equal in their rights and privileges.[19]

17 Smith translation from http://oll.libertyfund.org/titles/smith-an-inquiry-into-the-nature-and-causes-of-the-wealth-of-nations-cannan-ed-vol-2

18 Weber M. Agrarnaya istoriya drevnego mira. Moscow: Kuchkovo pole, 2001. p. 347.

19 Morgan, L. H. League of the Ho-de-no-sau-nee, or Iroquois. New York, 1922.

Justice

As we have already seen, in many languages the very word "justice" is derived from the word for "law", i.e., they have one and the same source. Even taking into consideration the fairly early secularization of the term introduced by Plato and then Aristotle in his *Nicomachean Ethics*, the term still directly refers to virtue and integrity. But let us pose an illustrative question: What virtue can there be when the right to access to natural resources such as water or land on the basis of a given agreement between indigenous peoples is annulled when they are altogether expelled from the lands on which their ancestors lived since time immemorial?

Attempts at addressing the question of justice have, nevertheless, been undertaken in the West. In this respect, rather indicative is John Rawls' *A Theory of Justice*[20], which was an attempt at developing a credible alternative to the political-philosophical school of utilitarianism. The author saw a serious problem in the main institutions of constitutional democracy which prompted him to develop his own model. It is important to note that Rawls was essentially daring to revise the ideas of the "founding fathers" of Western rights and freedoms, i.e., the social contract theories of John Locke, Jean-Jacques Rousseau and Immanuel Kant. Rawls' construct of society, however, was too ephemeral, as he proceeded from the premise that people have no intrinsic status and do not know their place in society. Thus, he rejected the thesis that man is directly shaped by society. The notion of redistributing wealth was also met with criticism on the part of liberal-minded scholars. Meanwhile, Rawls recognized that in addition to the most widespread notion of justice according to which members of society establish civil ties, other versions can exist as well insofar as the principles governing basic rights and obligations can themselves differ.

If we approach this issue from the standpoint of its relevance, then the problem is not so much in the philosophy of utilitarianism and the peculiarities of Anglo-Saxon thinking in which the right of precedent differs from continental legal school. The problem is that globalism is destructive by its nature, and these negative trends penetrate deep into different societies and cultures. As the German writer and cultural critic Friedrich Georg Jünger noted:

20 John Rawls. A Theory of Justice. Harvard University Press, 1971.

> Today many have the extremely distinct feeling that things are slipping away from us. A process of alienation is ongoing which often with lighting speed leaves the thinker awestruck. The materiality of existing reality is disappearing. In our language, the word "thing" (Ding) originally meant speech, or conversation. Ding was also the meeting place for this conversation for which the meeting was held, as well as the place where people gathered to talk. Things appeared thanks to this place. And insofar as things appear thanks to this place, then if this place disappears, then so do things...Jurists speak of property rights, and these property rights are reflected in property law (Sachenrecht), which necessarily correlates with individual rights. When an entity and corresponding law disappear and objects disappear, then the law regulating this sphere disappears as well.[21]

This was said in 1962. Needless to say, the situation has profoundly degenerated in the fifty years since. Therefore, it is high time to rethink both international law and other Western legislative templates, and open a space for introducing amendments based on the cultural traditions of the many peoples of this planet. If it proves difficult to arrive at a common denominator as the basis of a new international law, then such must be made open, flexible, and inclusive without lifeless regulations and secularistic restrictions. After all, the denominators can be very different, proof of which we will provide in the examples below.

The Andean Case: The Rights of Spirits and the Thinking Landscape

A vivid demonstration of the inadequacy of the Western legal system, including so-called international law, can be found in the case of those countries which have suffered from colonial conquests.[22] Even a cursory analysis of some states in Latin America[23] reveals

21 Friedrich Georg Junger. Sprache und Denken. Verlag Vittorio Klostermann, 1962. pp. 54-55.

22 Here we have in mind not only military campaigns with consequent subordination, but also so-called "mental occupation", when Western norms and values are adopted by the political elites of various countries voluntarily and then imposed on the population.

23 Unfortunately, even the very term "Latin America" has Eurocentric roots.

a dichotomy between the traditional law of indigenous peoples and national legislation, a situation which has given birth to deep internal conflict and contradictions.

Before the arrival of European conquerors, the empires of the Incas, Mayans, and Aztecs were lively examples of distinctive states with their own hierarchies, bureaucracies, and judicial systems. The conquistador invasion rather quickly destroyed these peoples' state systems and turned them into second class citizens under the rule of Spanish and Portuguese colonizers. The so-called Burgos laws adopted in Spain in December 1512 only formally granted the indigenous inhabitants of the New World freedom and property rights, while in reality forcing them to work for the benefit of the crown, for which the encomienda system was established with taxes in the form of subsistence farming later commuted to labor service. Also in effect for the indigenous peoples of the Americas was the Requierimiento or Spanish Requirement of 1513, according to which they were supposed to accept the Catholic religion. This demand ended with the following words:

> But, if you do not do this, and maliciously make delay in it, I certify to you that, with the help of God, we shall powerfully enter into your country, and shall make war against you in all ways and manners that we can, and shall subject you to the yoke and obedience of the Church and of their Highnesses; we shall take you and your wives and your children, and shall make slaves of them, and as such shall sell and dispose of them as their Highnesses may command; and we shall take away your goods, and shall do you all the mischief and damage that we can, as to vassals who do not obey, and refuse to receive their lord, and resist and contradict him.[24]

Although a number of thinkers, including Francisco de Vittorio, tried to defend the rights of the indigenous population and criticized European colonization (and the King and the Pope), it was obviously very difficult for these populations of South America, under the dual pressure of the secular government of Spain and the Vatican, to preserve their traditions and bring them into the 21st century in their entirety. The basic elements of these traditions have, however,

24 translation from https://en.wikipedia.org/wiki/Spanish_Requirement_of_1513

been retained in some regions largely thanks to the inaccessibility of their areas in the mountains, jungles, and selva of South America. The Quechua and Aymara people, for instance, still refer to the national legal system and legislation as la otra justicia, or the "other law", as opposed to their nuestra derecho, or "our law."[25]

True, this does not mean that there exists a monolithic, pan-Andean customary law of indigenous peoples.[26] However, it is possible to speak of a "customary law of the indigenous peoples of the Andes" by recognizing the peculiarities of its form and content. As long as the customary laws of the Quechua are desired to be kept, they must be applicable and responsive to changes in local goals. Insofar as they address practical needs, they must be able to adapt to changes in the needs of the community, yielding new tools to resolve new tasks, give way to problem solving, or develop improved methods.[27] Over the past 20 years, this has become the subject of extensive debate on changing national legislation, in particular for adopting a new constitution in Bolivia[28] and Ecuador. The essence of these questions, however, is much more profound insofar as they directly affect the identity of indigenous peoples, their beliefs, and traditions.

First and foremost, it must be noted that the Andean peoples' understanding of society and its functions differs from concepts found in the West (Europe and the US), the Middle East, Africa, and other regions. According to experts on Latin America ethnography, a special term exists to express the social formation among the Andean peoples

25 Brandt, Hans-Jurgen. Justicia Popular: Nativos, Campesinos. Lima: Fundación Friedrich Naumann, 1987.

26 Ambia, Abel Adrían. El Ayllu en el Perú Actual: Con un Estudio de las Normas Tradicionales de la Comunidad Campesina de Amaru, Calca, Cusco. Lima: Ediciones PUKARA, 1989; Drzewieniecki, Joanna. Indigenous People, Law, and Politics in Peru. Paper presented at the Meeting of the Latin American Studies Association, Washington DC, 1995.

27 Ardito, Wilfredo. The Right to Self-Regulation: Legal Pluralism and Human Rights in Peru. Journal of Legal Pluralism and Unofficial Law, 1997, 39, 1-42; Swiderska, Krystyna. Protecting Traditional Knowledge: A Framework Based on Customary Laws and Bio-Cultural Heritage Comparing and Supporting Endogenous Development, Leusden & Bern: University of Bern, Centre of Development and Environment, 2006.

28 The very name of the state was also changed, which is now called the Plurinational State of Bolivia.

(the Quechua and Aymara). This term, ayllu, is a very elastic concept which can refer to:

- the people inhabiting a common territory
- in some contexts, people in a greater region, while in others a smaller group opposed to another group in the same larger ayllu
- other social units.

Catherine Allen, an ethnographer of the Andean peoples, defines the ayllu as "an indigenous community or other social group whose members share a common trajectory."[29] Overall, it is rather difficult to determine what an ayllu is from a distance, and the more that one looks at Andean society, the more variable the term ayllu becomes. "The ayllu, the basic unit of Andean social organization, occurs in many different forms throughout the Andes. An ayllu is created when runa build a house or houses on a named place. The ayllu does not consist simply of the group of co-resident individuals, nor of the named place by itself: it exists only when these entities - peoples, houses, the place - are brought into relation to each other."[30] Furthermore: "It also seems natural that, as they arise from a non-Western worldview, in all times and places ayllu would prove difficult to filter through Euro-American conceptual (particularly historical and ethnographic) lenses. This is, perhaps, its most important characteristic of the Andean ayllu: its utter opacity to the epistemic supports of colonialism. This characteristic is key because it is where truly subversive potential lies."[31]

As is characteristic of traditional societies, ayllu have their own festivals which are observed with ritual ceremonies. But unlike many indigenous ethnic groups in different parts of the world, where the true meaning of such ceremonies has often been lost, the real meaning of the Andean peoples' festive ceremonies can be traced: "Festivals are important to

29 Allen, Catherine. The Hold Life Has. Coca and Cultural Identity in an Andean Community. Washington, DC: Smithsonian Institution Press, 2002.

30 Coca and Cocaine. Effects on People and Policy in Latin America, ed. by Deborah Pacini and Christine Franquemont, Cultural Survival Report 23, Latin American Studies Program (LASP), Cornell University, 1985. P. 40. http://pdf.usaid.gov/pdf_docs/PNABI435.pdf

31 Sam Grey. Decolonization as Relocalization: Conceptual and Strategic Frameworks of the Parque de la Papa, Qosqo. University of Victoria, 2011. P. 145.

the ayllu (community) and the strength of the ayllu's bonds between its people (runakuna) and its environment (tirakuna). Thus, a festival and the ritual practices that are performed during the festival are important to the well-being of the community."[32] The suffix "kuna" means not simply "more than one", but "a collective, a gestalt, something whole and unified but fundamentally various. Runakuna and tirakuna together are the Andes, in all its diverse iterations."[33] Thus, the whole surrounding environment of the Andes is a thinking being which is the lifeblood of the ayllu, i.e., the communities living there.

In this case, attempts at reading the epistemological lines at work here have shown that such earth-related practices are relationships for which the predominating ontological distinction between people and nature is inadequate.[34] It has been explained that practical activities on earth determine respect and affect the necessity of the maintenance of relations between people and other beings that create life in (many parts of) the Andes. These "other beings" besides humans include animals, plants, and the landscape. The latter, which has been the most commonly addressed in recent political issues, consists of a constellation of intelligent beings, known as the tirakuna, or earthly beings with individual physiognomies which are more or less known to the individuals who are interacting with them.

In other words, these are "titular earthly beings who are intentional, ceremonially accessible entities embodied in natural features. Locally, the main one of them is Ausangate, an object that is simultaneously a mountain and a more than natural (that is, living, but still material) personality."[35] Moreover, "the fact that these tirakuna are felt as presences, as personalities, gives them social and religious dimensions. The places of an individual's locality are like guardian deities; they

32 Jonathan Espitia, The Soul of the Festival: Order, Rituals, Street Food, and State Power. Chapel Hill, 2017. P. 18. https://cdr.lib.unc.edu/indexablecontent/uuid:295de068-bd76-4e7b-b3b1-4a4f0b3e165d

33 Sam Grey. Decolonization as Relocalization: Conceptual and Strategic Frameworks of the Parque de la Papa, Qosqo. University of Victoria, 2011. P. 149.

34 Abercrombie, Thomas. Pathways of Memory and Power: Ethnography and History among an Andean People. Madison: University of Wisconsin Press, 1998.

35 Marisol de la Cadena, Earth Beings: Ecologies of Practice Across Andean Worlds. Durham: Duke University Press, 2015.

are uywaqniyku, 'the ones who nurture us.' The relationship between members of a community and its tirakuna is said to be like the relationship between parents and children." The tirakuna "are said to watch over human behavior; they can control the weather, as well as health, luck, and prosperity of individuals according to their social and ritual comportment."[36]

Such tirakuna or earthly beings are presently recognized as political subjects in Chapter 7 of the 2008 Constitution of Ecuador, which grants rights to the Pachamama ("Source of Life").[37]In addition, the Pachamama is mentioned in the preamble of the Constitution of Ecuador along with the principle of sumak kawsay.[38] In the new Bolivian Constitution of 2009, we can also find elements from the traditional culture of the Andean peoples. In Article 8, Point 1, we read: "The State adopts and promotes the following as ethical, moral principles of the plural society: ama qhilla, ama llulla, ama suwa (do not be lazy, do not be a liar or a thief), suma qamaña (live well), ñandereko (live harmoniously), teko kavi (good life), ivi maraei (land without evil) and qhapaj ñan (noble path or life)."[39] Pachamama and Mother Earth are also mentioned in the preamble. Peru's Constitution, however, does not contain any elements of traditional law despite the fact that numerous studies of the Andean peoples have been undertaken on the country's territory.

In the Constitution of Venezuela (amended in 1999), there are clear guidelines indicated for the legal protection of indigenous ethnic communities and their traditions. Article 119 of Chapter VIII reads:

> The State recognizes the existence of native peoples and communities, their social, political and economic organization,

36 Coca and Cocaine. Effects on People and Policy in Latin America, ed. by Deborah Pacini and Christine Franquemont, Cultural Survival Report 23, Latin American Studies Program (LASP), Cornell University, 1985. P. 41. http://pdf.usaid.gov/pdf_docs/PNABI435.pdf

37 Gregg Mitman and Rob Nixon. Disciplines in Environmental Studies, Edited by Robert Emmett, Frank Zelko. RCC Perspectives, 2014/2, P. 62 http://www.environmentandsociety.org/sites/default/files/2014_i2_web.pdf

38 http://pdba.georgetown.edu/Constitutions/Ecuador/english08.html

39 Bolivia (Plurinational State of)'s Constitution of 2009, Oxford University Press, Inc, 2017. P. 8. https://www.constituteproject.org/constitution/Bolivia_2009.pdf

> their cultures, practices and customs, languages and religions, as well as their habitat and original rights to the lands they ancestrally and traditionally occupy, and which are necessary to develop and guarantee their way of life. It shall be the responsibility of the National Executive, with the participation of the native peoples, to demarcate and guarantee the right to collective ownership of their lands, which shall be inalienable, not subject to the law of limitations or distrait, and nontransferable, in accordance with this Constitution and the law.[40]

Overall, eight articles in the chapter are devoted, in addition to political, economic, and social rights, to traditional beliefs, cult places, and other aspects specific to the life of indigenous peoples.

The above remarks provide grounds for subsequent assumptions. Since Peru has not been deeply affected by the "left turn" in Latin America, whereas Hugo Chavez, Rafael Correa, and Evo Morales, under whom the Constitutions of Venezuela, Ecuador, and Bolivia were amended, are representatives of (relative) left wing ideology, it can be supposed that left ideology in Latin America is something altogether different from its European or Asian analogues. The interests of the indigenismo movement in Latin American countries have been at least partially linked to land rights (such as the landless peasants movement in Mexico), while the introduction of traditional laws into Venezuelan, Ecuadorian, and Bolivian legislation has relied on a more traditionalist approach which has numerous shades and interpretations. This can also be explained by a special approach to ecological issues (the relationship between the landscape and the community). Moreover, it should be noted that the Constitution of Venezuela was adopted almost immediately after Hugo Chavez claimed victory in the 1998 elections. This also explains the formalistic style of presentation in relation to indigenous peoples that differs from the Constitutions of Ecuador and Bolivia which employ terms from the lexicon of the Andean peoples.

Here we arrive at the peculiarities of the Andean peoples' dualism which does not end with a symbiosis of the runakuna and tirakuna, but instead boasts broader, unique attributes and is manifested in the social

40 Constitution of the Bolivarian Republic of Venezuela. P. 25. http://www.venezuelaemb.or.kr/english/ConstitutionoftheBolivarianingles.pdf

organization of their communities. In the words of the *Encyclopedia of Religion*'s entry on "Gender and South American Religions":

> Andean parallelism and complementarity are perhaps best illustrated by Pachamama and Pachatira. Pachamama, literally Mother Earth, is said to embody the generative forces of the earth and to sustain society by providing nourishment. She cannot, however, realize her procreative powers without a male celestial counterpart and is often paired with Illapa (or Rayo), the god of thunder and lightning, who dominates the heavens and provides the rain necessary for crop production. Pachamama is also inextricably linked with Pachatira, a temporal and material dimension of the earth associated with masculinity. Pachamama and Pachatira appear to represent different aspects of the pacha's nature as both a nurturing figure, yet also a potentially angry force that may punish people and requires their worship and sacrifice in exchange for sustaining them. Pachamama/Tirakuna may appear as distinct manifestations of Mother Earth with Tirakuna seen as sacred places identified as "Fathers" and Pachamama as the earth as a whole. Thus, rather than being completely separate, Pachamama/Tirakuna are distinct manifestations of a gendered Mother Earth.

Pierre Duviols observed[41] that gender parallelism transcended life so that when elite Andean people died, they were transformed into two entities: a mallqui, the mummy of the live person and the feminine half that represented the seed of future generations, and the huaca, the masculine half, a phallic rock that represented the inseminating force. Thus like the Pachamama/Tirakuna the individual reflected a unified whole that was nonetheless gender distinct. Similarly Andean couples are known as the single composite word, warmi-qhari (woman-man), suggesting that couples represent a unified whole. This assumption is reflected in the mandate that only couples may perform religious cargos—elective offices held for a one-year term by male community members charged with responsibility for overseeing civil and religious activities crucial to indigenous communities' survival—like that of fiesta sponsors.[42]

41 Duviols, Pierre. Cultura andina y repression: Procesos y visitas de idolatries y hechicerias. Cajatambo. Siglo XVII. Cusco, Peru, 1986.

42 Gender and Religion: Gender and South American Religions. http://www.encyclopedia.com/environment/encyclopedias-almanacs-

Such an approach sharply differs from those of the most well-known types of local power and self-government. With the emergence of democratic rule in Ancient Greece, we see women excluded from political life. In post-modern studies, this has been a source of criticism of masculinity and provoked the appearance of such a concept as Jacques Derrida's phallologocentrism. Contemporary advocates of feminism and women's emancipation, however, often forget of the traditional principles of equality, which to the outsider might appear to be but strange and outmoded relics, whereas an example of such is posed by the above-illustrated principles of gender roles among the Andean peoples.

In sociological, ecological, and cosmological terms, life in the Andes is maintained by three basic principles: rakinakuy (balance), yanantin (duality), and ayninakuy (reciprocity). Rakinakuy describes the proportion and balance in the human, natural, and sacred worlds, i.e., those characteristics which are not inherent but must be cultivated.[43] Rakinakuy is thus a key principle governing activities in such a complex, chaotic, and holistic system. Rengifo Vásquez describes this in the following: "harmonization means following the signs given by other living beings. Every living being is a sign for others."[44] The values of this balance follow the second principle of the Quechua, yanantin, which describes how all things in the cosmos naturally have a set of complementary opposites, or archetypes which form a pair.[45] None of the components of such a pair are perfect or complete by themselves, and there are no subordinate or unnecessary elements since each and every element is an integral part of a rhythm and just system as a whole. Yanantin also conceptually establishes a reciprocity of rights and duties.[46]

---

transcripts-and-maps/gender-and-religion-gender-and-south-american-religions

43 Gonzales, Tirso, & Gonzalez, Maria. From Colonial Encounter to Decolonizing Encounters. Culture and Nature Seen from the Andean Cosmovision of Ever: The Nurturance of Life as Whole. In Sarah Pilgrim & Jules Pretty (Eds.), Nature and Culture: Rebuilding Lost Connections, London & Washington: Earthscan, 2010. pp. 83-101.

44 Rengifo Vásquez, Grimaldo.The Ayllu. In Frédérique Apffel-Marglin & PRATEC (Eds.), Spirit of Regeneration: Andean Culture Confronting Western Notions of Development. New York & London: Zed Books, 1998. pp. 89-123.

45 Estremadoyro, Julieta. Domestic Violence in Andean Communities of Peru. Law Social Justice and Global Development, 2(1), 2001.

46 ANDES, Building Mechanisms for ABS based on Customary Quechua Norms: Access and Benefit Sharing among the Communities of the Potato Park. Cusco: Asociación para la Naturaleza y el Desarrollo Sostenible & the International

In the Quechuan view, a flow of energy connects everything in the material world, thus providing a kind of communication medium. The ability of a runakuna to receive, return, and direct these flows advantageously and participate in the exchange of creative influence is the basis of ayninakuy.[47] The latter is often characterized as the founding value of Quechuan society, its guiding spirit and the natural principle to which all of the Andean cosmos is subject.[48] According to Inge Bolin's study, this is "a distinctive feature of Andean life" and a "catalyst for responsible and dignified living."[49] Taken together, rakinakuy, yanantin, and ayninakuy do not constitute a set of rules, but rather provide an epistemological basis for all Quechuan values. In turn, these values shape laws, spiritual practices, and socio-economic organization.[50] It is not rules, but a general understanding of Andean concepts and common opinion which make certain types of behavior integral parts of a community's individual actions.[51] However, norms are not individually determined, as they are not simply "habits", but are approved by consensus and mutual participation in the system which they support.[52] Pierre Bourdieu specifies: "Thus the precepts of custom…have nothing in common with the transcendent rules of a juridical code: everyone is able, not so much to cite and recite them from memory, as to reproduce them (fairly accurately). It is because each agent has the means of acting as a judge of others and of himself that custom has a hold on him."[53] Thus, although these

---

Institute for Environment and Development, 2011a

47 Allen, Catherine J. Body and Soul in Quechua Thought. Journal of Latin American Lore, 1982, 8(2), 179-196.

48 Allen, Catherine J. To Be Quechua: The Symbolism of Coca Chewing in Highland Peru. American Ethnologist, 1981, 8(1), 157-171.

49 Bolin, Inge. Growing Up in a Culture of Respect: Child Rearing in Highland Peru. Austin: University of Texas Press, 2006, pp. 150, 152.

50 Argumedo, Alejandro. The Potato Park, Peru: Conserving Agrobiodiversity in an Andean Indigenous Biocultural Heritage Area. In Thora Amend, Jessica Brown, Ashish Kothari, Adrian Phillips & Sue Stolton (Eds.), Values of Protected Landscapes and Seascapes: Protected Landscapes and Agrobiodiversity Values, 2008. pp. 45-58.

51 Rist, Stephan, Burgoa, Freddy Delgado, & Wiesmann, Urs. The Role of Social Learning Processes in the Emergence and Development of Aymara Land Use Systems. Mountain Research and Development, 2003, 23(3), 263-270.

52 Ardito, Wilfredo. The Right to Self-Regulation: Legal Pluralism and Human Rights in Peru. Journal of Legal Pluralism and Unofficial Law, 1997, 39, 1-42.

53 Duviols, Pierre. Cultura andina y repression: Procesos y visitas de idolatries y hechicerias. Cajatambo. Siglo XVII. Cusco, Peru, 1986.

are not rules per se, and despite the fact that even the most durable Andean principles show a surprisingly low degree of formalization[54], rakinakuy, yanantin, and ayninakuy can be characterized as having a "judicial character" because they generate norms which define actions that people respect out of a sense of duty.

These, in brief, are some basic features of the worldview of the indigenous peoples of South America which codify social behavior and relations with other people and the surrounding landscape. Unlike the Anglo-Saxon utilitarian type of thinking in which the landscape is either a *limitrophus* that produces material goods or some kind of dead zone which must be overcome, the indigenous peoples of South America see the environment as just as much of a political subject as the local communities, and both live in an indivisible relationship.

The Rights of Peoples and Communes

Besides the example of traditional Andean law, we can present other old indigenous forms (or rudiments) which survive to this day in different countries. In Africa, there is the famous form of popular assembly with a thousand-year-old tradition known as the Palaver.[55] This specific model lacks any kind of regulations or restrictions for members, as the palaver aims at achieving consensus, thus featuring long discussions which for European consciousness might seem to be a strange relic. In the traditional communities of African countries, the palaver is convened in existentially important situations, such as when the existence of the community is under threat because of the sudden death of the leader, a raid or attack, natural disaster, or when issues of a moral nature arise concerning the conduct of a member of the community.

But Africa is not one homogenous whole. Islamic law (Sharia) is

54 Rist, Stephan, Burgoa, Freddy Delgado, & Wiesmann, Urs. The Role of Social Learning Processes in the Emergence and Development of Aymara Land Use Systems. Mountain Research and Development, 2003, 23(3), 263-270; Swiderska, Krystyna. Protecting Traditional Knowledge: A Framework Based on Customary Laws and Bio-Cultural Heritage Comparing and Supporting Endogenous Development, Leusden & Bern: University of Bern, Centre of Development and Environment, 2006. pp. 358-365.

55 Höffe O. Kritik der Freiheit. Das Grundproblem der Moderne. München, 2015,

currently widespread across some countries while in others, communities can be autonomous and self-governing. For example, many Berber communities in North Africa (who in fact call themselves Imazighen, which means "free people") have preserved a traditional hierarchy which is structured along religious lines. As a rule, the community leader is a Sufi order adept. The Imazighen have their own economic models and legal traditions which they preserved even during the spread of Sunnism. For example, the Berber system of jurisprudence uses customary law, or azerf, as long as such does not fundamentally violate the principles of Sharia. Also well known is the tradition of urf (an Arabic name) which is common among the Tuareg people. As for the Berbers' grassroots political organization, there are the Jamaats, or rural communities which are guided by social ceremonies, tribal traditions, the formation of alliances, and land-use deals.

Issues such as deep-seated traditional law must be handled very delicately, or else they can provoke social and political conflicts. For example, when in May 1930, France attempted to introduce the so-called Berber Dahir, i.e., take criminal jurisdiction in Berber areas off of the basis of Sharia, Muslim protests erupted across all of North Africa and the Middle East, mostly in cities, as such was interpreted as an attempt at Christianizing the Berbers and alienating them from the Muslim community.[56]

Furthermore, if we look to India, there we can see traditional Hindu law, which is rooted in the Laws of Manu (Manavadharmashastra), which make up part of Indian law as established by the Constitution of India

56 France's Berber policy represents another example of Western Orientalism. France actively pursued a policy of Berberism from 1890 to 1930 in Algeria and from 1913 to 1934 in the protectorate of Morocco in an attempt to create a special education and justice system, infrastructure, as well as reform the Jamaat tradition (in this context, village meetings). In Algeria this led to the formation of the Kabyle myth which appealed to the historical nuances of Berber society and aimed at abolishing Muslim institutions. French politicians considered the Kabyle to be the descendants of Gauls, Romans, Christian Berbers, and Vandals. At the first stage, the Berbers were more open to assimilating with the French, and the French fiercely defended their local customs and traditional laws, supporting the Jaamat against Sharia. After some time, however, the Kabyle underwent intense Arabization. An analogous situation took place in Morocco where, in 1915, traditional Berber law, or azerf, was recognized. By 1929, 72 Jaamat were established, covering two-thirds of the Muslim population. Conflict erupted with the Arabs living in Berber areas.

of 1949. Indian law, we should note, was part of the British colonial legal system, although even the laws for Hindus enacted by the English were largely based on early translations of the Sanskrit Dharmashastra treatises on the religious rules of conduct of the Hindus.[57] The contemporary legal system of India remains paradoxical. The current Constitution, which largely copies the US Constitution, speaks of the abolition of the "untouchable" category and the establishment of equality between castes and religions. Behind the scenes, however, divisions into varna obviously continue and untouchables are denied access to the corridors of power.[58] Moreover, Muslim law can also be found to be operating in parts of India in the form of religious or customary law.

A peculiar legal consciousness can be found in those states whose peoples are closely bound to the Christian tradition. Christianity has not preserved the tradition of synthesizing spiritual and secular rule as existed in Byzantium until its fall in the form of a balance called the symphony of powers (between the Emperor and the Patriarch). The last echoes of spiritual-secular rule were in Montenegro in the 19th century, where the country acquired the first features of a modern state under Petar Njegoš, who was both the metropolitan and the ruler.

As for Russia, the Russkaya Pravda (Russian Truth) from the early 11th century is recognized as the foundational historical written account of legal norms containing prescribed norms for criminal, hereditary, commercial, and procedural law. The Russkaya Pravda was the main source of legal, social, and economic relations for the Ancient Russian state before these rules were transferred to the Kormchaia Book, which was a reworked version of the Byzantine Nomocanon.

The Russian philologist Vladimir Kolesov has pointed to a link between the Russian words *pravo* ("law", "right"), *pravda* ("truth"), *pryamoy* ("straight", "direct"), and *pravednyi* ("righteous"). One truth

57 Herbert Cowell's definition of Hindu law in The Hindu Law: Being a Treatise on the Law Administered Exclusively to Hindus by the British Courts in India (Calcutta, Thacker, Spink and Co.: 1871), 6.

58 In recent time, the untouchables have often been used as tools of political pressure by external forces. The Dalits (the "oppressed" representing the lowest castes) movement in India has been supported by international organizations in the likes of George Soros' Open Society Foundations.

is not enough, as reflected in the Domostroy and encapsulated in the household phrase "to serve faithfully and honestly" (*sluzhit' veroy da pravdoy*). This means "not only in accordance with the rules of the household, but also necessarily eliminating the crooked and wicked. In this sense, truth is justice and is contrasted to crookedness. Proper behavior excludes that which is 'most advantageous' for oneself if such contradicts the common 'truth.' The notion of what is right involves not only positively affirming a right motion, but also rejecting a confused, twisted, and flawed one. And not only the motion (how to behave) but also its ethical evaluation."[59]

Although certain elements of Western legal thinking were introduced in Russia under Peter the Great's reforms and later, authentically Russian elements were preserved in addition to an understanding of the peculiarities of other peoples' legal schools. As the Russian philosopher and jurist Ivan Ilyin wrote:

> [H]uman legal consciousness arises irrationally, develops historically, and is subject to the influence of family, clan, religiosity, country, climate, national temperament, property distribution, and all other social, psychological, spiritual, and material factors. From this point of view, one could speak of, for example, a "sea" legal consciousness among the Greeks and English and a "continental" legal consciousness among Russians and the Chinese; a religious legal consciousness of the Mohammedans and the non-religious legal consciousness of modern socialists and communists; a tribal legal consciousness of the ancient civil community and the tribe-less legal consciousness of modern republics, etc. All of this means that state forms are peculiar to each people and entity, springing from their one of a kind sense of legal consciousness, and only political skygazers could imagine imposing their state system on other peoples or that there exists one state form that is 'best for all times and peoples'...All of this also means that a people's legal consciousness can and must be nurtured, and that this nurturing (or, if appropriate, re-educating) requires time, spiritual culture, pedagogical understanding and experience. There is nothing more dangerous and absurd than imposing a state form upon a

59 Kolesov V. Drevnyaya Rus. Nasledie v slove. Bitie i bit. Vol. 3. Spb, 2004. p. 312.

> people which does not fit their legal consciousness (for example, imposing a monarchy in Switzerland, a republic in Russia, a referendum in Persia, an aristocratic dictatorship in the United States, etc.).[60]

On a separate note, in the context of rights, it should be noted that all peoples have, since time immemorial, developed their own systems of preferential treatments for certain persons or groups. As follows, some have had more rights than others. Equal rights never existed before. In Russia, for example, since the time of the Russkaya Pravda, privileges were "granted" by the sovereign as exclusive rights, as manifestations of the ruler's mercy and "monarchical will." These were a kind of special "gift" or "tribute" for a restricted circle of people belonging to the upper strata. Privileges were codified in relevant statutes. Moreover, privileges could be not only acquired, but conquered. This, as a rule, is the case with those peoples who practiced predatory raiding. Over the course of a certain historical period, the vikings, Germanic peoples, Slavs, Turks, Bedouins, and many other peoples all practiced seizing others' goods, including livestock and people. In such cases, plunder was acquired by those who succeeded in grabbing anything of value, or loot was divided by the warlord amongst participants according to existing customs. Vestiges of these traditions have still been retained by various ethnoi.[61] This is a fact which should be taken into consideration without any moral interpretations.

Also of interest is the fact that some of the privileges previously enjoyed by the upper strata were taken from the private laws of these peoples and included in international law, therein applied to the states and entities representing them. For example, official diplomatic persons on the territories of other states have immunity. There can be no talk of the equality which liberal ideologues so hypocritically proclaim. The Convention on Privileges and Immunities of the United Nations (resolution 22A adopted by the UN General Assembly on February 13th, 1946) says: "The United Nations, its property and assets wherever located and by whomsoever held, shall enjoy immunity from every form of legal process except insofar as in any particular case it has expressly waived its immunity…It is, however,

60 Ilyin I. O monarchii I respublike // Voprosi philosophii № 4, 1989. p. 129.

61 The US, for instance, still resorts to the rule of force whenever it feels the need to, thus showing that such rudiments are amazingly resilient!

understood that no waiver of immunity shall extend to any measure of execution." Furthermore: "The premises of the United Nations shall be inviolable. The property and assets of the United Nations, wherever located and by whomsoever held, shall be immune from search, requisition, confiscation, expropriation, and any other form of interference, whether by executive, administrative, judicial, or legislative action. The archives of the United Nations, and in general all documents belonging to it or held by it, shall be inviolable wherever located." Thus, despite declarations of human rights and liberal political rhetoric, certain privileges very much still exist, albeit in the present era tied to political careers, not ancestry.

The Hypothesis of a Eurasian "Blessocracy"

In concluding the present chapter, we propose to consider another theoretical alternative to the concepts of Carl Schmitt, who employed the notion of the Nomos to construct his theory of geopolitical orders which substitute each other in different epochs. While paying tribute to this German genius, we cannot fail to mention the fact that he was, as a matter of course, subsumed by the European scientific paradigm and therefore interpreted the notion of Law in this context. If we criticize Eurocentrism and its Hellenic roots which formed the basis of Western European philosophy and politics, then we are compelled to thoroughly, comparatively analyze and revise even Schmittean theory. For example, from the standpoint of classical Eurasianism and those Russian philosophers who turned to Orthodoxy, a number of Schmitt's provisions might be controversial. The Russian publicist Vadim Kozhinov has argued that the definition of nomocracy as the rule of law is peculiar to the West, whereas Asian societies are "ethocracies", a term based on the Greek word ἦθος, or "moral" or "character."[62] Byzantium, meanwhile, is for Kozhinov an example of an ideocratic state.

The model of ideocracy was put forth within the framework of the conventional modernist paradigm in the early 20th century by one of the founders of Eurasianism, Nikolai Trubetzkoy, who believed that ideocracy is characterized by a common worldview and willingness on the part of ruling elites to serve one ruling idea representing "good for the totality of peoples inhabiting a given autarchic, special

62 Kozhinov V. «Chernosotentsi» I revolyutsiya. http://www.rus-sky.com/history/library/kozhinov.htm

world."[63] The philosopher and jurist Nikolai Alekseev, who also stood at the origins of Eurasianism, appealed to ideocracy ("eidocracy") in his works and developed an indigenous approach to Russian statehood and the Russian legal system, thereby proposing a model for a "draft and guarantee" state. Alekseev proposed a harmonious and "proportionate" approach to organizing both spheres of state life, the normative and attributive.[64] Overall, ideocracy might seem to be in tune with Schmitt's Nomos in form insofar as it appeals to great spaces, but its content is different.[65]

The Eurasianists proposed ideocracy for Russia-Eurasia, where the dominant religion is Orthodoxy featuring an adapted Byzantine heritage with a theological corpus that is full of complex and paradoxical texts. In this regard, we can present the example of Metropolitan of Kiev Hilarion's "Sermon on Law and Grace" written in the mid-11th century. Hilarion raised the question of the equality of peoples, a notion which strongly contradicted medieval theories of one people being chosen by God. In other words, his was a theory of a universal empire where "All lands, cities and men honour and glorify their teacher who brought them the Orthodox Faith."[66] It is known that Carl Schmitt had Catholic views, and while on broad issues he might not have touched on the heritage of the Vatican and its corresponding juridical provisions, it is impossible to deny the influence of religion. The same goes for Russia despite the agedness of the above-cited text and the noticeable superficial knowledge of Orthodoxy of most nominal, present-day Christian citizens of Russia, it would be imprudent to deny the influence on the political agenda exercised by the collective subconscious or that which has been accepted as part of strategic culture.

As a brief summary, we can take note of one main difference. Schmitt's Nomos expresses the idea of the Land of Law, whereas the ideocracy

---

63 Trubetzkoi N. Istoriya. Kultura. Yazik. Moscow: Progress, 1995. p. 441.

64 Alexeev N. Prusskiy narod I gosudarstvo. Moscow: Agraf, 1988.

65 Savin L. Carl Schmitt, Rossiya i 4-ya politicheskaya teoriya // Geopolitica.ru, 29.06.2017 https://www.geopolitica.ru/article/karl-shmitt-rossiya-i-chetvertaya-politicheskaya-teoriya

66 Translation from Duham university community https://community.dur.ac.uk/a.k.harrington/ilarion.html

of Russian-Eurasianist philosophy appeals to the Land of Grace. Of course, such an approach is idealistic and in need of proper adjustment to address the current situation and potentially take into account the need for ideological and spiritual systems with the potential of social mobilization and qualitative changes in legal consciousness. It follows that in developing a polycentric law in the international system, it is necessary to clearly understand what we are aiming for - substantiating Laws projected onto geographical space, or affirming poles of Grace?

7

Security and Sovereignty

Security and sovereignty are important and interrelated issues in the activities of any state. Founding documents, such as constitutions, often speak of the priority of defending a country's national sovereignty, and analogous provisions can be found in national security strategies and doctrines. However, both concepts - sovereignty and security - are not so unambiguous as they are treated in the Western liberal tradition. As an example, we can examine the Euro-Atlantic security system realized through NATO. This is a typical Western collective model featuring a distribution of burdens among participating countries, a system for planning responses to threats, and a leading state, the US, with a wide network of military bases abroad. Here we can see that, first of all, NATO countries have in fact conceded some of their sovereignty and decision making to the alliance's headquarters in Brussels. NATO membership automatically entails a certain attenuation of national sovereignty insofar as a participating country is obligated to fulfill the alliance's demands, which are often contrary to a country's own interests. This point is reflected in the organization's charter. Secondly, the practice of recent years (such as the migration crisis and terrorist attacks within EU countries) shows that NATO operations do not guarantee European citizens security, but are rather outdated, slow, reactive, and do not meet the challenges and realities of the current era. Something similar can be said about the EU, in which the security and sovereignty of each of this association's members can diverge from the security system and sovereignty of the Brussels bureaucracy. Moreover, the ability of an EU country to implement comprehensive national-level decisions is progressively restricted depending on economic, financial, and political indices. For example, Greece enjoys significantly less sovereignty than Germany, and Germany itself does not take important decisions independently.

Security is equally associated with both international relations and the domestic politics of a state, whether concerning administration, control over public order, or measures in emergency situations. Both of these interpretations are equally important, as historical precedents suggest that conflicts between proto-state formations that threatened the welfare and lives of entire peoples eventually resulted in the institutionalization of principles for security in international law. In both cases we are dealing with a continuity of the principles of Roman law in European countries, thanks to the colonial policies of which this model spread across the globe. This global security template, moreover, is constructed in the West's interests. For example, non-proliferation is synchronized with the interests of the US military-industrial complex, and military operations themselves are almost always connected to restructuring programs and the operations of certain contractors. The example of American troops' occupation of Afghanistan - which did not resolve local conflicts, but did lead to a significant increase in opium production - reflects not only the bankruptcy of the Western style of thinking in the sphere of security, but also the existence of double standards.

The emergence of new blocs and alliances engaged in handling issues of regional security (SCO, CSTO, the South American Defense Council within UNASUR, the African Union's military missions, EU attempts to establish an independent defense structure, etc.) suggest that multipolarity is growing beyond individual states or UN security forces. However, upon diving deeper into the essence of this matter, it turns out that security and sovereignty are more complex, ambiguous, and multifaceted issues.

Shepherds, Keepers, and Guards

First of all, the very word "security" (Russian: *bezopasnost'*) carries different semantic charges in different languages, a fact which points, firstly, to the inevitability of a logical "scissors effect" in attempts at translating ideas, and secondly, to the fact that every people has its own cultural core with deep, proto-historic roots. For example, in the majority of Romance languages, which are derivative from Latin, the word for security originates in the expression *se cura*, meaning "without worry." In the ancient Greek word *ασφάλεια* (from the root *σφάλλω*, meaning "to knock down", "to humble", "to mislead", or "to defeat"), the word has a different meaning, connoting stability, constancy, reliability, and fidelity. Thus, despite the apparent temporal and spatial proximity of Ancient Greek and Latin culture, we are dealing with completely different principles related to this expression.

In the Russian language, the word *opasnost* ("danger") is related to the verb *pasti*, which means "to graze," "to shepherd," or "to herd", and is used not only in relation to animals, but also one's subjects, thus implying a certain care for them. One can also find a much deeper meaning for security in Russian. In Rus, there existed a certain division for objects, goals, and issues and who was responsible for fulfilling entrusted respective functions. What's more, the idea of personal "salvation", or *spasenie*, which is important for Christians, was produced by means of the Old Church Slavonic verb *bliustisia*, or "to guard." In this case, however, "this refers not to protection, but rather to careful oversight or, as we would say today, to the supervisory functions of authority or simple human wishing. *Bliusti* means to observe, to be vigil, and simultaneously to be ready for incidents of any kind."[1] The word "to protect," or *okhraniat'* comes from *khraniti* or *khoronitisia*, i.e., "to conceal" or "to shelter." It is employed to mean "to cover." *Khraniti* means protection from without, whereas *bliustisya* is one's own safeguarding (the reflexive suffix *-sya* means "ownself"). There is also the term *storozhit'*, which refers exclusively to a guard, and is used only in the plural, thus relating to a collective action. We also have the term *sterech'*, which has several meanings, such as *bliusti*, or to observe, *storozhit'* or *sterech'*, *oberegat'* (also "to protect"), *okhrianiat'*, [*pred*]*osteregat'* ("to [fore]warn"), and *podsteregat'* ("to monitor").[2] A selfless attitude towards the act of defending is also apparently expressed in the pair of *bliusti-radeti*. The idea of serving unites the verbs *posobit'* ("to aid") and *sterech'*, in the former the point being effective assistance and in the latter that which should be "covered" as something of the highest value.[3]

Therefore, depending on the task at hand, there is a corresponding expression. In modern state terms, there are different services and levels of responsibility for security structures and departments which

1 Kolesov V. Drevnyaya Rus, Nasledie v slove. Bitie i bit. Vol. 3. SPb, 2004. p. 183.

2 Ibid, 187-188.

3 Ibid, 189.

deal with issues of security. From the point of view expressed here, we can assume that the presence in Russia of different services with what at first glance appear to be similar tasks is related to the structure of the Russian people's thinking, where on the level of language and in the unconscious we find a division into types of needed protection.

It is also telling that in the Russian language the word for security, *bezopasnost'*, harbors pastoral functions at its root, whereas in its modern version it bears a negative meaning. *Opasstvo* is caution or fear.[4] In Rus, "danger credentials" (*opasnye gramoty*) were called "protective credentials" (*okhrannye gramoty*), and only later did danger, or *opasnost'*, come to be associated with something negative. Thus, according to its inner logic, the word *bezopasnost'* actually means an absence of caution, whereas we now assign it the opposite meaning. In the Serbian language, security is *bezbednost'*, thus having a slightly different accent stressing an attempt to avoid *beda* ("something bad").

In modernity, security came to be associated first and foremost with military threats and the subversive operations of the agents of competing or hostile countries. The demarcation of the main paradigms of international relations is also mainly tied to interpretations of security issues. Which of these paradigms is characteristic of the thinking of a decision-making entity depends on the model response to potential threats.

According to the theory of the founder of the school of political realism, Hans Morgenthau, society is governed by objective laws, not good intentions, and international relations are defined as expressions of changing national interests in terms of force and beyond the morality of states. Thus, the main question of international relations boils down to whether a state's foreign policy empowers the nation. In this paradigm, understandings of possible threats and other factors related to security depend on interpretations of national interests, and change accordingly.

In the last third of the 20th century, new trends advanced within realism, such as structural realism or neorealism, the main advocates

4 Dyachenko G. (ed.) Polniy tserkovno-slavyanskiy slovar. Moscow: Otchiy dom, 2006. p. 384.

of which were Kenneth Waltz and Stephen Walt. In Walt's view, states form alliances in order to balance threats, not other states.[5] John Mearsheimer, who belongs to the school of offensive realism, believes that states exercise aggression not only in attempts to gain power and influence, but also for guaranteeing security while unsure as to the intentions of their rivals. In such a case, the state should not cease its efforts to increase its strength and security and should not relinquish sovereignty into the hands of other states.[6]

New aspects of security were revealed by Barry Buzan and Ole Waever, who are known for their concept of "securitization" and theory of complex regional security. In their opinion, the very notion of security is tied to survival: "Existential threat can only be understood in relation to the particular character of the referent object in question" (usually, but not necessarily, state, territory, and society).[7] Further: "The special nature of security threats justifies the use of extraordinary measures to handle them. The invocation of security has been the key to legitimizing the use of force, but more generally it has opened the way for the state to mobilize, or to take special powers, to handle existential threats." In the political sphere, Buzan and Waever write, "existential threats are traditionally defined in terms of the constituting principle - sovereignty, but sometimes also ideology - of the state. Sovereignty can be existentially threatened by anything that questions recognition, legitimacy, or governing authority." Other factors can be considered threats as well, for example: "The European Union (EU) can be existentially threatened by events that might undo its integration process."[8] Thus, according to these thinkers, security is a self-referencing practice since, in reality, an existential threat does not always become a security problem, but a problem presented or viewed as such a threat might become one.[9]

Rather controversial points can be distinguished in Buzan and Waever's elaborations. Their main theory of complex regional

5 Stephen Walt,The Origin of Alliances (New York: Cornell University Press, 1987).

6 John Mearsheimer, The Tragedy of Great Power Politics (New York: W. W. Norton, 2001).

7 Barry Buzan, Ole Waever and Wilde J. De, Security. A New Framework for Analysis (London: Lynne Reinner Publishers, Inc., 1998), 21.

8 Ibid, 22.

9 Ibid, 23.

security is that, despite globalization, the majority of security threats in international relations remain territorial in nature, and their severity directly depends on geographical space.[10] Earlier, Buzan and Waever stressed that "because most political and military threats travel easily over short distances than over long ones, insecurity is often associated with proximity."[11] The conclusions drawn on the basis of such a formulation can be contradictory. For example, the attack on the World Trade Center on September 11th, 2001 does not fall under the range of threats assessed by the authors, but nevertheless became the formal reason for intervention in Iraq and Afghanistan as well as the expansion of the US' military presence in Central Asia.

Russian scholars have also questioned Buzan and Waever's thesis that regional borders do not intersect, a point which implies that an actor can belong to only one region. Russian scholar Artyom Lukin has pointed out that, due to their geopolitical nature, some states might be actors in two or more regions. First and foremost, Russia is such an exception. According to Buzan and Waever, Russia has its own region (the post-Soviet space) which, together with the EU/Europe, forms a weakly bound super-complex. Their thesis that Russia is an external power in relation to East Asia is, in our opinion, not quite correct and essentially denies Russia the right to participate in security problem-solving in the East Asian security complex. In alleging such, Buzan and Waever "essentially abandon the cornerstone principle of their own theory, i.e., the primacy of territoriality."[12]

Nor are Buzan and Waever's elaborations consistent with the principles of geopolitics. Dale Walton has pointed to a new shift in global politics which he associates with the end of the post-Columbian epoch and the era of Pax Americana.[13] According to this view, changes in regional and global systems deeply affect regional security complexes, but the

---

10 Barry Buzan and Ole Waever, Regions and Powers: The Structure of International Security (Cambridge : Cambridge University Press, 2003), 70.

11 Barry Buzan, Ole Waever and Wilde J. De, Op. cit. P. 11.

12 Lukin A. Teoriya komplexov regionalnoy bezopasnosti i Vostochnaya Aziya // Oikumena 17, № 2 (2011). URL: http://www.ojkum.ru/arc/2011_02/2011_02_02.html

13 Dale Walton, Geopolitics and the Great Powers in the Twenty-first Century: Multipolarity and Revolution in Strategic Perspective (London and New York: Routledge, 2009).

main recognized Western authors in the field of geopolitics continue to think in the old paradigm of the post-Columbian epoch, in the best case offering new interpretive models for global leadership only for specialists from other regions, with few exceptions, to simply translate their ideas.

As we have already noted, the liberal paradigm in international relations theory sees foreign policy as a continuation of domestic policy. Hence, some of its contemporary adherents tend to assume that the liberal-democratic model should be imposed on other countries and regions. A striking example of such an approach is presented by the US' efforts to promote "democratic norms and values" in the international arena by means of what are often far from democratic methods.

The constructivists presume that social reality is not invariably given or predetermined. They believe that international relations scholarship is tied to the view that an exclusively Western civilization remains relatively closed to influences emanating from the rest of the world. Although constructivism, which appeared later than other theories, insists on the importance of cultures, languages, religions, ideologies, and other forms of knowledge, and recognizes the unique identity of each state, when it comes to security, this trend follows the realists and liberals in trying to synthesize their main provisions and enrich them with a number of elements.

As a result, all these theories of international relations are limited by a positivist approach which is rooted in the Western-centric paradigm of thinking directly related to the worldview of the Enlightenment. In this regard, we would like to commend those attempts at rethinking the concept of security undertaken by Martin Heidegger and Michel Foucault, who criticized this Eurocentric tradition. If the German philosopher approached this problem from the standpoint of ontology and etymology[14], then his French colleague tried to find a bifurcation point in European history with the formation of states and violence, an approach which also led him to interesting conclusions. Foucault considered security alongside concepts of normativity and disciplinarity.

14 It should be noted that in Heidegger's early works one finds the word die Sicherheit, which can be translated as "security", "safety", "guarantee", or "assurance", and was used in relation to a truly scientific method to indicate its reliability, i.e., the accuracy of the results obtained through such.

He concluded that "Mechanisms of security do not replace disciplinary mechanisms, which would have replaced juridico-legal mechanisms" and established a "system of correlation between juridico-legal mechanisms, disciplinary mechanisms, and mechanisms of security."[15]

Not too long ago, attempts began to be undertaken in international relations theory to rethink actors and international relations in world politics. Oran Young's theory[16] of mixed actors was followed by emergence theory, network-centrism, complexity, and others which have denied the claims to universality of preceding concepts, adjusting them to new scholarly approaches and "findings." Nevertheless, these theories continue the Western-centric model of utilizing knowledge in the political sphere. Moreover, academic analysis is often not synchronized with political practice, a reality which can be seen in the artificially provoked crises in Libya and Syria. Seeing as how military intervention in Libya was approved at the UN Security Council, the question arises as to the adequacy of the international legal system. Non-Western theories and practices, despite lying at the heart of many countries' statehoods, are perceived in recognized international and interstate platforms as anachronisms or as attempts to change the balance in a given state's favor. This has led to serious regional imbalances.

Another example of such a crisis can be seen in the case of Turkey. In recent years, this state's foreign policy has been marked by a distinct imbalance in strategy, national interests, and security issues. Firstly, by characterizing the neighboring regions of the Middle East and North Africa as unstable, stagnant, and potentially distressing, Ankara has not taken into account the significance of its historical and religious ties with these regions. Secondly, since it ideologically and strategically oriented itself towards the West following the Second World War because of a perceived threat from the USSR, Turkey has not reconsidered its views on the role and place of Russia in today's world (although recently we have observed a shift in Turkey's attitude towards Russia). Thirdly, the opinion

15 Michel Foucault, Security, Territory, Population: Lectures at the Collège de France, 1977-78 (London: Palgrave Macmillan, 2007), 22. http://www.azioni.nl/platform/wp-content/uploads/2013/04/Foucault-Security-Territory-Population.pdf.

16 Oran Young, "The Actors in World Politics" in The Analysis of International Politics, ed. John. Rosenau and M. A. East (New York : The Free Press, 1972), 125–144.

prevails in Turkey that the country's modern history is a result of the collapse of the Ottoman Empire and that similar threats remain relevant for the country to this day (mostly in the Kurdish provinces).[17] Experts have noted that these circumstances have rendered turkey's military security a high priority, which in turn has justified the influence of the military elite's decisions on Turkey's foreign policy. Alternative foreign policy concepts, however, have never been discussed, and foreign policy itself is considered to be related to "state" affairs, i.e., the military and civil bureaucracy, and not the "government of parties." This distinction in Turkey's political discourse has defined the status quo for a long time.[18]

The coup d'etat attempt that struck Turkey in July 2016 confirms this thesis. It is telling that external forces tried to organize this putsch by means of the military, which is supposed to be the foundation of security. The ensuing arrests, investigations, and purges in both military and political structures are inevitably leading to a change in decision-making in the national security sphere. However, the reorganization of Turkey's security apparatus and the preparation of new cadre could take some time, and Turkey is potentially vulnerable in this period.

It is also necessary to note that the strategies of some actors are directly or indirectly dependent on the strategies of others. Further complication of the system of international relations and the increase in unpredictability tied to it is the consequence of this "interaction" between different actors' strategies. Each actor constructs a model for strategy and pursues its own strategy and line of behavior. A mistaken understanding of an opponent's strategy leads to unpleasant surprises and unexpected turns of events.

An example of this is Russia and the Eurasian Economic Union project. While Moscow has been trying to create a security belt around itself in a broad sense, by economically subsidizing states in the post-Soviet space on its borders, and by proposing the establishment of clear mechanisms for economic cooperation (in the EEU decisions are adopted on a consensus basis, hence we are right to speak of a genuinely democratic approach in contrast to the dictatorial model of

17 Seufert G, Foreign Policy and Self-image. The Societal Basis of Strategy Shifts in Turkey (Stiftung Wissenschaft und Politik. Berlin, September 2012), 7.

18 Semih İ, "Public Opinion as a Determinant of the New Turkish Foreign Policy," Südosteuropa-Mitteilungen 50, no. 6. (2010), 40–45.

the Eurocommission in the EU), these efforts have been incorrectly interpreted and spun for Western public opinion. For example, Hillary Clinton, while US Secretary of State, asserted that the Eurasian Economic Union is an attempt to revive the Soviet Union, and numerous experts and scholars from the liberal camp have hurriedly claimed that this represents an "economic noose" and an attempt by Russia to expand its sphere of influence.

Russia's support for the Ukrainian government under Viktor Yanukovych's presidency and the West's (mainly the US') organization of a coup d'etat in February 2014 represent the apogee of the collision between two strategies. On the one hand is Russia's new approach towards its neighboring states based on mutual interests; on the other, we have the West's Cold War era thinking in which propaganda and the creation of an image of the "enemy" (with the aim of further subordinating it to the West's political will) are more important than cooperation. The referendum in Crimea and Russia's aid in maintaining law and order in order to prevent mass murder in the likes of what happened in Kiev in February 2014, Odessa in May of the same year, and the South-East Ukraine later (which led to the emergence of the Donetsk People Republic and Lugansk People Republic) is another example exposing the West's double standards. Whereas the West worships Vaclav Havel for allowing the peaceful partition of Czechoslovakia and pretends that the unification of Germany was a hallmark of democracy (no referendum was held), the West accepts other scenarios only when they benefit itself. In Ukraine, the result has been the undermining of political, economic, and social stability for years to come, and the US, EU and IMF's exploitation of the situation to initiate reforms in Ukraine that are creating unprecedented debt.

Further vivid examples of such deceptive strategies on the part of the West include numerous diplomatic and military surprises. States are led to believe that the obstacles to their opponents' political course are so great that they are insurmountable and, as a consequence, nothing is done to block their actions or prepare for them. This thereby provokes the enemy into exerting additional efforts to ensure success in this direction. In choosing one's strategy, it is necessary to take into account that knowledge of one party's real potential and the strategy of another are incomplete and not always adequate to the real state of affairs. Partial knowledge might provoke one side to take measures which it should have avoided, as such lead to a negative turn of events with the complete opposite of the desired effect.[19]

Finally, as has already been noted, the past thirty years have shown that globalization processes wield considerable influence on the geopolitical power of this or that country. This is a very complex phenomenon that has numerous dimensions. In his work, *Runaway World: How Globalization is Reshaping Our Lives*[20], Anthony Giddens writes that globalization has connected distant places in such a way that local events shape global ones, and vice versa. Thus, one small event in a given part of the world can trigger a chain reaction with repercussions reaching across the region or continent. Western experts believe that it is none other than the West that has the right and priority to direct globalization processes and indicate what other countries and peoples must do. Moreover, the West can deliberately produce provocations in order to justify interference in the domestic affairs of other states under the pretext of protecting human rights.

Attempts at political homogenization are tied to the need to ensure security. US Naval War College Professor Thomas Barnett, for instance, believes that liberal democratic and industrial capitalist countries have created the preconditions for establishing a global network, while the exclusion of a number of regions from the global information networks leaves certain risks due to the presence of a number of countries and peoples characterized by a different pattern of thinking than that of the center of globalization. It follows that a political culture similar to that of the West is supposed to be introduced in these countries.

The growing influence of transnational corporations, rating agencies, venture funds, etc. are also evident in ongoing globalization processes. We are confronted with a tendency on the part of a number of private companies to become new actors in international law (the so-called multistakeholder approach). The role of private military companies and non-governmental organizations in local conflicts also testifies to the erosion of the international security framework formed after the Second World War.

19 Arzumanyan R. Metaphora nelineynosti v sotsialnikh sistemah // 21St Vek 2 no. 4 (2004): 139. URL: http://www.noravank.am/upload/pdf/226_ru.pdf

20 Giddens A. Uskolzayushiy mir. Kak globalizatsiya menyaet nashu zhian. Moscow, 2004.

In these globalization processes, also visible are efforts at usurping the geopolitical capacities of other countries. On the one hand, private companies can undermine national sovereignty, while on the other some states can use these new opportunities to establish their hegemony in certain countries and regions. This leads to the deterioration of the political landscape. As an example, we can cite the operations of the Evian company in Bolivia, which has privatized key sources of drinking water, a move which has resulted in price hikes and the spread of infectious diseases. The American company Monsanto, which produces genetically-modified vegetables and fruits, is also known for its attempts to establish a monopoly over the agricultural industries of many countries. A group of pharmaceutical companies in the US, known as Big Pharma, is also trying to control global medication markets and dictate prices to consumers which, as a rule, often far exceed the prices offered by competitors.

These and other direct and indirect effects of globalization not only reshape definitions of state sovereignty, but blur the legal, political, and economic aspects. Especially relevant in recent time is the phenomenon of cyberspace in its various manifestations. While Russia, China, and a number of other countries insist on retaining national sovereignty over the Internet space within their state borders, another group of countries under the auspices of the US is trying to institutionalize a global character for the Internet, all the while maintaining the liberal culture of the Internet and keep control over its technological aspects in the hands of private companies most of which are to be found in the US.

Furthermore, globalization and the increasing influence of network culture are leading to changes to classical approaches to geopolitics. The fundamentals of geopolitics are changing. Like earlier with the reach for outer space, a new category of cosmic power has emerged, and cyberspace has become a new sphere of confrontation. This compels us to reconsider approaches that were previously considered the only correct and appropriate ones, and search for answers to new challenges and threats in new political conditions.

Insofar as there is no single unambiguous interpretation of the concept of security or other notions related to it, there can be no single model for international relations. It follows that there can be no single political system claiming universal recognition. International relations theories formulated in terms of realism, liberalism, Marxism, and constructivism, as well as the newest attempts at interpreting contemporary global politics in terms of feminism, postmodernism, traditionalism, neo-institutionalism, etc., are in a state of constant evolution and contradiction. Accordingly, speaking of any possibility of developing a single standard that could encompass the national interests of existing states and their security strategies and concepts is impossible. Instead, a more appropriate view is one that appreciates the coexistence and coevolution of multiple geopolitical systems with their own approaches to security and sovereignty and a system of mutual deterrent mechanisms which suits the concept of a polycentric world order.

Multifaceted Sovereignty

Now we need to consider in greater detail the concept of security as an originally Western European notion. It is believed that the French jurist Jean Bodin was the first to formulate the modern concept of sovereignty. In his 1576 work, *The Six Books of the Republic*, Bodin argued that the ruler or sovereign has the right to determine the law. Bodin's position was based on his own monarchical and Catholic convictions. Tellingly enough, Bodin sharply criticized the democratic form of governance, believed in the power of witchcraft, and directly participated in the inquisition processes against dozens of women, many of whom were burned at the stake.

In fact, the origination of the idea of sovereignty began even earlier. The division of Christianity into Western (Catholicism) and Eastern (Orthodox) and the division of the Roman Empire (also into Western and Eastern parts, the latter known as Byzantium) can be noted as catalyzers in this process.

The British politician, Labor Party ideologist, and author of the concept of "pluralistic democracy", Harold Laski, has also derived the notion of sovereignty from the phenomenon of the Christian Republic, with mention also also of the heritage of Imperial Rome. Laski writes that "Sovereignty, in the modern sense, is the progenitor of impalpable barriers from which the medieval thinker sought at all costs freedom", adding that the "*Republica Christiana* implied the worship of pervasive unity."[21] The relationship between the church (Papal Rome) and state authorities led to the formation of two schools of political thought. One insisted on the idea that if Christ is the ruler of the heavenly kingdom, then on Earth his counterpart is the Pope, being the vicar of Christ. According to this logic, all authority belongs to the Catholic Church. The Emperor can administer the empire, but obtains this right from Rome (the Pope). Thus was proclaimed "sacred law", *Jus divinum*, which asserted the ecumenical sovereignty of the church, and *Plenitudo Potestasis*, which implied full sovereignty over human affairs. The second school asserted the sacred right of kings, which resulted in confrontation between secular and spiritual authorities and further schisms. Siba N'Zatioula Grovogui has noted:

> [S]overeignty and self-determination have reflected the dominant European culture and functioned as a mediating ideology, reconciling the juridical means for attaining hegemony with the opposing need to project the rights and obligations created for the other as objectively derived from universal values…[M]edieval Christianity and papal interpretations of the Scriptures have defined the modern international order, including its hierarchical system and various forms of unequal subjectivities (or sovereignties). These hierarchies and subjectivities in turn have delineated the realm of international law from the Renaissance through the Enlightenment to the present…The first is that the classical episteme, to which the Renaissance merely contributed a new configuration, created the hierarchies underlying international relations and its norms…

Before Pope Innocent III emphasized the primacy of the papacy and the church in the late twelfth century, the dispute between the pope and the European rulers had been temporarily settled by the Concordat of Worms (1122). This agreement between Pope Calixtus and Emperor Henry V brought about a new modus vivendi between the church and temporal rulers within the Holy Roman Empire. It was a compromise that allowed the church to remain the ultimate spiritual but also political power while relegating to temporal Christian rulers certain lesser rights and prerogatives over their subjects. The church would

21 Laski, Harold Joseph. The foundations of sovereignty, and other essays, New York, Harcourt, Brace and company, 1921, P. 2. https://archive.org/details/foundationsofsov00lask/page/n4/mode/2up

no longer stand between the rulers and their subjects in reference to earthly matters.

The proclamation by Innocent III of papal plenitude and the supremacy of ecclesiastical authority within the Holy Roman Empire was a response to growing internal pressure for reform. Indeed, during the later Middle Ages the primacy of papal authority was undercut by theoretical debates over the nature of political authority within Europe itself. Several European monarchs, including King Edward I of England (1272-1307) and Philippe IV of France (1285-1314), successfully challenged Pope Boniface VIII, Innocent's successor, concerning the universality of papal imperial powers. Their objections presaged the sixteenth-century Protestant Reformation, when the papacy lost ecclesiastical authority over a large part of Western Christendom.

> The opposition of European monarchs to the authority of the pope was first framed in terms of the agency of imperium, purposefully defined as lordship (and later sovereignty) and dominium, the sphere of political influence over peoples, policy, and property. These concepts were understood in religious, legal, and political terms to be articulated around the identity of the various communities. Each secular ruler (monarch) who represented a community claimed to possess the right to sovereignty. This right was exercised against any domestic rival claim, and also abroad against the external encroachment of the papacy.
>
> The Concordat of Worms also constructed a political universe (respublica, or common order) in which the pope remained the suprema protesta: the only authority who acted independently of any external power but God. The pope was followed in this hierarchical universe by lesser European authorities (monarchs) who held their power by papal volition. The rest of humankind, forming the base of the pyramid, was incorporated into this temporal hierarchy by successive papal bulls. In the new order, the pope remained at the pinnacle, followed by European kings and their subjects. "Old World Infidels" (Chinese, Indians, and Muslims) came next, above Africans and, after 1492, the "New World Infidels."[22]

22 Siba N'Zatioula Grovogui, Sovereigns, Quasi Sovereigns, and Africans. Race and Self-Determination in International Law (University of Minnesota Press,

As we can see here, a racist approach was inherent in the formation of the Western European concept of sovereignty. In the Eastern Roman Empire, interestingly enough, the concept of a "symphony of powers" was developed in which the Emperor and the Patriarch exercised rule together, resolving secular and spiritual issues in accordance with their respective authority. The rudiments of such a model have been preserved in Russia where, although formally separate from the state, the Church plays an important role in public life, and the head of state regularly meets with the leadership of the Moscow Patriarchate to discuss a wide range of issues.

In the West, Thomas Hobbes contributed to the concept of royal sovereignty. Hobbes claimed that not only does the king declare the law, but establishes it, thus giving the sovereign absolute moral and political power. Like other social contract theorists, Hobbes argued that a king acquires his power from the people, which collectively, unconditionally relinquishes individual sovereignty and authority to the king.

The next stage in the development of the concept of sovereignty came with the religious Thirty Years War whose end marked the beginning of the Westphalian system of international relations. This system presumed the separation of religion and politics, which left certain problems lying in wait for the future. At the time, many states continued to have religious doctrines as state programs, and to this day there are a number of countries in which religion occupies the most important place in socio-economic life and is even encoded in constitutions.

In the 18th century, however, Jean-Jacques Rousseau assigned a collective identity, the people, as the sovereign, which introduced an antagonism between previous formulations and this new concept of sovereignty. As Carl Schmitt pointed out on this question:

> The people, the nation, the primordial force of any state – these always constitute new organs. From the infinite, incomprehensible abyss of the force [*Macht*] of the pouvoir constituant, new forms emerge incessantly, which it can destroy at any time and in which its power is never limited for good. It can will arbitrarily. The

---

1996): 16, 17-18.

> content of its willing has always the same legal value like the content of a constitutional definition. Therefore it can intervene arbitrarily – through legislation, through the administration of justice, or simply through concrete acts. It becomes the unlimited and illimitable bearer of the iura dominationis [rights/legal prerogatives of rulership], which do not even have to be restricted to cases of emergency.[23]

In Schmitt's works, the notion of sovereignty is considered in relation to the history of Western European countries up to the mid-20th century. As these states were engulfed by tumultuous events and evoked corresponding reactions, Schmitt analyzed in detail relevant issues of authority and law taken to their extreme, such as the principle of dictatorship. Schmitt writes: "From the perspective of sovereign dictatorship, the entire existing order is a situation that dictatorship will resolve through its own actions. Dictatorship does not suspend an existing constitution through a law based on the constitution – a constitutional law; rather it seeks to create conditions in which a constitution – a constitution that it regards as the true one – is made possible."[24]

Schmitt's deep study of these questions led succeeding authors and scholars to attribute this German scholar with the merit of being the most authoritative specialist on sovereignty. The Schmittean formula of "Sovereign is he who decides on the exception"[25] (Souverän ist, wer über den Ausnahmezustand entscheidet) indeed became one of the most prevalent theories. Schmitt stipulates: "Only this definition can do justice to a borderline concept."[26] Thus, the content of the legal and de facto highest authority is the main question, which Schmitt answers in the following: "The highest competence cannot be traceable to a person or to a socio-psychological power complex but only to the sovereign order in the unity of the system of norms."[27] Does this not mean that only those who can change the rules of the game on the

23 Carl Schmitt, Dictatorship: From the origin of the modern concept of sovereignty to proletarian class struggle (Polity Press, 2014), 123.

24 Ibid, 119.

25 Carl Schmitt, Political Theology: Four Chapters on the Concept of Sovereignty (MIT Press, 1985), 5.

26 Ibid.

27 Ibid, 19.

international arena can claim to wield sovereignty, and not those who follow regional or global leaders and serve their interests in exchange for patronage and privileges?

The Italian philosopher Giorgio Agamben took such considerations "to the edge" in his work *Homo Sacer: Sovereign Power and Bare Life*. Starting from Schmitt, Agamben proceeds to Giambattista Vico's notion, which is compared with features of positive and negative theology, the opposition between positive law (ius theticum) and the exception with its special status. In this context, Agamben attributes sovereign power the role of katechon, that which deters the coming of the Kingdom of the Antichrist. Here we arrive at the most ancient principle of sovereign power - Pindar's 169th fragment, the ambiguity of which suggests a mysterious character of the sovereign insofar as the law is directly linked to violence:

> The *nomos*, sovereign of all,
> Of mortals and immortals,
> Leads with the strongest hand,
> Justifying the most violent.[28]

Agamben thus concludes that "the sovereign nomos is the principle that, joining law and violence, threatens them with indistinction."[29] This intuition probably prompted Max Weber to argue that the state has the legitimate right to exercise violence.

Further on, Agamben trails in the wake of Western political thought, nevertheless still appealing to such heterodox authors as Walter Benjamin and Georges Bataille. In the end, in Agamben's opinion, the "fundamental activity of sovereign power is the production of bare life as originary political element and as threshold of articulation between nature and culture,"[30] and the (concentration) camp is the biopolitical paradigm of the West, not the city as in antiquity. In light of the current migration crisis in the EU, this interpretation might seem unfounded,

28 Translation from Giorgio Agamben, Homo Sacer: Sovereign Power and Bare Life (Stanford University Press, 1998), 30. The original Greek reads nomos, which has been translated as "custom" or "law."

29 Giorgio Agamben, Homo Sacer: Sovereign Power and Bare Life (Stanford University Press, 1998), 31.

30 Ibid, 181.

as numerous camps and shelters for refugees and migrants have stirred political debates that have been "embalmed" with a Brussels program of tolerance and multiculturalism, once again overriding the norms, values, and boundaries of political space and identity.

George Bataille's ideas are also of interest to our study, although he stipulates that he writes about a kind of sovereignty which has little to do with the sovereignty of states as defined in international law. Bataille argues that the distinguishing hallmark of sovereignty is "the consumption of wealth, as against labor and servitude, which produce wealth without consuming it."[31] Bataille suggests that "the sovereign (or the sovereign life) begins when, with the necessities ensured, the possibility of life opens up without limit."[32]

If we adapt these thoughts to current realities in international realities, the following questions arise: Is consumption as such a criterion of sovereignty? If yes, can it be associated not only with political elites, but also the population at large, thus developing a special index for consumption sovereignty? Can autarchy, i.e., self-sufficiency, even if only potential, mean real sovereignty? This in turn exposes the following paradox. A number of states have achieved certain heights of prosperity by virtue of military force and economic ties, whether through oil sales or commodity speculation. Any change to this system would lead to the collapse of the political system, and, in the case of geopolitical turmoil, those countries which are not sufficiently deeply integrated into the global economy and international processes would be more resistant to changes in their external environment.

As Bataille notes, in the bourgeois world, sovereign order is reduced to its utility through production. In anti-bourgeois doctrines, sovereignty is aimed at overcoming alienation, but interpretations of the means and end goals for such can vary. In Bataille's words: "Sovereignty often entails power, but then it is sovereignty that is power's end...[I]t is as though the negation of sovereignty were, in a sense, identical with sovereignty."[33] Another question thus arises: How can we interpret the acquiring of knowledge and levels of sovereignty?

31 Georges Bataille, The Accursed Share: Volumes II and III (Zone Books, 1993), 198.

32 Ibid.

33 Ibid, 356.

Even if we were to pass over Georges Bataille's remarks[34], it is nevertheless clear that the relationship between power and knowledge reflects criteria of sovereignty. Jens Bartelson suggests that knowledge and sovereignty are entangled logically and produce each other historically.[35] According to Bartelson, the era of modernity is characterized by an understanding that sovereign subjects are capable of constructing visions and concepts which create the world around them. They become the element of sovereignty, rather than the king. Political and social relations are perceived through their historicization, whereas sovereignty becomes an organizing principle of political reality. The state thus becomes a conceptual whole capable of assimilating political and social differences collected as an array of analogous relationships, and is a mediator between the public and private, between the subject and object. The sovereign state and the international system, thus, become opposing spheres of political reality.

But if in Europe under the influence of Christianity one approach to the full scope of power was developed, then in other places and under other religions similar conceptions developed along a different trajectory. In the period of early Islam, it was affirmed that political power belongs only to Allah, as according to Surah An-Nur 24:55: "Allah has promised those who have believed among you and done righteous deeds that He will surely grant them succession [to authority] upon the earth just as He granted it to those before them and that He will surely establish for them [therein] their religion which He has preferred for them and that He will surely substitute for them, after their fear, security, [for] they worship Me, not associating anything with Me."

Historical analysis shows that the ideas of secular Modernity, including its interpretations of the concept of sovereignty, in a definite manner influenced the reform of traditional Islam which led to the emergence of new forms known as "political Islam." For example, it has been noted:

---

34 In Bataille's view, death is also an important mark of sovereignty, since sovereignty must under certain circumstances break the prohibition on murder. As follows from this, states with the death penalty have full sovereignty.

35 Jens Bartelson, A Genealogy of Sovereignty (Cambridge: Cambridge University Press, 1995).

> the central rallying cry of the Sunni Islamist movement during the middle of the 20th century was the proclamation of God's exclusive sovereignty (*hakimiyya*) over the world and human legislation…what we might call "high utopian Islamism" rejected any form of comparison or similarity with modern Western ideals of governance. The common Abrahamic belief in God's cosmic, creative sovereignty—what we might call divine sovereignty as fact— leads to an uncompromising insistence on God's exclusive legislative and normative sovereignty."[36]

The famous Sunni thinker and one of the ideologists of the Mulsim Brotherhood, Sayyid Qutb said in this regard:

> If we look at the sources and foundations of modern ways of living, it becomes clear that the whole world is steeped in *Jahiliyyah* [ignorance] and all the marvellous material comforts and high-level inventions do not diminish this ignorance. This Jahiliyyah is based on rebellion against God's sovereignty on earth. It transfers to man one of the greatest attributes of God, namely sovereignty, and makes some men lords over others… [and now] takes the form of claiming that the right to create values, to legislate rules of collective behavior, and to choose any way of life rests with men, without regard to what God has prescribed.[37]

Such a view, however, is characteristic only for Sunnis. Imam Khomeini has commented: "The fundamental difference between Islamic government, on the one hand, and constitutional monarchies and republics, on the other, is this: whereas the representatives of the people or the monarch in such regimes engage in legislation, in Islam the legislative power and competence to establish laws belongs exclusively to Almighty God."[38]

---

36 Andrew F. March. Genealogies of Sovereignty in Islamic Political Theology. Social Research: An International Quarterly, Volume 80, Number 1, Spring 2013, pp. 293-320.

37 Qutb S. Milestones, 1964. P. 8. https://web.archive.org/web/20100813111858/http://web.youngmuslims.ca/online_library/books/milestones/hold/index_2.htm

38 Blake Archer Williams. An Introduction to Waliyic Islam. Sacred Communities and their Covenantal Dispensations. Lion of Najaf Publishers, 2017. P. 153.

Another example is Tibetan Buddhism, which since the era of Genghis Khan has developed a theory of unity of policy and religion. Buddhist monks believed that the state needs a force which sanctifies order, or else will constantly degrade under a secular regime. "Where Buddhism failed to ideologically subdue the institution of power, it made considerable efforts to adapt to the existing political ideology and become, if not its mainstay, then at least an essential part of it."[39]

This demonstrates a difference in approaches to sovereignty between different civilizational types which operate in different geographical spaces. However, collisions over defining sovereignty have arisen even in one and the same cultural-historical area. For example, two different definitions of sovereignty with mutually exclusive criteria once arose on the territory of present-day Italy. In Dante, political power has divine justification, whereas in Machiavelli sovereignty and power do not depend on moral or religious origin. Such interpretations compelled a single idea of sovereignty to be brought together in the European political space. On the other hand, the possibility has been left open for interpreting other models of sovereignty which continue to operate this day.

Indigenous Peoples and Sovereignty

Another telling case of sovereignty is that of indigenous peoples inhabiting the territory of a particular state, namely, the US. In the Western approach to this issue we can, once again, expose the problem of racism. For example, the US Supreme Court has "systematically stripped [Native American] tribes of the one attribute that is - perhaps above all else - associated with sovereign status: the power to assert control over events that take place on one's own territory."[40] In the study quoted, we are dealing with the Suquamish tribe in Washington state in particular.[41]

39 Martynov A.S. Buddhism I obshestvo v stranakh Centralnoy i Vostochnoy Azii //Buddhism, gosudarstvo I obshestvo v stranakh Centralnoy i Vostochnoy Azii v Srednie veka. Moscow, 1982. p. 11.

40 Katherine J. Florey, "India Country'S Borders: Territoriality, Immunity, and the Construction of Tribal Sovereignty," Boston College Law Review 51 (2010): 597. http://www.bc.edu/content/dam/files/schools/law/bclawreview/pdf/51_3/02_florey.pdf

41 Oliphant v. Suquamish Indian Tribe, 435 U.S. 191, 194 (1978).

Overall: "The territorial element of tribal sovereignty has never been simple, largely because courts have long employed a strikingly narrow conception of what constitutes tribal territory. For tribes, the power to regulate has long been based not on traditional geopolitical boundaries but on the tribal ownership status of particular parcels of land—a highly unorthodox way to conceive of sovereign power over territory."[42]

In the 1990's in the US, tribal sovereignty was juridically eroded and the security of tribal territories completely passed into the hands of the federal government and police. Thus, decisions which affect the interests and territories of Indian tribes in the US (for example, the Dakota Access Pipeline) often lead to mass protests, riots, and repression by security forces.[43]

Insofar as there is no perfect ground upon which to establish sovereignty, the relationship between ownership and political control is, in the very least, important for tribes to maintain some elements of traditional territorial sovereignty. While large portions of reservations consist of tribal land, especially roads, civic buildings, and community gathering places, a tribe can also claim significant authority over geographical areas that are most important to it.

Immunity

The concept of immunity is also part and parcel of international law and is directly connected to notions of sovereignty. In European and British legislation, the idea that the sovereign enjoys immunity from persecution in some circumstances has taken strong root in jurisprudence, at least since the days of medieval England. The earliest version of this doctrine applied only to domestic sovereign immunity, i.e., the idea that the king cannot be brought before the courts of his own country.[44]

42 Katherine J. Florey, "India Country'S Borders: Territoriality, Immunity, and the Construction of Tribal Sovereignty," Boston College Law Review 51 (2010): 597. http://www.bc.edu/content/dam/files/schools/law/bclawreview/pdf/51_3/02_florey.pdf

43 Dakota Access pipeline: the who, what and why of the Standing Rock protests", 3 November 2016. https://www.theguardian.com/us-news/2016/nov/03/north-dakota-access-oil-pipeline-protests-explainer

44 Nevada v. Hall, 440 U.S. 410, 415 (1979); U. Colo. L. Rev. 1, 2–5 (1972).

The origins of this doctrine have been the subject of much discussion. Sometimes they are said to have stemmed from the metaphysical notion of the infallibility of the king. But it is also possible that this doctrine arose out of a more mundane reality - the king was the lawgiver and the highest judicial body, hence no practical mechanism existed for challenging the king's actions in court.[45] After the doctrine of monarchical immunity was finally developed and asserted, a parallel concept of external sovereign immunity arose as the principle that the sovereign should have protection in other states' courts similar to what he enjoys in his own country. Although doctrines of internal and external sovereign immunity were supposed to assure analogous protection and have followed a parallel course of development when it comes to many issues, they also harbor important differences.[46] Firstly, they differ in terms of grounds or justification. Many justifications for internal sovereign immunity are focused on government organizations. Moreover, both federal and state sovereign immunities contain exceptions for prospective court sentences against official state entities that violate existing law. For example, foreign sovereign immunity, as recognized in the United States, is not subject to equivalent restriction, but includes a powerful exception. In 1952, the United States recognized a distinction between private and state acts of foreign sovereigns, recognizing immunity only for the latter.[47] Since 1976, this distinction has been codified in the Foreign Sovereign Immunities Act (FSIA), according to which foreign states are not immune from prosecution related to commercial activities based in the US.[48]

Western countries are a prime example of how the concept of sovereignty can be used to justify any actions on the international arena, as well as within a state, without taking into account the rule of precedent and political-historical continuity. As the scholar David Chandler has noted: "With the end of the Cold War, there rapidly developed increasingly interventionist regimes of international regulation, clearly exposing claims of international sovereign equality and in

45 David E. Engdahl, Immunity and Accountability for Positive Governmental Wrongs, 44 U. COLO. L. REv. I (1972-73).

46 Katherine Florey, Sovereign Immunity's Penumbras: Common Law, "Accident," and Policy in the Development of Sovereign Immunity Doctrine, 43 Wake Forest L. Rev. 765, 769–70 (2008).

47 Republic of Austria v. Altmann, 541 U.S. 677, 689 (2004).

48 28 U.S.C § 1605(a)(2) (2006).

the process forcing Western powers and international institutions to account for the outcomes of these regulatory practices. Once relations of sovereign equality were openly brought into question through aid conditionality and human rights intervention, the question was sharply posed of Western responsibility."[49]

In his work, *Ironies of Sovereignty: The European Union and the United States*, the famous American political scientist Robert Keohane noted: "Ironically, the US, from which the first republican critique of the concept of sovereignty emanated, has now become one of its staunchest defenders. Meanwhile, the European Union has moved away from the classical conception of external sovereignty." Keohane is also known as the author of the concept of "pooled sovereignty."[50]

Sovereignty and Supranational Bodies

Over the last hundred years, questions of sovereignty have continued to be twofold. The UN Charter asserts that all peoples have the right to self-determination, but also claims that the territory integrity of states is not up for questioning. In the 20th and 21st centuries, moreover, the verdict has spread that historical sovereignty has been "exhausted"[51] and, accordingly, that some states are restricted in what they can and cannot do. In the early 2000's, a number of countries and supra-governmental organizations tried to apply their own notions of progress and development to a number of countries with weak sovereignty, thereby essentially interfering in their domestic affairs and imposing methods of control. The impetus for this interpretation came when the International Commission on Intervention and State Sovereignty came to the conclusion that the right of states to sovereignty can coexist with external intervention and state-building.[52]

49 David Chandler, "International State-Building: Beyond Conditionality, Beyond Sovereignty", Guest Seminar, Royal Institute for International Relations (IRRI-KIIB), Brussels, 17 November 2005, 6.

50 Robert O. Keohane, " Ironies of Sovereignty: The European Union and the United States," JCMS: Journal of Common Market Studies 40, no. 4 (November 2002): 743–765.

51 Badie B and Smouts M. Le retourment du munde. Sociologie de la scene Internationale (Paris, 1992), 33-35.

52 International Commission on Intervention and State Sovereignty (ICISS), Responsibility to Protect (Ottawa: International Development Research Centre, 2001), 16.

In August 2004, for example, the US government created a department for state-building, called the Office of the Coordinator for Reconstruction and Stabilization.[53] Subsequently, in December 2004, the UN proposed the establishment of an intergovernmental peacekeeping commission for monitoring UN operations and rebuilding post-conflict states. This UN initiative, despite political disagreements between supporters of multilateral peace-building and unilateral preventative war, shows that these projects represent responses to the overall security situation. Barnett Rubin argues that "in the past half-century has been the replacement of global juridical imperialism by global juridical national sovereignty. The UN incorporates this organising principle in its charter. This structure has altered the options available to Great Powers for coping with security threats or challenges to their interests."[54] Meanwhile, it has been noted that "current standards fail on both a pragmatic and equitable level."[55]

Nevertheless, in December 2004, the High Level Group established by Kofi Annan in 2002, issued a report which proposed that the UN Security Council adopt the concept of "Responsibility to Protect", according to which interventions can be made on other states' territories to prevent violations of the norms of international law. In February 2005, the UK government's Strategy Unit issued a report entitled "Investing in Prevention - An International Strategy to Manage Risks of Instability and Improve Crisis Response" which considered state-building to be a key part of the "Partnership for Stability" agenda.[56] In March 2005, at a session of the high-level Development Assistance Committee of the OECD in Paris, ministers for country development agreed on a set of principles for "good international engagement" of "fragile states" with a focus on state-building as the primary objective.[57] In the same month, the Commission for Africa issued a report which welcomed

53 http://www.state.gov/documents/organization/43429.pdf

54 Barnett R. Rubin, "Constructing Sovereignty for Security," Survival: Global Politics and Strategy 93-106 (Winter 2005): 94.

55 Leslie Sturgeon, "Constructive sovereignty for indigenous peoples," Chicago Journal of International Law 6, no. 1 (2005): 455.

56 UK Prime Minister's Strategy Unit Report, Investing in Prevention - An International Strategy to Manage Risks of Instability and Improve Crisis Response, February 2005. http://www.strategy.gov.uk/downloads/work_areas/countries_at_risk/report/index.htm

57 OECD Principles for Good International Engagement in Fragile States. OECD

the fact that more than a quarter of bilateral aid to Africa had already been allocated directly for state-building potential. The report said that even international financial institutions, such as the World Bank and International Monetary Fund, had proposed to abandon earlier aspirations for development and economic growth and focus on more narrow frameworks of transparency and accountability.[58]

In December 2005, during the World Summit of the United Nations, all state members officially recognized the principle of "Responsibility to Protect" and agreed to establish the proposed peacekeeping commission for coordinating international operations in this field. In 2009, at the UN General Assembly, the UN Secretary General presented a report entitled "Implementing the Responsibility to Protect,"[59] despite the fact that to this day this concept does not have any legal basis and situations presenting legitimate grounds for international intervention have not been defined.

In the late 20th and early 21st century, the political agendas of numerous countries came to include terms and terminology which leave doubt as to the existence of full sovereignty for a number of states. Depending on the context and interests, the following terms were proposed:

- states with limited sovereignty;
- fragile states;
- phantom states;
- failed states;
- fraud states.

Nowadays, the term sovereignty is used almost exclusively to describe the attributes of a state, not its supreme ruler. A sovereign state is often described as free, independent, and claiming the right to regulate its economic life without the input of its neighbors and to indefinitely increase its armed forces. In this view, other states have no right to interfere in the internal affairs of a sovereign country. In

document DCD(2005)11/REV2, p.8.
http://www.oecd.org/dataoecd/4/25/35238282.pdf

58 Our Common Interest, Commission for Africa (11 March 2005), 374.
http://www.commissionforafrica.org/english/report/introduction.html

59 http://daccess-dds-ny.un.org/doc/UNDOC/GEN/N09/206/12/PDF/N0920612.pdf?

their foreign relations, they claim the right to pursue their own ideas of rights and to declare war. Such a description of sovereign states has been rejected by those who argue that international law is obligatory. Insofar as states are restricted by treaties and international obligations, the declaration of war has become an anachronism. The US carries out military operations without legal formalities, yet this does not reduce the serious and negative consequences of American interventions. In addition, the UN Charter asserts that the absolute freedom of sovereign states must be left in the past. In contemporary international practice, the United Nations is the main authority when it comes to restricting the exercise of sovereignty.

Ambiguous interpretations of sovereignty do not end there. Following Stephen Krasner, four types of sovereignty have been distinguished in the political sciences: domestic, legal, Westphalian, and interdependence. Domestic sovereignty is related to the organization of public authority over a state's territory, while interdependent sovereignty refers to the ability of states to regulate transborder flows. Legal or international sovereignty is based on formally independent states recognizing each other as equal actors in international relations, while Westphalian sovereignty is a state's right to determine its domestic policy without interference from the outside. In addition, we can mention the concept of restricted sovereignty, in which a given state comes under the tutelage of another country or group of states. We know from history that all of these forms of sovereignty interact with one another and adduce various compromises and deviations from norms. Those compromises which have become regular in international relations were christened by Stephen Krasner as "organized hypocrisy."[60] Of course, this "hypocrisy" directly impacts security.

John Maszka has proposed the concept of constructive sovereignty to address the heightening pressure exerted by globalization on state sovereignty. Maszka's theory argues that states are not the primary actors that comprise them. It follows that their preferences are not fixed. Insofar as states merely represent the preferences of their constituents, they will adhere only to those international norms which their electorates accept. Instead of pressuring, larger, more powerful international organizations which impose global norms from without,

60 Stephan Krasner, Sovereignty: Organized Hypocrisy (Princeton, NJ: Princeton University Press, 1999).

the theory of constructive sovereignty argues that changes must ultimately come from within, i.e., from the constituency of each state. Since states' voters are becoming increasingly international, they will be more receptive to international norms. Thus, international norms will become embedded and viewed as legitimate, and each state's sovereignty will be maintained and respected.[61]

The Weak and the Strong

Oddly enough, despite such an abundance of terminologies, all states can be determined on a scale of sovereignty with respect to geopolitical capacities and political practice finding expression in international and domestic affairs. Those subjects which are unrecognized or partially recognized by other states (including by UN member states), can be called countries with "limited sovereignty." Abkhazia, South Ossetia, Transnistria, Nagorno-Karabakh, the Donetsk People Republic, and the Lugansk People Republic are such states in the post-Soviet space with which Russia directly or indirectly (through mediation, such as in the case of Nagorno-Karabakh) deals. In fact, there are many more such states, and a significant factor in numerous such cases is support from one of the major actors of world politics. A classic example of this is Taiwan, which is not a UN member. China exerts all possible efforts to prevent this island from being recognized by other countries as an independent actor in international relations.

The Constitution of Bosnia and Herzegovina allows its constituents to hold citizenship of Bosnia and Herzegovina and the citizenship of another country if there exists a bilateral agreement with said country approved by the parliament of Bosnia and Herzegovina. The federation signed such an agreement with Croatia in 1998, and Republika Srpska did so with the Federal Republic of Yugoslavia in 2001.[62] Bosnia remains a pure example of a modern, non-sovereign democracy born out of the neo-liberal doctrine of democratic peace.[63] Such restrictions imposed

---

61 John Maszka, Constructive Sovereignty. A New International Relations Model for an Old Problem (LAMBERT Academic Publishing, 2010).

62 Mezhdunarodnie organizatsii i krizis na Balkanah: dokumenti. Vol. 3. Moscow: Indrik, 2000. P. 239.

63 Rummel R.J, "Libertarianism and International Violence," Journal of Conflict Resolution 27, no.1 (1983): 27-71; Russet B, Grasping the Democratic Peace: Principles for a Post Cold War World (Princeton: Princeton University Press,

on sovereignty yield serious dilemmas. After all, "the consolidation of peace and democracy is impossible without the responsibility of the people for its political and economic development, and without popular and civil sovereignty."[64] In addition, it has been argued that the sovereignty of one state has no significance without juxtaposition to the sovereignty of other states and, more importantly, without mutual respect of sovereign territory arising out of this recognition.[65]

John Hobson, whose ideas we cited earlier, has proposed the concept of "default" or "gradated sovereignty." Insofar as the principle of sovereignty is first and foremost linked to modern Western states which are implicitly understood to be "civilized," then the sovereignty of such countries is "full." But if a country belongs, in the West's understanding, to a civilization of barbarians or savages, then it has default sovereignty, i.e., such a country's sovereignty is recognized legally, but Western states treat such with distrust and suspicion, constantly calling into question whether this sovereignty can be "correctly" exercised or not. The need for control over such (un)civilized states demands putting pressure on them under various pretexts which more often than not reduces the extent of their sovereignty. Thus, one model exists legally, whereas in deed another can be seen in international relations.

Close to this idea is Alexandros Yannis' concept of suspended sovereignty.[66] In the exemplary precedents of Kosovo and East Timor, Yannis showed that law and reality no longer coincide in the consideration of the location of sovereign authority. Robert Jackson has more clearly expressed what sovereignty might be considering various limitations: "[Legal means] a sovereign state is not subordinate to another sovereign but is necessarily equal to it by international law

---

1993); Muravchic J, "Promoting Peace through Democracy " in Managing Global Chaos (Washington: Institute of Peace Press, 1996): 573-585.

64 Sokolova E. Bosniya I Hertsegovina: Opit nesuverennoy demokratii // Neprikosnovenniy zapas №6, 2007. http://www.intelros.ru/readroom/nz/nz_56/1926-ekaterina-sokolova.-bosnija-i.html

65 Wendt, A. (1992, Spring). Anarchy is What States Make of it: The Social Construction of Power Politics. International Organization, 46(2), 391-425. p. 400.

66 Alexandros Yannis, 'The Concept of Suspended Sovereignty in International Law and its Implications in International Politics', European Journal of International Law 13, no. 5, (2002): 1049.

- although, of course, not necessarily by international fact. Absolute in that sovereignty is either present or absent. When a country is sovereign it is independent categorically: there is no intermediate condition... Unitary [means] that a sovereign state is a supreme authority within its jurisdiction."[67] It follows, such historically known forms as colonies, protectorates, mandates, trusteeships, dominions, etc. cannot be said to wield sovereignty.

However, insofar as the conceptualization of sovereignty as potential capacity, not as formal juridical right to self-governance and international legal quality, creates a "continuum" of sovereignty or hierarchy of sovereignty, some states are considered more sovereign than others. Jackson therefore introduces the concept of quasi-states. In his opinion, the sovereignty granted to post-colonial countries is artificial, not because they continue to be under the influence of their former rulers, but because most of these countries do not have the capacity to regulate and control their societies on the same level as the states of the West. Therefore, such states have sovereignty de jure, but not de facto.

If there exist states with weak, limited, default, or gradated sovereignty, then their counterparts can be characterized as hyper-sovereign states. This category concerns a number of countries who use their geopolitical predominance and methods of indirect influence to go beyond traditional international relations with the aim of gaining certain economic, political, and image-enhancing dividends. Two examples of hyper-sovereignty are the US and Israel. Although these states' economic power and political roles are incomparable, both exceed and overstretch their normative sovereignty. The US uses supranational structures such as the UN and its relevant bodies to push American interests and exert pressure on other countries, as well as established mechanisms of global influence known as "liberal hegemony." One of these mechanisms is the use of the dollar as the world reserve currency, due to which all states, companies, and individuals who use the dollar as a means of payment are de facto aiding the US economy. A second element is financial and banking instruments such as stock quotes and rating agencies which can create artificial demand, supply, and collapse prices and currencies. As for coercive means, military might distributed across the world at

67 Robert Jackson, Quasi-states: Sovereignty, International Relations and the Third World (Cambridge: Cambridge University Press, 1990), 32.

numerous bases and installations is used alongside multilateral and bilateral military partnerships and cooperation schemes. Additional leverage is provided by the NATO bloc and regional agreements in the Asia-Pacific region and Latin America. Moreover, links between the industrial and scientific sectors and military technology allow for a number of countries to be subjected to a position of dependence on the US military-industrial complex. Finally, public diplomacy is directly integrated into the US foreign policy agenda, which allows for Washington's interests to be lobbied through education, reforms, election monitoring, consultations, and training.

Following the election of Donald Trump, American political scientists began to use the term "sovereignty on steroids." In his *Sovereignty Wars*, Stewart Patrick remarked that: "Sovereignty is among the most frequently invoked, polemical, and vexing concepts in politics—particularly American politics…Today the best measure of effective sovereignty is not the absence of foreign entanglements, but indeed the extensiveness of a country's links with the outside world."[68] Further, Patrick writes:

> The discourse over American sovereignty has only grown more heated over the past five decades. During the 1990s, Senator Jesse Helms (R-N.C.), chair of the Senate Foreign Relations Committee, angered a generation of liberal internationalists by blocking U.S. membership in multilateral treaties and withholding U.S. dues to the United Nations (UN) in an effort to impose reform on the world body. In more recent years, John Bolton, who served as U.S. ambassador to the UN under President George W. Bush, has warned of 'the coming war on sovereignty.' John Fonte of the conservative Hudson Institute frames the choice for the United States as a binary one in his book Sovereignty or Submission: Will Americans Rule Themselves or Be Ruled by Others? On Capitol Hill, meanwhile, more than two dozen senators have formed the 'Sovereignty Caucus.' According to Representative Doug Lamborn (R-Colo.), one of its cofounders, the group was established

68 Stewart M. Patrick, Trump's National Security Strategy: Sovereignty on Steroids, December 19, 2017 https://www.cfr.org/blog/trumps-national-security-strategy-sovereignty-steroids; Stewart Patrick, The Sovereignty Wars: Reconciling America with the World, Brookings Institution Press, 2017. [https://www.cfr.org/book/sovereignty-wars]

> to 'protect and defend the rights of American citizens and the interests of American institutions from the increasing influence of international organizations and multilateral agreements. It will promote policies and practices that protect U.S. self-determination, national sovereignty, and constitutional principles and defend American values from encroachment by transnational actors.'[69]

Israel can be counted as a hyper-sovereign power given its de facto occupation of and establishment of political, social, and other operations on the territories of a number of other states. This is done in violation of international law and UN resolutions. Nevertheless, the international community has not initiated an international isolation or boycott (although international campaigns constantly threaten and attempt such). In Israel's case, it is important to remember that we are faced with an actual occupation waged by military operations which has led to the deaths of a large number of victims among the civilian population.

In this context, experts have drawn attention to the fact that in international circles Palestine is seen as a sub-sovereign or pseudo-sovereign actor and, as such, the demands of the Palestinian leadership are not taken into serious consideration. The origins of this approach lie in the Balfour Declaration.[70] However, Palestinian "performative diplomacy" has been seen by many scholars and analysts as fairly successful. A number of actions, especially violent resistance and mass hunger strikes by political prisoners (such as in April 2017 when 1500 Palestinians in Israeli engaged in such a collective act of protest), have been appraised as acts of "bodily performance of communal sovereignty" capable of affecting the political agenda on the recognition of the independence of Palestine.[71]

Moving on, in the context of contemporary globalization problems, we can ascertain that many processes have a pronounced anti-sovereign orientation. These include:

---

69 Stewart Patrick, The Sovereignty Wars https://www.cfr.org/excerpt-sovereignty-wars

70 Khalidi, R. (2006). The Iron Cage: The Story of the Palestinian Struggle for Statehood. Boston: Beacon Press.

71 Catherine Charrett, Palestine in Britain: Sovereignty and Diplomacy After Balfour. JUN 22 2017. http://www.e-ir.info/2017/06/22/palestine-in-britain-sovereignty-and-diplomacy-after-balfour/

- some norms and demands of international legislation

- the activities of non-state actors (religious organizations, non-governmental organizations, international movements, transnational companies, organized crime, terrorist networks)

- pressure exerted by states with stable sovereignty on other countries (here we encounter the problem of default sovereignty)

In this context, the effects of globalization and innovations have introduced changes into national, social, political, and economic order.[72] In current international relations, state economic and military capabilities have been insufficient on their own, "or their use and expansion politically constrained."[73]

Professor Lorenzo Zucca of King's College London argues that the decline of state sovereignty can be explained through a naturalistic approach, which can also make sense of the emergence of transnational rules. In this scheme, when a state collapses and international organizations are incapable of providing an alternative, then interested economic and political groups insist on scenarios desirable and conducive to the uninterrupted functioning of transnational markets. Nevertheless, attempts can still be seen to be made to preserve the Westphalian system despite the obvious growth of its limitations.[74] Let us note that this naturalistic approach can be traced back to the Dutch philosopher Benedict Spinoza. As follows, sovereignty was "born" in the West, and the roots of its destruction can be found in the same place. This dilemma gives rise to disputes.

Moreover, insofar as the international system is in the process of transformation, ongoing changes cannot but affect the principles of sovereignty. For instance, the 2005 report of Great Britain's Overseas Development Institute discerned:

72 Saskia Sassen, Losing Control? Sovereignty in an Age of Globalization (New York, Columbia University Press, 1996).

73 Janice E Thomson, Mercenaries, Pirates, and Sovereigns (Princeton, NJ: Princeton University Press, 1994) , 67.

74 Lorenzo Zucca, "A Genealogy of State Sovereignt" http://www.academia.edu/9290370/A_Genealogy_of_State_Sovereignty

The consensus now emerging from global economic, military and political institutions signals that this gap between de jure sovereignty and de facto sovereignty is the key obstacle to ensuring global security and prosperity. The challenge is to harness the international system behind the goal of enhancing the sovereignty of states – that is, to enhance the capacity of these states to perform the functions that define them as states. Long-term partnerships must be created to prepare and then implement strategies to close this sovereignty gap.[75]

Nevertheless, many states are stubbornly resisting attempts and tendencies to reduce or degrade their sovereignty. In July 2017, Russia's Federation Council established the Temporary Commission for the Protection of State Sovereignty and Prevention of Interference in the Domestic Affairs of the Russian Federation.[76] China has also been closely monitoring processes on the international arena and the actions of other actors who might in one way or another threaten Chinese national sovereignty. Also noteworthy is the fact that in 2005, the idea of a Sovereign Wealth Fund appeared which has since, regardless of its assets and registration types (whether investment companies, pension funds, oil funds, etc.), been under the constant scrutiny of analysts and ratings.[77]

As we can see, both security and sovereignty have a wide range of interpretations. If security is inherent to different social formations, and if feudal and tribal associations were compelled to directly address this issue even before the era of the birth of national states, then the concept of sovereignty arose in the West, became entrenched in legal institutions, underwent various transformations, and is now used as a means for protesting and justifying state interests and national identity in a broad sense.

75 Ghani, Lockhart and Carnahan, Closing the Sovereignty Gap, UK Overseas Development Institute (ODI) working paper 253. London, 2005. P.4. https://www.odi.org/sites/odi.org.uk/files/odi-assets/publications-opinion-files/2482.pdf

76 http://www.council.gov.ru/structure/commissions/iccf_def/

77 https://www.swfinstitute.org/fund-rankings/

8

Economics and Religion

Security and sovereignty are logically followed by two additional phenomena which originally lay at the origin of all social formations, but which with the rise of modernity became separate objects of scientific study: economics and religion. Although it is now commonplace to examine economics and religion in isolation from each other, they are in fact closely interconnected, a point which will be demonstrated over the course of this chapter. Economics, of course, receives considerably more attention in social and state affairs, but it is this approach that is largely responsible for the emergence of regular crises, as economics cannot be an autonomous sphere of vital activities, and the transfer of excessive authority to economists can lead to serious imbalances.

Religion, Authority, and International Relations

As noted by Georgetown University Professor Shireen Hunter: "Religion affects the character of international relations the same way as do other value systems and ideologies by influencing the behavior of states and increasingly non-state actors. Moreover, although mostly unrecognized, as part of states and other actors value systems religion has always played a role in determining the character of the behavior of various international actors."[1]

The renowned philosopher and first Vice-President of India, Sarvepalli Radhakrishnan, said that in any religion, regardless of the type of society at hand, movements arise over the course of its development which differ from one another in their method of professing loyalty to

1 Shireen T. Hunter. Religion and International Affairs: From Neglect to Over-Emphasis// The Sacred and the Sovereign a compendium of pieces from e-IR on religion and international relations. P. 8

the institution of power (the ruler). In one way or another, all religions speak of values and obligations which must be realized in relation to others. "Religion," Radhakrishnan believes, "is a kind of life or experience. It is an insight into the nature of reality (darsana), or experience of reality (anubhava)."[2] It is "an independent functioning of the human mind, something unique, possessing an autonomous character. It is something inward and personal which unifies all values and organizes all experiences. It is the reaction to the whole of man to the whole of reality. [It] may be called spiritual life, as distinct from a merely intellectual or moral or aesthetic activity or a combination of them."[3] In other words, while there may exist a number of different definitions of religion, all of them speak of a certain system of values, restrictions, and obligations.

In this chapter, economics and religion[4] are introduced alongside each other in order to show both the general traits and cardinal differences in the types of economies and religious doctrines. The very etymology of the word "economy" shows that this discipline is something more complex than is now commonly considered. The term consists of two words: οἶκος, i.e., "home" or "homestead", and νόμος, or "rule" and "law."[5] It is obvious that the household, by its very nature, cannot be the same for different peoples insofar as laws themselves, as we demonstrated earlier, have ethnic and religious peculiarities. "The economy is not autonomous - it is but a projection of certain cognitive systems and philosophical principles."[6]

Today, enormous significance and attention is assigned to critiquing the neoliberal economic model, globalization, the operations of transnational corporations, the consequences and impact of the Bretton-Woods system and World Bank programs, as well as petrodollars, certain agreements, offshores, stock speculation, and cryptocurrencies. All of these elements, as part of the global system,

---

2 http://www.iep.utm.edu/radhakri/#SH2c

3 Sarvepalli Radhakrishnan. Recovery of Faith. New York: Harper and Brothers, 1955. P. 88-89.

4 We will also touch upon questions of religion in international relations and types of state power.

5 Earlier we examined the concept of "nomos" in greater detail.

6 Dugin A. K chetvertoy ekonomicheskoy teorii // Geopolitica.ru, 15.12.2017. https://www.geopolitica.ru/article/k-chetvertoy-ekonomicheskoy-teorii

are at once the legacy of the domination of a particular worldview. Many have discerned in this some kind of continuity traceable like a straight red line from the ideas of the founding father of political economy, Adam Smith, to Milton Friedman. In fairness, however, it should be noted that Adam Smith's ideas are often undeservingly criticized, insofar as they are attributed the predatory nature that underlay British imperialism. In fact, Adam Smith was a supporter of free trade, and some of his phraseologies, such as the "invisible hand", have been dealt distorted interpretations.

In book four, entitled "Of Systems of Political Economy", of his foundational work, *An Inquiry into the Nature and Causes of the Wealth of Nations*, Adam Smith writes that any person in possession of and investing capital in a given pursuit "intends only his own security; and by directing that industry in such a manner as its produce may be of the greatest value, he intends only his own gain, and he is in this, as in many other cases, led by an invisible hand to promote an end which was no part of his intention."[7] Here there is no talk whatsoever of the market in his thesis on the "invisible hand of the market" as is so widespread and attributed to Adam Smith. By "invisible hand", Smith was directly referring to divine intervention. This is confirmed by another, earlier work of Smith's, *The History of Astronomy*. In his description of ancient peoples' relationship with objects of nature in the section "Of the Origin of Philosophy", Smith notes that "every object of nature…is supposed to act by the direction of some invisible and designing power. The sea is spread out into a calm, or heaved into a storm, according to the good pleasure of Neptune."[8] Literally a few sentences later, Smith speaks of the "invisible hand of Jupiter." In his economic *magnum opus*, Smith was merely developing his old thesis of the "invisible hand" without any concrete exemplification.

The first study on the "invisible hand" appeared only in 1971.[9] Altogether recently, the term was used by the chairman of the US Federal Reserve, Ben Bernanke, who claimed that "Adam Smith

7 http://oll.libertyfund.org/titles/smith-an-inquiry-into-the-nature-and-causes-of-the-wealth-of-nations-cannan-ed-vol-2

8 https://portalconservador.com/livros/Adam-Smith-Essays-on-Philosophical-Subjects.pdf

9 A. Macfie, "The Invisible Hand of Jupiter," Journal of the History of Ideas 32 (1971): 595–99.

conceived of the free-market system as an 'invisible hand'", and that the "invisible-hand approach to regulation aims to align the incentives of market participants with the objectives of the regulator."[10] Yet Adam Smith was rather clear on the role of religion in economic and other activities: "the reverence of the people naturally preserves the established forms and ceremonies of religion, long after the circumstances which first introduced and rendered them reasonable are no more."[11]

It should be noted, however, that several centuries before the appearance of the works of this "founding father of modern economics", virtually all of the same ideas had been outlined by the Muslim scholar of Berber origin, Ibn Khaldun, in his work *Muqaddimah*.[12] Thus, the approach which assigns an exceptional role to the West in the development of the modern capitalist system can, on the one hand, be seen as simplistic, while on the other it is a telling instance of how, as with the transformation of political projects, economic models can also come to claim universality. Final global victory in the 20th century was claimed by liberal capitalism and its derivatives. Extremely interesting in this regard is that, in terms of political ideologies, if Marxism emerged out of classical liberalism (Karl Marx basically paraphrased Adam Smith with certain slight variations and his own additions), if fascism bet on the bourgeois-state system, and if it was liberalism that championed economics as rooted in a specific religious tradition, then attempts by other religions (whether official state religions or those professed by the majority of a country's citizens) at influencing socio-economic life on a global and even regional scale have failed. Even if in some countries' domestic policies one can still see attempts at pursuing unique moral and ethical positions directly concerning economic modes, there is no competition or alternative posed by religious economic systems on a global level.

The American scholars Michael Dreiling and Derek Darves similarly argue that "globalization is best understood as a 'historical project

10 Ben S. Bernanke, Financial Regulation and the Invisible Hand, April 11, 2007. https://www.federalreserve.gov/newsevents/speech/bernanke20070411a.htm

11 http://oll.libertyfund.org/titles/smith-an-inquiry-into-the-nature-and-causes-of-the-wealth-of-nations-cannan-ed-vol-2

12 Ibn Khaldun. Introduction (al-Mukaddima). https://smirnov.iph.ras.ru/win/publictn/texts_2/ikh_t.htm

rather than a culminating process.' Treating neoliberal trade policies as part of a much larger historical project - made and remade by collective actors - offers a more realistic and empirically grounded framework for exploring the intersection of class and state actors in the political articulation of globalization."[13] This historical project is inscribed in the general logic of the position of religious dynamics, not only political ones.

However, a detailed description of economic globalization and its actors and mechanisms is beyond the scope of this study, as a number of interesting and serious works have already been devoted to this topic. Our aim is reasoning through the necessity of heterodox approaches which differ from or are opposed to the widespread liberal-capitalist model and are founded on the fundamental ethical principles dealt with by religious canons. Although there have been attempts at applying heterodox economic models of a secular nature (such as Silvio Gesell's "free money" or the organization of anarchist syndicates) such projects have either not lasted long in practice or have been confined to the periphery of political-economic processes.

It is obvious that in listing the main world religions (without going into further divisions and fragmentations into denominations and sects), we should have around ten economic systems including those of the three Abrahamic religions, Hinduism, Daoism, Buddhism, shamanism, and paganism. We can add to these atheism (agnosticism) and faith in technological progress known in recent years as the singularity movement. However, the prevailing global economic system is a model which deliberately excludes any types of variations projected by various traditional religions besides those which accept double standards and mechanisms of usury. Max Weber, for example, introduced the formation of the capitalist system as founded on the Protestant ethic. However, there exist a number of Protestant sects which do not recognize each other and dispute the details of their creeds.

Moreover, for instance, if we examine this question more closely, we can see that Judaism has a clear doctrinal framework related to economic organization which can be implemented in societies even

13 Michael C. Dreiling, Derek Y. Darves. Agents of Neoliberal Globalization. Corporate Networks, State Structures, and Trade Policy. New York, NY : Cambridge University Press, 2016. P. 6.

where the predominant religion significantly differs. It should be noted that among the creationist religions, it is Judaism and Protestantism that became a kind of set of wings for the plane of liberal capitalism, which has extended its influence on a global scale. The contemporary Russian economist, Valentin Katasonov, has described this phenomenon with the term “monetary civilization”, noting that “Jews’ consciousness has been programmed for world domination, and this strategic goal has been tied to usury as a means of achieving this goal.”[14]

Judaism and *Homo Economicus*

Although it is commonplace to consider Judaism, Christianity, and Islam as “kindred” religions insofar as they are all monotheistic (another common name is “Abrahamic”), it is obvious that Judaism is a closed religion which does not accept the claims of other confessions to possessing knowledge of God. One very striking characteristic of the Jewish religion is its legal foundation. As is well known, Yahweh and the nation of Israel entered into a contract involving a number of conditions. Jews therefore receive rewards for fulfilling their obligations, and for violating this agreement they face punishment which can be exacted in both this world and beyond. All good deeds (*mitzvot*), as well as all sins (*aberoth*), are recorded in a kind of account which is calculated and assessed after death. In this regard, Judaism not only differs significantly from Christianity and Islam, but even contradicts them.

Yakov Bromberg pointed out that “the Christian notions - which are fundamental to the whole mystical-symbolic structure of the Church - of the First Coming taking place still in the earthly history of man, of the mercy and grace of the embrace of God and immortality as revealed to man not only in the Adamic genesis before the fall and in the final catastrophe of the judgement of the universe for eternity, but also already at some middle point along the suffering path of earthly mankind, are to the Jewish religious consciousness and mystical perception of the world thoroughly and irrevocably unacceptable.”[15]

Another famous scholar of Jewish heritage, Martin Buber, said: “The

14 Katasonov V. O procente: ssudnom, podsudnom, bezrassudnom. «Denezhnaya civilizatsiya» i sovremenniy krizis. Moscow: Kislorod, 2014. P. 45.

15 Bromberg Y. Evrei I Evraziya. Moscow: Agraf, 1998. p. 137 – 138.

prophets of Israel have never announced a God upon whom their hearers' striving for security reckoned. They have always aimed to shatter all security and to proclaim in the opened abyss of the final insecurity the unwished-for God who demands that His human creatures become real, they become human, and confounds all who imagine that they can take refuge in the certainty that the temple of God is in their midst."[16]

In his work, *The Ethics of Judaism*, Moritz Lazarus pointed out that Jewish law and Jewish ethics are equally integral parts of religious doctrine: the law is given by God, and it is in a moral sense good and pleasing to him. Moral law and divine judgement in Judaism thus constitute a unified whole. The German-Jewish philosopher Hermann Cohen, argues more directly: "Jewish doctrine of morality is an internal source, or more specifically speaking, an objective principle of the Jewish creed. Jewish ethics is the first principle of the Jewish religion. It is a cause, not a consequence, and can be isolated from Jewish religion only as far as an axiom can be isolated in a mathematical theorem…Between Jewish doctrine on morality and teachings on God there exists an inextricable, indissoluble unity…The Jewish doctrine of ethics is none other than the Jewish creed."[17]

Werner Sombart, in his famous work, *The Jews and Modern Capitalism*, noted the following in his attempt to reveal the essence of the Jewish people's nature in connection to economic models: "no matter which manifestations of the Jewish character we take into account, we always encounter this peculiarity which can be characterized as clearly expressed subjectivity…No word sounds more trustworthy for a Jew than the word *tahlis*, meaning goal or final result (Hebrew: תילכת). *Tahlis* must be something presupposing a certain operation - this is the meaning of the life of a Jew as a whole as well as of all his particular affairs, this is the content of [his] world."[18]

Sombart thus determined four features upon which the structure of the rather complex Jewish character is built:

16 Martin Buber on Psychology and Psychotherapy: Essays, Letters, and Dialogue ,42; Бубер М. Два образа веры. С. 493.

17 Hermann Cohen. Das Problem der judischen Sittenlehre. in the "Monatsschrift," xiii. 1899.

18 Zombart W. Evrei i ekonomika. SPb: Vladimir Dal, 2005. p. 474.

- intellectualism
- theologism
- voluntarism
- mobility.

Sombart added two more to these: restlessness (entrepreneurship) and adaptability. These qualities are tied to the religious worldview enshrined in the Jews' various didactic texts. For example: "Be flexible like a reed which the wind blows in all directions, for the Torah protects only he who is humble in spirit. Why is the Torah likened to water? To show that just as how water never flows upwards, but always strives lower, the Torah is kept only by he who is humble in his spirit."[19] Furthermore: "When you yield to the wave, it will pass and you will remain. When you begin to resist, it will carry you away."[20] Such flexibility, despite a certain code of conduct, makes Jews super-rational amidst their surroundings. In Sombart's words: "He becomes a German where such is profitable and an Italian if it suits his taste. He 'arranges' everything, penetrates everywhere, and he succeeds in everything that interests him: in Hungary he becomes a Hungarian nationalist, in Italy a supporter of irredentism, in France he takes up the position of antisemitism."[21]

Such "flexibility" can also be discerned in the following instance. In the Eha-Raba, there is a story entitled "Hadrian's Villainy", which tells of how Emperor Hadrian ordered the elimination of all Jews: "Soldiers surrounded the Jews and killed every single one. Hiding in the caves, they came out at night and found the bodies of the dead by their cadaverous smell, brought the bodies to their caves, and ate their meat."[22] Although this historical cannibalism was not ritual, but forced, the memory of this event recorded in legend is a kind of additional marker of the behavior of the Jewish people.

Interestingly enough, even changing religion has had virtually no influence on the conduct and structure of the Jewish ethos, as can be seen in examples of prominent economic figures. David Ricardo, who

19 Derech Erez Sutta. Cap. VIII. Ubers. Abr. Tawrogi, 1885, 38.

20 Midrash Rabba Gen. I c. 44. Ubers. Fromer. a. a. O. S. 128.

21 Zombart W. Evrei i ekonomika. SPb: Vladimir Dal,, 2005. p. 481.

22 Agada. Skazaniya, pritchi, izrecheniya Talmuda i Midrashey. Moscow.: Raritet, 1993. p. 192.

was by birth a Sephardic Jew but who converted to Protestantism (the Quaker sect), became famous as the founder of economic liberalism. Ricardo introduced the term "capitalism" into widespread circulation, whereas previously such had been a rather slang expression. Interestingly enough, another famous English statesman, Benjamin Disraeli, who used this term in his speeches and articles, was also a Spanish Jew by descent whose ancestors had moved to Italy and later Britain.

Rather tellingly, Hannah Arendt, in her book, *The Origins of Totalitarianism*, drew attention to the true motives of Disraeli's activities: "In his first novel, *Alroy* (1833), Disraeli evolved a plan for a Jewish Empire in which Jews would rule as a strictly separated class…In a new novel, *Coningsby*, he abandoned the dream of a Jewish Empire and unfolded a fantastic scheme according to which Jewish money dominates the rise and fall of courts and empires and rules supreme in diplomacy."[23] According to another scholar, Moses Hess (1812-1872), who was an old colleague of Karl Marx who mentored the latter in his philosophical and economic research, the final point in the process of "liberation" is the "Sabbath of History" following the rebirth of Israel. According to Marx, who, let us note, came from a family of rabbis, the final point was communism, which would have an international character and not be tied to any individual people.

Thus, we can see how a certain worldview came to supply the basis of both the modern capitalist system and an ideology long considered to be the former's antithesis. A particular ethos directly influences Jews' economic models, interpretations of wealth, welfare, poverty, etc. Nevertheless, in order to objectively assess this ethos, it is necessary to turn directly to the works of Jewish scholars and the interpreters of Jewish sacred texts.

In his book, *Economic Morality and Jewish Law*, Aaron Levine argues:

> Jewish law espouses what philosophers would call a deontological ethical system. Under that system, the moral rightness or wrongness of an action depends on its intrinsic qualities, and not, as in consequentialism, on the nature of its consequences. For

23 Hannah Arendt, The Origins of Totalitarianism (New York: Harcourt Brace & Company, 1979), pp. 75.

> Jewish law, it is all a matter of discovering the rule that applies to the situation at hand. The measure of the worthiness of an economic action is whether the action satisfies Jewish law's moral code, which prohibits the infliction of harm on one's fellow even if the harmful action would maximize society's wealth in the long run.[24]

Levine illustrates this "deontological" character of Jewish business ethics with the example of the code prohibiting lying. Levine points out that a lie is permitted when the motive of the liar is ending a conflict. The permissibility of such a lie, called *darkhei shalom* ("path of peace"), has numerous qualifications that have been interpreted by different schools of Judaism. For example, Rabbi Meir ha-Kohen Kagan (Hafetz Hayyim, Radun, 1838-1933) argued that a lie conducive to peace is permissible only when the goal cannot be achieved without lies.[25] The *darkhei shalom* motive, according to the modern Jerusalem Rabbi Nahum Yavruv, legitimizes the utterance of a lie even if the liar understands that the lie will ultimately be exposed and the accomplished peace will disintegrate. This is so, because a lie for temporary peace is also legitimate.[26] According to Rabbi Judah Ben Samuel He-Hasid (Regensburg, c. 1150-1217), a *darkhei shalom* lie is allowed only with respect to a past event. A lie concerning the present or future is, on the contrary, prohibited. The reasoning behind this is that lying about the present or future is more likely than the past to accustom a person to lying.[27]

Another school of thought headed by Maimonides (Rambam, Egypt, 1135-1204) makes no distinction between a lie regarding a past event and a lie concerning the present or future. If the motive is *darkhei shalom*, then a lie is allowable regardless of whether it concerns the past, present, or future.[28] According to the teachings of Rabbi Solomonem

24 Levine, Aaron. Economic Morality and Jewish Law, Oxford University Press, 2012. P. 15.

25 R. Israel Meir ha-Kohen Kagan, Sefer Hafetz Hayyim , Hilkhot Rekhilut 1:8.

26 R. Nahum Yavruv, Niv Sefatayyim , 4th ed., helek 1, kelal 2:25 (Jerusalem, 2005), p. 40.

27 R. Yavruv, Niv Sefatayyim , helek 1, kelal 2:26, pp. 40–41.

28 Maimonides, Mishneh Torah , Gezeilah va-Aveidah 14:13. R. Hayyim Palaggi (Turkey, 1788–1869) follows Maimonides' line. See R. Hayyim Palaggi, Lev Hayyim , vol. 1, Orah Hayyim , siman 5.

Jehiel Luria (Poland, 1510-1573), a lie is permissible only when *darkhei shalom* requires a one-time lie. If the achievement of peace is possible only through repeated lying, then such is impermissible.[29] In his appeal regarding prohibitions on lies and deceit, Rabbi Jonah ben Abraham Gerodni (Rabbenu Yona, Spain, 1200-1263) divides lies into nine groups in terms of gravity.[30] The fourth group includes people who lie because they "like to lie."[31] If someone "likes to lie", a lie is banned even if it is intended to achieve peace.[32] But if there exists such a group of people alongside other classifications, then it follows that, even if forbidden, there remains the possibility of lying. Such interpretations of the use of lying or special approaches to hiding true information are, of course, one of the main, characteristic features of the Jewish approach to economics.

Alongside this facet, however, are other important details, such as ritual obligations. In Jewish law (*Halakha*), an obligation is of the highest level when it is upheld through a formal, symbolic act called *kinyan*. In order to realize *kinyan*, rabbis have institutionalized various symbolic acts for a number of transactions.[33] The question of *kinyan* is the subject of the twelfth book of the code of Rambam's *Mishneh Torah* of the same name. In *kinyan sudar*, one person holds a handkerchief for another. By accepting the handkerchief, the other person acquires ownership of the handkerchief and thereby commits to completing the transaction. Once the *kinyan* is undertaken, a Jewish court can intervene if necessary to ensure that the person who accepted the handkerchief does his best to uphold his end of the transaction.[34] An exception to this is an employment contract in which a worker is obliged to perform only a specific task. The court will not force him to carry out the specific job, since a person cannot be forced to work against his will. Nevertheless, the employed worker can be subject to fines. In the case of public servants, it is inexcusable for public duties to be left unfulfilled; thus, a court can order him to carry out his

29 R. Yavruv, Niv Sefatayyim , helek 1, kelal 2:14, p. 34.

30 R. Jonah b. Abraham Gerondi, Sha'arei Teshuvah 3:175–186.

31 Ibid., 3:181.

32 R. Yavruv, Niv Sefatayyim , helek 1, kelal 2:18, p. 38; helek 2, siman 12, p. 30.

33 Maimonides, Mishneh Torah , Mekhirah 1:3–20.

34 R. Yaakov Yeshayahu Bloi, Pit'hei Hoshen: Likkutim u-Ve'urim ba-Halakhah be-Dinei Kinyanim,
Mekhirah u-Matanah 7:1 and n. 3 (Jerusalem, 1994), pp. 170–171.

work until he finds a replacement.[35] In some other cases, special ritual action is not required (for example, the *kinyan odita,* or acquisition of property through verbal agreement). These examples demonstrate how religious systems codify not only the behavior of individuals involved in economic activities, but also influence the broader regulation of labor relations.

The need to increase price over cost was also the subject of wide discussion among Jewish jurists. For example, an ancient Talmudic decree demands that the suppliers of staple foods limit their profits to no more than 20% in order to allow consumers to live without undue hardship.[36] This commandment is referred to as the ordinance of *hayyei nefesh*, or "essential dish."

Nevertheless, the most common criticism of the Jewish approach to economics concerns Jews practicing the issuance of loans at scaling interest rates. The Torah is clear on usury: Jews are prohibited from lending money at interest to their fellow believers, but can do so with regards to other peoples: "You may require payment from a foreigner, but you must cancel any debt your fellow Israelite owes you" (Deuteronomy 15:3). These methods have been systematized and extended on a global scale.

Also of interest is the Jewish view on selling birthrights, as this ties into understandings of hierarchies of authority and conceptualizations of the possibility of changing them from within. Levine writes:

> Jacob's strategic behavior of springing his offer on Esau to buy the birthright when he found Esau in a famished state should not be viewed as timing his offer to exploit Esau's weak condition. Instead, Jacob's conduct can be viewed as a means of distracting Esau to induce him to focus on the zero or negative value that he assigned to the birthright rather than on the value that Jacob assigned to the birthright. More fundamentally, given that Jacob

35 Tosefta , Bava Metzia 11:13; R. Solomon b. Simeon Duran (Rashbash , Algiers, ca. 1400–1467),
She'elot u-Teshuvot ha-Rashbash , no. 112.

36 As a point of comparison, in Byzantium items related to primary needs, such as bread and grain, had a fixed tax. Speculation and price-raising was strictly punished.

> is cited as the prototype of the person who has "no slander on his tongue," it stands to reason that Jacob did not engage in strategic conduct to obtain the birthright for a pittance. Quite to the contrary, Jacob had no interest in acquiring the birthright until he became aware through Esau's own declarations that Esau was unqualified to carry out the responsibilities of the birthright. Because Esau's famished state spurred him on to make declarations indicating that he was unworthy of the birthright, the motivational force to acquire the birthright and the opportunity to buy it for a pittance came together for Jacob at the same moment. Accordingly, Jacob seized the opportunity that was thrust upon him. Jacob's conduct was therefore not opportunistic, but was instead driven by a desire to remove the birthright privilege from unworthy hands as soon as possible.[37]

These remarks, in our opinion, allow us to better understand the essence of the Jewish approach to economics. Considering that the global economy has its spiritual roots in Judaism and Protestantism (the latter can hardly be called Christianity in the full sense of the word, since it lacks any apostolic succession and denies the institution of priesthood), knowledge of the various mechanisms of Jewish ethics is simply necessary.

Catholicism and Orthodoxy

The Catholic Church's view on the economy and other issues was rationalized by Thomas Aquinas, who taught that conservation, the maintaining of an orderly household, and frugality are basic economic virtues.[38] Usury was initially forbidden, as someone taking interest could be excommunicated according to the Second Lateran Council of 1139, but stipulations were subsequently introduced, such as allowing for interest to be taken as insurance fees. Pawnshops were also permitted, which gave additional impetus to speculation.

A characteristic feature of Catholicism is indulgence, i.e., the acquisition of forgiveness for one's sins from the reserves of "divine

37 Levine, Aaron. Economic Morality and Jewish Law, Oxford University Press, 2012. P. 59.

38 Rakhimov T. Ekonomika i providenie, ili Vospitanie dush chelovekov. Moscow: MSU, 2016. p. 53.

grace" in exchange for a certain payment. Such an approach allowed the wealthy to regularly "pay off" their sins, while the poor had no such capacity, thus contributing to social division within the Catholic Church. According to Valentin Katasonov, Catholicism's culpability in the formation of the modern capitalist system lies in its inculcation of rationalistic thinking in medieval man, the Catholic Church's use of its intellectual apparatus to develop trade and banking, and the emergence of the institution of legal entities under the patronage of the Vatican.[39]

In the East, interestingly enough, especially among Muslims, such an approach drew ire and led to criticism of everything European. Muhammad as-Sadr wrote: "The moral system inlayed in modern European economic discourse directly contradicts the ethics of the Muslim world, whose moral system is so profound that the search for its roots cannot be reduced to following elementary religious doctrine…A European always looks down at the earth, not to the heavens."[40] As-Sadr believes that, as a result of Western colonialism, Muslims developed an aversion to any systems and regimes established by the occupiers, even if they were sound and politically independent.[41] According to as-Sadr, a particular system of values developed in Europe which was built on the veneration of matter and wealth, in which the thirst for profit became deeply rooted in the European conscience. Coupled with the idea of freedom (by which he means negative freedom), this opened the way for competition, which came to be interpreted as natural selection (the law of the jungle).

Nevertheless, in fairness it must be noted that the theory of distributism (also known as distributivism or distributionism) also developed out of Christian Catholicism in the late 19th century based on the encyclicals of Pope Leo XIII and Pope Pius XI, i.e., *Rerum Novarum*, and *Quadragesimo anno* respectively. While the religious messages underlying such were essentially anti-capitalist, distributism is treated as a theory opposed to both socialism and capitalism (and imperialism). Its main principles are:

---

39 Katasonov V. Kapitalizm. Istoriya i ideologiya «denezhnoy civilizatsii». Moscow.: Institut russkoy civilizatsii. pp. 131 - 133.

40 As-Sadr M.-B. Nasha Ekonomika. Moscow: Al-Mustafa Universitet, 2012. p. 35.

41 Ibid, 30.

- Property is a fundamental right, but the means of production should be as widely distributed as possible. They should not be centralized or under government control (socialism), should not belong to a small group of individuals (plutocracy), nor to corporations (corporatocracy). This allows us to deduce that distributism rejects liberalism, Marxism, and fascism (the three political theories engaged in planetary struggle in the 20th century).

- Societies of artisans and culture stimulate and emphasize local traditions.

- Families with children are the primary unit of a functioning society. This is a central element of distributist theory, with the emphasis placed on multi-generational families which create deep genetic relations between communities, nations, etc. Thus, society's economic system should aim for the prosperity of the family unit which represents something whole and indivisible in the past, present, and future. As follows that distributism gives priority to the family rather than individuals.

- The principle of subsidiarity as expressed in the encyclical of Pope Pius XI: "it is an injustice and at the same time a grave evil and disturbance of right order to assign to a greater and higher association what lesser and subordinate organizations can do."[42] Subsidiarity is believed to be inherent to the Christian principle of "Give a man a fish, he will eat for a day; teach a man how to fish, and he will eat for life."

- Solidarity between independent local cooperatives, small family businesses, Christian corporations, and labor guilds as the economic motors of the state and society.

- Rejection of the banking system, or more precisely the profit-making means of modern banks, especially private ones, based on interest. Credit unions are proposed instead.

For some time, political parties in Europe which positioned themselves as Christian Democrats tried to promote the ideas of distributism

42 Pope Pius XI, Quadragesimo anno, 1931

in their platforms, but distributist theory itself was never given preference by any political ideology. There were, however, distributist anarchists, such as Dorothy Day, and one renowned supporter of distributist theory, the British writer Gilbert Chesterton, remarked in one of his works: "Property is merely the art of the democracy. It means that every man should have something that he can shape in his own image, as he is shaped in the image of heaven. But because he is not God, but only a graven image of God, his self-expression must deal with limits; properly with limits that are strict and even small."[43] At the present time, distributist organizations continue to operate in various countries.[44] As a rule, they are associated either with Christian societies, or centers supporting traditional family values.[45]

The Orthodox Christian approach to economic activity is less specific. In fact, no uniquely Orthodox economic doctrine exists, although the Church Fathers did consistently emphasize the moral side of economic dealings in connection with metaphysics. Saint Basil the Great said: "Make one's living for the present and the future and do not squander the latter for the sake of vile greed."[46] In one of the Bishop of Caesarea's sermons, one can discern a hinting at the necessity of labor and a criticism of hoarding: "Imitate the earth, man: bear fruit as does it, so as not to be worse to yourself than to the inanimate (earth)" and "do not nurture thyself with human calamities - do not turn the wrath of God to the end of multiplying your money."[47] In his commentary on the words of St. Luke, Basil the Great said: "Destroy the entire building which harbors covetousness, break the roof, tear down the walls, open the mold-covered wheat to the sun, free wealth from its bonds, open for all to see the dark vaults of mammon."[48] Isaac the Syrian said: "There is no other aid but of God."[49]

---

43 Chesterton, Gilbert Keith, What's Wrong with the World, 1920, p. 59.

44 http://distributistreview.com/

45 Allan Carlson, "A Distributist View Of The Global Economic Crisis": A Report, July 12, 2009 http://www.frontporchrepublic.com/2009/07/a-distributist-view-of-the-global-economic-crisis-a-report/

46 Vasil Velikiy. Izbrannie poucheniya. Moscow, 2003. p. 583.

47 Ibid, 594, 595.

48 Ibid, 559-600.

49 Isaak Sirin. Slova podvizhnicheskie. Moscow: Pravilo veri, 1998. p. 138.

Nonetheless, it is necessary to distinguish different movements within Orthodoxy. For example, in Rus in the 14th-15th centuries, the Church and the people were "divided" into Josephites (named after Joseph Volotsky) and "non-possessors" (those who supported the teachings of the Zavolzhsky elder Nil of Sora). The former supported the Church's maintaining of land holdings, temple decorations, libraries, etc., while the latter advocated ascetic life and the denunciation of vices, including even when they came from royal authority. This dispute concerned not only questions of property ownership and cooperation with (or the censure of) authorities, but also heretics.

After the Church split in the second half of the 17th century, the opponents of Patriarch Nikon's reforms, known as the Old Believers, also held different views from the new believers regarding not only theological questions related to the translation of prayer books (which was the reason for the split), but also on economics and everyday life.[50] Until the end of the 17th century, the everyday life of the Russian people was governed by the *Domostroy*, in which economic aspects were closely linked to spiritual activities. After Peter the Great embarked on a secular course, the abolition of the institution of the patriarchate and further pacification, the official position of the Orthodox Church changed. The Old Believers, however, remained faithful to all the established traditions, and enjoyed considerable respect from rulers even during times of persecution. For example, taking into consideration the importance of developing the Northern and Ural regions, Peter the Great granted privileges and preferences to Old Believers who developed mines. Given their highly moral lifestyle habits (for example, mutual aid, strict discipline, and bans on tobacco consumption), the economic output of the artels controlled by Old Believers was higher than those of the new believers. This could not but impact the government's attitude towards them, as can be seen in how Catherine II abolished discriminatory measures in order to avert the exodus of Old Believers out of the country (although persecution completely ceased only after the 1905 decree on religious tolerance). The success of the Old Believers is often associated with their use of community capital for developing production, trade, and actively employing innovations. By the early 20th century, many Old Believers in the Russian Empire were millionaires. However, it is often forgotten that it was precisely their religious doctrine that shaped the cornerstone

50 See Zenkovskiy S. Russkoe staroobryadchestvo. Two volumes. Moscow: Institut DI-DIK, 2006.

of their approach. Meanwhile: "With regard to the sick issue of interest, the Eastern Church kept to the following practice: condemning such in principle, while actually fighting only usury, but without imposing indiscriminate measures on all levers of interest, and without resorting to the help of secular authorities like the Catholic Church."[51]

There is currently no special chapter dedicated to the economy in the social doctrine of the Russian Orthodox Church. However, two sections deserve consideration. Section VI, "Labour and its fruits", reads:

> From a Christian perspective, labour in itself is not an absolute value. It is blessed when it represents co-working with the Lord and contribution to the realisation of His design for the world and man. However, labour is not something pleasing to God if it is intended to serve the egoistic interests of individual or human communities and to meet the sinful needs of the spirit and flesh… The Church blesses every work aimed to benefit people. At the same time, she does not give preference to any form of human work if it conforms to Christian moral standards…At the same time, by God's commandment workers are ordered to take care of those who for various reasons cannot earn their living, such as the weak, the sick, strangers (refugees), orphans and widows. The worker should share the fruits of his work with them, «that the Lord may bless thee in all the work of thine hands» (Deut. 24:19-22)…[The Church] calls upon society to ensure the equitable distribution of the fruits of labour, in which the rich support the poor, the healthy the sick, the able-bodied the elderly.[52]

Next logically follows the section on property, which reads:

> The Church is not someone who defines the rights to property. However, the material side of human life is not outside her field of vision. While calling to seek first «the kingdom of God and his righteousness» (Mt. 6:33), the Church does not forget about people's the need for «daily bread» (Mt. 6:11) and believes that every one should have resources sufficient for life in dignity. At

51 Ryabushinskiy V. Staroobryadchestvo i russkoe religioznoe chuvstvo. Moscow: Mosti kulturi, 2010. p. 152-153.

52 https://mospat.ru/ru/documents/social-concepts/vi/

> the same time, the Church warns against the extreme attraction to wealth, denouncing those who are carried away by «cares and riches and pleasures of this life» (Lk. 8:14). The Church in her attitude to property does not ignore the material needs, nor does she praise the opposite extreme, the aspiration for wealth as the ultimate goal and value of life. The status of a person in itself cannot be seen as an indication as to whether God is pleased with him… The Church urges Christians to see in property a God's gift given to be used for their own and their neighbours' benefit. At the same time, Holy Scripture recognises the human right to property and deplores any encroachment on it…The Church recognises the existence of various forms of ownership. Public, corporate, private and mixed forms of property have taken different roots in the course of historical development in various countries.[53]

Here we can see that, in fact, the Orthodox view on labor and property is polycentric - their forms depend on the traditions that have taken root in different regions, while overall, labor should be of a nature that pleases God and values solidarity at its heart for the sake of the functioning of social relations and mutual aid within the community (the city, state, etc.). Orthodoxy believes, moreover, that "there is no economy without divine providence, 'for from him and through him and for him are all things' (Romans 11:36). Whatever may happen to man, everything is a blessing either by virtue of providence or visitation. The choice of affairs is in the power of man, but its discharge depends on God."[54]

Islamic Economics

In recent times, there has been much talk about the phenomenon of Islamic economics as some kind of alternative to liberalism that can be applied on both the national and international levels. Perhaps Islamic thought contains more detailed formulations which exhibit a unity of the elements of economy, trade, governance, and religion. Western authors, meanwhile, also attribute to Arab Muslims a leading role in the birth of capitalism.[55]

53 https://mospat.ru/ru/documents/social-concepts/vii/

54 Rakhimov T. Ekonomika i providenie, ili Vospitanie dush chelovekov. Moscow: MSU, 2016. p. 180.

55 Benedikt Koehler. Early Islam and the Birth of Capitalism. London: Lexington

Undoubtedly, by the emergence of Islam and the Quran, this religion's followers had already developed certain moral attitudes regarding trade. After all, Islam initially spread among nomadic tribes and merchants. Surah 16:90 reads: "Indeed, Allah orders justice and good conduct and giving to relatives and forbids immorality and bad conduct and oppression. He admonishes you that perhaps you will be reminded." The Hadith also stress fair trade: "A righteous honest merchant will be with the Prophets and martyrs on the Day of Judgement."

In Islam, justice is construed as the totality of moral and social values entailing honesty, balance, and moderation.[56] This understanding is supposed to be automatically applied to trade and any other economic activity. Additionally, Islam features a strict division between *halal* (what is permissible) and *haram* (what is forbidden). The latter includes a clear prohibition on interest (*riba*). On the basis of the Hadith which says that "the Dirham and the Dinar have destroyed many a people before you and they will destroy you too"[57], Islam also prohibits and seeks to thwart the hoarding of cash by means of forcing an annual tax (*zakat*) for any accumulated cash money.

Additional important concepts are those of *gharar* ("hazard" or "risk") and *maisir* (gambling). There are several types of *gharar*, such as the sale of still unproduced goods, lack of access to examining a product, the exchange of inequivalent goods, the absence of real price, and randomness (or *hassat*, such as when the outcome of a transaction is determined by throwing stones). *Maisir* literally translates as "a game of chance", such as the lottery, but also applies to financial instruments such as swaps and futures.

The first Muslim author to employ an interdisciplinary approach in dealing with broad economic and legal issues was Abu Yusuf. Yusuf's work, *Kitab al-Kharaj*, is considered to be a practical guide to taxation which quotes a number of Hadith to support its theses. The famous Arab philosopher and Sufi, al-Ghazali, also touched on the topic of economic activities, but focused mainly on the ethical aspects of such. For example, with regards to profits for the treasury of the ruler, al-

Books, 2014

56 Zamir Iqbal, Abbas Mirakhor. Ethical Dimensions of Islamic Finance. Theory and Practice. Palgrave Macmillan, 2017, P. 66.

57 Al-Kulaini. Al-Kafi. Vol.2. Hadis 6.

Ghazali remarked: "Do not mix amongst our money a single dirham or coin of profit from trade, for this diminishes the dignity of the ruler, humiliates his name, mutilates his standing, and damages his repute in life and after death."[58] As mentioned earlier, Ibn Khaldun also contributed enormously to the development of Muslim economic thought. However, given his speculative approach, the majority of Ibn Khaldun's ideas can be considered universal (as has been noted by Western authors, such as Joseph Schumpeter).

Classical Muslim law included several types of taxes: *zakat* (from capable Muslims for the sake of the needy), *ushr* (one-tenth of harvests), *khums* (one-fifth of the spoils of war), *jizya* (tribute from infidels), and *kharaj* (a proportional land tax). There were also indirect taxes, such as the *mukus*. Prototypical bank checks were also used, known as *khatt-saraf*, as well as various instruments for transferring funds from one place to another, such as *suftaja* (a voucher of issued funds) and *hawala*. It should be noted that the ban on usury in Islamic countries was often circumvented through various legal loopholes (*hiyal*), or by transferring managerial functions to Jews.[59] A significant role in Islam is also played by the institution of *wakf*, or special philanthropic institutions.

The term "Islamic economy" was directly popularized by the Indian Muslim scholar Manazir Ahsan Gilani, in his self-titled book published in 1947 (written in Urdu).[60] In addition to this work, in which he considered a kind of ideal system that meets Islamic norms and ethics, this scholar wrote more than 10 books collectively entitled *Sultanul Qalam* ("King of the Pen") and *Mutakallime Millat* ("Philosopher of the Nation"). Gilani himself belonged to the Deobandi school, which was at once a renaissance movement within Sunni Islam - primarily Hanafi - and a reaction to British colonialism. In 1919, a large group of this movement's scholars established a political party, Jamiat Ulema-e-Hind, which opposed the Pakistani movement.

58 Al-Gazali. «Nastavlenie pravitelyam» i drugie sochineniya. Moscow: Ansar, 2008. p. 111.

59 Ray N.D. The Medieval Islamic System of Credit and Banking: Legal and Historical Considerations // Arab Law Quarterly. 1997, Vol. 12 No. 1. P. 48.

60 Sayyid Manazir Ahsan Gilani, Islami Muashiyaat, Hyderabad, 1947. http://www.aiourdubooks.net/islami-muashiyat-shaykh-syed-manazir-ahsan-gilani-r/

However, the notion of Islamic economics found widespread engagement only in the 1970's. To this day there is no generally accepted definition of Islamic economics. The famous Iraqi Islamic scholar, Muhammad Bakir as-Sadr, defined "Islamic economics" as the economic program of Islam which embodies the Islamic method of ordering economic life and including all the intellectual baggage which this program entails, including Islamic moral traditions, and scientific, economic, and historical thinking on issues of political economy and analyses of human societies.[61] In as-Sadr's opinion, Islamic economics is anchored on three main pillars:

1. The principle of combined ownership
2. The principle of economic freedom within a limited framework
3. The principle of social justice [62]

Sadr argues: "Shariah commands the regulation of all forms of economic and social activities which impede, from the point of view of Islam, the realization of the ideals and values on which Islam is founded."[63] Further: "The Islamic vision of social justice comprises two universal principles: the principle of universal solidarity, and the principle of social balance."[64] With this approach, "Islamic economics is at once a practical and moral economics in both the goals it aims to achieve, and in its methods of achieving them."[65] Insofar as, according to Islam, every person is endowed with *fitra* ("divine spark") which drives him towards perfection, there is subjective motivation to resolve social problems. A religious approach is the only correct solution, insofar as spiritual energy is capable of turning a person away from ephemeral pleasures. Finally, as-Sadr elaborates: "Islam envisions apportioning not on the basis of class struggle in society, but in light of the highest ideal of a prosperous society, on the basis of immutable moral values which presume the distribution of blessings in a form which ensures the implementation of these values and the embodiment of this ideal to eradicate human suffering and poverty to the greatest possible extent."[66]

61 As-Sadr M.-B. Nasha Ekonomika. Moscow: Al-Mustafa Universitet, 2012. p. 48.

62 Ibid 305.

63 As-Sadr M.-B. Nasha Ekonomika. Moscow: Al-Mustafa Universitet, 2012. p. 311.

64 Ibid, 315

65 Ibid, 316.

66 Ibid, 368.

The Russian scholar Renat Bekkin has distinguished three groups of scholars dealing with Islamic economics. The first is made up of conservatives who believe that the Quran and Sunnah have already formulated all the principles needed to regulate economic activity. The second group includes theologians and jurists who believe that Islamic economics is one of the Islamic sciences alongside *fiqh* (Muslim jurisprudence). The third group consists of scientists who consider Islamic economics as one of the trends of global economic thought.[67] There is also the opinion that Islamic economics is part of the comprehensive doctrine of Islam covering different aspects of life[68] - it is not a science.

The Pakistani scholar Asad Zaman has pointed out that, unlike the first Islamic ideologues, the second generation of Muslim pragmatists has striven until recently to seek compromise between Islam and capitalism and proclaim a "new Islamic economics" as capitalism minus interest plus *zakat*.[69] But this project has been unsuccessful.

Various instruments of Islamic banking are used in different countries today, such as gratuitous loans (*kard hasan*), deposit accounts (*amana, wadia*), investments under the name of *mudaraba* (the transfer of funds to management, the profits from which are shared by the parties in agreed proportions), *musharaka* (a type of joint enterprise), *salam* agreements (lending via a contractor's bank, which undertakes the delivery of goods of a certain quality by a certain deadline), *istisna* (contractor agreements), *ijara* (renting and leasing), and *taqaful* (insurance).

Attempts have also been undertaken to draw parallels between global economic integration and the Muslim vision of humanity. The renowned Saudi scholar who deals with Islamic banking, Mohammed Umer Chopra, argues that "the unity of humanity is an essential implication of the foundational Islamic notion of the Unity of God (*tawhid*). If God is one, then humanity is also one. Differences forged

---

67 Bekkin R. Islamskaya ekonomicheskaya model i sovremennost. Moscow.: Marjani, 2010. pp. 14 — 15.

68 As-Sadr M.-B. Nasha Ekonomika. Moscow: Al-Mustafa Universitet, 2012. p. 339.

69 Asad Zaman, What is Islamic Economics? January 17, 2016 https://tribune.com.pk/story/1029286/what-is-islamic-economics/

by nationality, race, and skin color are artificial and have no place in a religion which advocates human brotherhood."[70] At the same time, note is made of a lack of justice under the new global economic paradigm, which Muslim scholars hint at as pernicious in character.

However, even if we take into account such meticulously developed mechanisms for banning usury and other elements in accordance with the Quran, it is practically impossible for individuals or organizations to avoid participating in interest schemes by virtue of the interpenetration of different countries' economies and the influence of the global international system which is intrinsically liberal and usurious. Insofar as interest-bearing loans (and stock speculations) involve producers, banks, and states, this in one way or another reflects itself in the products and services that can be realized in Muslim countries. Unless the state or community pursues a completely closed type of economy (the closest example of which today is the DPRK), it is impossible to keep a clear conscience and avoid involvement in operations entailing interest. Otherwise, it would be necessary to apply some kind of ritualized approach to this problem. On the other hand, Orthodox Old Believers found a way out of this situation. Even while living considerably remotely (whether in the taiga or in the North), they had to in one way or another enter into dealings with new believers. On these occasions and even in everyday life (or on certain days, such as divine services on Sundays) a special penance was added to compensate for "worldly apostasization."

Buddhist Economics

Beyond the Abrahamic religions, other confessions have their own approaches to economic regulation. Sometimes, at least in theory, the name of a given religion is even evoked in order to reflect the particularities of the economic model of this or that region. The British economist of German origin, Ernst Friedrich Schumacher, developed an approach based on Buddhism and his personal experience in the government of Burma that became renowned as "Buddhist Economics", the main ideas of which he laid out in the article "Buddhist Economics" first published in 1996 and in the book *Small is Beautiful: A Study*

70 M. Umer Chapra. Islamic Economic Thought and the New Global Economy// Islamic Economic Studies, Vol.9, No.1, September 2001, P. 3. http://www.irti.org/English/Research/Documents/IES/111.pdf

of Economics as if People Mattered published in 1973. Overall, Schumacher's ideas are nature-centric. On these grounds he builds his critique of production and the consumerist approach: "Modern man does not experience himself as a part of nature but as an outside force destined to dominate and conquer it."[71] Further, he writes:

> The Buddhist point of view takes the function of work to be at least threefold: to give a man a chance to utilise and develop his faculties; to enable him to overcome his egocentredness by joining with other people in a common task; and to bring forth the goods and services needed for a becoming existence... Equally, to strive for leisure as an alternative to work would be considered a complete misunderstanding of one of the basic truths of human existence, namely that work and leisure are complementary parts of the same living process and cannot be separated without destroying the joy of work and the bliss of leisure... From the Buddhist point of view, there are therefore two types of mechanisation which must be clearly distinguished: one that enhances a man's skill and power and one that turns the work of man over to a mechanical slave, leaving man in a position of having to serve the slave...so the Buddhist economist would insist that a population basing its economic life on non-renewable fuels is living parasitically, on capital instead of income. Such a way of life could have no permanence and could therefore be justified only as a purely temporary expedient. As the world's resources of non-renewable fuels - coal, oil and natural gas - are exceedingly unevenly distributed over the globe and undoubtedly limited in quantity, it is clear that their exploitation at an ever-increasing rate is an act of violence against nature which must almost inevitably lead to violence between men.[72]

Schumacher argued that Buddhism represents a "Middle Way" and does not contradict physical well-being. He writes: "It is not wealth that stands in the way of liberation but the attachment to wealth; not the enjoyment of pleasurable things but the craving for them. The keynote of Buddhist economics, therefore, is simplicity and non-violence. From an economist's point of view, the marvel of the Buddhist way of life

71 Ernst Friedrich Schumacher, Small Is Beautiful: Economics as if People Mattered (New York: Harper Perennial, 2010), pp. 10.

72 Ibid, 90-91, 101-102.

is the utter rationality of its pattern - amazingly small means leading to extraordinarily satisfactory results."[73] Schumacher proposed to develop new approaches on this basis, but he did not say how and what precisely must be done in this direction.

According to the Sri Lankan economist Neville Karunatilake, "a Buddhist economic system has its foundations in the development of a co-operative and harmonious effort in group living. Selfishness and acquisitive pursuits have to be eliminated by developing man himself."[74] In the opinion of the Hungarian scholar Laszlo Zolnai, "Buddhist economics represents a minimizing framework where suffering, desires, violence, instrumental use, and self-interest have to be minimized."[75]

Zolnai proposed the following comparative table for Buddhist and Western economic models:

Western Economics	**Buddhist Economics**
Maximize profit	Minimize suffering
Maximize desires	Minimize desires
Maximize market	Minimize violence
Maximize instrumental use	Minimize instrumental use
Maximize self-interest	Minimize self-interest
bigger is better	small is beautiful
more is more	less is more

In 1972, the fourth king of Bhutan, Jigme Singye Wangchuck, promoted the idea of establishing a Gross National Happiness (GNH) index[76] which was based in Buddhist spiritual values and represented an antithesis to GDP which is based on material characteristics from a liberal-capitalist perspective. The Buddhist line of economics was also continued by the

73 Ibid, 95.

74 Karunatilake N. This Confused Society, 1976.

75 Laszlo Zsolnai. Buddhist Economics for Business. http://laszlo-zsolnai.net/sites/default/files/3/documents/Buddhist%20Economics%20for%20Business%20corrected.pdf

76 http://www.grossnationalhappiness.com/

Thai Buddhist monk of the Theravada school, Prayudh Payutto, who received international recognition for his work on various social issues. He also employed the idea of the "Middle Way" as a necessary condition for peace and sustainable economic development.[77]

The practical implementation of Buddhist economics on the international level, however, began relatively late compared to other theories and regional traditions in South-East Asian countries. Only in 2007 was the first conference on this topic organized by the Buddhist Economics Research Platform.

It must be noted, however, that not everything is so simple with the Buddhist approach as it might appear at first glance. Insofar as the philosophy of Buddhism is based on the idea of compassion for living beings and the path to enlightenment, any discussions of a political or economic nature revolve around these ideas in one way or another. The most important criterion for Buddhism are the consequences of "suffering" (दुःख, *duḥkha*) which can arise as a result of any action. In other words, the main question is whether duhkha will decrease or increase.

For example, following the appearance of GMO's, discussion began among Buddhists as to how to approach genetic engineering and food products with GMO's. One author has pointed out in this respect:

> From a Buddhist point of view, most technologies are neither good nor bad in themselves. Nor are they neutral. That is because technologies cannot be separated from the larger social, economic, and ecological contexts within which they are devised and applied. Since Buddhism does not privilege "the natural," including the natural selection that drives the evolutionary process, there is the possibility that in the future some GMO might actually serve to reduce duhkha. For that to happen, however, it's essential that the evaluation process not be distorted by other, more problematic motivations that make it more likely to increase duhkha.[78]

---

77 Payutto, Ven. P.A. Buddhist Economics: A Middle Way for the Market Place, Bangkok: Buddhadhamma Foundation, 1994. http://www.urbandharma.org/pdf/Buddhist_Economics.pdf.

78 David Loy, The Karma of GMO Food, 06/05/2014.

As we can see here, such a justification means that GMO's are quite acceptable to Buddhists.

Meanwhile, Muslims have no clear position on this issue. Some allow for the use of GMO products (although disagreements exist over the use of pork genes[79]), while others suggest that GMO's are strictly forbidden based on the following passage in the Quran: "For he [Satan] had said, 'I will surely take from among Your servants a specific portion. And I will mislead them, and I will arouse in them [sinful] desires, and I will command them so they will slit the ears of cattle, and I will command them so they will change the creation of Allah.' And whoever takes Satan as an ally instead of Allah has certainly sustained a clear loss" (Surah An-Nisa 4:118-119).[80] Similarly, Christians have articulated differing positions. If Catholics allow for the use of GMO's (as confirmed by a relevant congress in Rome in 1999), then Orthodox Christians (especially Old Believers) have an extremely negative position on GMO's.

The Ethnic Side of Economics

As we have seen in the works of Max Weber and Werner Sombart, the sciences initially paid much more attention to the interrelations between religion and economics, emphasizing fundamental differences in religious doctrines concerning loans, interest, taxes, and the systematization of categories of entities involved in economic operations. Although no emphasis was placed on them, ethnic components are also significant factors in economic models. It is obvious that some peoples are more inclined towards trade, while others are more predisposed towards production and crafts, and still others towards exploitation or innovation and invention. As pointed out by Émile Durkheim: "In the way in which we conclude and carry out contracts, we are forced to conform to rules which, although not sanctioned, either directly or indirectly, by any legal

---

https://www.huffingtonpost.com/david-loy/the-karma-of-gmo-food_b_5441104.html

79 GMO — izbagat li musulmanam? 23 Jan. 2014. http://islam-today.ru/zhenshhina_v_islame/krasota-i-zdorove/gmo-izbegat-li-musulmanam/

80 See: Quran o sozdanii klonov i GMO, 12 Jan. 2015. http://islamreview.ru/science-and-tech/koran-o-sozdanii-klonov-i-gmo/

code, are none the less mandatory."[81] Any collective economic activity inevitably leads to the concluding of certain agreements. Two types of such arrangements have been termed "organic" and "contractual" solidarity.

The French anthropologist Marcel Mauss drew attention to the fact that relatively recently there still existed a model of economics entirely different from that prevailing today. This is a reference not to mere exchange trading, but a more complex system of social relations in which not only people, but also spirits participated. Mauss noted:

> First, it is not individuals, but collectivities that mutually agree, exchange and contract; the 'persons' involved in a contract are corporate personalities such as clans, tribes, or families, which meet and compete either in groups on a physical terrain, or in the person of their chiefs, or in both ways at once. Moreover, what they exchange is not only goods and wealth, movable and immovable property, or economically useful things. Above all, they exchange ceremonies, feasts, rites, military services, women, children, dances, celebrations, fairs; the bargain is only one moment in these exchanges, and the circulation of wealth is only one term in a contract that goes much farther and lasts well beyond the exchange.[82]

What's more, there exists a special type of objects which are not subject to exchange or gifting, but which must be preserved. The purpose of such stored items (whether talismans, knowledge, or rituals) is the deep affirmation of identity and its continuity in time. Maurice Godelier explained such: "Furthermore they affirm the existence of differences of identity between individuals, between the groups which make u pa society or which want to situate themselves respectively within a set of neighboring societies linked by various kinds of exchanges."[83] Some scholars have attributed the function of the gift to a special form of sacrifice. However, a number of peoples have existed who were

81 Emile Dukrheim, The Division of Labor in Society (New York: The Free Press, 1997), pp. 162.

82 Marcel Mauss, "The Pioneer Sociologist Marcel Mauss on Gifts and Exchange (Essay on the Gift: Forms and Motives of Exchange in Archaic Societies, 1923), https://web.stanford.edu/class/ihum54/odyssey/mauss_gift.htm.

83 Maurice Godelier, The Enigma of the Gift (Cambridge: Polity Press, 1999), pp. 33.

mostly hunters and gatherers and did not practice sacrifices. Therefore, there must be another reason for giving gifts.

One such function of a gift is related to specific rituals for destroying property. Such a ritual was discovered among North American tribes in North and South America by European anthropologists and is known as the "potlatch." The peoples of North Asia, such as the Chukchi, Koryaks, and Eskimo, also arranged both mandatory and voluntary gift exchanges during long ceremonies, after which the remains of the feast were thrown into the sea or thrown to the wind, since it was believed that this would help return killed game for the next year.

The French philosopher Georges Bataille saw in this practice a solution to the problem of surplus. On the other hand, a gift by definition must be perceived as an acquisition: "Hence giving must become acquiring a power."[84] Potlatches, moreover, can vary. If a leader wants to emphasize his high status and wealth, he should be wasteful. But if the issue at hand is the marrying off of children and participating in fraternities, then exchanges and return potlatches are the case. Moreover, the destruction of food and property could ensure a family's advancement up the social ladder.

In Rus, such ritual affairs were most clearly manifested during periods of Christmas tides, especially during caroling. This custom continues to exist to this day, and it has archaic pagan roots. It is believed that during this period, when one year gives way to another, invisible gateways to the world beyond are opened whenceforth come the dead, who must be given generous gifts in order for abundance to be enjoyed in the new year. A number of traditional Russian festivals tied to agrarian or family cults also have the semblance of gift-giving.

Another form of social economy was founded on systems of mutual aid and collective labor. In Russia, various forms of collective labor and mutual aid have been practiced since time immemorial. The 6th century Byzantine historian Procopius of Caesarea (500-565) wrote: "These tribes, the Slavs and Antes…since olden days live in democracy and they consider happiness and misfortune in life to be a common matter." In pagan times, in order to restore a community's

84 Georges Bataille, The Accursed Share Volume I (New York: Zone Books, 1991), pp. 69.

prosperity, people who hid their crops or had a negative influence on the community were killed or expelled, thereby ruining them in advance. The well-known custom of *bratchina*, which arose among the Slavs as a collective form of worshiping the gods, was held either with the whole village or by several villages gathered together, where each family offered a tribute of products to meet social needs. The South Slavs have the famous institution of *primachestvo*, in which a family takes in an orphan. This was usually done by the elderly, who found it difficult to cope with economic affairs or had no heirs. Examples of such institutions have been reflected in fantastic forms in folk tales. Sometimes, the orphan chose his "social" parents who took him into their care.

After the Christianization of the Slavs appeared the practice of supporting widows, whereas in pagan times, as a rule, a woman was supposed to follow her husband to the other world almost immediately after his death. Among Russian peasants, mutual aid in labor was termed *toloki*, or *pomochey*. Another famous form of such cooperation was *supriaga* (which initially meant a "couple harnessed together", a "married couple", or "matrimony"), which was a traditional form of peasant mutual aid in Russia. The essence of *supriaga* was joining the working cattle, inventory, and workforce of a number of households to jointly carry out agricultural labor. Such mutual aid was especially needed in regions with hard soils or sloped agricultural holdings which required the use of heavy plows and several pairs of oxen or horses harnessed together. In this practice, one of the participants could supply the draft animals, while the other offered his agricultural tools and equipment, while a third provided the labor force. Such a form of aid is well-known not only in Russia, but among the peoples of the Caucasus, Transcaucasia, and Central Asia.

Here it should be noted that following the adoption of Orthodoxy in Rus, the economic life of society came to be based simultaneously on spiritual principles and reliance on the ancestral community. The term *Domostroy*, which is translated from the Greek word *oikonomia*, is related to this. "*Domostroy* is the appeal by man to the world and to other people - not directly, but through every man's relationship to God and through God."[85] At the end of the 19th century, amidst

85 Kolesov V. Drevnyaya Rus. Nasledie v slove. Bitie i bit. Spb, 2004. p. 10.

deepening stratification in property ownership in society, *supriaga* relations more often than not turned into “patronage and servitude.”[86]

In the Caucasus, collective labor for mutual aid could be employed for different types of work, whether agriculture, horticulture, or cattle breeding. Scholars have noted that “traditions of mutual aid took root in and penetrated the sphere of handicraft production as well. The processing of wool was done by women among all the peoples of Dagestan. Out of wool were manufactured rugs, carpets, *mafrashi*, *hurdzhiny*, *chuvaly*, *dumy*, as well as cloth, felt, and ware produced thereof - sweater socks, *arbabashi*, boots, slippers and the like, rope, belts for packs, etc.”[87] It can be said that both in the Caucasus and other regions, “the viability and resilience of a community was ensured to a considerable extent by the well-being of its constituent families. Hence the enormous importance which the community as a whole attached to the institution of mutual aid.”[88]

Beyond the organization of labor, scholars have also shown interest in attitudes towards material values and money. Some peoples particularly revere artifacts and media of exchange, while others treat money rather contemptuously, using such only when necessary as a means. For example, in Russian folklore the possession of money or its equivalents (silver and gold) was as a rule associated with negative characters (the greedy merchant, the robber, or impure forces), and the easy acquiring of money promised misfortune. Heroes spent their money irrationally - by handing out money to paupers or passers-by, buying unnecessary things, or spending on drink. One scholar thus summates: “It is as if money is foreign to the folk hero. Money is opposed not only to the traditional peasant lifestyle, but also the entire sphere of traditional, ordinary everyday life…It is as if money

86 Semenov Y. Vzaimopomosh // Socialno-ekonomicheskie otnosheniya i socionormativnaya kultura: svod etnograficheskih ponyatiy i terminov. Moscow: Nauka, 1986. p. 31.

87 Magomedov R. Obshestvenno-ekonomicheskiy i politicheskiy stroy Dagestana v XVIII– nachale XIX veka. Mahachkala: Dagestanskoe knizhnoe izdatelstvo, 1957. p. 105

88 Elmurzaeva A. Obichai vzaimopomoshi v hozyaistvennoy deyatelnosti narodov Dagestana. XIX – nachalo XX veка. Mahachkala: Chelovek I Nauka, 2009 // [URL]: http://cheloveknauka.com/obychay-vzaimopomoschi-v-hozyaystvennoy-deyatelnosti-narodov-dagestana-xix-nachalo-xx-veka.

was originally identified with something beyond everyday norms and familiar reality."[89] Such ethnic attitudes can be important not only to political-economic analyses, but also economic planning and international agreements on projects in the economic sphere.

Towards Financial-Economic Multipolarity

Nowadays, some states are trying to devise alternative economic models independently of the faith their citizens profess. For example, under the leadership of Supreme Leader Ayatollah Ali Khamenei, the Islamic Republic of Iran has launched a project to develop *Moqavemati* economics[90], which does not even mention any commitment to following Shariah, but whose essence consists in a completely opposite approach to that of the modern liberal-capitalist system. The foundation of Moqavemati economics is the family, followed by the local economy, the regional economy, the national level, and the global economy at the top of the pyramid. In proportional terms, the influence of the global economy on the lowest level is supposed to be as negligible as possible. This presumes changes in the functions of consumption, reliance on economic education and upbringing, models of local financing and traditional forms, cultural and territorial planning, the diversification of approaches to trading partners and payment methods, and avoiding the dollar system.

In this example, we can see that religion and value systems are presumed to be integral in theory as the expression of society's basic traditions, which can differ from state to state. The authors of Moqavemati economics propose such as a means to counter the global Western system and gradually escape the financial-economic control of the United States.

89 Bogdanov K. A. Dengi v folklore. SPb: Bell, 1995. p. 13

90 Ekonomika Mokavemati: Professor Khojatulla Abdolmaleki (Iran), 17.04.2017. https://www.geopolitica.ru/article/ekonomika-mokavemati-professor-hodzhatulla-abdolmaleki-iran

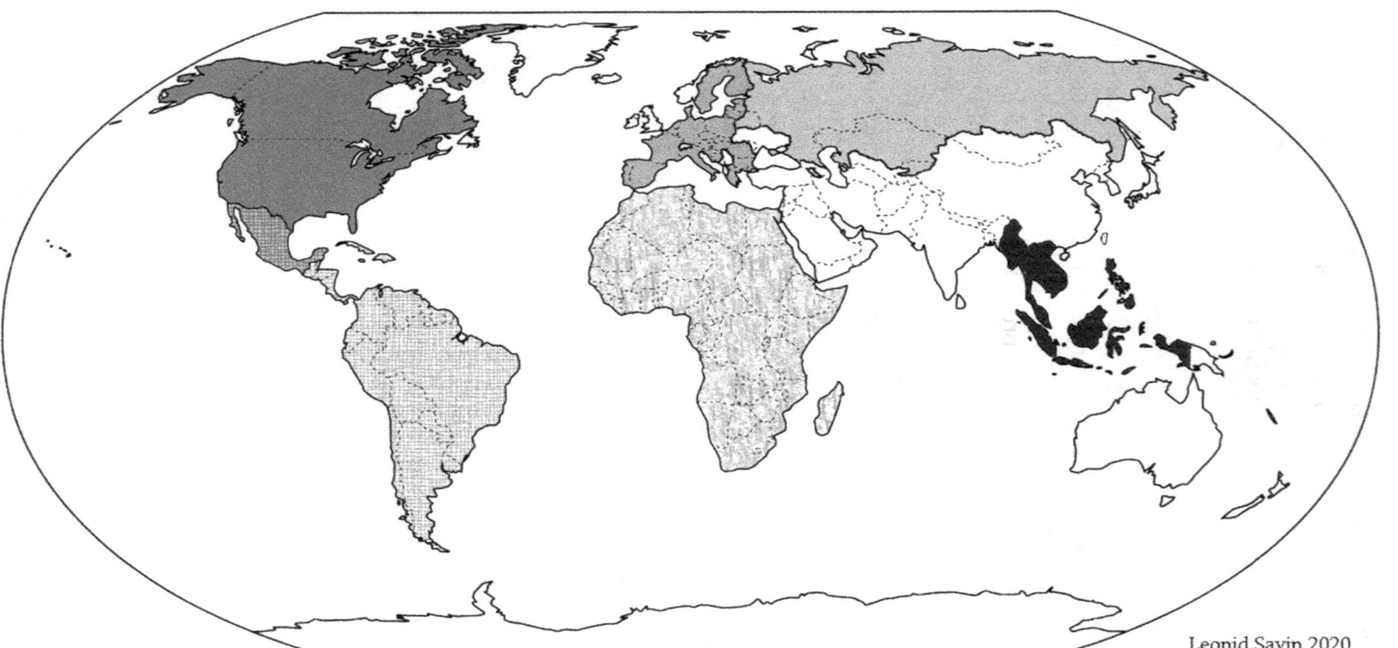

There are already large regional economic associations in the world with different operating principles: NAFTA, CELAC, EU, EAEU, African Union, ASEAN.

9

Power and the State

Taken together, the economy, sovereignty, religion, and security are expressions of power. But what is power? Are there universal criteria for defining this phenomenon? Robert Dahl prefaces this question: "one could set up an endless parade of great names from Plato and Aristotle through Machiavelli and Hobbes to Pareto and Weber to demonstrate that a large number of seminal social theorists have devoted a good deal of attention to power and the phenomena associated with it."[1] As in previous chapters, we will begin our study with etymological considerations.

In Plato's time, five types of power were known.[2] According to Plato, aristocracy (ἀριστοκρατία) and monarchy (βασιλεία) are the only correct form of governance, differing only in that in the former there are multiple rulers as opposed to one. This form is followed by four corrupt types of government. Timocracy (τιμοκρατία) is the unjust rule of respected citizens who obtained their authority not by virtue of their abilities, but because of their capacity to win power. Oligarchy (ὀλιγαρχία) is a worse type of power, that of the wealthy, in which the poor do not participate in governance. Democracy (δημοκρατία) is the unjust rule of the majority, while tyranny (τυραννὶς), the rule of only one person, is the most imperfect and unjust.

As we can see, in several of these cases a double-root term is used in which the function of power is presented as -κρατία, often used to refer to power without specifying how this power is concretely manifested. But the original meaning points to special properties. Κράτος means superiority either in battle or in assembly. This meaning, which is constant for Κράτος, is reinforced by some

1 Robert A. Dahl, "The Concept of Power", http://www.unc.edu/~fbaum/teaching/articles/Dahl_Power_1957.pdf

2 Plato. Phileb, Gosudarstvo, Timey, Kritiy. Moscow: Mysl', 1999.

examples of using the derivative word Κρατερός, which means "without equal", especially in battle.[3]

The French linguist Émile Benveniste offered detailed descriptions of other types of power which existed in the ancient world. Some of them, having undergone a certain transformation, continue to be associated with various instances of power. For example, the Latin word *rex*, which became a symbol of royal power, is derived from *reg-*, a study of the original meaning of which (*rego* means "to spread" or "to extend") leads one to suppose that *rex* is a priest rather than a king in the modern sense, i.e., a figure wielding power to delineate the location of a future city or determine the features of the legal order.

Yet in Iran one finds a different situation in which the designation of the autocrat had nothing to do with the Latin *rex*. Royal power was designated with the Persian title *xsayatiya xsayatiyanam*, i.e., *shahan shah*, or "king of kings" - a figure wielding royal power *xsay. Vazraka-*, the epithet for the Achaemenid kings also characterizing the god Ahuramazda and the Earth, shows that the king's power was essentially sacred.[4] The Avestan *xsatra* is etymologically close to the Sanskrit word *ksatra*, from which came the word *ksatriya*,i.e., the warrior caste. The special Persian form *xsassa* means both power and the area over which such power is extended - in other words: kingly power and the kingdom.[5]

In Ancient Greek, there were two ways to refer to a king: βᾰσῐλεύς and ϝάναξ. The first carried out magical-religious functions and wielded the scepter as a symbol of power, originally the walking staff of the messenger who delivered authoritative word. ϝάναξ means "holder of power." This term was known since Mycenaean times and is associated with the gods. "*Wanaks* is seen as the wielder of royal dignity, even if it is not possible to determine the parameters of the area subject to him…The title *wanakta* means absolute quality."[6]

3 Benvenist E. Slovar indoevropeyskih socialnikh terminov. Moscow: Progress-Univers, 1995. p. 284.

4 Ibid, 254.

5 Ibid, 255.

6 Ibid, 259.

The Greek word ἀρχή (which, as shown earlier, Plato used to refer to oligarchy), is also associated with power. In ancient translations in Rus, it was translated as the Slavonic поконъ (*pokon'*), but after the 10th century also known as power (*vlast'*).[7] ἀρχή meant both "beginning", "grounding", "end", "limit", "power", and "empire" (the foundational essence of statehood). *Pokon'* also means "custom", or "manner of the people", and this word is found among the Slavs most often of all in precisely this sense.[8] In the first Russian Constitution, known as the Russkaya Pravda ("Russian Truth" or "Russian Justice"), this word is encountered quite often. Interestingly enough, both вождь (*vozhd'*, "chief") and руководитель (*rukovoditel'*, "leader") are also both called поконьникъ (*pokon'nik'*), a fact which reflects the function of "he who first begins an endeavor". At that historical moment, power belonged to the tribe, not the individual, and the chief disposed of this power on behalf of everyone.

The Essence and Functions of Power

In the epoch of modernity, various attempts have been made to scientifically and expressly define the phenomenon of power and its various manifestations. The German sociologist Max Weber argued that "power is the probability that one actor within social relations will be able to achieve his own against opposition." In his book *The Theory of Social and Economic Organization*, Weber distinguishes three types of authority:

> There are three pure types of legitimate authority. The validity of their claims to legitimacy may be based on:
>
> 1. Rational grounds - resting on a belief in the 'legality' of patterns of normative rules and the right of those elevated to authority under such rules to issue commands (legal authority).
>
> 2. Traditional grounds - resting on an established belief in the sanctity of immemorial traditions and the legitimacy of the status of those exercising authority under them (traditional authority); or finally,

7 Evseev I. Kniga proroka Daniila v drevneslavyanskom perevode. M., 1905, p. 160.

8 Kolesov V. Drevnyaya Rus. Nasledie v slove. Mir cheloveka. SPb, 2000. p. 281.

3. Charismatic grounds - resting on devotion to the specific and exceptional sanctity, heroism or exemplary character of an individual person, and of the normative patterns or order revealed or ordained by him (charismatic authority).[9]

The liberal philosopher Raymond Aron argued that "Power is first of all, in the broadest sense, the capacity to act, to produce, to destroy"[10]

Less abstract definitions of power naturally include the subject who exercises power. The conservative Spanish philosopher Donoso Cortes suggested that "God, physical nature, and man are three exceptional entities whom philosophers could grant universal supremacy and all-encompassing domination in the world, or not grant them."[11] From this "trinity", Cortes deduces three political schools - two types of idealism (divine and human) and materialism related to nature. Benedict Spinoza concretized how the divine can manifest itself in political power: "God has no special kingdom among men, except in so far as He reigns through earthly potentates."[12] Another conservative thinker from France, Joseph de Maistre, added that a large people can never be ruled by government alone, but always needs someone or something else.[13] De Maistre cites as an example Turkey governed with the help of the Quran, and China, where the wise sayings and religion of Confucius were a kind of instrument of influence over the popular masses.

According to Friedrich Nietzsche, power is an attitude rather than an essence. Man (the actor) can do little other than have the will to power. Only the natural forces of being personified in becoming represent the highest form of power, whose forms differ insofar as wills to power differ in the likes of philosophy, morals, metaphysics, and art. These are divided into negative and positive and have their own levels of gradation (the will to freedom, the will to justice, etc.).

---

9 Max Weber, The Theory of Social and Economic Organization (New York: Oxford University Press, 1947), 328.

10 Raymond Aron. Peace and War: A Theory of International Relations, Garden City, N.Y.: Anchor Press, 1973. P. 47.

11 Cortes, Juan Donoso. Sochineniya. SPb: Vladimir Dal, 2006. p. 387.

12 http://www.sacred-texts.com/phi/spinoza/treat/tpt27.htm

13 Mest, de J. Sochineniya. SPb: Vladimir Dal, 2007. p. 40.

On Nietzsche's will to power, Heidegger pointed out that for Nietzsche himself the "'will to power' designates the basic character of beings; any being which is, insofar as it is, is will to power."[14] Working through the process of deconstructing Nietzschean philosophy, Heidegger arrives at the *in-sich stande Wollen* formula: "Willing itself is mastery over [something], which reaches out beyond itself; will is intrinsically power. And power is willing that is constant in itself."[15] In connection with this, Heidegger notes that German realism interpreted being as will. This is the "Schopenhauer effect" resultant of the collapse of German idealism, whereas Nietzsche refused to participate in the profanation and further subversion of such. In summary, Heidegger points out that power means three phenomena simultaneously: force or readiness for action (δύναμις), the exercising of domination (ἐνέργεια) and actualization (ἐντελέχια).[16] It should be noted that ἐνέργεια and δύναμις have often been translated into Latin as *actus* and *potentia*, i.e., as actuality and possibility.

Interestingly enough, Heidegger's reflections on these Ancient Greek terms correlate with the antique Russian understanding of power. Kolesov points out:

> In Rus in the 10th century, the word *volost'/vlast'* was polysemantic. It meant possibility, force, or the right to act. In the 11th century, *volost'* (and *vlast'*) was primarily *vladenie* (rural *volost'*). Starting at the end of the 11th century, this fused and simultaneous concept of power, dominion, and the ruler was unfolded into two in accordance with the conditions and requirements of feudal relations. *Volost'* became the domain and *vlast'* became force and the right to wield it. This very distribution of variants contains much of interest: the concrete (land rule) is termed with the Russian word *volost'* while the abstract (force and power) with the Slavic *vlast'*. This new form comes from and is sanctified by the church and is called by the high book term *vlast'*.[17]

14 Heidegger M. Niezsche. Vol. 1. SPb: Vladimir Dal, 2006. p. 39.

15 Ibid, p. 43-44.

16 Ibid, 65-66.

17 Kolesov V. Drevnyaya Rus. Nasledie v slove. Mir cheloveka. SPb, 2000. p. 276.

We should also recall Montesquieu's formula voiced in his *The Spirit of the Laws* (1748) that "the power of climate is the first power on earth."[18] This definition formed the foundation of geographical determinism and the later development of geopolitical ideas. If weather conditions affected the social organization and behavior of people, then this must also be reflected in peoples' psychologies and political systems. For example, on slavery Montesquieu argues that "the effeminacy of the people in hot climates has almost always rendered them slaves, and that the bravery of those in cold climates has enabled them to maintain their liberties", an expression which might sound too "Manichaean", but nevertheless contains a grain of truth.

The Russian legal scholar N.M. Korkunov, who referred to himself as of the Western positivist school, considered power as a dialectical phenomenon: "Only consciousness of dependence, not the reality of such, is required for ruling…power is force conditioned by the subservient's consciousness of dependence…State power is force conditioned by consciousness of dependence on the state."[19]

In the opinion of the American sociologist James Coleman: "The power of an actor resides in his control of valuable events."[20] Self-control is perhaps equally important for power. In the form of a parable, the famous Persian Muslim scholar al-Ghazali said that wise, good, and just rulers' "power over themselves and severity towards themselves was greater than over others."[21] The Norwegian scholar Stein Ringer argues that "power is something at the disposal of a certain person…Power is either there or not; you either have it or you don't; it does not appear when you begin to behave in a certain way. It precedes behavior."[22] Ringer also admits that it is altogether difficult to explain political culture, i.e., the space where the distribution of power takes place.

---

18 Monteskie Sh. O duhe zakonov. http://oll.libertyfund.org/titles/montesquieu-complete-works-vol-1-the-spirit-of-laws

19 Korkunov N. Russkoe gosudarstvennoe pravo, T.1. SPb, 1901. p. 24.

20 Coleman J.S. Foundations of Social Theory. Cambridge, MA: Harvard University Press, 1990. p. 133.

21 http://www.vostlit.info/Texts/Dokumenty/Persien/XI/Gazali/text12.phtml

22 Stein Ringer. Nation of Devils. Democratic Leadership and the Problem of Obedience. Yale University Press, 2013. p. 89.

If we trace economic theories of power, then the ideas of Friedrich von Wieser must be mentioned. Wiser was one of the founders of the Austrian school of economics who rejected classical liberalism and insisted that freedom must be kept within an orderly system.[23] Although Wieser stressed the importance of the role of entrepreneurs, whom he compared to heroic personalities, in a state's economic life, he nevertheless conceptually emphasized the systematic approach. This fundamentally differs from the proposals of Thomas Hobbes set out in his *Leviathan*.

If there is no single, universally recognized definition of power, then can we at least speak of power functioning the same way everywhere? Even in liberal societies that are culturally and historically close in type, there exist different types of governance - such as monarchical in Britain and republican in the USA. Moreover, even in one country there can be attempts at distinct methods of exercising power: for example, the concepts of soft, hard, smart, and sharp power have appeared in the US.[24] Joseph Nye's conceptualization of smart power is not original, however, as the Spanish philosopher José Ortega y Gasset expressed the idea more concisely in his *Invertebrate Spain*: "To command and rule is not merely to persuade or coerce someone. True dominion presumes a complex combination of both. Moral suasion and material compulsion are intimately linked in every act of command."[25] In addition, it has been customary to consider three projections of power and influence - symbolic, structural, and instrumental.

There have also been attempts at reframing power not only in function but also in essence. For example, the notion of "potestarity" introduced by the Soviet ethnologist Yulian Bromley, who adhered to the Marxist paradigm, was couched in the corresponding ideological environment - potestarity as a term denoted a pre-state organization of power characteristic of pre-class and early class societies.[26] Many modern scholars studying the peoples of Africa, Asia, and Latin America

23 Friedrich von Wieser. Das Gesetz der Macht, 1926.

24 CSIS Commission on Smart Power : a smarter, more secure America / cochairs, Richard L.Armitage, Joseph S. Nye, Jr. Washington, CSIS Press, 2007; Walter Russell Mead. Power, Terror, Peace, and War. America's Grand Strategy in a World at Risk. New York: Vintage Books, 2004.

25 Ortega-y-Gasset J. Vosstanie mass. Moscow: AST, 2001. p. 278.

26 Bromley Y. Ocherki teorii etnosa. Moscow: Nauka, 1983.

use this term despite the area of their analysis being specific states. This speaks to the fact that mechanisms for exercising power in these regions differ significantly, and that additional taxonomy is needed to somehow mark inter-tribal relations and bring out their differences with secular, modern conceptions of power that originally arose in Western Europe and spread to other places, where traditional customs, imported models (through colonial or post-colonial practices) and international law have been uniquely combined. It is already obvious that over the past few decades "altogether original models of political power and bizarre state-legal systems have appeared on the African continent and a rather complex configuration of the political space has taken shape in whose areas power relations have acquired previously unknown, unique forms."[27] Similar metamorphoses have taken and are taking place on other continents.

We also need to take into account the fact that the characteristics of power have changed in the conditions of postmodernity. Referencing Foucault, Antonio Negri has argued that power is never a coherent, stable, unitary entity, but is a sum of 'power relations' involving complex historical circumstances and numerous consequences: power is the field of powers.[28] Approximately 100 years ago in his work *The Transformation of Democracy*, Vilfredo Pareto remarked: "Who is now interested in theories of equilibrium of power? Who determines the correct equilibrium between State's rights and individual rights? Can an Ethical State of which people speak so respectfully (despite obvious irony), really be found? Certainly, the Hegelian State is the product of a very vivid imagination and yet has survived wear and tear of poetic and metaphysical sociology. Working people are more interested in the tangible benefits of high wages, progressive taxes, and increased leisure time than in metaphysics…"[29] Pareto's observations on the centripetal and centrifugal forces that vibrate and change a country or regions' political unity led him to conclude that there is some kind of social law of elite rotation. Such an approach

---

27 Gevelong L. Konturi transformiruyusheysya vlasti // Sovremennaya Afrika. Metamorfozi politicheskoy vlasti. Moscow: Vostochnaya literatura, 2009. p. 447.

28 Negri A. Trud mnozhestva i tkan biopolitiki // Siniy divan, 2008. № 12. http://www.intelros.ru/pdf/siniy_divan/12/6.pdf

29 Vilfredo Pareto, The Transformation of Democracy (New Brunswick/London: Transaction Books, 1984), 30

might be justified for secularist countries, but what is to be done with those states which have retained sacred institutions of power, even if only with nominal functions? In this case, we are left with another hierarchical structure handed down over processes of political transformation and perturbations.

Another interwar Italian author, Agostino Lanzillo, pointed out: "European nations are faced with the task of being simultaneously warlike and mercantile, democratic and militaristic…How society will adapt in practice to these two equally imperative demands, we do not know."[30] However, we do know that the 20th century passed through the crucible of two world wars and the duel between liberalism, communism, and fascism. Thus, these remarks remain relevant to this today despite certain changes in political actions and rhetoric. Left movements no longer fight for workers rights, but for the legalization of narcotics and same-sex marriages, while in many countries the right now serves the interests of patron states, not their own people. The impression is made that to this day no suitable, sustainable model has been developed which might be universal for different countries and peoples not even as a rigid template, but as a set of possibilities and limitations already inherent to political associations and their ancient or relatively young cultures. Nevertheless, the first steps in this direction have been made. Interesting theories and philosophical insights have bounced around through the works of different authors, some of whom belong to the Western political tradition and others who represent the peoples of other regions of the world. We will consider what in our opinion are some of the most interesting of these ideas in a later chapter.

Politeía

The first classical "debates" on state systems are usually attributed to Ancient Greek philosophy. Plato and Aristotle are considered the first authors to have systematized ideas about the state. However, the importance of these philosophers' works should not be exaggerated. Before Plato's time there existed powerful states in the likes of Elam, Babylon, Media, and Lydia which bordered the Hellenic city-states and the territories under their control in Western Asia, and which developed their own philosophical and religious systems. Cyrus the

30 Lanzillo A. La disfatta del socialismo: Critica della guerra e del socialismo. Liberia della Voce. Firenze, 1919. P. 270.

Great, during the expansion of the Persian Empire, spread not only his own power, but also the culture of Zoroastrianism. It is well known that this public religion clearly divided society into four castes: priests, the military aristocracy, peasants, and artisans. The Cyrus Cylinder written in Babylonian speaks of the "liberator" and "father", and mentions that he received power over the peoples from the god Marduk. Cyrus was praised as "of an eternal line of kingship, whose rule Bêl and Nabu love, whose kingship they desire for their hearts' pleasure." In other words, Ancient Greece, which is considered to be the cradle of political theory as such, was by no means the only space with the capacity for effective rule and governance.

Ancient Egypt is another such state which significantly influenced Ancient Greece. In his *Histories*, Herodotus says that "all the names of the gods came to Hellas from Egypt", a point which indirectly points towards the priority assigned to Egypt among the Hellenic peoples.[31] What's more, in his description of Egypt, Herodotus noted that the country's inhabitants did not adopt their customs from other countries. Also mentioned are the merits of King Sesostris, who divided the land between all Egyptians, collected taxes, measured plots, and conquered a number of peoples. These are clear signs of statehood.

Ancient China can also serve as an example. The era of legendary emperors from the fifth millennium BC was followed by the Xia Dynasty (2205-1766 BC) and the Shang Dynasty (1765-1123 BC) whose state is known to have already had an apparatus of officials. In view of the small number of reliable sources, the system of power under the Shang court has been called "proto-bureaucratic" by the famous Sionologist Harley Creel.[32] It is under the the Zhou Dynasty (1123-222 BC) that was born what the Chinese tradition is most known for: numerous important elements of state administration, the concept of the Mandate of Heaven, the "canonical works", and Confucianism (Confucius lived during the reign of Zhou). Returning to the Ancient Greek philosophers, it bears mentioning that they were by no means united. Aristotle and Plato were the biggest opponents in their views. Aristotle argued that the state in its very nature is a certain myriad. Suggesting that growing unity leads to the disappearance

31 Herodot. Istoriya. Moscow: Akademicheskiy proekt, 2014. p. 219.

32 Kril H. Stanovlenie gosudarstvennoy vlasti v Kitae. Imperiya Zapadnaya Chzhou. SPb.: Evraziya, 2001. p. 35.

of the state, Aristotle said in his critique of Plato's ideal state: "a lesser degree of unity is more desirable than a greater." In his third book of *Politics*, Aristotle voiced the brief formula that "the state is a collection of citizens" and immediately proposed to define citizen as he who participates in the judicial system and popular assembly: "Accordingly we lay it down that those are citizens who participate in office in this manner. Such more or less is the definition of 'citizen' that would best fit with all of those to whom the name is applied."[33]

This compels us to issue a few remarks about "citizens." Although by citizens was originally understood persons with certain rights, these rights have changed over the course of history. For example, universal suffrage from a certain age was not in place in all countries in the 20th century, and women received the right to vote on an equal basis with men in the US in 1920, in the UK in 1928, Spain in 1931, in France in 1945, and in Switzerland only in 1991 (the right to vote was introduced gradually only at the canton level starting in 1960). In Russia, universal suffrage was introduced in 1917 and in Finland in 1906 (as part of the Russian Empire until 1917). Although some politicians try to justify this fact by saying that political rights and freedoms were granted earlier in the West, especially in the US, this example clearly shows that this is not so.

According to the British sociologist T.H. Marshall, "Citizenship is a status bestowed on those who are full members of a community."[34] Such an interpretation does not correspond to reality, however, but rather refers to the era of Ancient Greece, where suffrage was only for free adult men (slaves, children, women, and foreigners were excluded). Marshall himself has analyzed the distribution of citizenship among white, working-able adult males in his works. But here appears the concept of "post-national" citizenship tied to globalization processes.[35] This gives rise to a variety of forms of citizenship such as cultural, minority, environmental, cosmopolitan, consumer, and mobile citizenship.[36]

---

33 http://www.perseus.tufts.edu/hopper/text?doc=Perseus:abo:tlg,0086,035:3 ; Aristotel. Sochineniya Vol. 4. Moscow: Mysl', 1984. p. 404-405, 444-445.

34 Marshall T., Bottomore T. Citizenship and Social Class. L.: Pluto, 1992. P. 18.

35 Soysal Y. Limits of Citizenship. Chicago (IL): University of Chicago Press, 1994.

36 Urry, John. Sociology beyond societies. Mobilities for the twenty-first century. London: Routledge, 2000. p. 239.

Going back to antiquity, however, it must be noted that the notion of the state was then associated with the *polis* (the city), but in Plato and Aristotle's era the notion of *politeia* or state system was also widespread. This was a broader concept which to this day is used in political science and analyses. Politeia can manifest itself in diverse forms even with differing content. For example, in the East there was the schema of power relations in the politeia system known as *mandala*. It is believed that until the 19th century in South-East Asia there were special conditions for interactions between power structures which might be called "sovereignty of hierarchical layers."[37] Therefore, it is better to not use the Western conception of the state, but speak of a "politeia in Mandala form." Mandala "represented a particular and often unstable political situation in a vaguely definable geographical era without fixed boundaries and where smaller centers tended to look in all directions for security. Mandalas would expand and contract..."[38]

In Indian texts, one often encounters the term *saptanga,* which means a "seven-limbed" kingdom. According to Kautilya, of the seven elements (*anga*) of the kingdom, four are material - the *dravyapraktri* (a stronghold, the countryside, the treasury, the army) - and three are human - the *purusa-praktri* (the king, the *amatya* companions, and the ally Mitra). The exercise of royal power (*rajatva*), i.e., the activity of the sovereign, or politics, is understood as a synonym for the rotation of the wheel (*cakgram vartate*). The wheel itself (or *chakra,* often introduced in Sanskrit texts as a conceptual image of the world order in its various aspects) can be understood as the theoretical designation of the scope of royal power. In most cases, this sphere is the kingdom (*rajyam*) or the Mandala realm which might be understood either as a concrete state or as the whole world (*cakra*).[39] Mandala is the principle upon which is formed the structure of any state or kingdom.[40] This is the unification of territory under a dominant ruler and his allies (the number of which

37 Thongchai Winichakul. Siam Mapped. A history of the Geo-Body of Nation. Silkworm Books, 1995. P. 88.

38 Wolters O.W. History, Culture, and Religion in Southeast Asian Perspectives. Singapore: Institute of Southeast Asian Studies, 1982. pp. 16-17, 27-28.

39 Lelyukhin D. Kontseptsiya idealnogo tsarstva v «Arthashastre» Kautili i problema strukturi drevneindiyskogo gosudarstva // Gosudarstvo v istorii obshestva (k probleme kriteriev gosudarstvennosti). Moscow: Institut Vostokovedeniya RAN, 2001. p. 27.

40 Ibid, 29.

does not matter) and a political - and to a certain extent the unified - state structured in many ways analogously to the seven-limbed kingdom. Here we can add that in Asia the defense of religion and the acquisition of supreme power were one and the same mission.[41]

This phenomenon can be found to this day in Asian state systems. For example, the official philosophical foundation of the Indonesian state is the concept of Pancasila, a term consisting of two Javanese words of Sanskrit origin: *panca*, meaning five, and *sila* or principles. The five principles are monotheism, just and civilized humanity, the unity of Indonesia, and democracy and social justice for all. Ignoring these principles is a violation of the law. For example, insofar as Indonesians are supposed to be religious, being an atheist is simply prohibited.

In Ancient China, the magic of numerical and color values, the four cardinal directions, and natural elements (the five primary elements, or Wu Xing) played a significant role in statehood and administration. Ancient textual sources on the Shun period contain a characteristically traditional maxim which likens the state structure to the structure of the human being: the sovereign is the head; dignitaries or officials are the hands and legs, ears, and eyes.[42] Such views, although subject to transformation, continue to exist on a deep level in the state system of the People's Republic of China.

However, even at first glance the most homogenous regions can harbor numerous contradictions. The famous American political scientist Charles Tilly began his work on the emergence of modern European states with posing the question: "What accounts for the great variation over time and space in the kinds of states that have prevailed in Europe since AD 990, and why did European states eventually converge on different variants of the national state?"[43] Giovanni Palazzo interprets the word "state" to have four different

---

41 S. J. Tambiah. World Conqueror and World Renouncer: A Study of Buddhism and Polity in Thailand against a Historical Background, Cambridge Studies in Social and Cultural Anthropology, 1977; Sunait Chutintaranond. Cakravartin: The Ideology of traditional Warfare in Siam and Burma, 1548-1605. Cornell University, 1990.

42 Vasiliev S. Drevniy Kitay. Moscow, 1995. p. 191.

43 Charles Tilly, Coercion, Capital, and European States, AD 990-1990 (Cambridge: Basil Blackwell, 1990), 5.

meanings: (1) dominium, i.e., a certain area; (2) jurisdiction, or a set of norms, customs, rules, and laws; (3) a situation in life, i.e, a social status; and (4) a quality opposed to change. According to Palazzo, a republic therefore represents a stability of territory, jurisdiction, and status of individuals.[44] Obviously, all the elements needed to ensure such stability will vary depending on place.

The aims of the state can also differ. If Aristotle said that the goal of a state is communication, then for Thomas Hobbes the aim is security, insofar as such is not guaranteed by natural laws, and as such concerns both internal security amidst the waging of "war of all against all" in society, and protection from external enemies.

If we look at Russian history, then the state in the original sense of the word is not an area, but power itself, power of the sovereign over all that falls into the orbit of his stateness (*derzhavstvo*). Hence all the later formations starting in the 16th century of the sovereign "household" state, state "management", and the meaning of the adjective state in its modern meaning which has been known in Russia since the 17th century.[45] The *derzhava*, as power by means of strength and force, is bestowed upon the chosen usually by a deity, because all supreme power lies with God.[46] In some sense, this model resembles the Asian Mandala insofar as the "*derzhava* is the heavenly force which holds (*derzhit*) the whole world."[47] Unlike Mandala, where the supreme ruler rotates the wheel even symbolically, the *derzhava* is a power at rest.[48] This concept is directly related to the term *Katechon* (ὁ κατέχων) which means "restraining."[49] This doctrine was transformed into a political theory in Byzantium which established the symphony

44 Giovanni Antonio Palazzo. Discorso del governo e delia ragion vera di Stato. Napoli: per G.B. Sottile, 1604.

45 Kolesov V. Drevnyaya Rus. Nasledie v slove. Mir cheloveka. Spb, 2000. p. 284.

46 Ibid, 288.

47 Ibid, 292.

48 Hence the symbol of one of the royal regalia: the derzhava was symbolized with an orb with a cross on top which the tsar (the imperator) brandished at palace ceremonies alongside a scepter.

49 See the Apostle Paul's 2 Thessalonians 2:7: τὸ γὰρ μυστήριον ἤδη ἐνεργεῖται τῆς ἀνομίας, μόνον ὁ κατέχων ἄρτι ἕως ἐκ μέσου γένηται ("For the secret power of lawlessness is already at work; but the one who now holds it back will continue to do so till he is taken out of the way.").

of powers, a kind of harmonious alliance of rulers in the persons of the emperor and the patriarch.[50]

Such cooperation is by no means limited to between spiritual and secular authorities. In the 19th century, Adam Muller wrote that the state itself is "an alliance between past and subsequent generations", thus affirming a kind of link between a people and the power system developed by their representatives.[51]

For the first geopoliticians of the European continentalist school, the state was a geographical organism, a spatial phenomenon, and territorial dominion. At the same time, the Swedish legal scholar Rudolf Kjellen argued that the state is both a subject of law and a society with an economy.[52] Friedrich Ratzel more simply suggested that the state is a kind of humanized and organized land.[53]

According to Carl Schmitt, there exist three types of states - jurisdiction, governmental, and administrative. In his *Legality and Legitimacy*, Schmitt writes: "The ethos of the jurisdiction state is that the judge renders judgement directly in the name of law and justice...The governmental state does not have so much an ethos as a great pathos. Its principle became most visible in the government of the absolute princes...The administrative state can call on factual necessity, the condition of things, the force of circumstances, the necessity of the moment, and other non-normative, situation-specific justifications."[54] In another work from 1931, *The Guardian of the Constitution*, Schmitt points out the tripartite character of power in the state: Pluralism denotes the power of many quantities over state's formation of will; polycracy is possible on the basis of withdrawal from the state and gaining independence in relation to state will; in federalism, both aspects are united in the antithesis ...".[55]

---

50 See Flavius Justinianus Imperator. Novellae, ed. R. Scholl and W. Kroll, Corpus iuris civilis, vol. 3. - Berlin: Weidmann, 1895 (repr. 1968). - Nov. 6 pr.

51 Muller A. Elemente der Staatskunst, 1809.

52 Kjellen R. Gosudarstvo kak forma zhizni. Moscow: Rosspen, 2008. p. 94.

53 Ratzel F. Politische Geographie. 2. Aufl. Berlin, 1903.

54 Carl Schmitt, Legality and Legitimacy (Durham/London: Duke University Press, 2004), pp. 8-9.

55 Schmitt C. Gosudarstvo. Pravo i politika. Moscow: Territoriya budushego, 2013. p. 113.

Another triplicity can be traced in the historical transformation of the state and society as mutually bound together in a dialectical development which passed through three states: from the absolutist state of the 17th and 18th centuries through the neutral state of the liberal 19th century to the total state of state and society being identical.[56] In the latter type, the economy, culture, security and logistics are tied together - all spheres of common human life are permeated by the state. This, of course, mainly applies to European state entities.

A rather paradoxical judgement on the state can be found in Ortega y Gasset's *Revolt of the Masses*, where the Spanish philosopher speaks of the modern state as the highest threat, as a product of the bourgeoisie becoming a "monstrous machine of unthinkable possibilities."[57] Unlike Carl Schmitt or Ernst Junger[58], who spoke of processes later defined as manifestations of totalitarianism in somewhat aloof and dry language, Ortega y Gasset was afraid of the suppression of individual freedom and the strengthened role of police.

The sociologist Zygmunt Bauman introduced[59] several metaphors to describe the activities of the state. Until modern times in Europe there existed the "hunter-state", which did not give society any final form and did not interfere in the privacy of its subjects. Disciplinary power was exercised within communities themselves, so there was no need for surveillance from a unified body. Then came the "gardener-state", which began to pay serious attention to form and order, with which cultivating, cutting, and eradicating became the main functions of the state, in which the leading role would be played by legislative power determining what must be supported or eliminated.

It is only obvious that in the era of postmodernity there is no longer any need for the hunter or the gardener. Given widespread consumer culture in the West, the conclusion begs itself that we have witnessed the appearance of the "mall-state" which creates interconnected cycles of redistribution (after all, everything is bought and sold) and the illusion of care under which, in Jean Baudrillard's expression,

56 Ibid, 123.

57 Ortega-y-Gasset J. Vosstanie mass. Moscow: AST, 2001. p. 112.

58 Schmitt and Junger were friends, and in his The Guardian of the Constitution, Schmitt cites Junger's Total Mobilization.

59 Bauman Z. Legislators and Interpreters. Cambridge: Polity, 1987

social relations are smeared with an institutional smile.[60] Bauman's conceptualization rests on a spatial sense referring to one type of terrain. Foresters and gardeners are associated with vegetation which must be looked after and cared for. But what about the possibility of a shepherd-state (referring to the traditional nomadic cultures of some peoples and to the metaphor we examined in our chapter on security), or a builder-state? Forests and gardens in need of care cannot be found everywhere, and houses, roads, palaces, fortresses, warehouses and communications systems, bridges, and dams can be built. What about a "fisherman-state" or the "hunter-state"? Both are clear manifestations of supporting a biological balance in nature through repressive measures. And what about the "oasis-keeper-state" which is of no small importance to peoples inhabiting deserts?

Other definitions of the state exist as well. Stein Ringer argues that the "State as such" is a center of political power and political institutions operating "above."[61] But such a definition is only adequate for certain geographical reasons. Karl van Wolferen dedicates the second chapter of his *The Enigma of Japanese Power* to the peculiar power relations in a country which eludes European understandings of statehood. Japan is an "elusive state" with power "out of focus" which, although it can be called a nation with a common language and sense of community, does not have a clearly defined group of those in power. What exists in Japan in terms of political parties does not meet Western logic. While there might formally be several parties, within one party can exist a coalition of political cliques, or *habatsu*. The rivalry between bureaucrats and open jealousy between agencies and ministries does not lend to analyzing Japan's official apparatus as a hierarchy. There is also the *zaikai,* or circle of business functionaries who, world-famous by virtue of various corporations, are in fact dependent in their operations on bureaucrats. This circle is constantly replenished with retired bureaucrats, a phenomenon called *amakudari* or "descent from heaven." *Amakudari* is vital for the functioning of corporations insofar as personal connections to officialdom and knowing policy priorities are indispensable. Van Wolferen writes: "Power in Japan is thus diffused over a number of semi-self-contained, semi-mutually

60 Baudrillard J. Obshestvo potrebleniya. Ego mifi i strukturi. Moscow: Respublika, 2006. p. 205.

61 Stein Ringer. Nation of Devils. Democratic Leadership and the Problem of Obedience. Yale University Press, 2013. p. . 83

dependent bodies which are neither responsible to an electorate nor, ultimately, subservient to one another. While all these bodies share aspects of government, it is impossible to find one among them that gives the others their mandate. No one has final responsibility for national policy or can decide national questions in emergencies."[62]

This could be called a serious drawback, but it could also be called an advantage, for if it is extremely difficult to determine the real source of power, then it is impossible to destroy such. On these grounds, Karel van Wolferen calls Japan not a state, and not a society, but a system: "The System presents a variety of apparent paradoxes. It has no strong leadership, yet it creates the impression abroad of a purposeful giant bent on economic conquest of the world. It has no political centre, yet domestically it always succeeds in bringing antagonistic groups within its folds. The System is elusive. It eludes the grasp of Westerners who want to deal with it."[63]

Similarly "elusive" systems can be found in other places as well. Is Russia not one such enigma in the eyes of the West? Although the Western world and Russia have had contact since the Middle Ages, something has prevented the West from grasping the essence of this country which subsequently expanded to the East and which has over time acquired such frighteningly large dimensions and military power that have allowed it to talk on equal terms with the strongest European states and even defeat them in military conflicts (the widely-believed invisible Swedish army of Charles XII was defeated by Peter the Great at Poltava in 1709, and a little more than a hundred years later the army of Napoleon Bonaparte that had conquered virtually all of Europe also suffered defeat at the hands of Russian troops).

Overall, we can say that the state is the highest expression of the creativity of the people who created it. It has both protective functions (for its traditions, histories, external borders, interests, citizens) and repressive functions. The latter can be projected onto a certain people's representatives if their actions are contrary to the aspirations of the ruling elites. This people might also be outside the borders of

62 Karel van Wolferen, the Enigma of Japanese Power: People and Politics in a Stateless Nation (New York: Alfred A. Knopf, 1989), 84-85.

63 Karel van Wolferen, the Enigma of Japanese Power: People and Politics in a Stateless Nation (New York: Alfred A. Knopf, 1989), p. 108.

a state and pose a certain threat, or be a collective member of society within a country. The supreme art of managing a state inhabited by different ethnoi rests in creating an organic symbiosis which maintains a balance of forces that suits all sides.

Borders

Questions of statehood are inevitably connected to the notion of borders, i.e., provisionally or specially established lines that mark where the power of one state ends and where the authority of another begins. Checkpoints through which communications pass have been traditional border lines, initially created to regulate the flow of people entering and leaving, tax collections, and strongpoints for defending territory. This special place has always attracted the attention of philosophers, political theorists, and those practically engaged in dealing with risk and security factors. A border is also a place of gravitation between two sides for conducting trade, a place through which a neighboring country can be visited, or a line that is violated for going to war with a neighbor.

Historical experience shows that many current borders, especially those in post-colonial countries, were established without taking into account the interests of the peoples living there. Because of such border-drawing, tribes, ethnic groups, and related clans have been cut into pieces. Those who wish to restore their integrity are inevitably faced with accusations of separatism, threatening state integrity, and attempting to change borders.

The Durand Line continues to this day to provoke problems with Afghanistan and Pakistan - in some places the border passes through established villages.[64] The Durand Line was imposed as a result of Britain's failure to occupy Afghanistan from the direction of previously occupied India. The government of Afghanistan refuses to recognize the line to this day.

The Kurds, who live in four different states, continue to cherish the dream of a Greater Kurdistan in which their people will become a single national entity. The irony is that throughout history Kurdish

64 Pakistan recognized it as official international border, but Afghanistan not.

groups have never been united. The very landscape contributed to their division, not cohesion, with each Kurdish tribe, and later Kurdish emirates, having their own leaders and interests. Even after acquiring broad autonomy in Iraq following the overthrow of Saddam Hussein, the existence of separate policies among local clans has remained obvious - Barzani's party has been oriented towards Turkey, whereas the Talabani have leaned towards Iran. We also have to take into consideration the armed civil conflict known as the Birakuji between Kurds in the mid-1990's.

The retired American military officer Ralph Peters, taking into account the inconveniences of the post-colonial heritage and the real topoi of ethnic identities, has proposed that the Middle East's borders be changed, with some countries benefitting from gaining territories and others losing land.[65] Granted, Peters' proposal is not entirely logical. In Peters' plan, Lebanon would expand at the expense of Syria's coastal strip, yet Lebanon is multi-ethnic and multi-confessional, inhabited by Shia, Sunni, Maronites, and Orthodox Christians. If Lebanon would become a federation in these new borders, then why should such not be applied to other countries as well? Northern Syria would also be extended at the expense of the province of Hatay, which became part of Turkey in 1939 under dubious circumstances (the region passed to Syria after the First World War in 1918, but Syria at the time was a French protectorate). Or it could be decreased if we take into account the Turkomen inhabiting the country, and their distribution is not compact to begin with. The Syrian Armenians living mainly in the North of the country would also be allocated a separate, administrative and political unit.

Old conflicts of an economic, not ethnic nature, have also continuously sparked discussions over the demarcation or moving of borders for many years. The Saltpetre War, also known as the Second Pacific War or Guano War (1879-1884) led to Bolivia losing access to the sea, and saw Chile, supported by Great Britain, occupying Bolivian and Peruvian ports and cities. The Peruvian province of Tacna was returned in 1929, but Bolivia lost the province of Antofagasta. Negotiations between Bolivia and Chile on returning the former's sea access continue to this day.

65 http://armedforcesjournal.com/peters-blood-borders-map/

If we look at the map of the United States of America, we can also see that some states' administrative borders are surprisingly, absolutely straight, introduced abstractly without taking into account the natural landscape and other peculiarities. This is the consequence of the Frontier strategy, in which conquered territory was considered a *tabula rasa* on which any geometric shapes could be imposed to delimit the jurisdiction of the new rulers.

Yet even such a notion as natural borders is a complex and ambiguous issue. One of the first Russian geopoliticians and Pan-Slavist, Ivan Dusinsky, drew attention to the inconsistency of the concept of natural borders in the works of 19th century European authors. Dusinsky cites Pradier-Fodéré, who remarked that "the idea and expression of a natural border was invented by modern politicians to justify their most unjust, greedy desires. The words 'natural border' do not correspond to anything real. Everything is a natural border, and nothing is a natural border. The Rhine is no more a natural boundary than the Seine or the Loire."[66] Further, he writes: "It is also worth noting that while French internationalists, distorting the notion of a natural border beyond recognition, might strive to prove that a natural border is a linguistic border, then German scholars will reject even this understanding, not without reason noting that the transition from one language to another usually does not occur suddenly, and borders are usually the sites of mixed, transitional dialects, which means that no such natural boundary exists."[67] Nevertheless, in an attempt to clearly define this controversial notion, Dusinsky posits that the "term 'natural border' (limes naturalis s. occupatorius) means a border coinciding with any large natural partition existing on the earth's surface and a sharp, difficultly passable feature bisecting the face of the earth."[68] Dusinsky suggested that even large rivers can only by a stretch be called natural borders since they do not disconnect but connect banks. Only high mountain ranges and deserts, seas, and oceans which are difficult to cross can be considered natural borders upon which states can rely. But a border as such, according to Dusinsky, is a result of a sum of coincidences. Here we can recall Heidegger's saying: "The bridge

66 Dusinskiy I. Geopolitika Rossii. Moscow, 2003. p. 125.

67 Ibid, 127-128.

68 Ibid, 129.

gathers the earth as landscape around the stream."[69] A bridge connects banks and reorganizes the life of people on both sides of a river.

If we further pursue the topic of dialects and borderline ethnic situations, then we arrive at the matter of socio-political miscegenation or "hybrid forms." Nestor Garcia Canclini, the author of the book *Hybrid Cultures*, draws a connection between borders, space, and processes of social hybridization. He writes: "Borders between countries and large cities are distinct as contexts which define specific formats, styles, and contradictions of hybridization. Rigid borders established by modern states have become porous. Some cultures can now be interpreted to be stable, with clear restrictions based on the occupation of territory. But the diversity of possibilities for hybridity does not mean uncertainty or unlimited freedom. Hybridization takes place in certain historical and social conditions among production and consumption systems which sometimes act as restrictions, which can be seen in the lives of many migrants."[70] By hybridization Canclini means socio-cultural processes in which structures or practices that existed imperceptibly beforehand are combined to create new structures, objects, and methods. Thus, borders as such, under new conditions with the existence of states and societies, become hybrid. Canclini's approach can be characterized as an attempt at overcoming the legacy of modernity, especially for states in whose political processes have begun to show the cultural impulses inherent to their land and whose population needs active mobility at this new historical stage.[71]

It is only obvious that different countries have different dynamics for the role of borders tied to historically developed traditions (cultural, religious, political). For example, in Latin America, one discovers an entirely different characterization of borders than in the EU or South-East Asia. Carlos Reboratti writes: "A border is what ecologists call an ecoton, a combination of characteristics of different social systems.

---

69 Heidegger M. Basic Writings / ed. by D.Farell Krell. L.: Routledge, 1993.

70 García Canclini, Néstor. Culturas híbridas: Estrategias para entrar y salir de la modernidad. México: Grijalbo, 1989.

71 Martín-Barbero, Jesús. Sobre "Culturas híbridas. Estrategias para entrar y salir de la modernidad". Reseña en: Magazín Dominical, No. 445, El Espectador, Noviembre 3 de 1991.
http://nestorgarciacanclini.net/hibridacion-e-interculturalidad/73-resena-sobre-culturas-hibridas-estrategias-para-entrar-y-salir-de-la-modernidad

We can say that a border is a kind of ecoton of culture. As an ecoton, it should be seen not as a line of division, as is usually the case, but as something opposite. A border is a line of union, an arena of symbiosis. At a border, as a rule, are visible such marginal things which occur in two 'central' systems, but this does not mean that it divides - it unites."[72] Different countries are trying to resolve the problem of such unification by abolishing border regimes as such (such as the Schengen Zone), or by creating special border zones where visas are unnecessary or the rules of transit for certain groups of persons are simplified (usually for those living in a borderland region).

Maritime borders are of a different nature. Alfred Thayer Mahan believed that the sea not only divides, but unites, which is a fully logical argument for Mahan, who belonged to the opposite geopolitical camp which bet on sea power. Maritime boundaries implicitly entail disputes over the extent of the continental shelf which defines the size of a sovereign economic zone. This automatically becomes a source of political frictions. This is especially relevant in those places, where natural resources, especially oil and gas, are deposited. Experts and politicians have suggested that the Arctic will soon figure on the agenda of all states capable of accessing or indirectly having ties to this region, since countries with access to the Arctic Ocean might be able to expand the size of their exclusive economic zones by 150 nautical miles if they prove that the Arctic shelf is a continuation of their land territory. However, opinions on the division of maritime territories are widely different. According to the median linear method, partition is done on the principle of equidistance of the boundary line from adjacent states' coastline (or coastline base points). According to the sectoral method, the pole is considered to be a point from which straight lines are drawn along the longitude. In theory, a mixed approach could be applied. But the UN Convention on the Law of the Sea does not regulate the specific means for demarcating lines between neighboring states besides references to mutual consent and the principle of justice.[73]

---

72 Reboratti, Carlos. La Frontera Vacía: Hacia nuevas formas de valoración territorial en América Latina. En: Revista Andes. Salta: Cephia. Universidad Nacional de Salta.1992. N° 5.

73 Konishev V., Sergunin A. Arktika v mezhdunarodnoi politike. Sotrudnichestvo ili sopernishestvo? Moscow: RISI, 2011. p. 43.

Comparative Cratology - Three Case Studies

Now we will briefly consider case studies in the formation of power structures in the US, Russia, and Iran. These countries are vivid examples of the extent to which approaches to designing power, organizing institutions of power, and distributing authority can differ. We do not intend to analyze the instruments of power realization that are identical among them or seek similar models within institutions. First of all, the emergence of statehood was markedly different in each of these three countries. Secondly, in inquiring into these examples of distinct peculiarities and specificities in the embodiment of different ideas in mechanisms of power, it is easier to demonstrate the impossibility of reducing to a common denominator what might appear to be merely utilitarian and universal functions related to apparatuses of subordination, coercion, and distribution.

The United States

The United States of America is a relatively young state which was founded upon the traditions of the Enlightenment in combination with various nostalgic elements from the Roman Republic (most pronounced in the architecture of this country's institutions of power, such as the Capitol and the White House). The United States has developed a tradition of applying multiple theories of power, such as concerning competition between interest groups, or pluralism, class theory, and power-elite accord. Various theorists of these models display differences which allow for the creation of various mixed models that cannot be attributed to only one of these three ideal types.

According to pluralist theory, individual citizens join together with like-minded compatriots to solve problems that seem important to them. This is how interest groups are formed. These interest groups compete fairly for power and the state, which is the arena, not an actor. State decisions are made by legal representatives reflecting the opinion of the majority of citizens, and the actual process of state decision-making is done in "black box" style. Pluralism completely ignores the existence and role of non-governmental power in society. Robert Dahl's notion of polyarchy[74] takes into account the existence

74 Dahl, Robert A. Pluralist democracy in the United States: conflict and consent, 968; Polyarchy: participation and opposition. — New Haven: Yale University Press, 1971.

of an elite in the US, but believes that these elites are fragmented and compete with one another in such a way that active parts of the public can also participate. The core of pluralism, whether naive or otherwise, is the belief that in the conditions of democracy, strong and organized private interest groups can constantly influence government. Pluralism presumes the presence of an active population constantly engaged in public discussions.

Class theory explains the actions of the state in terms of the interests and dominating position of the dominant economic class. In this theory, the real source of social power is capital, and the state exists to protect this capital in one form or another. Contemporary class theories differ to varying degrees from the traditional model proposed by Karl Marx. For example, the sociologist William Domhoff has developed the "instrumentalist" model of "class domination." His theory provides for the presence of a ruling business upper class, and includes elements of elite and class theory, ultimately arguing in favor of the ruling class actively influencing politics and deciding all affairs in the political arena by different means.[75] In this case, the ruling class is divided into "class segments" based in different interests related to such factors as regional and sectoral industries. The alliances between these different class segments and their striving to achieve influence and control over policy are taken to largely explain the actions of the state in question.

Domhoff also introduces the concept of a "ruling class network" behind policy planning. This network uses the ruling class to mobilize efforts for business interests to influence policies that are of importance to it. Domhoff's methodology, which presupposes the dominance of a business class, also includes inquiry into data confirming the influence and participation of individual members of the business elite - thus, the higher echelons of power make decisions in favor of the business class not only because "they rule", but because of the business elite's very impact and active participation.

The central idea of this elite theory is that power rests in the hands of a small part of the elite which makes important decisions for society but is not accountable to the latter. Beyond this basic consensus, proponents of

75 Domhoff G.W. Who Rules America? New York: McGraw-Hill, 2002; The Power Elite and the State: How Policy Is Made in America. New York: Transaction Publishers, 1990.

this theory vary considerably in their particular positions. The classical theory of elites argues that the elites maintain their power thanks to their advantages as an organized minority over the unorganized majority. One of this theory's authors, the American sociologist Charles Wright Mills, argues that the power of the elite rests in their control over the upper echelons of public institutions.[76] Elite theory scholars also differ in their assessments of elites' cohesion, the degree of harmonization of the "rules of the game" that might be agreed upon between elites, and the balance of to what extent the elite acts egotistically and to what extent it operates in the interests of society or certain social groups.

Regardless of which of these theories is taken as a reference point, it can be said that a characteristic feature of the American system of power is the so-called "iron triangles", or relationships between the legislature, the bureaucracy, and lobbying groups which form a kind of "mutual responsibility" within the elite. However, if bureaucracies and legislative authorities can be found in any country, then lobbying groups is a phenomenon of an exclusively Anglo-Saxon character despite its recent global reach. The institutions of lobbyism were formed by a circulatory system of iron triangles and became part of the political culture in this country.[77] The term itself comes from the word "lobbies" and originated in Britain. As the honorary president of the ATTAC-France NGO, Susan George, writes:

This practice takes its name from the foyer of the House of Commons, where people with special interests, and often stuffed envelopes, waited to ambush and catch entering or exiting deputies...After a couple of centuries of this practice, these unelected people became famous largely as more informed and quasi-legal actors on the outskirts of the state. Their offices occupy entire neighborhoods in Washington (K-Street) and the EU quarter in Brussels. They often go through "revolving doors" - after their career in politics they know better than anyone else whom to approach and how to change the minds of authorities or legislators. They have improved their methods, they are paying more than ever, and they get results. Lobbying pays off.[78]

---

76 C. Wright Mills, The Power Elite, 1956; Power, Politics and People, New York, 1963.

77 Savin L., Fedorchenko S, Shwartz O. Setecentrichnie metodi v gosudarstvennom upravlenii, Moscow: Institut ekonomiki I zakonodatelstva, 2015.

78 George S. Gosudarstvo korporatsiy – rost nelegitimnoy vlasti I ugroza demokratii // Geopolitika № 24.

The legal foundation for lobbying in the United States is the First Amendment to the Constitution, which guarantees the right to freedom of speech and access to Congress. This Amendment was adopted on September 17, 1787, and to this day is used to justify the interference of private capital and oligarchy (including transnational ones) in legislative processes.[79] In the US, corporations have actively intervened in politics to the point of completely merging. In Ratnikov's words: "Big business did not hesitate to use both illegal methods, including bribery, and fully legal ones, such as sponsoring politicians, public organizations, and the press. Congressmen, Senators, justices, and high-ranking officials were entangled in a network of different lobbying structures by the beginning of the 20th century. During the US presidential campaign of 1912, the future winner, Woodrow Wilson, claimed that the US government is nothing more than a servant of interests groups deprived of its own will."[80]

The very term "lobbying" has broad interpretations. Lobbying or "lobbyism" has been defined as: a particular system and practice of the organization of certain social groups through targeted influence on legislative and executive organs of power; the activities of legal entities and individuals aimed at influencing federal bodies of state power to use their authority on lawmaking; pressure put on power and decision-makers by various so-called pressure groups; or a multi-level phenomenon crowned by a politician (or group of politicians) proposing and implementing a decision.[81]

Indeed, the US presidency is directly bound to the workings of the "iron triangle" and lobbying institutions without which it would be impossible to hold caucuses in the form in which they are held in the US. The same can be said regarding the Senate and House of Representatives of the US Congress. In a global historical context, however, the emergence of US institutions of power and American political culture had a rather negative character, as for Great Britain and the old monarchical regimes of Europe who saw in the North American revolution a threat to their existence, as well as for, of course, the indigenous peoples of North America whose social structures and centuries of experience in administration, distribution, regulating relations, waging wars,

---

79 Savin L. Couching voina. Moscow: Evraziyskoe dvizhenie, 2017. p. 133.

80 Ratnikov A. Prohozhaya vlasti. 25 Oct. 2013. http://lenta.ru/articles/2013/10/24/

81 Menshenina M., Panteleeva M, Lobbizm. Ekaterinburg: Ural universitet, 2016. p. 12.

and peace practices were steamrolled by the Frontier and were only "inherited" at a later stage by a small group of cultural anthropologists. The rich heritage of the North American Indian world[82] turned out to be unwanted by the bearers of Puritanical ethics who built the New World in line with their own metaphysical beliefs and pragmatic calculations.

Russia

The American historian and professor at Columbia University, Richard Wortman, who is considered one of the US' leading specialists on Russia, begins the Russian edition of his *Scenarios of Power: Myth and Ceremony in Russian Monarchy: From Peter the Great to the Abdication of Nicholas II* with the following argument: "In Russia, visions of supreme power have since the very beginning been identified with the notion of empire; this identification was preserved in later periods, when the sole, real sovereign was the emperor who wielded full and rounded power."[83] Wortman's style of presentation is altogether eloquent, with chapters bearing decorative titles such as "Minerva Triumphant" (about Catherine the Great), "The Angel on the Throne" and "The Blessed Tsar" (Alexander the First), "Epitomes of the Nation" (Nicholas the First), etc. However, the previous quotation might engender the false impression that the Russian emperors wielded absolute power like European monarchs. Unfortunately, to this day in the West many perceive this as so and thereby contribute to the continuous formation of political prejudices. It should be noted that Wortman does not speak of other authorities which have existed in Russia which, even if not absolute, were operative and effective. For example, the princes of Rus had advisory bodies since pagan times which represented prototypes of the future Duma. As Vasily Kliuchevsky writes of the Duma: "Closed off from society by the sovereign above and dyaks from below, it [the Duma] was a constitutional institution with extensive political influence, but without a constitutional charter; it is a governmental place with a wide range of affairs, but without a chancellory or archive."[84]

---

82 Korotaev A. Kulturno-politicheskaya slozhnost kak faktor raspredeleniya mifologicheskih motivov v Novom Svete// Vlast v aborigennoi Amerike. Moscow: Nauka, 2006. p. 329 — 352.

83 Wartman R. Scenarii vlasti. Mifi i ceremonii russkoy monarhii ot Petra Velikogo do smerti Nikolaya I. Moscow: OGI, 2002. Vol.1. p. 31.

84 Klyuchevskiy V. O gosudarstvennosti v Rossii. Moscow: Mysl', 2003. p. 5.

What's more, before the establishment of the Russian Empire as such, during the times of princely fragmentation there arose the phenomenon of two consultative structures existing alongside each other: the Duma and the Veche. These political forces competed with one another and differed in their socio-political interests. Relations between them were based on mutual agreement, a contract, or "order" (*ryad*). Different regions had different definitions, rules, and regulations. For example, the "judicial board in Pskov is called 'lord' in the Pskov Judicial Charter…One might think that the boyar council was called thusly as well."[85] The later centralization of the Russian state, its expansion, and the emergence of new administrative divisions all introduced new regulations and functions for those wielding and representing power.

In Ivan IV's Oprichnina we saw an attempt at reforming the power system over the confrontation of two institutions - the tsar and the boyars. But it cannot be said that the previous structure of the boyar Duma was completely liquidated as is portrayed in some works on Ivan the Terrible era in Russian history. Instead: "Under one supreme power operated two parallel administrations, two orders of central and regional institutions, *zemsky* and *oprichny*."[86] Under Peter the Great, the boyar Duma gradually evolved into "an institution of a different nature when circumstances forced it to act individually, apart from the sovereign."[87] Even then there was no monarchical absolutism typical of various European regimes. A number of powers were delegated to the Senate which, in the absence of the emperor in the capital, had provisions for acting in one case or another.

If we sum up the peculiarities of the formation of the legislature in Rus, the conclusion can be drawn that the "system and significance of the Duma was a matter of *narodnosti* (folk or national identity) which took shape in the 15th century in the region of Oka and the Upper Volga. This *narodnost'* was formed with the old Russian population's retreat deep into our plain from the southern and south-western borderlands in the face of triumphant enemies."[88] Further, according to Kliuchevsky:

85 Ibid, 158.

86 Ibid, 271.

87 Ibid, 367.

88 Ibid, 427.

> By virtue of its system and the nature of its operations, the Moscow boyar Duma was an establishment of the very fact which served as the starting point for the history of the Muscovite state. This state began as a military alliance of the local rulers of Great Russia under the leadership of the most central of them, an alliance induced by the formation of Great Russian *narodnosti* and its struggle for existence and independence. The Duma became the head of this union with the significance of being a military-legislative council of local allied sovereigns with their free boyar servants, who gathered in Moscow under the leadership of this new leader."[89]

The clergy has also wielded strong influence in the history of Russian statehood. The institution of the Patriarchate of the Russian Orthodox Church existed until virtually the end of the 18th century, and spiritual power played a significant role not only in the life of parishioners, but also in matters of taxation and loans. Only with the Church schism and Peter the Great's reforms was secular power elevated to supreme status. But even under the Holy Governing Synod established in 1700 as an alternative post of the Patriarch, the church remained an influential institution. The emperor's representative to the Synod was the Procurator, and the Synod dealt not only with church issues, but also the adoption of final decision in divorce cases, defrocking, the traditions of anathematization of the laity, as well as the spiritual enlightenment of the people. This institution existed in such a form up until 1918, when a new Patriarch was elected in Russia.[90]

Following the separation of Church and state and the final victory of the Bolsheviks, in addition to executive authority there came into existence commissarial supervision and later party bodies which monitored the correctness of decision-execution. For example, the formal leaders of the Soviet state (the supreme officials *de jure*) were Vladimir Lenin, Lev Kamenev, Yakov Sverdlov, Mikhail Vladimirsky, Mikhail Kalinin, Nikolay Shvernik, Kliment Voroshilov, Leonid Brezhnev, Anastas

89 Ibid, 431.

90 It is telling that after the collapse of the USSR, the Russian Orthodox Church once again restored its position. Although the institution of the Patriarchate was restored under Soviet power with Patriarch Tikhon elected in 1917, practically immediately afterwards the Church was subject to persecution, and from 1925 to 1943 the functions of the patriarchal vicar were performed by metropolitans. In 1943, the new Patriarch Sergius was elected. This justifies the proverbial saying that "no holy place remains empty."

Mikoyan, Nikolai Podgorny, etc, whereas the broadest authorities were *de facto* delegated to the General Secretaries of the Communist Party - Joseph Stalin, Nikita Khrushchev, Leonid Brezhnev, Yuri Andropov, Konstantin Chernenko, and Mikhail Gorbachev - who were perceived as the leaders of the Soviet Union both within the country and abroad. Tellingly enough, even under the ruling classist-Marxist doctrine which spoke of the proletariat's role in struggling against the oppression of capitalism, the USSR wielded a vertical power structure similar to that of the Russian Empire. Although workers and peasants' soviets did operate and elections of people's deputies were regularly held, the country was in fact an autocratic power based on the popular masses. This was particularly pronounced during the rule of Joseph Stalin. An interesting model for conceptualizing the Soviet state under Stalin has been proposed by Alexander Dugin in his book *Sociology of Russian Society*, which conceives of the Soviet state as autocratic, popular or folk, socialist, independent, orderly, mighty, and messianic.[91]

If we consider the final years of the Soviet Union under Mikhail Gorbachev as a departure from this system, as his reforms led to the country's collapse, and if we examine Boris Yeltsin's presidency's orientation towards the West and associated neoliberal IMF reforms within Russia, then Vladimir Putin's rise to head of state, and the accompanying restoration of vertical power alongside progressive and rather restrained rejections of the Western political and administrative model, appear to mark a return to Russian traditions of rule. The role of the security forces around Vladimir Putin and the State Duma's informal subordination to the Presidential Administration's decrees resemble the boyar Duma of the Muscovite Principality united around the military-political leader.

To conclude our brief analysis of the power structure in Russia, we consider it necessary to reproduce the interesting observation of Michel Foucault on the distinctive features of power in both Russia and the West. In a lecture on shepherding from February 15th, 1978, Foucault quotes Nikolai Gogol's 1846 letter to Zhukovsky, in which Gogol illustrated his vision of the ideal Christian tsar imbued with love for all people, who weeps, cries, and prays for his people, and in so doing reconciles all the state's castes. On this basis, Foucault

91 Dugin A. Sotsiologiya russkogo obshestva. Rossiya mezhdu Haosom I Logosom. Moscow: Academic project, 2011. p. 400-401.

concluded that such a Christian Sovereign is not characteristic of the West, or in his words: "the Western sovereign is Caesar, not Christ; the Western Pasteur is not Caesar, but Christ."[92]

Iran

The statehood of modern Iran has deep roots in ancient times. The Persian Empire of the Achaemenid era was once the largest state in Eurasia. Indeed, the very idea of empire originated there. Numerous Ancient Greek philosophical conceptions, including Plato's parable of the cave, as well as Jewish dogma such as the concept of the Moshiach (the Savior), were also originally born in the Persian Empire and were elements of Zoroastrianism. Alexander the Great merely imitated the Persians in creating his own empire, seizing their control over numerous peoples by military force. Mongol and Turkic dynasties later ruled Persia (Iran). Only after the spread of Islam, and especially the Islamic Revolution in 1979, did it become justifiable to speak of political Shiism as the basis of the power system in Iran.

Of interest in this regard is the fact that Shiism was originally a political party which was transformed in the 70 years between the death of Hussein (680) and the Abbasid dynasty (749/750) into a religious movement. "The cult of the martyrdom of the Imams Ali and Hussein was the initial point upon which Shiism transformed into a religious current."[93] According to the Shiite tradition, we are currently in the time of the Great Occultation (Ghaibat al-Kubra) of the 12th Imam, "henceforth deeds are in the will of God." Shiite theology posits that this "occultation" or "concealment" will end only with the End Times (Akhir Al Zama) when the Mahdi, the eschatological deliverer of humanity from social and political oppression, will return to establish a just order on earth.[94]

It should be emphasized that Shiite Muslims associate the coming of the Mahdi with the same aspirations which Christians have for the Second Coming of Jesus Christ. As in Christianity, the Mahdi's main opponent will be the Dajjal, the Islamic Antichrist, the personification

92 Fuko M. Bezopasnost, territoriya, naselenie. SPb: Nauka, 2011. p. 217.

93 Petrushevskiy I. Islam v Irane v VII-XV vekah. Moscow-Leningrad, 1966, p.46.

94 Motahhari M. Iran i Islam. SPb, 2008. p. 42.

of worldly Evil and ignorance (*jahl*). The coming of the Mahdi, just as in the Christian case, is a profound mystery whose timing is unknown but whose imminent coming is indicated by certain signs. Insofar as the concealment of the Imam means that Muslims have no visible leader, the "translation" of the Imams' will into concrete political reality is the prerogative of theologians, the Fuqaha or Maraji. Iran's administrative system bears the name *Welayat-e Faqih*, i.e., "Guardianship" or "Governance" of the "Islamic Jurist."

The meaning of Welayat-e Faqih originally consisted of instructing a community on theological, legal (in Islamic law, or Sharia) and doctrinal matters. However, with the Islamic Revolution of 1979 this system was spread to the political sphere of the Iranian state. The role of Ayatollah Ruhollah Musavi Khomeini in this revolution was paramount. In his book *Islamic Government*, the ideas of which laid the basis of the Islamic Republic of Iran's state system, Khomeini writes:

> [W]ere God not to appoint an Imam over men to maintain law and order, to serve the people faithfully as a vigilant trustee, religion would fall victim to obsolescence and decay. Its rites and institutions would vanish; the customs and ordinances of Islam would be transformed or even deformed. Heretical innovators would add things to religion and atheists and unbelievers would subtract things from it, presenting it to the Muslims in an accurate manner. For we see that men are prey to defects...Moreover, they disagree with each other, having varying inclinations and discordant states. If God, therefore, had not appointed over men one who would maintain order and law and protect the revelation brought by the Prophet(s), in the manner we have described, men would have fallen prey to corruption; the institutions, laws, customs, and ordinances of Islam would be transformed; and faith and its content would be completely changed, resulting in the corruption of all of humanity.[95]

Khomeini stresses: "The fundamental difference between Islamic government, on the one hand, and constitutional monarchies and republics, on the other, is this: whereas the representatives of the people or the monarch in such regimes engage in legislation, in

95 http://www.iranchamber.com/history/rkhomeini/books/velayat_faqeeh.pdf

Islam the legislative power and competence to establish laws belongs exclusively to God Almighty."[96]

Khomeini also introduced the concept of *rahbar-e enghelab-e eslami*, or the "leader of the Islamic revolution, the bearer of religious and secular power." In Khomeini's vision of *Welayat-e Faqih*, the "supreme leader" is the supreme interpretation of divine laws who simultaneously exercises a high degree of control over secular state power, the army, and security forces. Only the power of God and the "concealed" Imam Mahdi are above him. Therefore, the doctrine of *Welayat-e Faqih* represents a traditionalist theory of theocratic governance. The very word *welayat* can be translated as "sovereignty", "rule", "reign", "regency", "guardianship", or "jurisdiction." In the context of the Shiite notion of the Imamate, *Welayat* "in this context means a sovereignty that implies the legitimate right to govern: a guardianship-type of governance."[97] *Faqih* is the singular form of *Foqaha*, or the theologians and doctors of Islamic law. However, as pointed out by Abdollah Javadi-Amoli in his book *Welayat-e Faqih*, the faqih does not mean one figure or group, but rather an institution that rules during the period of occultation.

A similar interpretation of the doctrine of *Welayat-e Faqih* has been proposed by Salehi Najafabadi, whose attention was focused on the role of the people and the administration in the election of the *Welayat-e Faqih*. The main point of Salehi Najafabadi's doctrine is the people's recognition of the legality of interpretation of this authority as contained in the doctrine of *Welayat-e Faqih*. He notes that interpretations of this doctrine have been dominated by judgements predicated on "abstract" Ahbars and Hadiths which exclude the interests of the people supposed to form the basis of the authority of the foqaha. Najafabadi thus proposed to replace the old principle of "divine predestination" of the faqih with a new, legal, social agreement between the Shiite community and the appointed faqih who takes upon himself sacred obligations with respect to the nation. In other words, Najafabadi attempted to lend legitimacy to the *welayat rahbar* as an expression of the interests of the people, and tried to turn the *welayat* into an institution of people's power, asserting the right of

96 Blake Archer Williams. An Introduction to Waliyic Islam. Sacred Communities and their Covanantal Dispansations. Lion of Najaf Publishers, 2017. P. 153.

97 Ibid. P. 5.

the people to remove an elected rahbar if he is revealed to lack the leadership qualities demanded by Islam.[98] This case study and such conclusions demonstrate that among Iranian Shiite intellectuals one can find supporters of a more participatory version of political life in Iran which still aims to comply with the established norms of Islam and Sharia.

98 Rakhmanova F. Princip «velayate fakih» v Islamskoy Respublike Iran. http://www.idmedina.ru/books/materials/turkology/1/islam_rahmanova.htm

10

Ethnoi, Peoples, and Nations

"Peoples" are not often considered in the political sciences, except for when it comes to the precedents of national-liberation movements in various countries, or in discussions of populism, which has become especially relevant in recent time in connection with the profound processes that are currently transforming the political landscape of EU countries. Meanwhile, ethnology and ethnography operate with different concepts, whereas sociology is more concerned with strata, classes, and processes within society.

The influence of the Enlightenment has instilled not only in Europe, but also other regions the belief that ever since the emergence of the concept of "nation", this new "institution" offers answers to all questions ranging from the economy to public administration. But this has not been the case. It is not by chance that the 20th century saw the re-emergence of great interest in ethnology and cultural anthropology, in the study of the life of different nationalities and autochthonous ethnic groups that have lived autonomously for a long time without being tied to the world of modernity. Such have come to be seen not only as "exotic", but as references for understanding others' own actions, identity, social structure, and so on. Even during the period of the collapse of empires and the formation of nation-states in Europe in tandem with the formation of nationalism as a state ideology, a number of thinkers repeatedly called to revive the past order or called for destroying the contemporary bourgeois-modernist order. Such convictions were simultaneously expressed by thinkers who influenced the development of liberal thought (e.g., the "noble savage" of Jean-Jacques Rousseau) as well as by conservative-oriented critics of modern culture (as exemplified in Friedrich Nietzsche's radical style).

Questions of gender relations (patriarchal or matriarchal systems being the most well-known manifestations of gender-political particularities), the status of leaders (allogenic and autochthonous elites), the structuring of society along phratry (dual or more complex organizations), castes, or classes (by pedigree or property qualification), the order of kindred ties which in turn shape such phenomena as xenopohobia and xenophilia - all of these factors have not disappeared in the era of globalization. Although they no longer play a significant role in the social or political lives of some states, in the majority of countries they still exert a greater or lesser influence. The largest democracy in the world, as India is often termed, maintains a caste system to this day. Even if all citizens of India are equal on the legal level, there is de facto no equality between them.

There are grounds to believe that the efforts of those liberal-globalist forces to spread a monolithic civil culture which strives to neutralize these differences are unlikely to succeed in the coming decades. Careful attention to ethnic diversity and national traditions will be a key feature of balanced and successful policies. To this end, however, it is necessary to delve into and understand the relevant terminological apparatus and the particularities of ethnic, folk, and national (and nationalist) categories.

Ethnos

In examining the history of human societies deep into past centuries, numerous theories inevitably come to mind which speak of primeval-communal and tribal structures of human organization succeeded by the birth of slave-owning and feudal societies. However, although such claims may be universally accepted, they are rather superficial and are founded on theories of evolution and Western-centric understandings of history.

As Franz Boas and Claude Levi-Strauss convincingly showed, even "primitive societies" in the modern understanding of the term have been discovered to display fairly complex structures and mechanisms for perceiving and reacting to processes, which puzzle contemporary scholars. The concept of "tribe" likely owes its origin to the tribes which, according to legend, Romulus established in Ancient Rome. There were originally three "tribes" - the Albans, Sabines, and Etruscans, although the third is considered foreign, as the language and other traits of the Etruscans differed from the first two. But the sixth king of Rome, Servius Tullius, altered this principle by introducing restrictions on relocation within the city (due to the fact that the Etruscan tribe was constantly expanding by means of influx from the outside) and by adding another tribe and 15 rural tribes. Subsequent regulation of the tribes up to the point of the end of the Roman Republic was based on balancing between city and agricultural communities. Other countries have had their own unique criteria for tribal differences based on linguistic, territorial, military, and other principles. Thus, when one hears talk of the current twists and turns in the "tribal politics" of, for example, the Middle East, such ought to be specified as different from the "tribal politics" of other states in, for example, South-East Asia or tropical Africa.

Another concept connected to the formation of peoples is that of "ethnos." In Russian scholarship, the term "ethnos" was coined by the Russian anthropologist and ethnographer Sergey Shirokogorov, who is considered to be the founder of the Russian school of ethnology. Shirokogorov defined the ethnos as "a group of people who speak the same language, recognize their common origin, and have a set of customs and lifestyles which are preserved and sanctified by traditions which differ from the customs of other groups."[1] He believed that the main bases for the classification of ethnoi are: "first of all, anthropological or somatic characteristics, i.e., peculiarities of the structure of the body - the skeleton and soft parts - and color, and trademarks unconsciously recognized by the ethnos group; secondly, ethnographical characteristics, i.e., sets of customs and lifestyles; and, finally, thirdly, linguistic characteristics, i.e., the language of the ethnos."[2]

A similar characterization was supplied by the major representative of the Soviet Marxist school of ethnology, Yulian Bromley. For him, the ethnos "is a stable group of people that has historically formed on a definite territory and which has relatively common and stable particularities of language, culture, and psyche, as well as a consciousness of their unity and difference from other such entities, all of which are established in its self-name."[3]

1 Shirokogorov S. Etnos: Issledovanie osnovnih printsipov izmeneniya etnicheskih I etnografichaskih yavleniy. Shankhai: Dalnevostochniy universitet, 1923, p. 30.

2 Ibid, 37.

3 Bromley Y. Ocherki teorii etnosa. Moscow: Nauka, 1983. p. 12.

Such definitions allow for one to identify the fundamental markers of ethnoi: "territory, history, language, culture, the peculiarities of their psyche, and national self-consciousness."[4] At the same time, it is necessary to note that "neither somatic qualities (i.e., anthropological characteristics) nor language and religion are necessarily decisive factors in defining an ethnos. Different ethnoi can arise out of a single ethnogenetic, linguistic, and cultural substrate but, for certain historical reasons, can even reside in eternal antagonism towards one another..And, vice versa, a very diverse ethno-linguistic substrate can give birth to an absolutely different ethnos, even one which is drawn to an ethnic element which is completely alien to the local cultural-historical landscape."[5] As follows, an ethnos as such is a very complex phenomenon despite its seemingly intuitive simplicity.

Yulian Bromley also proposed to divide ethnoi into two categories. In the first case is an ethnos in the narrow sense of the term which "can be defined as a totality of people that has historically formed on a definite territory and which has relatively common and stable traits (including language) in culture, and psyche, as well as a consciousness of their unity and difference from other such entities, i.e., self-consciousness."[6] Bromley suggested the term *ethnikos* to distinguish this diversity of ethnoi among others. At the same time, it was stressed that this whole set of ethnic properties could be preserved when a group of people of this or that people moved to a new territory. Bromley cited as an example Ukrainians living in Canada, particularly those who moved there at the end of the 19th century. The second category was said to be exemplified by individual territorial-political communities which present themselves as autonomous macro-units. Such ethnosociological organisms, in addition to a cultural component, also boast territorial, economic, social, and political community. The direct carrier of ethnic culture is the *ethnophor*. The *ethnophor* establishes the laws of the gathering and division of people along ethnic lines, and is the direct heir and co-creator of national culture. The peculiarity of the *ethnophor* is that it cannot independently ensure the intergenerational reproduction of ethnic properties. In other words, the *ethnophor* needs to be surrounded by others similar to it, which makes the ethnos an ethnos. The *ethnophor*

4 Latyshina D., Khairullin R. Etnopedagogika. Moscow: Urait, 2014. p. 32.

5 Asatryan G. Etnicheskaya kompozitsya Irana. От «Aryiskogo prostora» do Azerbaidjanskogo mifa. Erevan: Kavkazskiy centr iranistiki, 2012. p. 76.

6 Bromley Y, Podolniy R. Chelovechestvo – eto narodi. Moscow: Mysl', 1990. p. 32.

is the individual bearer of a certain ethnic culture and national psyche. It is a kind of atom out of which ethnoi are built.

The original Ancient Greek term *ethnos* did not cover all categories of people with a common language and cultural traditions living on a definite territory. In Ancient Greek, in addition to *ethnos*, one finds several other types of associations of people, such as *demos (δῆμος)*, *laos (*Λάος), and *okhlos* (οχλος). How do these types differ? The French linguist Émile Benveniste offers the following definitions:

> *Demos* designated both a division of land and the people who inhabit it...*Laos* is warrior community which is defined by its relationship to the chief, the "shepherd", or the "leader." The shepherd never rules over the *demos*, only over the *laos*. Meanwhile, the *demos* is a community of people united only by common social conditions, whereas *laos* designates the individual ties between a group of people and their leader...*ethnos* refers not only to people, but to animals as well as bees.[7]

Okhlos, meanwhile, meant the people as "a crowd, mob, or mass."[8] In modern sciences, as a rule, ethnoi are not defined by taking into account bees and and fauna; rather, it is customary to refer to an ethos as a group of people with a common language, cultural traditions, and historical past. In the Septuagint (the Old Testament texts translated into Ancient Greek), the word *ethne* was used to translate the Jewish term *goyim*, which meant peoples other than the Jews.[9]

Ethnocentrism

In the context of international relations, it is important to consider such a notion as ethnocentrism. The term "ethnocentrism" was introduced into scholarly circulation by the American sociologist William Sumner in 1906, who described such as attitudes of prejudice or distrust towards outsiders who can exist even within the given social group.

7 Benvenist E. Slovar socialnikh indoevropeyskikh terminov. Moscow: Progress, 1995. p. 297.

8 Weisman A. Grechesko-russkiy slovar. Moscow: Greko-latinskiy kabinet Shichalina, 1991. p. 916.

9 Tonkin E., McDonald M., Chapman M. History and Ethnicity. London: Routlege, 1989. P. 11.

Sumner formulated a by all means fruitful conception of the influence of hostile surroundings or external aggression on the internal cohesion of society[10], also pointing out:

> The exigencies of war with outsiders are what make peace inside, lest internal discord should weaken the we-group for war. These exigencies also make government and law in the in-group, in order to prevent quarrels and enforce discipline. Thus war and peace have reacted on each other and developed each other, one within the group, the other in the intergroup relation. The closer the neighbors, and the stronger they are, the intenser is the warfare, and then the intenser is the internal organization and discipline of each. Sentiments are produced to correspond. Loyalty to the group, sacrifice for it, hatred and contempt for outsiders, brotherhood within, warlikeness without,—all grow together, common products of the same situation. These relations and sentiments constitute a social philosophy. It is sanctified by connection with religion. Men of an others-group are outsiders with whose ancestors the ancestors of the we-group waged war. The ghosts of the latter will see with pleasure their descendants keep up the fight, and will help them. Virtue consists in killing, plundering, and enslaving outsiders.[11]

The limitations of Sumner's theory can be seen in numerous rituals related to the "domestication" of foreign culture - ranging from Shamanic practices of exorcizing foreign spirits, to "reading" eyes, and acts of cannibalism, insofar as the eating of an enemy's flesh has been considered among many peoples to be directly tied to the acquisition of additional spiritual power. A foreign "others-group" can be adapted to the needs of the we-group and even be metaphysically "conquered" even if the others-group is stronger and more numerous. A characteristic example of the latter can be seen in cargo cults, according to which white people are the spirits of the dead ancestors of some Pacific island peoples, whom the latter are tasked with caring for.

In one way or another, we can see here the interrelationship between ethnocentric perception and strategy, which has given birth to the

10 Sumner W. G. War // WSPSA, 1964.

11 Sumner W., Folkways. New-York: Dover, Inc., 1959. http://www.gutenberg.org/files/24253/24253-h/24253-h.htm

concept of strategic culture. Ethnocentrism can also be reformed into a national idea or initially have claims to special status. This is particularly characteristic of ethno-religious societies. Under certain circumstances, ethnocentrism can be transformed into an even broader array of ideological markers and convictions. For example, contemporary Eurocentrism represents a complex phenomenon based on the ideas of the Enlightenment in tandem with incorporating the suppressed ethnocentrisms of the peoples belonging to the European Union. Ken Booth considered the model of ethnocentrism on the state level without reference to a particular people. Booth noted:

> When thinking about the rational behaviour of others, strategists tend to project their own cultural values...but it should be apparent that one can only predict the behaviour of 'a rational man' if both observer and observed share the same values, have the same set of priorities, and have similar logical powers. Ethnocentric perceptions interfere with this process: they mean that one's own values and sense of priorities are projected onto the other. By this process ethnocentrism undermines the central act in strategy, that of estimating how others will see the world and then will think and act.[12]

Ken Booth's theory is directly associated with the school of political realism in international relations. Nevertheless, in considering the "we vs. others" opposition, it is very difficult to speak of any total purity of ethnic groups, especially as the interpenetration of ideas and the mutual exchange of cultural traditions has been ongoing for a very long time. "The creolization or hybridization of culture is the result of complex, uneven, and imbalanced processes of social interaction, often stretched out over several centuries, and processes which have generated many societies of human civilization."[13] This is all the more obvious in the case of those modern nation-states which do not have a single ethnically homogenous subject. In one way or another, ethnic minorities always exist, even if they use the language of the majority for everyday communication. The Kashubians in Poland, the Lusatian Sorbs in Germany, the Sami in Finland, and the Vlachs (or

---

12 Ken Booth, Strategy and Ethnocentrism. New York: Homes & Meier Publishers, 1979, p 65.

13 Urry, John. Sociology beyond societies. Mobilities for the twenty-first century. London: Routledge, 2000. p.222.

Aromanians) in Macedonia are examples which illustrate the deep heterogeneity of modern European states. Turkey is inhabited by more than 40 ethnic groups. In the latter case, it is widely believed that there is merely the Turkish majority and several minorities such as Kurds, Armenians, Greeks, and Circassians (the collective name for multiple North Caucasian nationalities). But even among the Turks we can differentiate, for example, the Anatolians. Overall, the Turkish people itself took shape over the course of ethnogenesis among Asian, Caucasian, Balkan, and Slavic tribes.

In the 20th century, international relations was dominated by the Western approach, which relies on a modernist understanding of nation-states in which ethnic nuances are not usually taken into account. This resulted in the confusion of concepts and the acceptance of politically incorrect decisions. The American political scientist Walker Connor was obviously mistaken in believing that *ethnos* is the Greek equivalent of the word "nation", and that the very term "ethno-nationalism" is tautological.[14] An ethnos is a natural community, while a nation is a socio-political community. "This fact is another example of the numerous misconceptions of Western scientific thought as it has entangled itself in a labyrinth of terms and definitions."[15]

Meanwhile, ethnic studies and theories of nations and nationalisms often have similar points of departure, namely, that such is a group community within which there are systematic ties based on language, solidarity, mythology, and often common perceptions of external threats and/or enemies.

The theory of constructivism also represents a speculative model that can be applied to both ethnoi and nations. According to this theory, the ethnos is a construct created by the intellectual influence of certain entities, such as cultural or power elites. In this case, "ethnic" traditions can be either artificially created and enforced through manipulation or attempted to be "recreated" on the basis of historical materials.

---

14 Connor W. A Few Cautionary Notes on the History and Future of Ethnonational Conflicts // Facing ethnic conflicts: Toward a New Realism / Ed. by A. Wimmer. Lanham: Rowman & Littlefield Publishers, 2004. P. 23–24

15 Savin L. Paradoxi natsionalizma I etnokonflikti // Geopolitica.ru http://geopolitica.ru/article/paradoksy-nacionalizma-i-etnokonflikty#.VYmrldK8PGc.

For example, Fredrik Barth conceptualizes and defines ethnicity in the framework of constructivism as the broadest category of social identity, as a situational phenomenon created by means of symbolic distinction which highlight the contractual nature of borders between ethnic categories. In this perspective, an ethnos is born when a group of people engages in self-determination vis-a-vis other communities. On the basis of self-identification, this group pursues the appropriate marking of cultural borders. When these issues become politicized, one can speak of a transition from ethnoconstructivism to nationalism. Classic examples of such constructivism are Croatian, Kosovo, and Ukrainian nationalisms.

As in the case of constructivism, theories of primordialism and instrumentalism can be applied not only to analyze an ethnos, but also to describe a nation. Rogers Brubaker, for instance, proposes a broader view of the interrelationship between the ethnos and nation. He believes:

> Ethnicity, race and nation should be conceptualized not as substances or things or entities or organisms or collective individuals—as the imagery of discrete, concrete, tangible, bounded and enduring 'groups' encourages us to do—but rather in relational, processual, dynamic, eventful and disaggregated terms. This means thinking of ethnicity, race and nation not in terms of substantial groups or entities but in terms of practical categories, cultural idioms, cognitive schemas, discursive frames, organizational routines, institutional forms, political projects and contingent events.[16]

Terminological Paradoxes

It is interesting to note that the concepts of "people" and "nation" have developed in parallel, often resulting in their confusion. Such a fate has also befallen the terms "nationality" and "national." It is well known that the expression "national interests" refers primarily to the state, whereas categories of "nationality" are often employed to

16 Rogerbs Brubaker, "Ethnicity without Groups", Arch.europ.sociol.,XLIII: 2 (2002): 167. http://bev.berkeley.edu/Ethnic%20Religious%20Conflict/Ethnic%20and%20Religious%20Conflict/1%20Identity/Ethnicity%20without%20Groups%20Brubaker.pdf ; Брубейкер Р. Этничность без границ. p. 29

refer to peoples. But what if multiple peoples inhabit a state? Whose interests are "national"?

If we take an historical approach, then we see that, for instance, Emperor Frederick II's 1486 law on the Peace of the Land used the term *Sacrum Imperium Romanium Nationis Germanicae* (*Heiliges römisches Reich deutscher Nation*). In his 1512 address to the Reichstag, Maximilian I first officially used the term "Holy Roman Empire of the German Nation" (Heiliges Römisches Reich Deutscher Nation).[17] The precedent of the concept of nationality thus appears to belong to the Germans. According to Gérard Noiriel, the substantive "nationality" circulated in France significantly later than the substantive with the same root "nation." The "birth" of the term in French is connected with the translation of the 1815 work *Deutsches Volkthum* by one of the founders of German ethnography, Friedrich Jan.[18]

However, *Volksthum* is an artificial term invented by Jan himself. Moreover, it should be clearly understood that in German, the term *Volk* means "people", not "nation." By *Volksthum*, Jan understood a force that united individuals into a group and shapes them into a whole. Noiriel also draws attention to the polysemy of the term "nationality" in French, which carries different semantic charges in different contexts. Interestingly enough, the term "nationalism" was recorded in French before "nationality", in 1798, when it was used by Abbot Barruel to criticize Jacobinism: "Nationalism ousts love for one's neighbors…It allows for the despising of foreigners and cheating and hurting them."[19] Meanwhile, in France the term "nation" was directly related to the state as the *État-nation*. At the end of the 18th century, post-revolutionary France was compelled to forge a new civil society out of the wreckage of the estates and various regional ethnoi and thus prevent further disintegration. The central nerve of unification processes was found in contrasting France to other countries and peoples, even those with common historical roots.

---

17 Winkler H. A. Germany: 1789-1933. — Oxford: Oxford University Press, 2006. — Vol. 1. — P. 9 -10.

18 Noiriel G. Etat, Nation et Immigration. Paris, 2005.

19 Filippova E. Chto takoe Frantsiya? Kto takie frantsuzi? // Nacionalizm v mirovoi istorii. Moscow: Nauka, 2007. P. 182.

In the 19th century, nationalism was raised as the flag of many European states, including both monarchies and republics. And, of course, it became a template and powerful catalyst for peoples seeking to gain independence (such as against Ottoman rule in the Balkans).

As for philosophical and metaphysical views, the German philosopher Johann Herder, who is considered one of the foundational thinkers of the Counter-enlightenment, argued that peoples are thoughts of God. In contrast to his compatriots, who followed a common trend in clearly suggesting that the European race was superior to others, Herder for his part followed the humanistic tradition of his time based on historical development; he clearly opposed the rationalists (hence his polemic with Kant, and Fichte's rejection of his ideas), and criticized all ideas related to "national superiority" and the domination of some peoples over others. In his words: "Race refers to a difference of origin, which in this case does not exist, or in each of these countries, and under each of these complexions, comprises the most different races. For every nation is one people, having it's own national form, as well as it's own language..."[20] Herder further develops this idea in the eighth book of his voluminous study, *Outlines of a Philosophy of the History of Man*, remarking: "Their own mode of representing things is the more deeply imprinted on every nation, because it is adapted to themselves, is suitable to their own earth and sky, springs from their mode of living, and has been handed down to them from father to son. What is most astonishing to a foreigner they believe they most clearly comprehend; he laughs at things, on which they arc most serious."[21]

At the same time, Herder emphasized: "Thus nations modify themselves, according to time, place, and their internal character: each bears in itself the standard of it's perfection, totally independent of all comparison with that of others."[22] Friedrich Nietzsche, for his part, said that a people is something which "understands itself"[23]

20 John Godfrey Herder, Outlines of a Philosophy of the History of Man (London: Luke Hanfard, 1803), 298

21 Johann Gottfried v. Herder, Outlines of a Philosophy of the History of Man (Bergman, London/New York: 1800/1966), 197.

22 Ibid, 452.

23 Beyond Good and Evil, Aphorism 268

THE NATION-STATE PROJECT

Virtually the whole 20th century passed under the signboard of nation-states. The United Nations is presently considered the most authoritative inter-state tribune. However, are all states "national" in the original meaning of the word? Why are federal entities such as Brazil and Russia and more or less mono-ethnic countries like Poland or Lichtenstein given equal signs in the context of the UN? Do we still find ourselves in a state of illusion as to the "nation" and the "national"? Why is this label still so stable at the same time as many of the European countries where the very concept of nation arose, now have political elites who deliberately condemn manifestations of "nationalist aspirations"? What are the differences and commonalities between "nation", "nationality", and "nationalism"?

The 20th century English philosopher Ernest Barker proposed a global scheme of political organization in which each nation is a state and each state a nation. In the early 20th century, the German historian Friedrich Meineke also divided nations into two types: nation-states and "cultural nations." At the same time, ideas of racial nationalism were developed, and in 1926 the Romanian eugenicist and social hygienist Iuliu Moldovan published his book *Biopolitics*, which has been described as a manifesto for the creation of a totalitarian eugenic state operating on biological principles.[24] Moldovan's book described the nation as a living organism which functions according to biological laws and in which physical qualities and symbols of innate virtue are passed down from generation to generation.

Arthur Moeller van den Bruck noted the problematic nature of the notion of "nation" in the case of German culture, pointing out that the word nation "refers rather to some kind of state of mind or…state formation, such as a Reich or Empire, while both represent something much bigger than a mere 'nation-state.'"[25] According to Max Weber, the nation is "a specific sentiment of solidarity in the face of other groups. Thus, the concept belongs in the sphere of values."[26] At the

24 Iuliu Moldovan, Biopolitica, Cluj, 1926.

25 Mohler A. Die konservative Revolution in Deutschland 1918-1932. Ein Handbuch, Darmstadt, 1989. S. 15.

26 Max Weber, Economy and Society: An Outline of Interpretive Sociology, ed. Guenther Roth and Claus Wittich, 2 vols. (New York: Bedminster, 1968) 2: 2, p. 922.

same time, Weber argued that the "the meaning of the terms 'nation' and 'national' is not unambiguous. Such is imparted with some kind of common quality which constitutes society, whereas the sole goal towards which strives what we call by the collective name 'nationality' is independent statehood."[27]

Anthony Giddens argues that a nation exists only when "a state has a unified administrative reach over the territory over which its sovereignty is claimed."[28] Margaret Canovan, on the other hand, says that the majority of democracies are single-nation nation-states. In order for a state to function properly, she argues, there should be sufficient "feeling" of solidarity between its citizens, and nationhood is the best candidate for creating and maintaining such solidarity. In Canovan's words:

> Thus, a nation is a polity that feels like a community, or conversely a cultural or ethnic community politically mobilized; it cannot exist without subjective identification, and therefore is to some extent dependent on free individual choice, but that choice is nevertheless experienced as a destiny transcending individuality; it turns political institutions into a kind of extended family inheritance, although the kinship ties in question are highly metaphorical; it is a contingent historical product that feels like part of the order of nation; it links individual and community, past and present,; it gives to cold institutional structures an aura of warm, intimate togetherness.[29]

David Miller describes the nation as "a group of people who recognize each other as belonging to one and the same community, who recognize special obligations to each other, and who strive towards political autonomy by virtue of characteristics which they think they share. Usually, this means a common history and attachment to a geographical place and social culture which differs from their neighbors."[30]

27 Weber M. Gesammelte Aufsatze zur Soziologie und Sozialpolitik. Tubingen, 1924. p. 487.

28 Giddens, Nation-State and Violence, volume 2 of A Contemporary Critique of Historical Materialism (Cambridge: Polity Press, 1985), p. 119.

29 Margaret Canovan, Nationhood and Political Theory (Cheltenham, UK: Edward Elgar, 1996), p. 69.

30 David Miller, "Secession and the Principle of Nationality," in Jocelyne Couture, Kai Nielsen, Michel Seymour (eds.) Rethinking Nationalism (Calgary, Alberta: University of Calgary Press, 1996), p. 266.

The German scholar and political scientist Kurt Hübner suggested that a nation is an individual historical and cultural form with a particular historical fate which, like the fate of any entity, can be "told."[31] According to Hübner, the development and formation of the idea of the "nation" has been linked to concepts of the state and sovereignty, but Montesquieu, in his *The Spirit of the Laws*, introduced a kind of denominator by pointing to the common spirit of a given people. This supplied the first clear definition of a nation as a cultural community formed by natural and historical realities.[32] In his history of Osnabrück, Justus Möser developed Montesquieu's idea and laid the foundation for Romantic philosophy affirming the unity of the past, present, and future. He was followed by Herder and his above-mentioned idea that every people has its own "norms, laws, and views of happiness."[33] As follows, there is no universal form of state, and every nation harbors its own blissful center, just as every ball has its own center of gravity. Humboldt subsequently employed biological and organicist categories. In Humboldt's understanding, nations are *Gestalten* and "individuals," towards which an individual person relates as does a leaf to a tree.

The German philosopher Fichte's ideas on the interrelationship between people and language are rather interesting in this regard. Ficthe argued that it is not a people that speaks a language, but a language that speaks through a people. A people is an integral whole of people living with one another in a society and perpetually reproducing themselves in a natural and spiritual way which is, all together, governed by some kind of law of Divine providence of this whole.[34]

The poet and philosopher Novalis considered the state as a "*macroanthropos*" whose substantive carrier is a people. Such a view is close to that of the historian Jules Michelet who, in his *History of France*, assigned countries criteria of personality. In this view, a country has its own character which differs from that of its neighbors and reflects on its past. The country is personified in the nation, which is capable of experiencing the same feelings that a human can, such as pride, shame, happiness, ecstasy, etc.[35]

---

31 Hubner K. Naciya: ot zabveniya k vozrozhdeniyu. Moscow: Kanon+, 2001. p. 52. It is important to note that Hübner's original work was titled *Das Nationale*.

32 Ibid, 121.

33 Ibid, 125.

34 Fichtes. Werke. Berlin, 1971. Bd. VII. p. 381.

35 Filippova E. Chto takoe Frantsiya? Kto takie frantsuzi? // Nacionalizm v

In summarizing the issues confronting the creation of "neutral states" and attempts at unification into something bigger, as in the example of the European Union, Hübner points out that the "notion of a nation can be defined approximately thus: it is a community brought together by feeling, an adequate expression of which can be the neutral state which, as follows, regularly tries to generate a state out of itself."[36] Hübner also insists that "not only the identity of the individual, but also the identity of a nation is a necessary condition for human coexistence."[37] Thus, Hübner speaks of two types of identity - synchronic and diachronic - although both are difficult to define. Thus, "The identity of a nation at a given point in time is characterized by a structured multitude of systems."[38] Therefore, the nation can be a nation-state, a sub-nation, or a cultural nation. A nation-state exists if a nation represents a homogenous totality and has the dominant role in a state. If a state is comprised of multiple people, then this concept implies a unified consciousness. A sub-nation is a nation molded in the likes of national diversity. "Cultural nation" is a term applied regardless of state system.[39] In Hübner's view, a nation is defined by its history. Two nations can therefore speak the same language, but nevertheless not be identical. The example of Latin America is one such case. Thus, Hübner concludes that "identification with a nation is not an act or will or free decision. It is fate."[40]

Hübner published his works just on the eve of the establishment of the European Union, when discussions were ongoing and European integration processes had been launched. Criticizing "contemporary philosophers' blind trampling over the soil of the classical Enlightenment" by hollering about "individual rights" and forgetting about community and history, Hübner concluded that "he who is incapable of revealing the essence of national ties is shut off from access to the higher connection which not only ensures the outward unity of Europe, but holds it together in its depths."[41]

---

mirovoi istorii. Moscow: Nauka, 2007. P. 178.

36 Hubner K. Naciya: ot zabveniya k vozrozhdeniyu. Moscow: Kanon+, 2001. p. 484.

37 Ibid, 291.

38 Ibid, 293.

39 Ibid, 295.

40 Ibid, 345.

41 Ibid, 385.

Stein Ringen defines a nation as a synthesis of people and country. In this view, the nation-state is a country in the form of a political object. Such an approach is quite concise, but it does not reveal the very essence. What's more, historically speaking, nations and nationalisms have been subject to different interpretations.

The American professor Ronald Grigor Suny from the University of Chicago defines a nation as "a group of people who imagines itself to be a political community that is distinct from the rest of humankind, believes that it shares characteristics, perhaps origins, values, historical experiences, language, territory, or any of many other elements, and on the basis of their defined culture deserves self-determination, which usually entails control of its own territory (the "homeland") and a state of its own."[42]

The Many Faces of Nationalism

Although there exist different definitions of nation and nationalism, the initial conditions which gave birth to both nations and nationalisms were the same, namely, the project of the Enlightenment of Western European modernity. The starting point was set precisely there, and later variations (of which there have only been a few) have all been inextricably tied to the cultural particularities, including perceptions of power and statehood, belonging to the peoples who claimed European leadership.

Fernand Braudel recounts that nationalism was the spawn of bourgeois urban culture at the junction of the late Middle Ages and the early Renaissance. At the same time, however, this "Western" nationalism has led scholars of science and technology to deny or downplay Europe's borrowing from China[43] - and, of course, not only China, but other regions of the world which Western European political entities tried to mercilessly exploit at the first given opportunity. According to Alexander Wolfheze:

> In essence, Modern "nations" primarily represent bio-cultural residues, left over in the wreckage of the Traditional order.

42 English translation from http://www.dartmouth.edu/~crn/crn_papers/Suny4.pdf

43 Brodel F. Materialnaya civilizatsiya, ekonomika i kapitalizm, XV-XVIII vv. Vol.1. Strukturi povsednevnosti: vozmozhnoe i nevozmozhnoe. Moscow: Ves mir, 2007. p.354.

> Even where coherent genetic, religious, cultural and linguistic units still existed as *material* realities, however, Modernist Nationalism retains its essential character of a *psychological* phenomenon: it serves as mental "cement", absorbing and shaping the allegiances of populations to the governing elites of the new Nation-States. Operating under the aegis of the ephemeral ideologies of Modernity, these elites had no choice but to resort to psychological trickery. Initially, the Modern Nation-States primarily defined themselves in opposition to the older dynastic states that they sought to replace (e.g. "Germany" and "Italy" as opposed to the Hapsburg Empire, "Greece" and "Serbia" as opposed to the Ottoman Empire). Modernist nationalist ideology assures the allegiance of the workers" and peasant masses to the Nation-State government, even if, in fact, these governments are merely the tools of the bourgeois elite. Nationalist ideologies project the illusion of freedom, equality and brotherhood on all members of the nation.[44]

It is no coincidence that in the late 19th century, Konstantin Leontiev noted in his article "National Policy as a Tool of World Revolution" that "the movement of modern political nationalism is nothing other than the spread of cosmopolitan democratization modified only in method."[45] In Wolfheze's assessment: "Nationalism's primary host was the bourgeois class of merchants and intelligentsia and its spread was greatly facilitated by two other sure symptoms of Modernity: mass literacy and mass education."[46]

The Dutch scholar Alexander Wolfheze thus describes the formation of two types of nationalism in 19th century Europe. The first is directly tied to Romanticism, which "involved an emotional and instinctive reaction against the calculating rationalism imposed upon economic and socio-political life by early Capitalist practice and Enlightenment thought."[47] This type of romantic nationalism was associated with

44 Alexander Wolfheze. The Sunset of Tradition and the Origin of the Great War. Cambridge Scholars Publishing, 2018. P. 271.

45 Leontiev K. Vostok, Rossiya, slavyanstvo. Filosofskaya i politicheskaya publitsistika. Duhovnaya proza (1872 — 1891). Moscow: Respublika, 1996. p. 513.

46 Alexander Wolfheze. The Sunset of Tradition and the Origin of the Great War. Cambridge Scholars Publishing, 2018. P. 273.

47 Ibid, 276.

symbolic motives, idealized visions of the nation, and folkloric popular traditions, heroic archetypes, and mystical ideals, all of which revolved around the "nation" as the source of inspiration. It should be noted that such a type of nationalism was conservative and reactionary, and opposed the modernist liberal ideology of the bourgeoisie that had gained strength at the time. Wolfheze continues:

From 1870 onwards, the idealist content of European Nationalisms was increasingly replaced by materialist content: these transformed Nationalisms re-defined national identity and self-interest in terms of socio-political Social-Darwinism and biological racialism... The most important characteristic of Hyper-Nationalism was its basic *irrationality*, which, given the increasing influence of "public sentiment" on policy making, tended to destabilize international politics... In the Traditional monarchies of Europe the rise of irrational Hyper-Nationalism resulted in an all-permeating atmosphere of deep fatalism and existential fear.[48]

Thus, "The phenomenon of Hyper-Nationalism provides the single most powerful example of the ultimately sub-rational and maliciously-subversive nature of all Modern ideological constructs."[49] The British economist John Atkins Hobson has arrived at the same conclusion from a somewhat different perspective. Hobson writes:

> Turning from this territorial and dynastic nationalism to the spirit of racial, linguistic, and economic solidarity which has been the underlying motive, we find a still more remarkable movement. Local particularism on the one hand, vague cosmopolitanism upon the other, yielded to a ferment of nationalist sentiment, manifesting itself among the weaker peoples not merely in a sturdy and heroic resistance against political absorption or territorial nationalism, but in a passionate revival of decaying customs, language, literature, and art; while it bred in more dominant peoples strange ambitions of national "destiny" and an attendant spirit of Chauvinism.[50]

---

48 Ibid, 277-278, 279.

49 Ibid, 282.

50 English text from http://oll.libertyfund.org/titles/hobson-imperialism-a-study ;

In Hobson's opinion: "The older nationalism was primarily an inclusive sentiment; its natural relation to the same sentiment in another people was lack of sympathy, not open hostility."[51]

The new nationalism was different: first it destroyed empires, and then began employing the methods of imperialism, provoking antagonisms between peoples and unleashing wars over resources, markets, and territories. When national-liberation movements flared up across the Ottoman Empire, their leaders had no idea that their main, future enemy would not be the old empire of Turko-Muslim rule, but their own brothers-in-arms, who immediately after winning their freedom began to claim the territories of their neighbors. Amidst these showdowns, Macedonia in its ethnic borders lost part of its historical lands to Bulgaria (Pirin Macedonia) as well as access to the sea, which was taken by Greece, which, in order to subsequently alter the demographic composition of Aegean Macedonia, resettled Greeks from Asia Minor there following the Greco-Turkish War of 1919-1922.

These conclusions are confirmed by the French social philosopher, Raymon Aron, who argued that the "ideal type of nation-state is that of political unity, all the citizens of which have the same culture and display a desire to live together and independently."[52] But the problem is that this is an idealized view, whereas reality is completely different. For example, what should the criteria in this case be for a monolithic culture? If different vernaculars and dialects, not to mention different kinds of traditional music, dances, clothing, and crafts (all of which are both immaterial and material manifestations of culture), can co-exist in one country, then is it even worth arguing that this state is not a nation-state, specifically if certain groups of its citizens do not manifest a desire to live with the rest of the population? The posing of such a question might seem strange, but it has serious grounds. Pre-2014 Ukraine was "united and gathered" and was composed of numerous regional cultural and historical traditions (which were inscribed in the national culture), and according to official statistics, Ukraine was inhabited by around 100 ethnic groups. The course towards radical nationalization (which had begun earlier) has since led to inter-ethnic conflicts and a number of regions declaring independence. Moreover,

51 Ibidem.

52 Aron R. Izbrannoe: Izmereniya politicheskogo soznaniya. Moscow: Rosspen, 2004. p. 98.

it is hard to speak of any kind of remaining "national unity" on what remains of Ukraine's territory.

Aron posed the right questions as to the essence of "nations" and "nationalism"more than half a century ago when he juxtaposed "a majestic understanding of the role of the nation, or ordinary devotion to the unique values which it embodies."[53] The 19th century showed just what can underly such values, especially when the political and economic capacities of neighboring countries varied, thus yielding the temptation to change the existing layout of borders. Then, in Aron's words, "our nationalism was condemned by another as imperialist…As expansion was taken to be the natural law of states, nationalism easily began to slide towards imperialism, and ideology, as it seemed, began to serve the will to power."[54] This remark of Aron's can easily be confirmed not only by the events of the 19th century, but by recent conflicts as well. When the independent state of Croatia was established during the Second World War, the first thing that supporters of the Ustaše regime did was wage genocide against other ethnic groups, including seizing the territories that they inhabited. Later, Kosovo nationalism grew out of the demographic explosion of the Albanian minority in Yugoslavia and rose as a result of support from the West. Apologists of Ukrainian nationalism argue that the borders of their ideal and imaginary Ukraine extend to the Caucasus and central black earth regions of Russia in the East, while also claiming part of Belarusian lands in the north as well as the territories of neighboring states to the west. The anthem of the Ukrainian even mentions the San and Don rivers, the first of which is in Poland, and the second in Russia.

According to Greenfeld, nationalism is "modern culture. It is the symbolic blueprint of modern reality, the way we see, and thereby construct the world around us." Nationalism "is a fundamentally secular and humanistic consciousness based on the principles of popular sovereignty and egalitarianism." Further, in Greenfeld's opinion, "To claim that nationalism is the modern culture is tantamount to saying that it represents the cultural foundation of modern social structure, economics, politics, international relations, educations, art science, family relations, and so on and so forth."[55]

53 Ibid, p. 99.

54 Ibid.

55 Greenfeld L. Nations and Nationalism. 2005. Vol. 11. №3.

Insofar as "nation" is generally understood to mean the spiritual, cultural, social and political community of one people, then out of the discourse on "nation" and "nationalism" arise additional notions that are crucial to state and international activities, such as "national interests" and "national values." In turn, these are tied to scholarly schools of international relations. Therefore, if one sees the borders of their imagined nation far beyond the boundaries of their existing state, then this affects the work of the entire state machine and society to the extent that nationalist ideas penetrate the latter. Thus, in general terms, nationalism can be defined as "an ideological concept and derivative political practice based on the fact that collective communities that fall under the term nation are natural and legitimate foundations for the organization of states, their economic, social, and cultural life. Members of a nation should demonstrate their devotion, while the state and leaders insist upon and put above all else the interests of the nation."[56] Nationalism isolates culture in order to focus attention on it in its anthropological metathesis as a way of life and in its aesthetic meaning in art.[57] As a rule, nationalism is usually divided into civic and ethnic nationalisms. The American sociologist of Jewish origins, Hans Kohn, has proposed the additional term "political nationalism", while the American social psychologist and professor Michael Billig has introduced the term "banal nationalism." At the same time, one can encounter discussions of "liberal", "state", and "cultural" nationalisms.

In his 1944 work, Hans Kohn differentiated nationalisms according to geographical-civilizational type, thus proposing to distinguish between Western and Eastern forms of nationalism. Kohn's ideas were developed to link civic nationalism to Western Europe, ethnic nationalism to Eastern Europe, and to juxtapose between liberal and universalist nationalism on the one hand, and ethnic and particularist (referring to specific values), non-liberal nationalism on the other. The criteria for nation and nationalism, what's more, can vary greatly depending on region, historical traditions, and cultural and worldview foundations. In this regard, the main criteria of the Western type of nationalism are: (1) the existence of nations as self-sufficient units; (2)

56 Nacionalizm v mirovoi istorii, Moscow: Nauka, 2007. p. 24

57 Gregory Jusdanis, The End of Literary Narratives? in Novel and Nation in the Muslim World. Literary Contributions and National Identities (ed. Elisabeth Özdalga, Daniella Kuzmanovic) Palgrave Macmillan, 2015. P. 21.

the right to self-determination; (3) the nation as the source of authority; (4) self-identification; (5) solidarity; (6) universal education; and (7) the nation as the highest value.

Modernists thus argue that nations and nationalism emerged with the development of capitalism. As old collective identities, such as religion and tribe, were either destroyed or saw their roles rapidly reduced, a new identity was chosen to replace them which is associated with a unified culture and, to a certain extent, planned political economy. The modernist school includes the theorists of constructivism, which presents the ethnos as a construct created by the intellectual influence of individuals (cultural and power elites). Thus, by means of manipulation, "ethnic" traditions are artificially created and inculcated. The Western theorists of this school include Benedict Anderson, Pierre Bourdieu, Ernest Gellner, Eric Hobsbaum, and the American sociologist Roger Brubaker.

Ernest Gellner identified the following imperatives that compelled modernist nationality to be formed out of ethnic identity: (1) a politically centralized industrial society, which is (2) mobile in terms of its prevalence on a time scale from several generations to several days; (3) a growing need for effective means of communication for the transmission of diverse and complex information; (4) the requirement of long-term training for a significant proportion of professions; and (5) this training is based on a common set of basic knowledge and skills that can be acquired only within the cultural infrastructure of a major political unity, and are impossible in an isolated family or village.[58]

Modernist theories are becoming less effective in our day and age. The German sociologist Niklas Luhmann, citing Benedict Anderson's argument that the nation is first and foremost "an imaginary unity which should be imparted with reality"[59], adds that the notion of "nation" earlier justified military conscription (and death in war) without assuming special preferences from the state for citizens in return (for example, universal suffrage). But now, according to Luhmann, we are in the final phase of this idea which now produces more harm than good. Such "harm" can also be detected in the serious

58 Gellner E. Natsii i natsionalizm. p. 35.

59 Luman N. Samoopisaniya. Moscow: Logos/Gnosis, 2009. p. 198.

problem of ethnonationalism, upon which is often superimposed religious identity. Ethnonationalism has repeatedly led to outbreaks of violence in various countries, such as in the USSR during its collapse, and later in Russia. As a rule, these are artificial constructs, vivid examples of which include the contemporary ideology of Ukrainian nationalism and attempts at creating a "Russian nationalism" which has an essentially anti-state character.

On the other hand, a correct approach to ethnicity can allow for a state system to be constructed in which each people would feel safe, would be in demand for the state, and would have the opportunity to exercise freedom of creativity. As the Russian sociologist and ethnologist Svetlana Lurie writes: "ethnicity remains, but thanks to some mechanisms, all have found a common language both together and separately."[60]

Attempts at formulating this were undertaken by the Eurasianists in the 20th century. In his article, "On True and False Nationalism"[61], Nikolai Trubetzkoy identified several false versions of nationalism. The first is when the identity of a culture is of no significance, and only the seizure of state independence is of interest. Insofar as state independence by itself, according to Trubetzkoy, is meaningless, and seeing as how some national movements sacrifice themselves for such, then such a nationalism is not only a false one, but is harmful and is driven by petty vanity. Another form of false nationalism is militant chauvinism, which denies the equal value of other peoples and cultures. The third type of false nationalism comes from cultural conservatism, which equates national identity to historical artifacts and previously established values. Such a type of nationalism leads to cultural stagnation, because it denies the possibility of peoples' psyche changing. All three of these types of false nationalism can combine with one another to produce mixed types. True nationalism, for Trubetzkoy, is built on self-recognition. For example, Trubetzkoy called the USSR a particular, multi-ethnic nation which wielded its own kind of nationalism. This "Eurasian nationalism" was said to be based on common historical destiny, not ethnic, linguistic, or religious kinship.

60 Lurie S. Imperium. Tsennostniy i etnopsihologicheskiy podhod. Moscow: AIRO-XXI, 2012. p. 224.

61 Trubetzkoy N. Ob istinnom i lozhnom nacionalizme/ / Ishod k Vostoku. Predchuvstviya i sversheniya. Utverzhdeniya evraziytsev. Sophia, 1921, p. 71-85.

Overall, the Eurasianist school insisted on authenticity and represented a case of relativism[62] which stood in contrast to the social and economic evolutionists, who insisted on progress and the backwardness of social formations and thereby laid the foundations for race theory and the division of all peoples into "civilized" and "barbaric." The Eurasianist approach offers the possibility to develop positive approaches to "national" issues.

The methodology of deconstruction can offer an additional alternative to understandings of the concept of "nation." The Latin word *natio*, from which "nation" descends, primarily encompasses the notion of "birth." *Natio*, after all, meant the goddess of birth. The very root *nat-* refers to natural origin. It follows, nation is none other than "those born" or "the totality of the born." Another Latin term semantically similar is *genitus* (birth), which is related to the term *gens* (kin, clan, or *narodnost'* in Russian, i.e., "nationality" or the "quality of being of a people"). In its original interpretation, international law is *jus gentium*, not *inter-national*. Such etymological subtleties have unfortunately been forgotten, but they can serve as additional grounds for redefining the various concepts that appear to be inadequate in the present period.

Nations and Nationalism Beyond Europe

The "non-West" has also developed its own concepts of nation and nationalist ideologies. Although the influence of Western modernity has been by all means glaring, more than once attempts been made to develop original, authentic concepts with references to preceding philosophers and theologians. To begin, let us consider several concepts from the Arab world and Muslim thinkers.

The Arab philosopher Abd al-Rahman al-Kawakibi defined "nation" not as a "collection of sleeping creatures, the totality of the slaves of the usurper-ruler", but as a "community of people bound together by commonality of race, language, homeland, and laws."[63] Abd Al-Aziz Duri has posited that the concept of an "Arab nation" consists of four interrelated identities. The first is the current understanding, which

62 Relativism is an analytical method which affirms that all knowledge and convictions are relative.

63 Aliev A. «Nacionalnoe» i «religioznoe» v sisteme mezhgosudarstvennih otnosheniy Irana i Iraka v XX veke. Moscow, 2006. p.79.

is based on ethnic principles, including tribal structure, and the role of Islam in the Arab geographical space. In addition, he numbers the philosophical thought and literary work of various Arab writers, as well as popular consciousness. Duri points out that the idea of an Arab nation first arose in the late Umayyad era, when the empire began to encounter external threats.[64] Duri identifies the referential source of such to be a statement by Abd al-Hamid, secretary to Marwan Ibn Muhammad, in his work *Ila I-Kuttab*, where he draws an analogy between the Umayyads and the Arab Empire and writes: "Do not let even a strand of the Arab Empire fall into the hands of a non-Arab clique."[65] Al-Tawhidi (d. 1024) in turn argued that the Arabs compose a nation with their own special qualities and virtues.[66]

A more detailed and structured understanding of the nation was offered by Ibn Khaldun. In his opinion, there should be more than one condition, be it religion or ethnos, for the foundation of a nation. Environmental factors influence way of life, skin color, and other physical peculiarities as well as the formation of character and various habits. In the example of various pre-Islamic peoples, Ibn Khaldun shows that the disappearance of a state does not necessarily entail the disappearance of a nation, which depends on a people's spirit of solidarity (*asabiyyah*).[67] Language is also an important factor. According to Ibn Khaldun, one does not need to be an ethnic Arab, as the very use of the Arabic language is enough to not doubt one's belonging to the Arab nation. Ibn Khaldun thus divides the Arabs into several groups: the "lost" tribes (*ba'ida*), the "pure" Arabs (*ariba*) and the "assimilated" Arabs (*musta'riba*), and the "followers" of the Arabs (*tahi'a*), all of whom can be called Arabs insofar as they speak Arabic.[68]

---

64 A.A. Duri, The Historical Formation of the Arab Nation. A Study in Identity and Consciousness. Volume I. Beckenham: Centre for Arabic Unity Studies, Croom Helm, 1987, P. 97.

65 'Abd al-Hamid al-Katib, Ila l-Kuttab, ed. Muhammad Kurd 'Ali in his Rasa'il al-bulagha', 2nd ed. (Dar al-kutub al-misriya, Cairo, 1913), p. 221.

66 A.A. Duri, The Historical Formation of the Arab Nation. A Study in Identity and Consciousness. Volume I. Beckenham: Centre for Arabic Unity Studies, Croom Helm, 1987, P. 106

67 Ibn Khaldun, Muqaddima, Vol. I (Bulaq, Cairo, AH 1247) 123.

68 A.A. Duri, The Historical Formation of the Arab Nation. A Study in Identity and Consciousness. Volume I. Beckenham: Centre for Arabic Unity Studies, Croom Helm, 1987. P. 112.

The Grand Mufti of Russia, Rawil Gaynetdin, has suggested that for Muslims the notion of "nation" is related to such terms as (1) *shaab*, or a people united by common territory, and language, (2) *qabila*, or a tribe unified by kinship ties, and (3) *Ummah*, i.e., a community or large group of people united by ties of spiritual kinship and religious confession.[69]

The term Ummah is most widespread and is used in many countries to emphasize unity among Muslims. However, such an interpretation appeared only in the 20th century. Earlier, Al-Farabi (d. 950) drew a distinction between the Ummah, by which he designated "nation" in an ethnic sense, and *milla*, referring to followers of a particular religion. Al-Masudi (d. 956) upheld the same distinction.[70] This point is indirectly confirmed by the Turkish word for "nationality", *milliyet*, which is a loan from Arabic inherited during the era of the Ottoman Empire, whose subjects included not only Turks, but also Arabs, berbers, Kurds, Slavs, and other peoples.

In G.G. Kosach's opinion, Arab-Muslim culture, the self-consciousness of such and the psychology of such as a stable group, can be identified as the Arab nation (*al-ummah al-Arabiya*). Such is qualified as an eternal, unified community wielding a natural space, i.e., the "Arab fatherland" (*al-Watan al-Arabiy*).[71] This space was once united, which thus lends grounds to speak of the possibility of its reconstruction, and stretched from the Atlantic Ocean to the Persian gulf. The "Arab fatherland" was not and has not become a single state, but the peoples inhabiting this space's countries are the peoples composing the "Arab nation." Here it is necessary to distinguish between Arabic two terms: *bilyad*, which denotes a political and socio-cultural reality, and *al-qutr*, which refers to a temporal reality that can be abolished or liquidated. In these terms, the reconstruction of unity (*al-Wahda*) of Arabs is the task of an Arab national movement.

---

69 Gainutdin R. Islam i natsiya // Vera. Etnos. Natsiya. Religiozniy komponent etnicheskogo soznaniya. Moscow: Kulturnaya revolutsiya, 2009. p. 219.

70 A.A. Duri, The Historical Formation of the Arab Nation. A Study in Identity and Consciousness. Volume I. Beckenham: Centre for Arabic Unity Studies, Croom Helm, 1987. P. 110.

71 Kosach G. Arabskiy nacionalizm ili arabskie nacionalizmi: doktrina, etnonim, varianti diskursa. Natsionalizm v mirovoy istorii. Moscow: Nauka, 2007. p. 259.

In the modern era, one "apologist" of Arab nationalism was the Syrian Christian N. Azuri, who in 1905 published the pamphlet *Reveil de la Nation Arabe dans l'Asie Turque* in Paris. In this work, Azuri proclaimed the self-determination of the Arab national movement and demanded independence from the Ottoman Empire. These ideas developed in the context of liberation movements in different regions and accordingly acquired unique variations. In the context of 20th century secularism, the main emphasis was therefore on Arab, rather than Muslim identity. In 1950, in his work *Arabism above All*, Sati al-Husri remarked that "Arabism is belonging to a geographical space, the 'Arab homeland', and appealing to the Arabic language as the language of communication and mutual understanding. Arabism stands above religious restrictions."[72]

The Iranian view of the nation also boasts its own unique features. Before the Islamic Revolution, Iran under the Shah was heavily influenced by Western scholarly theories, which effectively formed the dominant school. "In the dialectic of the confrontation between the mainly Western ideology of nationalism and Islamic traditionalism, a new approach took shape which found expression in the ideas of Morteza Motahhari...Motahhari presented the nation as an evolving community residing in constant motion. He thus denied the existence of any permanent and unchanging foundations that are immanent to a nation and which form its 'spirit.'"[73]

Ayatollah Motahhari based his theory on the notion that Iranians have historically manifested an intrinsic "natural morality" - when the Zoroastrian religion became untenable, it was defeated by Islam. When the Iranians became Muslims, this contributed to the development of "natural talents", the establishment of social justice, and the spiritual and social unity of the Iranian people. Islam did not supplant the historical and civilizational subjectivity of the Iranian nation, but rather acted as the pivotal element of this subjectivity. If we take into account the flourishing of all kinds of religious-philosophical

72 Ibid, 319.

73 Gibadullin I. Dialektika vzaimodeistviya islamskoy ideologii i iranskogo natsionalizma na primere idey ayatolli Mortazi Motahhari. Natsii i nacionalizm v musulmanskom mire (na primere Turcii, Irana, Afganistana, Pakistana, etnicheskogo Kurdistana, sosednih stran i regionov), Moscow: IV RAN, 2014. p. 16. http://book.ivran.ru/f/nations-n20141117f.pdf

schools in Iran after the spread of Islam, including Sufi traditions and the development of various forms of visual art, then this explanation is quite logical and rational. Motahhari recognized the existence of an Iranian nation and even established such as exceptional, thus lending the notion of nation content which is not restricted to national frameworks, but rather assumes the level of pan-Islamic unity and, further, presupposes solidarity between anti-imperialist forces around the world.[74]

The concept of "returning to self", in Motahhari's opinion, was the unique allegory of national awakening and the rebirth of the Iranian people when it realized that it "had its own doctrine and independent thought and is capable of standing on its feet and relying on its own strength."[75] Discussing the "return to self", Motahhari uses allegories to define the situation in Iranian society, in particular "confusion", "self-alienation" (*khodbakhtegi*) and "stupor" (*estesba*) to describe the psychological mood of Iranians in the pre-revolutionary period under the influence of Western colonialism. Motahhari argues that the worst form of colonialism is cultural (*este'mar-e farhangi*), where "in order to take advantage of someone, they take away their individuality and place before all what they believe to be their own, and then leave them to be fascinated by what the colonizers have offered."[76]

Besides Ayatollah Morteza Motahhari, the main theoreticians of Iranian religious-national identity were Ali Shariati and Mehdi Bazargan. If for Motahhari a moderate and peaceful nationalism leading towards cooperation and social ties between people is consistent with Iranian-Islamic national identity[77], then Ali Shariati defined the nation and nationality in terms of culture and therefore saw a close link between these terms and religion. Following this line, Shariati argued that over the past 14 centuries the two histories of Islam and Iran have been so mingled that it is impossible to seek out an Iranian identity without Islam or an Islamic identity without the strong Iranian presence within it. In Shariati's opinion, these two elements, *Irān-e Eslāmi*, together

74 Ibid, p. 17.

75 Motahhari M. On the Islamic Revolution (Peyramoon-e Enghelab-e Eslami), Tehran, Sadra Publications 1993, P. 45.

76 Ibidem. P. 160 – 161.

77 Mortażā Moṭahhari, Ḵadamāt-e moteqābel-e Eslām wa Irān, 8th ed., Qom, 1978. pp. 62-67.

constitute Iranian identity. Therefore, Shariati believed that cultural and national alienation can only be overcome by confidence in the Iranian nation and the support of its Shiite culture.[78] During the critical transition between the fall of the Shah and the rise of the Islamic Republic, Bazargan remarked that "opposing Islam and Iranian nationalism to one another is tantamount to destroying ourselves. Denying Iranian identity and holding nationalism to be non-religious is an integral part of the anti-Iranian movement and is the work of anti-revolutionaries."[79]

The London University professor of Iranian origin Arshin Adib-Moghaddam uses the term "psycho-nationalism" to describe the phenomenon of the Iranian nation. A member of the Iranian diaspora raised in the West and a supporter of liberal ideas, Adib-Moghaddam believes that Iranian society has developed differently than European societies:

> In fact, in Europe the nation as an idea to die for was invented in the laboratories of the enlightenment and the book traces this ideological history. In Persia, the idea of a coherent nation was institutionalised in the 16th century by the Safavid Dynasty. As in any other country…the birth of the so-called nation was rather arbitrary, violent and full of myths about natural origins and roots.[80]

Adib-Moghaddan writes in his book, *Psycho-nationalism: Global Thought, Iranian Imaginations:* The Iranian revolution was a hybrid phenomenon. The revolutionaries were not nationalists in the traditional sense of the term. In fact, the leader of the Iranian revolution Ayatollah Khomeini was against the forms of Persian nationalism espoused by the ancient regime. And yet, the Iranian state, as it was institutionalised after the revolution couldn't fully escape the legacies of psycho-nationalism in the country. The political formula for power remained similar. There was a clear boundary between the sanctioned ideology of the state and those placed outside of it. The state adopted a sacrosanct hegemonic position that demanded the sacrifice of the populace for the

78 Ali Šariʿati, Bāzšenāsi-e howiyat-e irāni-eslāmi, Tehran, 1982. 72-73.

79 Mehdi Bāzargān, "Nahżat-e żedd-e irāni," in Keyhān, 23 Šahrivar 1359/14 September 1980, cited in Dr. Maḥmud Afšār, "Waḥdat-e melli wa tamā-miyat-e arżi," Ayanda 6/9-12, 1980, p. 655.

80 Interview – Arshin Adib-Moghaddam, E-IR, July 26, 2018 http://www.e-ir.info/2018/07/26/interview-arshin-adib-moghaddam-2/

sake of the nation, codified in terms of the "oppressed", the umma or Iranians more specifically. Of course, the tropes and metaphors changed from the Shah's orthodox Persian nationalism and they took a rather more potent religious, theocratic and explicitly transcendental colouring after the revolution. But this emphasis on the nation as a sacred project continued and the state remained the sanctioned ideal that everyone should be cognitively obliged to. This is psycho-nationalism par excellence. Yet at the same time there is a nuance and difference to the situation in Europe and North America. In Iran, psycho-nationalism is not imbued with a systematic grammar of racism. This genealogical and biological emphasis on difference that was developed in the laboratories of the European enlightenment, never really turned into a systematic movement in Persia, not least because Muslim political thought and philosophy is – at its ideational epicentre – anti-racist.[81]

But psycho-nationalism is not an exclusively Persian-Iranian invention. In Adib-Moghaddam's opinion, psycho-nationalism is in contrast to traditional studies of nationalism, focused on the cognitive impact of the form of mental violence and represents the psychology of a way in which the nation is constantly invented and introjected into our thinking as something for which one should kill and die. It is thanks to such psycho-nationalism and the sub- or unconscious of societies susceptible to it that Europe is seeing the resurgence of right-wing movements.

In the 19th century, India was also home to numerous discussions on identity and the country's place in the world. "Indian nationalists genuinely 'imagined' [their] nation, first and foremost because a united country of India, especially within the borders of the modern republic…had never existed before."[82] The ideology and practice of Indian nationalism began with Westernized activists taking up the study of history, cultures, and languages. This initial stage was accompanied by Bengali reformers' establishment of the Society for the Acquisition of General Knowledge in Kolkata in 1838. One prominent figure of this reform movement was Krishna Mohan Banerjee, a Bengali brahmin

81 Arshin Adib-Moghaddam, Psycho-nationalism: Global Thought, Iranian Imaginations. Cambridge University Press, 2017.

82 Vanina E. Proshloe vo imya budushego. Indiyskiy nacionalizm i istoriya (seredina XIX - seredina XX века). Nacionalizm v mirovoy istorii. Moscow: Nauka, 2007. p. 491.

who adopted Christianity as a sign of protest. In his treatise *On the Nature and Importance of Historical Studies*, Banerjee called for the rationalization of historical knowledge to search for means to exalt the country and its people.[83]

In his 1902 work *The Voice of India*[84], Maithili Sharan Gupt used the term *Hindu jati* and employed the traditional epic narrative approach to idealize the past, which is followed by a decline described in the Mahabharata, with the spread of Buddhism and Jainism, the invasion of "non-Aryans" and the arrival of Muslims, and the Hindu homeland resultantly plunging into darkness. The concept of *Jati* was proposed to mean "nation." The fallaciousness of this was pointed out in 1913 by B.C. Pal, who argued that the notion of nation did not exist in pre-colonial India.[85] Pal is correct from an etymological point of view, since the term *Jati* is the distorted English form of *Jaatihi* (जातिः in Sanskrit), which means descent, caste, or class. In 1909, however, Mahatma Gandhi argued: "We were one nation before they [the English] came to India." In Gandhi's words, Indians' "farseeing ancestors…saw that India was one undivided land so made by nature. They, therefore, argued that it must be one nation. Arguing thus, they established holy places in various parts of India, and fired the people with an idea of nationality in a manner unknown in other parts of the world."[86] It should be noted that Gandhi specifically used the term *Swaraj*. Thus, the notion of Indian nationalism was directly associated with the concept of *swaraj*, which can be translated as "self-governance." *Swaraj* represents "a metabolic principle as well as a principle of political action."[87] Aurobindo Ghose, an Indian philosopher and one of the founders of the national liberation movement, argued that "nationalism came to the people as a religion…nationalism lives by virtue of the divine force encapsulated in it…Nationalism is immortal, because it originates not from man, but is god manifesting himself."[88]

83 Banerjee K.M. On the Nature and Importance of Historical Studies; Delivered...

84 Gupta M. Bharat bharati. Chirganv, 1954.

85 Pal B.C. Nationalism and Politics // Life and Works of Lal, Bal and Pal. P. 295.

86 Gandhi M.K. Hind Swaraj // The Moral and Political Writings of Mahatma Gandhi / Ed. R. Iyer. Oxford, 1986. Vol. I. P. 221.

87 Joseph S. Alter. Gandhis Body. Sex, Diet, and the Politics of Nationalism, University of Pennsylvania Press, 2000, XI.

88 Erasov B. Socialno-kulturnie traditsii i obshestvennoe soznanie v razvivayushihsya stranah Azii i Afriki странах Азии и Африки. Moscow:

Another important element of Indian nationalism is Hindutva, a notion derived from the book of the same name written by Vinayak Damodar Savarkar, the ideologist of Hindu communalism, while in prison in 1923. Savarkar considered Hindutva as a set of principal, generic features of the constructed Hindu "nation", belonging to which is determined on the basis of territory, blood (Aryan descent), culture (classical Sanskrit), and religion (Hinduism).[89] According to Savarkar, the whole subcontinent is the birthplace of "one nation" - that of the Vedic Aryans. Religion was assigned a less important role in the theories of Madhav Sadashiv Golwalkar, who believed that the Aryans did not come to India, but were the indigenous population. Despite the emergence of other religions, he called the Hindus the most noble people. Both Savarkar and Golwalkar picked up the idea of an "Aryan race" that had been developed by European Orientalists, writers, and theorists.

At the same time, however, India has seen the parallel development of concepts of both Hindu and Muslim nations, the latter of which was actively employed in the creation of the independent state of Pakistan. Moreover, other theorists have insisted on the priority of Bengali culture. Chattopadhyay, for instance, said that "Bengali genius has shone most brightly."[90]

States and Nations in the 21st Century

In practically all states, governments in one way or another try to "catalogue" all the ethnoi existing on the territory of their country. Insofar as there exist very few mono-ethnic states, and insofar as, in the very least, there are state-forming peoples and minorities, state authorities have an interest in constantly controlling and receiving reliable information on processes related to this or that ethnos, especially if its representatives live abroad. "States try to grasp their citizens through a classification network and identify in both ethnic as well as other (gender, social, religions, etc.) regards."[91]

Nauka, 1982. p. 142.

89 Vanina E. Proshloe vo imya budushego. Indiyskiy nacionalizm i istoriya (seredina XIX - seredina XX века). Nacionalizm v mirovoy istorii. Moscow: Nauka, 2007. p. 512-513.

90 Ibid, p. 507.

91 Scott J. C. Seeing Like a State. p. 83

In the early 20th century, Carl Schmitt wrote: "It [the nation] can will arbitrarily. The content of its willing has always the same legal value like the content of a constitutional definition. Therefore it can intervene arbitrarily – through legislation, through the administration of justice, or simply through concrete acts. It becomes the unlimited and illimitable bearer of the iura dominationis [rights/legal prerogatives of rulership], which do not even have to be restricted to cases of emergency."[92] Now, however, the situation is different.

The role of national policies differ depending on the structure and type of state. In one case, the nationalism of one group can be supported to the detriment of others, whereas in another case, the identity of all groups is eroded. For example, "ethnic nationalism in Latvia is a functional tool of the ruling elite for preserving ethnopolitical stratification and inequality, and is also a necessary peripheral means for maintaining European economic inequality in the conditions of economic crisis."[93] As for another example, in the words of Michael Mann: "When we talk about 'African nationalism,' for example, that is not really an accurate label, for it was a racial protest movement against the white colonial power…Their own identity was racial rather than national. But as they developed their state they tried to develop a national identity and a nation-state. Since they thought that successful countries were nation-states, they sought to emulate them."[94]

The EU model, as well, as predicated on the erasure of traditional national identities, has also been oriented towards the creation of artificial groups. In particular, in 1993 the Norwegian Ministry of Defense, Johan Holst, proposed to deter nationalism by providing citizens with numerous identities (from "local" to "European") and by creating communities across borders.[95] Since then, studies have shown that certain efforts to destroy previous identities have borne fruit. For example, the majority of students from Eastern European countries who

92 Carl Schmitt, Dictatorship: From the origin of the modern concept of sovereignty to proletarian class struggle (Polity, 2014), p. 123.

93 Rodin Y. Etnopoliticheskie konflikti i natsionalnaya identichnost Latvii. Riga, 2013. p. 54.

94 Michael Mann, Power in the 21st Century: Conversations with John A. Hall (Polity, 2011). pp. 46,47.

95 Holst J. J. European Security in the Era of Ambiguity. Norwegian Atlantic Committee. P. 3

have passed through the ERASMUS program prefer to call themselves "Europeans", as opposed to Bulgarians, Hungarians, etc.[96]

Be that as it may, to conclude this chapter, it is necessary to make one last important remark. For the majority of states in the world, the term "nation" is of foreign origin. Western Europe, where "the nation" and "nationalism" ultimately took shape out of Hellenistic philosophy and Roman law, is in geographical terms but a small peninsula of Eurasia. But over the past several centuries, the whole world has come to internalize this small peninsula's narrative.

96 Oborune K. Becoming more European after ERASMUS? The Impact of the ERASMUS Programme on Political and Cultural Identity // Epiphany, 6 (1), 2005.

11

Strategic Cultures and Civilizations

Although the concept of "nation" has different interpretations, it remains an altogether narrow notion that is limited by both a temporal range (the epoch of Modernity), the spatial habitat of a given people, as well as what are often rigidly fixed borders. With "peoples" too, as a rule, a dilemma often arises. A characteristic example of such is the case of Latin America. For instance, the Quechua Indian tribes live across the territories of Peru, Bolivia, Ecuador, Argentina, Colombia, and Chile. At the same time, these countries are inhabited by the descendants of Spanish colonizers. Another example is that of the confrontation between Taiwan and China, or between the Republic of Korea and the Democratic People's Republic of Korea. These cases are rather paradoxical, since they concern one people that once lived together in a single political space. Hence, in recent time theories of nations and nationalism have increasingly referred to "identity politics", which is a broader concept that can, in the very least, be applied to more narrow definitions, such as with regards to religious groups or ethno-tribal organizations.

The Psychological Particularities of Peoples and Strategic Culture

Identity, as related to state power, historical traditions, customs, religion, ethnic groups, and national interests, is encapsulated in the umbrella concept of "strategic culture." Although the latter, in its classical understanding, is related to war and conflict (as its very name suggests)[1], there is every reason to consider strategic culture as something larger than military-political thinking, defense planning,

1 If war is taken as a norm intrinsic to humanity as such, then there is nothing strange in the posing of such an equation.

or the use of armed force.[2] First and foremost, this idea is tied to the theory of realism in international relations, insofar as it speaks of the right of might, the rational actions of the state as akin to man, as well as national interests. However, as strange as this may sound, strategic culture does not evaporate in those states which assert liberal values and employ the theory of liberalism in international relations. Strategic culture may be less pronounced in these states, and its elements may be veiled by specific rhetoric which covers concepts that are common to and widespread in different cultures and regions. But this does not detract from the practical actions of states and their consequences. At the same time, some states may manifest similar strategic cultures, which can allow them to unify into a group even if they otherwise consist of different peoples speaking different languages.

Strategic culture is commonly understood to be "a persistent system of values held in common by the leaders or group of leaders of a state concerning the use of military force."[3] Strategic culture is therefore directly related to conflict, as, according to one of this concept's authors, Alastair Johnston, strategic culture is centered around responses to three key issues: the role of war in international relations, the nature of enemies and the threats which they might pose, and the use of force.[4] This concept is therefore extremely important for inter-state and international relations, especially during periods in which an existing order is transformed or the balance of forces is altered. Strategic culture is also tied to questions of sovereignty and security, economics and political systems, as well as religion and ethnic traditions. Johnston, basing himself on the work of Clifford Geertz, offers the following development of the notion: "Strategic culture is an integrated 'system of symbols (e.g., argumentation structures, languages, analogies, metaphors) which acts to establish pervasive and longlasting strategic preferences by formulating concepts of the role and efficacy of military force in interstate political affairs, and

2 As an alternative, we propose the term "Inmost Strategic Culture." This qualification points to the deepest and innermost elements of state strategy associated with the ethnic and ideological systems of peoples.

3 Andrew Scobell, "Soldiers, Statesmen, Strategic Culture and China's 1950 Intervention in Korea" // Journal of Contemporary China 8, no. 2, Spring 1999. P. 479

4 Alastair Iain Johnston, Cultural Realism: Strategic Culture and Grand Strategy in Chinese History, Princeton: Princeton University Press, 1995.

by clothing these conceptions with such an aura of factuality that the strategic preferences seem uniquely realistic and efficacious." [5]

The term "strategic culture" itself was introduced into modern political science in the late 1970's by Jack Snyder who, in a special study commissioned by the Pentagon, claimed that the Soviet approach to nuclear strategy differed significantly from the American approach.[6] However, the Iranian scholar Cyrus Faizee notes in his work that:

> [E]ven in old times great enemies had a strategic culture and respected its principles as by enmity, they meant to show a logical level of hostility, not a savage and uncivilized behaviour aiming to exterminate the resources and achievements of human civilization. We already know that the United States and the Soviet Union reached the maximum level of ideological animosity during John F. Kennedy's presidency, but finally the leaders of the two countries observed the limits of hostility and tried to rationalize it. Perhaps the main reason for this behaviour was that such an excessive degree of enmity was not "constructive" and could degenerate into a duel which would destroy the whole world.[7]

If we attempt to overcome the American view on strategic culture, which is focused on questions of organizing war and handling conflict-related decisions, then, arriving at the deeper level of "inmost strategic culture", we can "spin" the potential for conflict in a positive direction, avoid mistakes, misunderstanding, and bias, and act according to the principle of "win-win", not a zero-sum game.

The concept of strategic culture appeared relatively late. However, a number of scholars before spoke of differences in the psychology of peoples as playing a leading role in the shaping of behavior, including in the international arena. Usually mentioned in this regard are the

---

5 Alistair Iain Johnston, Thinking about Strategic Culture// International Security 19, no. 4 (1995): 46; Clifford Geertz, The Interpretation of Cultures. New York: Basic Books, 1973.

6 Jack Snyder, The Soviet Strategic Culture: Implications for Limited Nuclear Operations, R-2154-AF. Santa Monica: RAND, September 1977.

7 Cyrus Faizee, Strategic Culture in the Confrontation between Iran and Israel-United States// 26 February 2012 http://www.tisri.org/default-1059.aspx

Ancient Greek thinker Thucydides and the Chinese philosopher Sun Tzu, who are known for their works on military operations, their analysis of the reasons for the outbreak of such, and their tactical and strategic cunning. The father of medicine, Hippocrates, also said that differences in the character of people depend on climate and geography. The Byzantine Emperor Maurice, in his work *Strategikon* (dated to the 7th century A.D) on the art of war, devotes one of the chapters to techniques of warfare among different peoples. However, it is only after the emergence of psychology as a science, with its anthropological branch, that we can speak of the beginning of systematic analysis of the "conceptual fields" of different peoples, such as with regards to the use of military force.

The initiators of such a special branch of psychology were Moritz Lazarus and Heymann Steinthal, who in 1860 treated "folk psychology" (*Völkerpsychologie*) or "folk spirit" as a special, closed entity which expresses the psychic convergence of the individuals belonging to a certain nation, and as their self-consciousness itself. This "folk psychology" was supposed to be discoverable by way of the comparative study of language, mythology, morality, and culture. Lazarus and Steinthal tried to prove that language, religion, law, art, science, lifestyle, mores, etc. acquire ultimate expression in the psychology of a given people as the bearer of the collective mind, will, feelings, character, temperament, etc. According to this understanding, all phenomena of social life are a kind of "emanation of the folk spirit." The task of the psychology of peoples as an autonomous science is therefore to psychologically discern the essence of the spirit of a people, and reveal the laws in line with which the spiritual activities of peoples operate. In the opinion of these authors, folk psychology "rests in the following tasks: (1) psychologically discerning the essence of a folk spirit and its actions; (2) discovering the laws according to which the internal, spiritual, or ideal activity of a people proceeds in life, art, and science; and (3) discovering the grounds, causes, and reasons for the emergence, development, and destruction of the peculiarities of this or that people."[8]

Wilhelm Wundt imparted this trend with a more realistic view by proposing a program of empirical studies of language, myths, and customs, a kind of "sociological of everyday consciousness." In his

8 Shpet G. Vvedenie v etnicheskuyu psihologiyu. SPb: Aleteya, 1996. pp.19–20.

version of folk psychology, the latter is treated as a descriptive science which does not claim to discover or establish any laws, but instead records the peculiarities of the "deep layers" of the spiritual life of people. For Wundt, folk consciousness is a "creative synthesis" of individual consciousnesses that generates a qualitatively new reality to be found in the products of supra-individual activities. According to Wundt, there is a rather clear triadic structure observable in such products related to language, myths, and customs. Wundt pointed out: "Language, myths, and customs are common spiritual[9] phenomena so closely fused with one another that one of them is unthinkable without the other…Customs expresses in actions those views of life which lurk in myths and are made into common property through language. And these actions in turn make more durable and further develop the ideas from which they stem."[10]

At the turn of the 19th-20th centuries, ethnopsychology did not exercise particular influence on military strategy and policies. However, interest in ethnopsychology rose dramatically during the Second World War. Impetus was given to the instrumentalization of ethnographical and anthropological studies to serve military and political strategy following the publication of *The Chrysanthemum and the Sword* by the American anthropologist Ruth Benedict. The latter book studied the worldview of the Japanese people in response to the demand for such by Washington during the Second World War. As Ruth Benedict herself admitted, she was assigned to study Japan in June 1944. The author concluded: "The Japanese are, to the highest degree, both aggressive and unaggressive, both militaristic and aesthetic, both insolent and polite, rigid and adaptable, submissive and resentful of being pushed around, loyal and treacherous, brave and timid, conservative and hospitable to new ways. They are terribly concerned about what other people will think of their behavior, and they are also overcome by guilt when other people know nothing of their misstep."[11] Thus emerged one variant of distinguishing between peoples in the case of Japan and the West, in this case concerning two types of culture: guilt and shame. In the 1960's, the famous

9 In English translations of Wundt's works, the adjective "spiritual" is replaced with the term "mental."

10 Wundt W. Problemi psihologii narodov. Moscow: Librokom, 2010. p. 226.

11 Ruth Benedict, The Chrysanthemum and the Sword: Patterns of Japanese Culture (New York: Mariner/Houghton Mifflin, 2005), 2-3.

Japanese professor and specialist on international relations, Kinhide Mushakoji also suggested that Western and Eastern societies have different perceptions in processes of communication.[12] Moreover, Japan is also home to the phenomenon of *amae*, which is characteristic of hierarchical relationships. This term was introduced into wide circulation by the psychologist Takeo Doi in 1971 in his book *The Anatomy of Dependence*, and the word *amae* itself can be translated as "dependence on the benevolence of others." This is one of the foundational concepts for understanding Japanese society.

Negotiations proceed differently in the highly-contextual societies of the East than they do in the low-contextual societies of the West. The Western active style (or *erabi* style, from the verb "to choose") is distinguished by its unwavering belief that a person is free to manipulate the environment for the sake of his own goals. The Japanese "harmonizing" style (or *awase* style, from the verb "to adjust" or "to attune") reflects the notion that a person is capable of controlling the environment, but presupposes a unity with it. The Japanese language, according to the scholar and translator Kunihiro Masao, is first and foremost interested in feeling out the mood of the interlocutor so that a course of action can be developed on the basis of impressions.[13] The Japanese thus rely less on explicit linguistic expressions than on intuitive, non-verbal communication. Because of the pressure exerted by the structure of the "vertical society", opinions are expressed as impersonally as possible, and generally in line with group consensus. Kunihiro, however, probably pays too much attention to the uniqueness of the Japanese language, whereas it is the Japanese "worldview", conveyed in both oral and non-verbal language, that might be misunderstood by people from other national cultures.[14]

---

12 Kinhide, Mushakoji, "The Cultural Premises of Japanese Diplomacy," originally published in Japanese in 1967. Reprinted in The Silent Power, The Simul Press, Tokyo, Japan, 1976

13 Kunihiro, Masao, "The Japanese Language and Intercultural Communication," originally published in Japanese in 1967. Reprinted in The Silent Power, TheSimul Press, Tokyo, Japan, 1976.

14 Verner Bickley, Cross-cultural, cross-national education: the greatest resource. Culture Learning Institute Report Vol. 5, No. 4, East-West Culture Learning Institute, Honolulu, Hawaii, Oстober 1978. P. 4. https://scholarspace.manoa.hawaii.edu/bitstream/10125/17432/1/CultureLearningInstituteReport_1978_v5_n4%5Bpdfa%5D.pdf

Richard Nisbett categorically states that a kind of complex whole, understood more collectively rather than in parts, and subject more to collective than to individual control, is typical of the Asian world. For a typical Westerner, the world is a relatively simple living space consisting of discreet objects which are perceived regardless of context and subject to personal, individual control. Thus, in his opinion, "American children are learning that the world is mostly a place with objects, Japanese children that the world is mostly about relationships."[15]

Furthermore, if for a Western person all events take place thanks to an actor, then for an Easterner, "happenings" are the result of concerted actions by several entities or the interaction of a person with some field of forces. In addition to this approach, which is structured around an opposition between West and East (in this case represented by Japan), there are a number of other models of characteristics that can be applied to analyze conflict situations and political planning, as well as to understand the fact that there exists a plurality of different societies and civilizations.

Not One, But Many

John Gray argues that "the propensity to cultural difference is a primordial attribute of the human species; human identities are plural and diverse in their very natures, as natural languages are plural and diverse, and they are always variations on particular forms of common life, never exemplars of universal humanity."[16] Gray considers the various currents of the Counter-Enlightenment of the 18th-19th centuries to be the beginning of an alternative philosophical anthropology which affirms that human nature is only partially determined; otherwise, people are capable of self-determination and creating diverse and unique forms of identity. Thus, Gray introduces the term "agonistic liberalism" as "an application in political philosophy of the moral theory of value-pluralism – the theory that there is an irreducible diversity of ultimate values (goods, excellences, options, reasons for action and so forth) and that when these values come into conflict or competition with one another there is no overarching

15 Richard Nisbett, The Geography of Thought: How Asians and Westerners Think Differently...and Why (New York: Free Press, 2003), 150.

16 John Gray, Enlightenment's Wake: Politics and Culture at the Close of the Modern Age (New York: Routledge, 1995) ,98.

standard or principle, no common currency or measure, whereby such conflicts can be arbitrated or resolved."[17]

Pluralism of values has been discussed by the modern philosopher Joseph Raz as "ultimate and ineliminable." Raz argues: "Value pluralism is the doctrine which denies that such a reduction [to the value of feeling happy, or having one's desires satisfied] is possible. It takes the plurality of valuable activities and ways of life to be ultimate and ineliminable."[18] As for well-defined typologies, the American sociologist Talcott Parsons proposed a division into four types of society:

- A society of a universal model for achievement, which is characterized by the aspiration of a large portion of the population to achieve success. The functioning of this type of society is determined by the instrumental values and actions of people pursuing a concrete benefit, as well as by status and role characteristics of people, and their chances at promotion and a career. The US is seen as an example of this type of society.

- A society of a universal model for ascription, which is characterized by a tendency towards the establishment of totalitarian and authoritarian regimes which dictate to the population values and behavioral norms in all spheres of life-activities, and which exercise rigid social control. The status and role characteristics of people are determined depending on the results of collective actions. According to the American sociologist, the Soviet Union and Fascist Germany were examples of this type of society.

- A society of a particularistic model for achievement, characterized by a desire on the part of the majority of the population to achieve particular goals in various spheres of life-activities. The economy of this type of society is, as a rule, monocultural. The status and roles of people are determined by family and communal relations. Ancient China might serve as an historical example of this type of society.

17 Ibid, 103.

18 Quoted in ibid, 104; Joseph Raz, Ethics in the Public Domain: Essays in the Morality of Law and Politics, Oxford: Clarendon Press, 1994.

- A society of particularistic model for ascription, in which there is no orientation towards achievements, and where ascriptions have a restricted character, as the population is characterized by a passive and even negative attitude towards work. Statuses and roles are determined by traditional ways of life and established dictatorial regimes. Typical examples of this societal type are said to be Latin American countries.

Not only sociologists, but also specialists on various types of conflicts continue to appeal to Parsons' ideas to this day.

Another American sociologist, Edward Hall, proposed the terms "high-context" and "low-context" cultures, according to which the former conduct communication in a way so that the greater part of information is present in a general context and is internalized by the parties involved (i.e., knowledge passes from the subjective to the objective for society), and the information directly transmitted by means of words or symbols is relatively small. In low-context cultures, communication is constructed in the opposite manner. Basic information is conveyed verbally, and the general context carries a lower volume of information. Therefore, the different sides have no internalized community. High-context cultures therefore rely more on context than words. For them, order, the observance of hierarchy, and respect for status are more significant, and the history of previous relationships and common rituals, traditions, and future are important. Low-context cultures prefer verbal communication, and strive to express their thoughts as accurately as possible. Of course, the qualifiers "high" and "low" are relative terms and are not loaded. High-context cultures include: African and Arab countries, Brazil, China, Francophone Canada, France, Greece, India, Indonesia, Italy, Japan, Korea, Latin America, Pakistan, Iran, Russia, the Southern states of the US, Thailand, Turkey, Vietnam, and the countries of the Southern and Eastern Slavs. Among low-context cultures figure: Australia, Holland, Anglophone Canada, England, Finland, Germany, Switzerland, the Northern states of the US, Sweden, and Norway. It is important to note that both types of culture can coexist within one country and, as follows, there is the potential for mutual misunderstanding and conflicts.

As we can see, Parsons' cultural paradigms and Hall's contextual cultures point towards the necessary existence of different models for socio-political affairs. In this light, the theory of liberalism in international relations, which until recently claimed to be universal, a priori cannot be accepted as a global mechanism for regulating political processes in the world. The sociologist Ann Swidler proposed a more complex model for relationships between culture and state behavior grounded in the culture of "action strategies." Swidler defines culture in general as consisting of "symbolic vehicles of meaning, including beliefs, ritual practices, art forms, and ceremonies, as well as informal cultural practices such as language, gossip, stories, and rituals of daily life."[19] In view of this approach, the variability of societies increases even more significantly.

The psychological sciences associated with management and leadership must also be taken into account in state administration. The most successful organizations are those which demonstrate a strong cultural foundation that is not always revealed to the external observer. Organizational psychology, as shown in the work of Edgar Schein, suggests that only those organizations with leaders who know their culture and develop it can be the strongest. Organizational psychology also affirms that most organizations are not conscious of their culture and, as follows, either lose it over time, or their leaders lose control.[20] The maintenance of culture in all of its diversity, and its adaptation to changing conditions, is therefore an art.

Civilizations

Even more problematic, in our opinion, is the term "civilization", which is, on the one hand, associated with identity, but which also possesses a wider geographical and historical scale. If we pose the question of a comparative analysis of the term "civilization", then, according to the International Society for the Comparative Study of Civilizations, there exist approximately thirty definitions of this phenomenon, some of which are directly contradictory. Therefore "civilization" is a complex, debatable, and open question.

Conclusions on the fate of the future world order depend on which side of civilizational theory we stand. Nevertheless, if we engage in

19 Ann Swidler, "Culture in Action: Symbols and Strategies," American Sociological Review 51, no.2 (April 1986): 273.

20 Edgar Schein, Organizational Culture and Leadership. Volume 2 of The Jossey-Bass Business & Management Series. Edition 4, John Wiley & Sons, 2010

a retrospective analysis, then three seminal typologies are obvious at the heart of civilizational theories. The first is the notion of civilization as some kind of social formation of "better quality." This quality "belongs" to Western societies, hence the confrontation between "Western civilization" and the "backwardness" of all other countries and peoples. The second theory, related to the first, expresses the contrast between Western civilization and the rest from the standpoint of criticizing the West. Value assessments, as a rule, change, and now the West looks like a dead-end of human evolution. As a rule, such theories are typical among Muslim thinkers, but some Western scholars too have recognized the decadence of Western civilization. The third theory argues that there exists not one (Western), and not two (Western decadent and its opposite) civilizations, but that the world is home to (and always has been) a number of different civilizations, some of which are similar, others of which differ sharply. Civilizations can exercise mutual influence, enter into conflicts, and/or find themselves in a state of symbiosis.

Civilization as a Discursive Tool of Western Politics

The notion of civilization was introduced into broad scholarly circulation in the late 18th century by the Scottish philosopher Adam Ferguson, who meant by this a stage in the development of human society characterized by the existence of social classes, cities, writing, and other phenomena. The preceding stages, according to this thinker, were savagery and barbarism. In his *Essay on the History of Civil Society*, Ferguson remarked: "This progress in the case of man is continued to a greater extent than in that of any other animal. Not only the individual advances from infancy to manhood, but the species itself from rudeness to civilization."[21] A similar approach was subsequently taken up by many scholars, especially in Soviet times, due to the fact that this view was maintained by Friedrich Engels. This imperative wields influence to this very day, hence such expressions as "civilizational approach", and "civilized society", etc. Around the same time, a similar idea was expressed by the English scholar, John Boswell.

21 https://oll.libertyfund.org/titles/ferguson-an-essay-on-the-history-of-civil-society; Accessed in Russian in: Benvenist E. Civilization. Contribution a l'histoire du mot // Obshaya lingvistika. Moscow: URSS, 2010.

The German sociologist Norbert Elias argued that the concept of civilization "expresses the self-consciousness of the West", and: "By this term Western society seeks to describe what constitutes its special character and what it is proud of: the level of its technology, the nature of its manners, the development of its scientific knowledge or view of the world, and much more."[22] Elias notes further:

> But 'civilization' does not mean the same thing to different Western nations. Above all, there is a great difference between the English and French use of the word, on the one hand, and the German use of it, on the other. For the former, the concept sums up in a single term their pride in the significance of their own nations for the progress of the West and of humankind. But in German usage, *Zivilisation* means something which is indeed useful, but nevertheless only a value of the second rank.[23]

As is characteristic of the German school, Elias shares Spengler's distinctions between culture and civilization, suggesting that civilization signifies a process or, at the very least, the result of a process. If civilization "plays down" national differences, insofar as the "concept of civilization has the function of giving expression to the continuously expansionist tendency of colonizing groups, the concept of *Kultur* mirrors the self-consciousness of a nation which had constantly to seek out and constitute its boundaries anew, in a political as well as a spiritual sense, and again and again had to ask itself: 'What really is our identity?'"[24]

Examining the origins of the contrast between culture and civilization, Elias cites Kant's 1784 *Idea for a Universal History from a Cosmopolitan Point of View*, which reads: "The ideal of morality belongs to culture; its use for some simulacrum of morality in the love of honor and outward decorum constitutes mere civilization." In other words, according to Kant, civilization is a special kind of behavior, even if it is artificially created with the aim of legitimizing social status.

---

22 Norbert Elias, The Civilizing Process: Sociogenetic and Psychogenetic Investigations (Oxford: Blackwell, 2000), 5.

23 Ibid, 6.

24 Ibid, 7.

The sociogenesis of the notion of "civilization" is seen analogously in France. "The first literary evidence of the development of the verb *civiliser* into the concept *civilisation* is to be found, according to present-day findings, in the work of the elder Mirabeau in the 1760s."[25] Maribeau wrote:

> I marvel to see how our learned views, false on all points, are wrong on what we take to be civilization. If they were asked what civilization is, most people would answer: softening of manners, urbanity, politeness, and a dissemination of knowledge such that propriety is established in place of laws of detail: all that only presents me with the mask of virtue and not its face, and civilization does nothing for society if it does not give it both the form and the substance of virtue.

Elias thus summates:

> Concepts such as *politesse* or *civilité* had, before the concept *civilization* was formed and established, practically the same function as the new concept: to express the self-image of the European upper class in relation to others whom its members considered simpler or more primitive, and at the same time to characterize the specific kind of behaviour through which this upper class felt itself different from all simpler and more primitive people."[26]

This, let us note, means that people from the very same state or nation were seen as backward "barbarians" in the eyes of court-aristocratic and bourgeois circles. If earlier the upper class in all regions of Europe fundamentally opposed the lower strata, the "mobs", then in the epoch of bourgeois revolutions, the idea appeared that all of society could be "finished up" and led to the state of "civilization." It was often under this idea that the bourgeoning bourgeoisie fought against caste restrictions and everything that might interfere with their trade and interests. "The consciousness of their own superiority, the consciousness of this 'civilization', from now on serves at least those nations which have become colonial conquerors, and therefore a kind of upper class to large

25 Ibid, 33-34.

26 Ibid, 34.

sections of the non-European world, as a justification of their rule, to the same degree that earlier the ancestors of the concept of civilization, *politesse and civilité*, had served the courtly-aristocratic upper class as a justification of theirs."[27] Thus, Elias argues that "civilization" was needed by the West in order to extend its power and influence to other regions of the world through a system of coercion and subordination in various forms. He emphasizes: "In this way civilizing structures are constantly expanding within Western society; both the upper and lower strata are tending to become a kind of upper stratum and the centre of a network of interdependencies spreading over wider and wider areas, both populated and unpopulated[28], of the rest of the world."[29] The "spread of civilization" is therefore the penetration of Western institutions and behavioral standards into other countries. Non-Western countries can voluntarily join this process insofar as they see the need for their own survival, the point of which is not only the borrowing of technical skills, but also forms of "civilized" behavior which allow them to enter the network of interdependencies. But the center of this network remains occupied by the people of the West.

In fact, what Norbert Elias was describing is what is now called "globalization", although the latter author arrived at these conclusions in the interwar period. In the present time, criticisms of Western civilization in its "exclusive form" have only intensified. For example, Raymond Aaron notes that "suspected, explicit racism could not endlessly resist the opening up of the greatness of other civilizations or the obvious fragility of European supremacy."[30] Hamid Dabashi from Columbia University argues that the idea of Western civilization was for European nations a kind of umbrella structure asserting the universal identity of European national cultures and to "unify these cultures against their colonial consequences." Dabashi thus surmises:

> Islamic, Indian, or African civilizations were invented contrapuntally by Orientalism, as the intelligence arm of

27 Ibid, 43.

28 The Russian translations reads "colonized and un-colonized": Elias N. O processe civilizatsii. Vol. 2. Moscow: Universitetskaya kniga, 2001. p. 256.

29 Norbert Elias, The Civilizing Process: Sociogenetic and Psychogenetic Investigations (Oxford: Blackwell, 2000), 381.

30 Aron R. Izbrannoe: Izmereniya politicheskogo soznaniya. Moscow: Rosspen, 2004. p. 97.

> colonialism, in order to match, balance and thus authenticate 'The Western Civilization.' All non-western civilizations were therefore invented exactly as such, as negational formulations of the western, thus authenticating the western. Hegel subjected all his preceding human history into civilizational stages leading to the Western Civilization, thus in effect infantilizing, Orientalizing, exoticizing and abnormalizing the entire human history...[31]

Western civilization itself, in the opinion of Western scholars, is the product of the mixing of two traditions that arose in the ancient world: the Judeo-Christian and the Greco-Roman.[32] Insofar as the apogee of Western civilization is represented by the US, the theories of American scholars have constantly been analyzed in terms of their possible justifications for the US' geopolitical dominance. Such was the lot of the American historian Carroll Quigley, who believed expansion to be a necessary element in the history of civilizations. Quigley distinguished seven stages of development: (1) mixture, (2) gestation, (3) territorial expansion, (4) conflict, (5) universal empire, (6) decay, (7) invasion and conquest. Insofar as Quigley's works coincided with the Cold War, his theory was associated with the Anglo-Saxon civilizational paradigm inclined towards external aggression. Quigley argued: "After centuries of expansion our society is now organized so that it cannot subsist; it must expand or it will collapse."[33]

Metahistorical Analysis

In his work *The Decline of the West*, Oswald Spengler unequivocally denies that the world's space is homogenous from the standpoint of anthropology, sociology, and politics. Spengler writes: 'Mankind,' however, has no aim, no idea, no plan... 'Mankind' is...an empty word. But conjure away the phantom, break the magic circle, and at once there emerges an astonishing wealth of actual forms."[34] Spengler speaks

31 Dabashi Hamid. For the last time: civilizations. Rethinking civilizational analysis// Intern. sociology - L., 2001. - Vol. 16, N3 (Special issue), P. 364.

32 Marvin Perry. Western Civilization. A Brief History. Volume 2: From 1400s. Boston: Wadsworth, 2013. P. XXV

33 Quigley C. The Evolution of Civilizations: An Introduction to Historical Analysis. Indianapolis, 1961. p. 141.

34 Oswald Spengler, The Decline of the West (New York: Alfred A Knopf, 1926), pp. 21.

of a "a number of mighty Cultures...each stamping its material, its mankind, in its own image; each having its own idea, its own passions, its own life, will and feeling."[35] For Spengler, moreover, culture and civilization are different. When a culture stagnates and ceases to be active, it turns into a civilization. Spengler says: "The Civilization is the inevitable destiny of the Culture...Civilizations are the most external and artificial states of which a species of developed humanity is capable. They are a conclusion...They are an end, irrevocable, yet by inward necessity reached again and again."[36]

Is this indeed the case? While it can definitely be said that there exists an Alanian-Ossetian culture, has it turned into a civilization? Has it become petrified to the point of becoming part of a civilization covering the Caucasus region? What about the cultures of the Basques, the Kurds, the various Finno-Ugric ethnoi? After all, they are unique, alive, and active, but have we heard of the presence of civilizations of these peoples?

Spengler falls into the trap of linear time and progress. For example, he proposes to understand the Romans exclusively as heirs of the Hellenes. He also considers expansion, including by dint of military force, to be a fundamental marker of civilization or, as Spengler put it, "Imperialism is Civilization unadulterated."[37] Expansion is therefore seen by Spengler as a tendency of any mature civilization.

Spengler also rather arrogantly and haughtily believed that his *The Decline of the West* was some kind of "non-philosophical philosophy" of the future, "the last that West Europe will know."[38] Despite Spengler's erudition, the extensive materials that he summoned to his work, and despite the fact that his works peaked a certain interest that continues to this day, it was nonetheless Martin Heidegger that would put a period behind Western philosophy - and more convincingly and scientifically soundly.

The superficiality of Spengler's arguments can be traced in his attempt

35 Ibid.

36 Ibid, 31.

37 Ibid, 36.

38 Ibid, 45.

to mark cultures with certain tags. Following Friedrich Nietzsche, Spengler proposed to distinguish three types of culture, which he called Apollonian, Faustian, and Magian. Apollonian culture refers to an ancient epoch in which, in Spengler's view, the single, corporeal body was the ideal type of "expression-space" or duration.[39] The Faustian is based on pure, limitless space, and its "body" is Western Culture. The Magian soul, according to Spengler, is "aloof", such as "Arabian Culture with its algebra, astrology and alchemy, its mosaics, and arabesques, its caliphates and mosques, and the sacraments and scriptures of the Persian, Jewish, Christian, 'post-Classical', and Manichaean religions", and "Kismet."[40]

However, the idea of infinity is rather characteristic of the Indian tradition, which, along with other Eastern cultures, does not fit into Spengler's triad. Indeed, the attempt to sweep Arabic culture out into the periphery betrays an overt Eurocentrism, whereas historically Europeans borrowed many ideas and technological innovations from the Arabs.

Moreover, although he criticizes Hegel in the beginning of the first volume of *The Decline of the West* for having "declared so naively that he meant to ignore those peoples which did not fit into his scheme of history"[41], Spengler himself did not want to note the influence of Asian cultures, and he completely "forgot" Africa and pre-Columbian America. The only justification for such is the name of the book itself, insofar as it deals mainly with Europe and the West. However, this inconsistency is also evident in the second volume, where Spengler postulates: "For me, the 'people' is a unit of the soul…Neither unity of speech nor physical descent is decisive."[42] According to Spengler, peoples can change their language, race, name, and country of origin, and a people differs from a population by means of the inner experiencing of the concept of "We." Only a few paragraphs later, Spengler offers a definition of race which rejects the Darwinian approach, and reflects his definition of a people: "In race there is nothing material, but something cosmic

39 Such a case is, in the very least, demonstrated by Spengler's own superficial knowledge of the works of ancient philosophers.

40 Oswald Spengler, The Decline of the West (New York: Alfred A Knopf, 1926), pp. 183, 307.

41 Ibid, 22.

42 Ibid, 165.

and directional, the felt harmony of a Destiny, the single cadence of the march of historical Being."[43]

How, then, can peoples change their race? One attempt at adjusting this approach or, more precisely, at developing a broader conceptualization, was undertaken by Arnold Toynbee. Like Spengler, Toynbee denies that there exists only one single civilization or mankind. Toynbee writes: "This thesis of the unity of civilization is a misconception into which modern Western historians have been led by the influence of their social environment."[44] Toynbee points to three main factors that have led to this interpretation. The first factor is that modern Western civilization has spread its economic system across the whole world, which has been accompanied by political unification. The UN is seen as part of the Western political system. The second reason is the mistaken thesis of continuity - for example, Minoan civilization is seen as the beginning of the Hellenic, and the Hellenistic is treated as the embryo of Western civilization. Thus arises the illusion of linearity according to which the sources of Western civilization can be traced back to the "primitive society' of the Neolithic. The third problem is that of a selectivity towards different societies, some of whom, for one reason or another, are not fitted into the civilizational framework invented by Western scholars, and are excluded from the picture as "barbaric" or "decadent." For example, from this point of view Orthodox Christianity is a kind of temporary "growth" on the body of Western society. "Having exhausted its function, this growth atrophied and disappeared, just as the gills and tail are shed by a tadpole at the stage of turning into a frog,"[45], Toynbee writes, adding that the "egocentric illusion in Western consciousness" is compacted by the false notion of the 'unchanging East' encompassing Islam, Hinduism, and Far Eastern civilization under the nondescript epithet 'oriental.'[46]

Here it is also possible to mention the Shamanism and Tengrism of Asian Siberia and Mongolia, the scattered pockets of Zoroastrianism from Iran and Tajikistan to India, and the various Polynesian cults. In Western consciousness, all of the latter are treated as exotic, archaic

43 Ibid, 165.

44 Arnold J. Toynbee, a Study of History: Abridgment of Volumes I-VI by DC. Somervell (Oxford: Oxford University Press, 1987), p. 114.

45 Ibid, 88.

46 Ibid, 116.

remnants, not living traditions directly tied to the socio-political structures of many countries.

Another observation made by this British scholar concerned monotheistic religion, coupled with his important hinting at the polycentricity of cultures. "A uniform understanding of a one true God is impossible, for human nature is stamped with fruitful diversity, which is the hallmark of divine works."[47] Another, no less important thesis of Toynbee's was his pointing out that Western culture is in crisis, and has lost its authority and monopoly:

> [The societies of the species called civilizations will have fulfilled their function when once they have brought a mature higher religion to birth; and, on this showing, our own Western post-Christian secular civilization might at best be a superfluous repetition of the pre-Christian Graeco-Roman one, and at worst a pernicious back-sliding from the path of spiritual progress. In our Western world of today, the worship of Leviathan— the self-worship of the tribe— is a religion to which all of us pay some measure of allegiance; and this tribal religion is, of course, sheer idolatry.[48]

Elsewhere, Toynbee suggests: "In the quarter of a millennium that has passed since the revolution of the 17th century, modern Western civilization has shown not only its light side, but also its dark side, and in our time this dark side is darker than the darkest spot on the pages of Western history of the middle ages and even the era of religious wars."[49]

With these remarks in mind, let us return to consider how Toynbee defined civilization. In total, Toynbee numbered 23 flourishing civilizations, four delayed in earlier stages of development, and five underdeveloped civilizations. The first generation of civilizations includes the Egyptian, the Andean, the Sumerian, the Minoan, Indic, the Shang, and Mayan. The second generation of civilizations is related to these early ones: the Babylonian (based on the Sumerian), the Hittite

47 Ibid, 539.

48 Arnold Toynbee, Civilization on Trial (New York: Oxford University Press, 1948), 235.

49 A. Toynbee. Civilizatsiya pered sudom istorii (Moscow: Airis-Press, 2003), p. 214.

(also based on the Sumerian), the Hellenic (based on the Minoan), the Syriac (also Minoan), Indian (Indic), the Chinese (Shang), the Yucatan (Mayan), and the Mexican (also based on the Mayan). The third generation, which is of direct relevance to modern peoples and states, is represented by the Orthodox Christian (based on the Hellenic), the Russian branch of the Orthodox Christian (Hellenic) civilization, Western civilization (also traced back to the Hellenic), Arab Muslim (based on the Syriac), Iranian Muslim (also Syriac), Hindu (Indian), the Far Eastern (Chinese), and the Japanese branch of the Far East (Chinese). Eskimo, nomadic, Ottoman, and Spartan civilizations are discerned as having been held up in their development, while the First Syriac, the Far Eastern Christian, the Far Western Christian, and Scandinavian civilizations, as well as the constellation of medieval city-states, are "abortive civilizations."

Even a superficial analysis of this category shows that Toynbee's methodology is quite controversial. Toynbee justified his approach with the caveat that his criteria for identifying civilizations are not uniform: "In some cases this is material culture, in others religion, and in still others, race."[50] But obvious questions still arise. Why is Iranian civilization said to belong to Syriac, and not Persian civilization? How is Scythian culture to be characterized? As is well known, there were both nomadic and sedentary Scythians. And why have the peoples of the Caucasus, the autochthonous cultures of Southern Latin America and the Pacific Ocean disappeared from the historical map? Where are the peoples and cultures of Sub-Saharan Africa? It is quite telling that Toynbee did not figure black Africa into his list at all, even though he repeatedly mentioned different African peoples, such as in the context of their oppression by the West. In the end, Toynbee counted five remaining civilizations in the 20th century: Western civilization, Orthodox-Christian, Islamic, Hindu, and Far Eastern. Thus, he writes that "though the [Western] unification of the world has been finally achieved within a Western framework, the present Western ascendancy in the world is certain not to last."[51]

If anything, Toynbee's opinion on Russia is of interest. Toynbee believed that Russia had "beheld" three civilizations in its history:

50 Ibid, 234.

51 Ibid, 158.

Scandinavian, Byzantine, and Western, the latter of which Russia experienced in two forms - Liberal and Marxist. The impact of Asian civilization, or rather the phenomenon of the Golden Horde and its influence on the formation of Russian statehood, is completely overlooked. Nevertheless, Toynbee's futuristic prognosis has turned out rather correct, as when he wrote:

> But we do not know what effect this political heirloom in Russia's Byzantine heritage is going to have on Russia's fortunes now that she has to make the momentous choice between taking her place in a Western world or holding aloof and trying to build up an anti-Western counter-world of her own. We may guess that Russia's ultimate decision will be deeply influenced by the sense of orthodoxy and sense of destiny which she has also inherited from her Byzantine past. Under the Hammer and Sickle, as under the Cross, Russia is still 'Holy Russia' and Moscow still 'The Third Rome.' *Tamen usque recurret*.[52]

Toynbee is also quoted as saying: "In 1961 it is still impossible to predict whether 20th century Western communist ideology will achieve greater successes than 17th century Western liberal ideology in casting Byzantine civilization out of Russia."[53] Today, we can definitely affirm that Byzantinism has, in updated form, reemerged and seized a revanche in Russia.

After Arnold Toynbee, the topic of civilizations was taken up in a new study, in its relationship to material culture and economics, by the French historian Fernand Braudel. Unlike Oswald Spengler, Braudel did not divide culture and civilization, but considered them equal. More precisely, Braudel considered culture to be the primordial achievements of man, and civilization to be the further success of such. In the first volume of his principal study, *Civilization and Capitalism, 15th-18th Century*, Braudel calls civilizations "strange collections of commodities, symbols, illusions, fantasms and intellectual schemas."[54] In the second volume, Braudel elaborates further: "Civilizations or cultures - either

52 Ibid, 182-183.

53 Moetis Meotida, "Toynbee o Rossii i Zapade" (10/23/2006) https://meotis.livejournal.com/74898.html

54 Fernand Braudel, Civilization and Capitalism, 15th-18th Century, Volume I: The Structure of Everyday Life (University of California Press, 1992), 333

word can legitimately be used in this context - are great reservoirs of habits, constraints, accumulated lore, accepted practice and statements which may seem, to the individual, personal and spontaneous, but which have really been handed down from a great distance. They are as much our inheritance as the language we speak."[55]

Like Toynbee, Braudel was rather skeptical of Western society, pointing out much of the West's lexicon's borrowing from the Muslim world and East:

> This is suggested by the Islamic words taken into the western vocabulary: douane = customs (Italian *doana*, from the Arabic), *fonduk*, *magasin*, *mohatra* (forward selling, immediately followed by resale, which the fourteenth-century Latin texts relating to usury called *contractus mohatrae*). and further evidence comes from the gifts Europe received from the East: silk, rice, sugar cane, paper, cotton, Arabic numerals, the abacus, Greek science rediscovered through Islam, gunpowder, the compass - all of them precious goods which Europe passed on in turn. To admit the existence of these borrowings means turning one's back on traditional accounts of the history of the West as pioneering genius, spontaneous inventor, journeying alone along the road towards scientific and technical rationality.[56]

At the end of the second volume, Braudel poses the question: "After all why should one civilization be more intelligent and rational than another for all time?"[57] A more critical approach contends that civilization is the accumulated experience and fully deserved result of experience and misconception, that civilization is the sum of experience which, partially in the form of explicit knowledge, is passed down from generation to generation, evermore embodied in the tools and institutions proving its viability.[58]

Less widely known than Toynbee and Braudel is the Polish historian and philosopher Feliks Koneczny, who defined civilization as a

55 Fernand Braudel, Civilization and Capitalism, 15th-18th Century, Volume II: The Wheels of Commerce (University of California Press, 1992), 555.

56 Ibid, 556.

57 Ibid, 581.

58 Hayek F.A. The Constitution of Liberty. Chicago, 4 Aufl. 1971. S. 60.

method of the structuring of collective life. Koneczny did not associate civilizational types with certain races or nations and, interestingly enough, Koneczny related Poles to the Turanian civilizational type, and Germans to the Jewish type, while ethnic Jews themselves could represent the Latin type of civilization. Koneczny considered early 20th century Europe to be the site of clashes between the Latin, Turanian, and Jewish civilizations, while he saw Byzantine civilization as being in deep crisis. Koneczny proposed the current existence of nine civilizations, seven of which are historical civilizations (Chinese, Brahmin, Jewish, Turanian, Byzantine, Latin, and Arab) and two are local (Berber and Tibetan). Overall, in this thinker's opinion, a total of 22 historical civilizations have existed.[59] Koneczny attempted to develop the systems approach to the theory of civilizations, giving due credit to the contributions of the French historian François Pierre Guillaume Guizot, who in the early 19th century published his two books *A General History of Civilization in Europe* and *A History of Civilization in France*. It is important to note that Koneczny's scientific methodology was based on a plural approach.[60]

Continuing the topic of the multiplicity of civilizations, according to the classification of the Polish-American scholar Andrew Targowski there are currently eight civilizations in existence in the world: the Chinese, Hindu, Islamic, Japanese, Buddhist, Eastern, African, and Western. Targowski distinguishes four sub-divisions of the latter: Western-West, Western-Center, Western-Latin, and Western-Jewish. Meanwhile, the Czech sociologist Jaroslav Krejci correlates the term civilization with cultural and socio-economic structure, ethnicity, and statehood, leading to a list of "civilizations" which are quite differentiated despite many of them having common roots and similar traits.[61]

If we add to these classifications the criterion of way of life, then the picture becomes even more complex. For example, if we distinguish

59 Dianova V. Teoriya civilizatsiy Felixa Konechnogo: svoeobrazie i smislovie paralleli. // Vestnik Associatsii filosofskih fakultetov i otdeleniy, 6(1), 2015. pp. 155-166.

60 Feliks Koneczny, O wielości cywilizacyj, Gebethner & Wolff, Kraków 1935. English translation (abridged) On the Plurality of Civilisations, Polonica Publications, London 1962, Antyk, Komorów, 2012

61 Jaroslav Krejci. The Paths of Civilization : Understanding the Currents of History, Gordonsville: Palgrave MacMillan, 2004.

there to be a nomadic civilization, then it would be no less reasonable to raise the question of hunter-gatherer civilizations, such as in Australia, that of the Arctic sea-hunters and fishermen, and so on. In other words, all types of human cultures could be characterized as civilizations.[62]

Dual Typologies of Civilizations

Radical Islamic ideologies typically divide the world into two types of civilizations - Islamic society and the *Jahiliyyah*, the latter including all Western societies and their surrogates. The follower of Sajjid Kutb, A. Yassin, argued that "Western civilization is devoid of any values besides pragmatic ones considered in money and investments... Their religion is military power, strategic balance, strategic interests, and geopolitical domination."[63] Another Muslim thinker, Abul A'la al-Maududi, believes that Islamic society submitted to Divine law is the only true human civilization. This civilization is opposed to the civilization of ignorance and barbarism that has forgotten God. According to al-Maududi, there exist five elements of civilization: (1) a worldview, (2) a life purpose, (3) metaphysical principles and philosophy, (4) a public education program, and (5) a social system. Interestingly enough, if we exclude the Muslim factor, then the first three elements fit other religions, such as Christianity, Judaism, and Buddhism, as well. According to al-Maududi, language, ethnos, history, and traditions do not define a civilization, but rather the main, causative factors of civilization are the metaphysical, ontological, and eschatological views of a people.[64]

Among other such theories which propose a dichotomous approach, the ideas of the Moroccan Islamic philosopher and thinker Taha Abdul Rahman are rather interesting. Rahman is considered to be a unique modern thinker insofar as he worked to create a project based on "pure concepts" from the Islamic heritage, free from the influence of the West. Abdul Rahman's central idea was that there exist two types of civilizations the civilization of the logos (word) and the civilization of action. These are *alqawl* (لوقلا) or "to speak", and *alfiel* (لعفلا), or "to do", respectively.

62 Kulpin E. 3zolotaya Orda: Sudbi pokoleniy. Moscow: INSAN. 2006. p. 88.

63 Quoted in: El Ayubi M. L'image de l'Occident dans le discours islamiste // Homme et societe. - P., 1994. № 144. P. 88.

64 Mutmaz Ali Muhammad. An exploration into Western and Islamic concepts of development and civilization // Hamdard Islamicus. - Karachi, 2002. Vol. 25, № 3. P. 18.

Abdul Rahman believed that the idea of a "dialogue of civilizations" is incorrect, since it is tied to such notions as intercultural dialogue or inter-religious dialogue, and he was a harsh critic of the West, which he accused of creating a hegemonic civilization that denies all others, the very denial of which means that dialogue is impossible. Against the offensive of the hegemonic civilization of the West, which operates, among other things, by means of terror, Abdul Rahman proposed his own version of dialogue. "Correctional Dialogue" (يميوقتلا راوحلا) is founded on a critique of the cultural values of Western civilization through the very means that support this civilization. This "unique civilization" is supposed to support the contributions of others and to not try to force them to change their values. The second path, which is applicable to countering terror, is "Negotiated Dialogue" (يضوافتلا راوحلا) which aims to ensure that no single civilization can claim absolute truth. This entails the creation of a balance of power between different players. If this balance is broken, then violence returns. Between correctional and negotiated dialogue, there exists a dialectical relationship. If the first overcomes the second, then we have a higher civilization; in the reverse, a decline sets in. Interestingly enough, the Arabic language harbors a close conceptual and etymological relationship between the words "religion", or *din*, "city", or *madinah*, and "civilization", *tamaddun*.[65]

Another example of juxtaposing confrontational civilizations can be seen in the studies of the French anthropologist Louis Dumont, who considered the opposition between Western and non-Western civilizations. In his work *Homo Hierarchicus*, Dumont contrasted Western egalitarian society to Indian hierarchical society, and showed that the caste system in India is a sign of its civilizational unity in diversity. If in the West the presence of a caste system is perceived as a "relic" or "degeneracy", then Dumont, on the contrary, presents it as a civilizational scheme. In this view, the normative equality and individualism of the Western understanding are indices of decline and backwardness. Therefore, for Dumont, modern Western civilization - where spiritual authority is subordinated to political power, and where the latter's representatives are often frauds and opportunists - is an "abnormal civilization."[66]

---

65 Afro-Aziatskiy mir: problemi civilizatsionnogo analiza. Issue 2. Regionalnie civilizatsii. Moscow: INIAN RAN, 2004. p. 78.

66 Dumont L. Homo Hierarchicus: the Caste System and its Implications. Chicago, 1980.

The concept of Axial-Age Civilizations can also be examined in this group of theories under consideration. "Axial-Age Civilizations" is often taken to refer to the Greek, Jewish, Persian, Indian, and Chinese civilizations. Excluded from this list of civilizations, and assigned to the list of "non-axial" or "pre-axial" civilizations are all the rest, including both ancient societies and those which do not fit the criteria of the model of "axial civilizations." This model, and the theory of axial time, were developed by Karl Jaspers. Although Jaspers belongs to modernist Western European philosophy, his ideas do not bear clear conclusions on the future of the West and the world. On the one hand, Jaspers argued that "The West knows, with unique forcefulness, the postulate that man must shape his world"[67], in which we can see a typically Eurocentric approach. On the other hand, in Jasper's opinion, what the future order of human life "will be like in universal peace must depend upon the various orders with their origins in history; the manifold pattern of life will be determined by the remoulding imposed upon it by technological conditions."[68] Jaspers wrote:

> A new world cannot arise out of the crisis through the work of the rational life-order as such. What is needful is that the human being shall achieve something more than he brings to pass in the life-order, shall achieve it by way of the State as expressive of the will towards the whole, by the State to which the life-order has become nothing but a means - and also through mental creation, whereby he grows aware of his own being…the State in and by itself falls short of his hopes, and merely offers scope for the realisation of possibilities…He has to go back to the very beginning, to human existence, out of which the State and the mind derive blood and reality.[69]

Jaspers' concern for the West is shared by modern authors who define the present traumatic shifts in the world political system as signs of a new transformation of Axial Time. For the latter, the main question is whether this directly represents a sign of the collapse of Western civilization and how such will affect other civilizations. The fatalists among the latter simply admit that Western civilization is "fragile and perishable" and

67 Karl Jaspers, The Origin and Goal of History (New Haven: Yale University Press, 1965), 63.

68 Ibid, 199.

69 Karl Jaspers, Man in the Modern Age (New York: Routledge, 2010).

that "Western people, despite their extraordinary accomplishments, were never more than a step or two away from barbarism."[70]

Theories of Civilizations in the Context of Post-Modernity and Globalization

In his work, *Civilizations: Culture, Ambition, and the Transformation of Nature*, Professor Felipe Fernandez-Armesto posits: "Loosely used, «a civilization» means an area, group, or period distinguished, in the mind of the person using the term, by striking continuities in ways of life and thought and feeling."[71] Alongside this affirmation, the author points to a number of problems which arise when one tries to pursue a definition for a concrete civilization. "One way of getting round this problem", Fernandez-Armesto writes, "is to insist that there are particular continuities which distinguish civilizations, such as a common religion or ideology or sense of belonging to a «world order»; or a common writing system or mutually intelligible languages... or some combination of such features."[72] Ultimately, Fernandez-Armesto proposes to define civilization as a type of relations with the natural environment, in which the latter are modified to meet human needs. In his opinion, there are two mistakes often associated with understandings of civilization: the "diffusionist illusion" and "self-deception about the past." Fernandez-Armesto writes:

> People have traditionally talked about civilization "spreading" from place to place and not happening by other means...Yet, in reality, civilization is an ordinary thing, an impulse so widespread that it has again transformed almost every habitable environment...Our received wisdom about prehistoric times was formulated in the late nineteenth and early twentieth centuries, when Europe was enjoying her own great imperial age. The experience of those times convinced self-appointed imperial master-races that civilization was something which descended from superior to inferior peoples.[73]

---

70 Marvin Perry. Western Civilization. A Brief History. Volume 2: From 1400s. Boston: Wadsworth, 2013. P. xvii, 18.

71 Felipe Fernandez-Armesto, Civilizations: Culture, Ambition, and the Transformation of Nature (New York: Free Press, 2001), p. 12.

72 Ibid, 12-13.

73 Ibid, 183-184.

Also noted is the influence of thalassocracy on the formation of societies: "The sea can shape island civilizations either by confining them or by linking them to other lands. Either way, proximity to the sea is such a powerful feature of any environment which includes it that it dwarfs all other features...Nearness to the shore molds one's outlook and affects the way one thinks."[74] Further, Fernandez-Armesto arrives at a definition of Western civilization: "When people nowadays speak of "Western civilization," they mean, essentially, an Atlantic community comprising parts of Western Europe and much or most of the Americas. The creation of this ocean-spanning world has been a curious departure in the history of civilization."[75]

If we approach this question from the perspective of communications theory, then the conclusion can be drawn that civilizations create connections, i.e., an order between thousands of cultural goods which are in fact disparate, motley, and at first glance alien to one another - from goods related to spiritual life and the mind to objects and tools of everyday life.[76] An interesting understanding of civilization in this regard has been proposed by University of Pennsylvania Professor Randall Collins in his article "Civilizations as zones of prestige and social contact."[77] On the one hand, Collins' approach can be treated as Western-centric, insofar as he speaks of civilizations as structures which are bigger than societies and states, which radiate a certain influence that attracts people from the periphery. These people outside of the civilizational center draw their identity or formulate their ideas about it as something attractive. "Missionaries" are sent from the civilizational centers to the peripheries, the hinterlands. All of this clearly resembles the colonial policies of European states and the US. On the other hand, Collins argues that, first of all, civilization as a "zone of prestige" can have several centers. Second of all, civilizations are not static, but active, and their locations can accordingly change. Thirdly, all civilizational zones of prestige interact with other civilizational zones. The decisive influence of Chinese civilization on

74 Ibid, 276.

75 Ibid, 404.

76 Savarkar V.D. Samagra Savarkar Wangmaya (Writings of Swatantriya Veer Savarkar), Pune, 1964. Vol. VI. 521.

77 Collins R. Civilizations as zones of prestige and social contact. Rethinking civilizational analysis// Intern. sociology - L., 2001. - Vol. 16, N3 (Special issue), P. 421-437.

the formation of Japanese civilization, and relations between Western and Islamic civilizations, which continue into the 21st century, are cited as examples of such.

Johann Arnason proposes to analyze the main structural components that define civilization as (1) a cultural interpretation of the world; (2) institutional 'constellations' in political and economic life; (3) and representative ideologies in the strategies and self-consciousness of the socio-political elites.[78] The first, cultural element is important for understanding the basic conditions of the divergence of different societies' historical paths. Arnason also proposes to consider civilizational complexes as "families of societies", or "sociocultural frameworks within which smaller units can organize themselves in a more or less autonomous fashion, and elaborate their variations on shared themes."[79] The author also notes that "clearly demarcated regions of historical importance are sometimes characterized by enduring multi-civilizational constellations."[80] In addition, elsewhere Arnason remarks: "It is permissible to assume the existence of a diversity of civilizational formations, some of which will resemble 'civilization' in the habitual sense of this term more than others."[81] In the opinion of the author, such an approach establishes the prerequisites for inter-civilizational analysis and thereby, inter-civilizational relations.

As a tool for civilizational analysis, the American sociologist Benjamin Nelson proposes to employ a typology of structures of consciousness. Nelson distinguishes three types: sacro-magical, religious, and rational. The first is characterized by a sense of collective responsibility for possible violations of unity. In the second type, words and deeds must necessarily match the spiritual world, i.e., the Logos. Both collective and individual participation in social rituals and rites are important here. The third, rational type appears when religious consciousness weakens.[82]

---

78 Arnason J.P. Civilizational patterns and its sources/ Rethinking civilizational analysis // Intern. sociology - L., 2001. - Vol. 16, N3 (Special issue), P. 387-405.

79 Ibid, 394.

80 Ibid, 397.

81 Arnason J. Ponimanie civilizatsionnoy dinamiki: vvodnie zamechaniya. p. 20. http://www.jourssa.ru/sites/all/files/volumes/2012_6/Arnason_2012_6.pdf

82 Nelson B. On the roads to modernity: conscience, science and civilizations. Selected writings / Ed. By Toby E. Haff. - Totowa, Rowman and Littlefeld, 1981.

Professor Hayward Alker of the University of South Carolina criticizes Huntington's approach and develops Toynbee and Braudel's, also integrating Hegel's theory of dialectics. Although the possibility of conflicts is not denied, it is presumed that there are variations of domination, continuity, adjustment, interpenetration, mutually-stimulating coexistence, assimilation, and creative synthesis.[83] Alker also importantly contributed to international relations theory by pointing out the provincial character of Anglo-Saxon models.[84]

In a 1998 article, Israeli scholars Eisenstadt and Schluchter put forward the theory that the era of early modernity was not merely intrinsic to Western countries, but that there existed multiple early modernities. Insofar as there have been several modernities in the world, and not one European version, their development follows different trajectories. Thus, each civilization is heterogenous, polycentric, and has its own dynamics of development. In the present period, all of them are linked to one another.[85]

Robert Cox believes that civilizations are forms of large-scale identity which are compelled to confront a homogenizing and alienating globalization: "Civilizations represent continuities in human thought and practices through which different human groups attempt to grapple with their consciousness of present problems."[86] According to Cox: "Western consciousness has been split between a dominant universalistic perspective that sees civilization as a Western civilization encompassing the whole world, and a pluralistic perspective that sees Western civilization (variously defined) as coexisting with and interacting with other civilizations."[87] Such a posing of the question is characteristic of the state of postmodernity. Tonomura Naohiko also posits an altogether postmodernist thesis that civilization means a "social revolution" and "revolution in consciousness."[88]

---

83 Alker H.R. If not Huntington's "civilizations", then whose?// Review. - Binghamton, 1995. Vol. 18, N4. P.533-562.

84 Alker H.R. and T.J. Biersteker. The Dialectics of World Order: International Studies Quarterly. 1984. Vol. 28. № 2

85 Eisenstadt Sh., Schluchter W. Paths to early modernites. A comparative view// Dedalus. Cambridge (Mass), 1988. Vol. 127, N3. P. 1-18.

86 Robert W. Cox, "Civilizations and the twenty-first century: some theoretical considerations", 106.

87 Ibid, 109.

88 Tonomura Naohiko. What is feudalism? - Definition, complex, civilization // Comparative civilizations review. Carlisle, 1999. N 11. P. 52.

The Russian-Eurasian Civilizational School

Insofar as a number of Russian scholars and researchers have engaged in the study of civilizations, it makes sense to single out these theories in a separate sub-chapter. The first Russian to raise the question of civilization was the Slavophile Nikolai Danilevsky. His book, *Russia and Europe*, published in 1869, was dedicated to Russia's relations with European states as united into something whole not only in a geographical sense, but also culturally, historically, and politically.[89] Danilevsky constantly appeals to the historical development and unique identity of peoples. He contrasts modern "Romano-Germanic" civilization to Greek and Roman civilization of the Mediterranean basin. Danilevsky writes that Ancient Hellenic culture developed across parts of Asia, Africa, and Europe, and does not exclusively belong to the latter. Romano-Germanic civilization, however, usurped the historical achievements of other peoples and established itself as equivalent to the European geographical space. Thus, "Europe is Germano-Roman civilization."[90] Furthermore, in the chapter "Is European Civilization Universal?", Danilevsky ironically speaks as if from the position of a Westerner: "There is no salvation outside of progressive, European, universal civilization; there cannot even be any civilization outside of it whatsoever, because outside of it there is no progress. To affirm the opposite is an evil heresy."[91] Then, just as ironically, Danilevsky switches to the opposite perspective: "Asia has absolutely more countries suitable for culture than its Western peninsula, and only in a relative sense (towards the entire space) should it yield."[92] Here follows the example of the high culture and technology of Ancient China.

The reason for the pondering of the existence of civilization outside of Romano-Germanic or European forms of culture taken to be universal, Danilevsky identifies in an inadequate view on continuity which assigns history a more progressive form in the West. "Progress, as follows, does not constitute the exclusive privilege of the West, or Europe, but stagnation the exclusive stigma of the East, or Asia."[93]

89 Danilevskiy N. Rossiya i Evropa. Moscow: Institut russkoy civilizatsii, 2011.

90 Danilevskiy N. Rossiya i Evropa. Klassika geopolitiki, XIX vek, Moscow: AST, 2003. p. 337.

91 Ibid.

92 Ibid, 353.

93 Ibid, 356.

A misunderstanding of the most general principles of the historical process and a nebulous vision of the historical phenomenon called "progress" is therefore the problem at hand.[94]

Danilevsky proposed to define civilizations as culturo-historical types, and identified five laws of their development. The first law speaks to the unique identity of culturo-historical types on the basis of the closeness of a family of peoples speaking the same or similar languages. The second law affirms the need for political independence, thanks to which a civilization can develop. The third law suggests that the elements of one culturo-historical type are not transmitted to peoples of a different type. The fourth law testifies that civilization, as peculiar to a culturo-historical type, only attains completeness, diversity, and wealth when its ethnographic elements, its constituents, are diverse. They should not be absorbed by one political center but, exercising independence, constitute a federation or political system of states. The final, fifth law is that the period of civilization of each culturo-historical type is comparatively brief, and drains the latter's strength. Danilevsky thus adhered to an organicist theory and often compared peoples to biological organisms. He even characterized the methods of the spread of civilizations as (1) "transplantation" (via colonization), (2) "vaccination" (following the example of a bud or stalk of plant); and (3) "fertilizing" (in his opinion, this is how Egypt and Phoenicia influenced Greece, Greece Rome, and Rome Greece up to the point of Romano-Germanic Europe).[95]

An appeal to civilizations can also be found in the works of Konstantin Leontiev. For example, Leontiev writes that Byzantium as a state spent its life in a defensive position but, as a civilization and religious culture, reigned for a long period of time and extensively, even acquiring whole new worlds, such as Russia and other Slavs.[96] Leontiev thus considered religion to be the backbone of civilization, without which a civilization is vulnerable to collapse or absorption by a different civilization. "Religion, prevailing in any given people, is here a cornerstone for guarding the durable and actual."[97]

---

94 Ibid.

95 Ibid, pp. 374-375.

96 Leontiev K. Vostok, Rossiya i Slavyanstvo. Moscow: Respublika, 1996. p. 149.

97 Ibid, 222.

Another important figure relevant to our study is Lev Mechnikov, the brother of the famous biologist and Nobel Prize winner Ilya Mechnikov. Although his works were published in European countries, one of his fundamental works was dedicated to a comparative historical analysis of different civilizations. The book was published in 1889 in France, thanks to the efforts of his friend, the famous French geographer Jacques Élisée Reclus, for whom Mechnikov worked as a secretary, and who wrote the preface for the French edition of the book. It is known that Friedrich Ratzel spoke enthusiastically about the book, as did many Russian scholars and philosophers. The book appeared in Russian only in 1898. Despite the fact that the title employs the word civilization in a singular sense, Mechnikov's conception speaks of a plurality of civilizations that have developed near bodies of water. Mechnikov rejected the concept of linear time, according to which the development of societies proceeds along a straight line, and instead pointed to the complexity of clear classifications, insofar as the subjective sympathies of a scholar and various contingencies make any assessment contradictory, unproven, and arbitrary.

In defining the notion of civilization, Mechnikov adheres to the manner of Pierre Mougeolle[98], who believed such to be "one of the most complex, which covers a totality of discoveries made by man, and all inventions; it determines the sum of ideas in circulation, and the sum of technological obtainments; this notion also expresses a degree of improvement in science, art, and industrial technology; it shows the state of the familial and social system, and all existing social institutions in general."[99] Such an approach exhibits a clear anthropocentrism influenced by Enlightenment ideas. However, although Mechnikov cited the positivists and evolutionists, he rejected Darwin's idea of selection and competition, instead contrasting it to Karl Baer's theory of morphological criteria for organic phenomena and degree of differentiation. In other words, Mechnikov was a proponent of the organicist school, but with a focus on cooperation, not struggle, for survival. Mechnikov believed that at an earlier stage in history, despotism and violence were necessary for the economic and political organization of societies, but with technological development, anarchic demes will become a more adequate form for social groups. In Mechnikov's opinion, only such unions or alliances of

98 Mougeolle P. Statique des Civilisations. Paris, 1883.

99 Mechnikov L. Civilizatsiya i bolshie istoricheskie reki. Moscow: Airis Press, 2013. p. 91.

the highest type strive for the preservation and unlimited development of the human species, which becomes much more important than previous types of social organizations which maintained the lives of individuals and groups. It is also important to note that Mechnikov spoke of the presence of a number of such unions, but did not assert any need for the creation of a single structure for the purpose of working in the interests of all of mankind, as globalists argue.

In examining the historical development of various societies, Mechnikov departed from conventional schemes. For example, besides the four most famous types associated with rivers - the Nile, the Tigris, the Euphrates, the Indus and Ganges, the Huang He and the Yangtze - he added another civilization in Asia: "the country between the mountains of the Hindu Kush and the present Caspian Sea had its own center of civilization which arose independently of the above-mentioned four great civilizations of antiquity."[100] Since the valleys of the Oksa and the Syr Darya (the "Yakhsha Arta") had no outlet to the ocean, Mechnikov believed that the peoples inhabiting this area later gravitated towards the Mesopotamian zone.

Black Africa is practically absent from Mechnikov's civilizational analysis, the reason being that he considered only the Old World. To visualize this phenomenon he illustrated the Congo-Nile axis, running from Madagascar on the eastern coast to Gibralter in North-West Africa. Everything to the left of this axis was not dealt with in Mechnikov's work. Parallel to the Congo-Nile axis, he drew another line which he called the border of the Mediterranean zone, starting in the South a little to the right of the Strait of Hormuz and in the North dividing the Baltic Sea in half. Such a region, which includes parts of Europe, Asia, and Africa, can hardly be called a whole.[101]

The Russian Eurasianist movement in European emigration also contributed to the development of theories of civilizations. In particular, Konstantin Chkheidze put forth the notion of "pan-regions." In geopolitics this term is attributed to Karl Haushofer, but Chkheidze proposed such a model somewhat earlier.[102] Chkheidze's text was devoted to analyzing

---

100 Ibid, 203.

101 Ibid, 217.

102 Karl Haushofer's book The Geopolitics of Pan-Ideas was published in 1931, whereas Konstantin Chkheidze's article "The League of Nations and Continental

the functioning of the League of Nations established just before, which he suggested was incapable of being a "world government" (which indeed happened), and Chkheidze also pointed towards the emergence of a "coordinative-subordinative" government of a United States of Europe, i.e., the future European Union. In addition, he observed parallel processes in world politics: (1) the differentiation of state autonomy, religion, race, and economics along various lines; and (2) the integration of a new type, that of a union of nations into a "continental-state."

Chkheidze pointed out that such a union is "characterized by two important foundations: material and spiritual. The material foundation includes such features as geographical, economic (related to production and consumption), financial (capital, currency uniformity, customs union), and transport. The spiritual foundation is composed of racial psyche, cultural heritage, and commonality of impending historical tasks."[103] By these aspects, Chkheidze meant essentially "unity of historical fate." As for the concrete manifestations of different civilizations, Chkheidze wrote: "The correctness of theoretical provisions on culturo-historical types is acting with newfound persuasiveness in the processes forming continental-states; in these processes there is a coincidence of place-development and unity of historical fate; the combination of these points creates new culturo-historical types." In addition, contemporary international processes allowed Chkheidze to conclude that "the true, ontological nature of world order does not coincide with the superficial, phenomenological phenomena of world life."

It is important to note that at the same time that many ideologists and political scientists were discussing the "national idea" and the secular states replacing the empires rooted in the Christian and Muslim religions, Chkheidze anticipated the emergence of Muslim civilization: "Regardless of how the current governments of Muslim countries relate to Islam, one cannot deny the enormous influence which Islam has and is exercising in the sense of 'stamping' human material." Pan-European, Pan-American, and Pan-Asian worlds were

States" appeared in 1927. Given that Hausehofer mentions the ideas of "Eurasian Pan-Slavism", cites Danilevsky, and mentions the Eurasianists as a "political sect", it is possible that Haushofer borrowed various ideas from the Eurasianists.

103 Chheidze K. Liga natsiy i gosudarstva-matriki // Evraziyskaya chronika, Issue VIII, Paris, 1927, pp. 32-35.

also evoked. So was, of course, Russia-Eurasia, as a continental-state representing a unity of geopolitical, ethnic, and culturo-political systems towards which adjacent countries gravitate. In Chkheidze's words: "In this sense, we can speak of competition between Pan-European, Pan-Asian, and Pan-Eurasian worlds." As we can see, many of the provisions set out in a small publication by Konstantin Chkheidze, like other insights of the Eurasianists, have since found embodiment in history and practice.

The famous sociologist Pitirim Sorokin also studied civilizational processes. In his assessment, Western society or "civilization" is not homogenous: "The total sum of the social and cultural phenomena of Western society and culture have never been integrated into one, uniform system."[104] In turn, Sorokin proposed a theory according to which there exist ideational, idealistic, and sensate systems. These manifest themselves in art, science, ethics, philosophy, and systems of law and religion. According to Sorokin, the succession of ideational, idealistic, and sensate domination took place in the likes of the mythical phases of the Gold, Silver, and Iron ages. It follows, in antiquity things were better, and now they are worse and, as one can glean from his works, these experiences pertain mainly to the Western world. Sorokin's *Social and Cultural Dynamics* also contains a call for a radical conservative revolution: "In the madness of decadent thinking, the man of sensate society today is once again destroying his own sensual home which he erected so proudly over the past five centuries. Sensate ethics and law are once again at an impasse marking the end of the present epoch. Without a transition to ideational ethics and law, and without a new absolutization and universalization of values, society will not be able to avoid this dead-end."[105]

Overall, if we speak of the foundations of Russian civilization, then it should be noted that in the Russian traditions (The *Russkii* and *Rossiiskii*), civilizational stability might be interpreted as a co-existence of different confessional traditions. The definition of *Rossiiskii* civilization as Orthodox does not seem quite sufficient even though, without a doubt, no other religion can compete with Orthodoxy

104 Sorokin P. Chelovek. Civilizatsiya. Obshestvo. Moscow: Politizdat, 1992.

105 Ibid, 504.

in terms of strength and degree of influence in the history and culture of Russia. At the same time, it is impossible not to recognize the contributions of other religious traditions, such as Islam, Judaism, Buddhism, Protestantism, and the national religions, a point which testifies to the mutual influence, mutual enrichment, and joint creation and defense of common values and state structures in this single geographical, political, economic, and spiritual space. This creates a sense of belonging to and complicity with a single, unified historical fate with archetypical visions that are common to the consciousness of different ethno-confessional communities.[106]

Global Geopolitics and Etymology

Without a doubt, Samuel Huntington was the first author to politicize the concept of civilizations by introducing it into the context of geopolitical confrontation. In our view, although Huntington's definition of civilization clearly bears a certain ethno-sociological shade, it most closely of all conveys the idea that socio-political formations can be taken as definite centers of power insisting on common interests and values in international relations. In his *The Clash of Civilizations*, Huntington writes:

> A civilization is thus the highest cultural grouping of people and the broadest level of cultural identity people have short of that which distinguished humans from other species. It is defined both by common objective elements, such as language, history, religion, customs, institutions, and by the subjective self-identification of people...Civilizations are the biggest 'we' within which we feel culturally at home as distinguished from all the other 'thems' out there.[107]

It is no coincidence that Alexander Dugin, in his study *The Theory of the Multipolar World*[108], points to Huntington as the author who came closest of all (although not close enough) to conceptualizing

106 Mchedlova M. Vera i kulturno-civilizatsionnaya identichnost: novie grani religioznosti v Rossii i Evrope // Vera. Etnos. Natsiya. Religiozniy komponent etnicheskogo soznaniya. Moscow: Kulturnaya revolutsiya, 2009. p. 365.

107 Samuel P. Huntington, The Clash of Civilizations and the Remaking of World Order (New York: Simon & Schuster/Rockefeller Center, 1996), 43.

108 Dugin A. Teoriya mnogopolyarnogo mira. Moscow: Evraziyskoe dvizhenie, 2012.

what might be considered a "pole" in the new system of international relations. Civilization can therefore be called a collective community, united by a belonging to the same spiritual, historical, cultural, mental, and symbolic tradition whose members recognize their closeness to one another independent of national, class, political, and ideological affiliations.[109] However, in order to fulfill the conditions necessary to function as a center of strength, common geopolitical conditions are also needed, a point which has been suggested by Russian scholars.[110] This brings us to the "place-development" or topogenesis of peoples.

The term *mestorazvitie* ("place-development", topogenesis) was proposed by the founding father of Eurasianism, the geographer Petr Savitsky, to explain the totality of geographical, ethnic, economic, historical, and other peculiarities that compose a single whole.[111] This neologism very organically conveys the interrelationship between landscape, culture, and peoples in the broadest possible sense. It is no coincidence that this term was later developed and interpreted by Lev Gumilev in his work *Ethnogenesis and the Biosphere of the Earth.*[112] In describing the legal and political framework of such, we inevitably arrive at the concept of large spaces (*Grossraum*) of the German jurist and geopolitician Carl Schmitt.

To conclude this chapter, we would like to embark on a brief etymological excursion similar to those that we have pursued throughout our study. If we take the English word "civilization", then in accordance with its structure (the suffix "-tion"), it should denote either a process or state. Yet as we have pointed out, it is precisely the understanding of civilization as a process that was proposed by the German sociologist and founder of figurative sociology, Norbert Elias, who devotes his work *The Civilizing Process*[113] to this question. If we adopt such a model then, as a rule, the structure of world politics and international relations changes completely. Globalization - and this term, let us note, is used exclusively to denote a process - figures as a special stage of the "civilizational process" with its

109 Ibid, 103.

110 Frolov E. Problema civilizatsiy v istoricheskom processe // Vestnik Sankt Peterburgskogo Unuversiteta. Seria 2: ИIstoriya. — 2006. № 2. pp. 96 -100.

111 Savitskiy P. Kontinent Evraziya. Moscow: Agraf, 1997.

112 Gumilev L. Ethnogenez i biosphera zemli. Moscow: Airis-Press, 2012.

113 Norbert Elias. Uber den Prozess der Zivilisation. Basel, 1939.

own characteristics, patterns, and laws. The same can be done with the English term "nation", and move from its binding to an ethnos and state borders to the dynamics of peoples and cultures. It is no coincidence that many thinkers have disputed the definition of "nation", and still do. But we can note in this context that the original Latin word *civilis*, meaning "civil", "state", or, according to its etymological features, is close to the notion of "movement" (the second form of the verb *cieo - civi* means to set into motion, to excite, to shake, to oscillate).[114] In other languages, we find a somewhat different semantic charge. In Chinese, *Wen* means "culture", "civilization", or "upbringing" in a substantive sense, akin to "cultureness" or "civilizationness." *Wen* can refer to both man (*ren wen*), Heaven (*tian wen*), and *Earth* (*di wen*). The Ancient Greek *paideia* might also be considered as an ideological standard for a certain civilizational community.

As we can see, the notion of civilization is complex, multifaceted, and can have different meanings depending on context. Some modern states might be assigned the status of civilization, while in some regions it is quite difficult to draw civilizational boundaries between groups of states. What's more, sometimes a civilization can exist and develop independently of states and methods of political governance. For example, examining the historical vicissitudes of the Chinese dynasties, Marcel Granet concluded: "They thus reached the stage of forming what I will call a grouping of civilization, an active and powerful grouping, without however believing themselves under the obligation to give to the State and to the idea of the State that prestige and authority in which the Western mind very readily sees the indispensable protective armour of all national life."[115] We should also recall Masakazu Yamazaki's 1996 claim[116] that a new Asian civilization is now in the making, which might include not only the Chinese and Japanese civilizations (according to a different typology), but also other societies of South-East Asia and the Pacific region.

114 Dvoretskiy I. Latino-russkiy slovar. Moscow: Russkiy yazik, 2000. p. 139.

115 Marcel Granet, Chinese Civilization (New York: Meridian, 1958), pp. 5-6.

116 Yamazaki M. Asia, a civilization in the making// Foreign Affairs. 1996 Vol. 75 N4, P. 106-118.

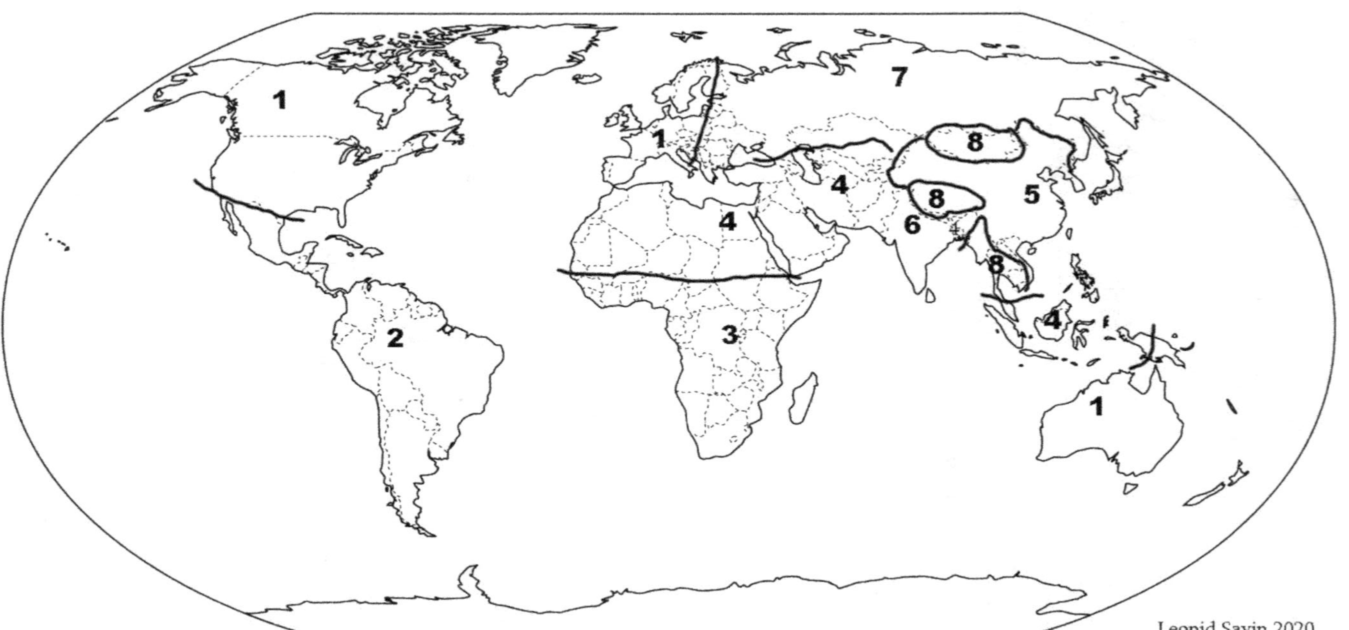

According to Huntington, there are nine civilizations in the world: Western, Latin American, African, Islamic, Sin, Hindu, Orthodox, Buddhist, Japanese. At the same time, Western, Buddhist and Islamic are not monolithic, but are divided into regional parts.

12

Forming an Alternative

In the preceding chapters, with the aid of numerous examples, we examined a number of fundamentals and phenomena directly related to the structure of the world's societies and states. Despite the enormous differences between cultures and traditions, a point which we have also illustrated with diverse case studies, international politics in the form that it is presented and exists today is essentially a Western invention. It is the manifestation of Western civilization, with minor "adjustments" across various regions, and these adjustments are considered by the West itself to be some kind of "relic." This situation is exacerbated by the fact that many intellectuals of the Global South (the countries of Asia, Africa, and Latin America) continue to imitate the Western system.

For example, Hamid Dabashi has critically analyzed the role played by "comprador intellectuals" in aiding the global dominance of American imperialism. In his groundbreaking book on the relationship between race and colonialism, *Black Skin, White Masks*[1], Franz Fanon studied the traumatic consequences of the feeling of inferiority endured by colonized people, and explored how often this complex has led them to identify with the ideology of colonial rule. Dabashi's book *Brown Skin, White Masks*[2] raised further questions posed by Fanon's work, and extended Fanon's views to the context of the present world. Dabashi shows how intellectuals who migrate to the West are often used by the imperial power to inform the public about the situation back in their home countries. This was the case with the many Iraqis in emigration in the West who were used to justify the invasion of Iraq. Indeed, Dabashi demonstrates that this is an ordinary phenomenon giving rise to his study of why and how many migrant intellectuals contribute to the maintenance of imperialism. *Brown Skin, White Masks* radically altered

1 Frantz Fanon, Black Skin, White Masks, Grove Press, 2008.

2 Hamid Dabashi, Brown Skin, White Masks. Pluto Press, 2011.

Eduard Said's notion of "intellectual exile" to the point of demonstrating the characteristically negative influence of intellectual migration. Dabashi studied the ideology of cultural superiority and presented an account of how migrant intellectuals - "homeless compradors" and "guns for hire" - consistently betray any idea of their homeland or home country so that the most dubious imperial projects (primarily of the US and Great Britain) are met with approval.

If we analyze the publications of journals such as *Foreign Affairs*, we find that Dabashi's hypothesis is altogether adequate, as many of the critical publications aimed against certain states, and more specifically against their political leadership and system, are authored either by natives of these countries themselves or by second or third generation migrants. Anyone with an Iranian name can call for pressure to be put on the leadership of Iran in the name of the Iranian people, just as anyone with a Russian name can describe the "horrors in Russia" without ever having stepped foot in the Russian Federation and with knowledge drawn from what are most frequently dubious sources. The presence of clearly "national" and "ethnic" names among such publications' authors creates the illusion that the criticism being voiced therein is from within the opposition or, in the very least, from an informed person. This hardly ever corresponds to reality.

Although certain efforts were made in the 20th century to expose Western Neo-colonialism (political, cultural, intellectual, and spiritual), few have succeeded in translating authentic models of national systems into reality. On the level of world politics, these attempts have been looked upon as something "exotic", or as some kind of "remnants" that will sooner or later be incorporated into the global system through transformation, if one follows the theory of hegemony of Antonio Gramsci.

Nevertheless, there is consensus among contemporary liberal theoreticians and practitioners that the time of their ideology's global dominance has come to an end. The liberal world system is collapsing. From their point of view, the world awaits chaos and fragmentation. Whatever may have been the successes of globalization, its parallel effect of the exchange of knowledge and the creation of stable information flows between previously closed regions has turned out to be astoundingly effective. The ideas of a number of Western scholars, who have hitherto been intentionally marginalized for their critical (and generally justified) views on the Western liberal system and its political mechanisms, especially the destructive consequences for societies, cultural dignity, and the surrounding environment, have been supported and developed in other countries. At the same time, numerous concepts devised by the apologists of liberalism, such as Paul Krugman, who received the Nobel Prize in Economic Sciences in 2008 for his theory of "economies of scale", have been discredited by reality itself, thereby opening up the way for more adequate and multilateral analyses. Some of these figures, such as the former director of the World Bank, Joseph Stiglitz, have themselves begun to expose the flaws of globalization and neoliberal practices. The Mexican scholar Carlos Antonio Agirre Rohas has observed on this matter: "the terminal crisis of capitalist civilization means the overthrow and destruction of all the structures of the capitalist system, from the geographical and territorial constructs of its numerous and artificial national maps to the global structure of modern knowledge and cultures existing today."[3] Now Western liberal authors themselves are taking note of the necessity of a paradigm-change in thinking in international relations and world politics.

Critiquing the "One World" Model

As Charles Hauss has noted, our political consciousness follows a certain model of behavior: "It is thus all but impossible to avoid thinking in adversarial, 'we' versus 'they' terms, which psychologists call the 'image of the enemy.' 'We' are good; 'they' are dangerous… We also view the political process in largely zero-sum or win-lose terms. We expect politics to be more or less like an athletic event, with clear winners and losers." However, Hauss recognizes that there do exist such "games" with "positive-sum or win-win outcomes." Although Hauss presumes that such an approach to politics is hardly likely to become the norm in Western society in the near future, he suggests that "conventional wisdom can be changed." Historically, such shifts have often been given impetus by crisis situations.[4] More than 100 years ago, the British economist John Atkins Hobson wrote:

3 Agirre Rojas C.A. Latinskaya America na rasputie. Socialnie dvizheniya i smert sovremennoy politiki. Moscow: Krug, 2012. p. 57.

4 Comparative Politics. Domestic Responses to Global Challenges. Wadsworth/Thomson Learning. Belmont, CA. 2003. P. 510

> In particular, the trend of liberal sentiment regarding government of lower races is undergoing a marked change. The notion that there exists one sound, just, rational system of government, suitable for all sorts and conditions of men, embodied in the elective representative institutions of Great Britain, and that our duty was to impose this system as soon as possible, and with the least possible modifications, upon lower races, without any regard to their past history and their present capabilities and sentiments, is tending to disappear in this country, though the new headstrong Imperialism of America is still exposed to the taunt that «Americans think the United States has a mission to carry 'canned' civilisation to the heathen.»[5]

Nowadays philosophical constructs which expose the ideas of Liberalism in different forms and historical manifestations have begun to be on the rise in the ratings of scholarly studies and publications. While some scholars are directing their research lenses to identifying the results of the present crisis, others are engaged in analyzing the deep cause-and-effect relations behind it. For example, John Gray has suggested: "The world-historical failure of the Enlightenment project – in political terms, the collapse and ruin, in the late twentieth century, of the secular, rationalist and universalist political movements, liberal as well as Marxist… suggests the falsity of the philosophical anthropology upon which the Enlightenment project rested."[6] In Gray's opinion, "political allegiance – at least when it is comparatively stable – presupposes a common cultural identity, which is reflected in the polity to which allegiance is given; political order, including that of a liberal state, rests upon a pre-political order of common culture."[7] In Gray's analysis: "In political milieux which harbour a diversity of cultural traditions and identities, such as we find in most parts of the world today, the institutional forms best suited to a *modus vivendi* may well not be the individualist institutions of liberal civil society but rather those of political and legal pluralism, in which the fundamental units are not individuals but communities."[8] The latter observation points towards the necessity of rejecting the Liberal political model, including parliamentarianism, insofar as the very idea of

5 English text from: https://oll.libertyfund.org/titles/hobson-imperialism-a-study

6 John Gray, Enlightenment's Wake: Politics and Culture at the Close of the Modern Age (New York: Routledge, 1995), p. 98.

7 Ibid., 120.

8 Ibid., 203.

citizens granting representatives the right to make decisions on different matters leads to alienation, corruption, and other negative side-effects.

To address the question of the ongoing global confrontation, it is worth mentioning the American historian John Lukacs, who saw the planetary battle between directive (communist) and liberal (capitalist) societies to be a clash between two versions of nationalism. The "Iron Age", nevertheless, ended with the collapse of both ideologies. Hinting at the diversity of civilizations and the necessity of pursuing pluralism in political systems, Lukacs noted that "the character of a people molds their institutions more than their institutions mold, or influence, their characters."[9] Lukacs thus described the unsuccessful attempts at creating monogenic political structures in Europe following the First World War in the following manner: these jackets of import cut did not fit on the stocky figures of their temporary owners. The seams soon parted, the clothes were not worn for a long time. This type of parliamentary liberalism belonged to the nineteenth century, but not to the twentieth.[10]

With regards to homogeneity, the Italian philosopher Giorgio Agamben suggested that the notion of a uniform world for all living beings is an illusion. As an example, Agamben cited the ideas of the founding father of ecology, Jakob von Uexküll, who proved that "a unitary world does not exist, just as a space and a time that are equal for all living things do not exist."[11] In turn, Agamben argued for a distinction between the surrounding environment (*Umgebung*), that is objective space in which we see living beings in movement, and the surrounding world (*Umwelt*), which consists of a more or less broad range of elements. In Agamben's words: "The *Umgebung* is our own *Umwelt*, to which Uexküll does not attribute any particular privilege and which, as such, can also vary according to the point of view from which we observe it…Every environment is a closed unity in itself, which results from the selective sampling of a series of elements or 'marks' in the *Umgebung*, which, in turn, is nothing other than man's environment."[12] As follows, the historical development of the diverse

9 John Lukacs, The End of the Twentieth Century and the End of the Modern Age (Ticknor & Fields, 1993), 75.

10 Ibid. p. 135.

11 Agamben G. Otkritoe. Chelovek i zhivotnoe. Moscow: RGGU, 2012. p. 52.

12 Ibid. p. 53. Giorgio Agamben, The Open: Man and Animal (Stanford University Press, 2003), 40-41.

surrounding world also unfolds along diverse vectors.

Anthropologists, by virtue of their professional obligations, have been more sensitive towards different cultures to which they do not belong. For instance, Claude Lévi-Strauss noted:

> "One has to be very naive or dishonest to imagine that men choose their beliefs independently of their situation. Far from the forms of social existence being determined by political systems, it is they which give meanings to the ideologies by which they are expressed…At the moment, the misunderstanding between East and West is primarily semantic: the concepts or 'signifiers' that we try to propagate in the East refer to 'signifieds' which are different there or non-existent."[13]

In the 1950's, the American anthropologist Julian Steward argued in his book, *Theory of Cultural Change: The Methodology of Multilinear Evolution*, that the culturo-historical patterns and changes which happen in societies must be studied not in the form of one universal culture of so-called humanity, but in terms of different cultures. Steward argued: "What is lost in universality will be gained in concreteness and specificity."[14] Further, Steward posited: "Twentieth-century research has accumulated a mass of evidence which overwhelmingly supports the contention that particular cultures diverge significantly from one another and do not pass through unilinear stages."[15] More recently, Piotr Sztompka has noted: "Hence evolution must be treated as multilinear, and this in two senses. First, in the inter-societal sense: evolution runs along different paths in various societies, because of the unique conditions in which they find themselves. Second, in the intra-societal sense: the evolution of various social fields (culture, economy, politics, art, law etc.) follows different courses and employs different mechanisms."[16]

Therefore, societies remain diverse both in their primordial state and over the process of their development, despite attempts at political and ideological unification, and this applies to legal, economic, as well as

---

13 Claude Levi-Strauss, Tristes Tropiques (New York: Penguin, 2012).

14 Julian Haynes Steward, Theory of Culture Change. The Methodology of Multilinear Evolution. University of Illinois Press, Urbana 1955. P. 19.

15 Ibid. P. 28.

16 Piotr Sztompka, The Sociology of Social Change (Oxford: Blackwell, 1993), p. 115.

political systems. Even if one were to propose that there exists some kind of unity arising from generally accepted scientific concepts, this unity itself would not be homogenous. In Raymond Aaron's words, "Unity and diversity in the political world are not so much opposite as complementary features of a situation."[17] In the 20th century, states were heterogenous in terms of their different sizes and political systems, and their coexistence compelled the employment of pluralistic interpretation. As Michael Mann has pointed out: "There are alternatives…The Anglophones, Nordics, Continental Europeans (with Mediterranean countries separating somewhat from their northern neighbors in recent years), Latin Americans, East Asians - and there may be more, too - [manifest] distinctive trajectories of development."[18]

Indeed, there already exists quite a lot of such alternatives. Despite attempts by unipolarists and the neoliberal political cartel to hang on to their hegemony, new approaches and non-liberal philosophical concepts that are applicable in political practice are not only being introduced into international discourse, but are beginning to claim certain institutional algorithms in the field of foreign policy strategies. These approaches are by all means diverse. For example, the German political scientist Alexander Wendt has proposed applying the discourse of quantum physics to describe international relations.[19] In the present chapter, we will restrict ourselves to examining several models which fit the general idea behind this book, namely, Neopluralism in international relations, synthesis theory, and non-Western theories of international relations. As for new, critical political theories, several concepts will be examined, namely, those of aesthetic politics, the Fourth Political Theory, and political sustainability theory.

Neopluralism

The theory of neopluralism is associated with the American scholar Robert Dahl and his 1961 work *Who Governs? Democracy and*

17 Aron R. Izbrannoe: Izmereniya politicheskogo soznaniya. Moscow: Rosspen, 2004. p. 145.

18 Michael Mann, Power in the 21st Century: Conversations with John A. Hall (Cambridge: Polity Press, 2011), p. 58.

19 Wendt, A. E. (2015). Quantum Mind and Social Science. Unifying Physical and Social Ontology. Cambridge: Cambridge University Press.

Power in an American City.[20] In the 1950's and '60's, Dahl developed the theory of pluralism and also became known for his concept of "polyarchic democracy", both of which terms were applied by Dahl to the state system, not to international relations. However, the basic conditions of polyarchy can also be applied on the international level. The four main principles of such are:

- To come to power and to maintain power, violent means of coercion ought not to be used.
- Society should be dynamic, modern, and organized on pluralistic principles.
- Conflict potential should be balanced with tolerance.
- A political culture and system of convictions predisposed towards the ideas of democracy and polyarchy must be in place.

The discussions which followed Dahl's publication led William Connolly, in his 1969 article "The challenge to pluralist theory", to criticize Dahl for too simplistic an approach. In his opinion, society is the site of constant competition between various groups over the establishment of political influence, and each group has certain opportunities to attempt to limit other groups in the achievement of political goals. On the international level, this order is violated by powerful multinational interests and dominant states.[21] Both Dahl and Connolly's approaches have one common provision, namely, that they describe the actions of groups or actors. To this day, discussions continue over these theories' adjustment to contemporary realities.[22] The neopluralist school is now a rather large group consisting of several fields engaged in the study of lobbyism[23], unions and social

20 Hunter, Floyd; Dahl, Robert A. (March 1962). "Who Governs: Democracy and Power in an American City". Administrative Science Quarterly. Johnson Graduate School of Management, Cornell University. 6 (4): 517–519.

21 William E. Connolly, Democracy, pluralism & political theory, Routledge: New York, 2007

22 Henrik Enroth. Beyond unity in plurality: Rethinking the pluralist legacy, Contemporary Political Theory, November 2010, Volume 9, Issue 4, pp 458–476.

23 Walker JL. 1983. The origins and maintenance of interest groups in America. Am. Polit. Sci. Rev. 77:390–406

movements[24], as well as networks.[25] The peak of the neopluralist school's activities was in the US in the 1970's-'90's. Andrew McFarland postulates on this school: "Political processes or neopluralist theories assume that persons being studied are aware of their own interests, and thus neopluralism is limited in its treatment of situations some call hegemony, that is, domination through cultural indoctrination."[26]

The new approach to pluralism in the sphere of world politics shows the importance of searching for creative resolutions in international relations, conflict situations, integration projects, and foreign policy. In his *Rethinking World Politics. A Theory of Transnational Neopluralism*, Philip Cerny argues that the paradigm of neopluralism arises out of globalization itself, which stirs economic competition between societies in new ways. Thus, neopluralism demands not dominance and centralized power, but "orchestration" and "political choreography."[27] Cerny postulates four scenarios for future global politics. The first entails that current political actors will adequately respond to current historical challenges and will develop a type of governance in the style of *raison du monde*. The second scenario is of the same spirit, but the leading driving force will be transnational social movements, which will establish a consensus on international rules and cosmopolitan legal practices. In the third scenario, governmental structures will merge with capital, as a result of which state-capitalist actors will compete with one another to yield a "disciplinary neoliberalism." In the final count, this scenario means the shift of power from political agents to economic ones, and thereby might lead to what Cerny calls a "governmentality gap", which bodes sorry consequences for the social world.[28] The fourth envisioned scenario is a New Middle Ages, which would be the result of the weakening of the nation-state system in the

---

24 Chong D. 1991. Collective Action and the Civil Rights Movement. Chicago: Univ. Chicago Press; Lichbach MI. 1995. The Rebel's Dilemma. AnnArbor: Univ. Mich. Press.

25 Heclo H. Issue networks and the executive establishment. In The New American Political System, ed. A King, Washington, DC: American Enterpise Institute, 1978. pp. 87–124.

26 Andrew S. McFarland. Neopluralism. P. 62. http://www.u.arizona.edu/~zshipley/pol431/Neopluralism.pdf

27 Philip G. Cerny. Rethinking World Politics. A Theory of Transnational Neopluralism. Oxford: Oxford University Press, 2010. P. 63.

28 Ibid. P. 305.

absence of any capability on the part of any categories of actors to acquire more power than others to influence international processes. This would lead not to chaos, but to "durable disorder."[29] Although these future scenarios remain speculative concepts, a combination of all of these scenarios in one way or another is quite possible. For developing an effective approach, however, it is more important to determine the rational mechanisms for such "political choreography", especially as certain forces clearly wish to take the place of, if not the choreographer, the lead dancer.

A more balanced approach has been proposed by Jeffrey Checkel, who suggests that a transition from monism to (semi-)pluralism in international relations theory has been well underway since the 1990's.[30] Checkel suggests that the landscape of leading publications has noticeably changed as key theorists have begun to change their discourse, signaling a turn towards pluralism. In 1997, the leading international relations journal in Europe, *European Journal of International Relations*, published a conceptual essay by one of the most recognized theorists in the field of international relations, the Uruguayan Professor Emanuel Adler. The latter's article defended the position of an intermediate point of view between two conventionally opposing paradigms.[31] Adler would develop the idea of pluralism in his other works[32], among which his collaboration with Peter Katzenstein is significant from the standpoint of civilizational theories[33], insofar

29 bid. P. 305.

30 Checkel, Jeffrey T. 2010. Theoretical Synthesis in IR: Possibilities and Limits, Simons Papers in Security and Development, 6, School for International Studies, Simon Fraser University, Vancouver, Canada. https://core.ac.uk/download/pdf/56378965.pdf

31 Adler, Emanuel (1997) „Seizing the Middle Ground: Constructivism in World Politics," European Journal of International Relations 3 (3): 319-63.

32 Emanuel Adler, Communitarian International Relations: The Epistemic Foundations of International Relations (London and New York: Routledge, 2005); Emanuel Adler and Vincent Pouliot, "International Practices: Introduction and Framework," in Emanuel Adler and Vincent Pouliot, eds. International Practices (New Cambridge and New York: Cambridge University Press, 2011); Emanuel Adler, "Constructivism in International Relations: Sources, Contributions, and Debates" in Walter Carlsnaes, Thomas Risse, and Beth A. Simmons, eds., Second Edition, Handbook of International Relations (London: Sage, 2012).

33 Emanuel Adler, "Europe as a Civilizational Community of Practice," in

as such a methodological approach undermines the monopoly of the Western liberal school.

Synthesis Theory

Synthesis theory organically arises out of the theory of neopluralism. The above-mentioned Jeffrey Checkel and many of his scholarly colleagues have for many years studied "using international institutions in Europe as their laboratory and a domain of application bridge-building strategy, they theorized the mechanisms of institutional socialization, from both rational-choice and constructivist perspectives."[34] Checkel et al. have developed a synthetic theory of bridge-building which promises "more compelling answers and a better picture of reality."[35] In this context, bridge-building means "not just developing scope conditions for when, say, rationalist or constructivist mechanisms prevail, but translating across very different philosophical commitments."[36] Yet Checkel himself admits: "There is no global community of IR bridge builders. Rather, with a few important exceptions in Canada and Germany, the debate over synthesis and pluralism has largely been an American one."[37] Naturally, the question arises as to just how effective such debates can be for creating practical tools. At the very least, there has been no clear sign that the figures engaged in important foreign-policy decision-making in the US have employed Checkel and his colleagues' theoretical innovations.

On the basis of a synthetic approach, the Cypriote author Nikos Lekakis has proposed an alternative path allowing one to avoid the

---

Peter Katzenstein, ed. Civilizations in World Politics: Plural and Pluralist Perspectives (New York and London: Routledge, 2009).

34 Checkel, Jeffrey T. (2007) „Constructivism and EU Politics," in Knud Erik Joergensen, Mark Pollack, Ben Rosamond (eds), Handbook of European Union Politics. London: Sage Publications.

35 Fearon, James and Wendt, Alexander (2002) „Rationalism v. Constructivism: A Skeptical View," in Walter Carlsnaes, Thomas Risse, Beth Simmons (eds), Handbook of International Relations. London: Sage Publications. P. 68

36 Checkel, Jeffrey T. 2010. Theoretical Synthesis in IR: Possibilities and Limits, Simons Papers in Security and Development, 6, School for International Studies, Simon Fraser University, Vancouver, Canada. P.18 https://core.ac.uk/download/pdf/56378965.pdf

37 Ibidem. P. 25.

inadequacies of the major paradigms of international relations.[38] In Lekakis' opinion, such an approach facilitates clear analysis of the role of national-level subjects in foreign policy and can help ensure more reliable research results. Lekakis explains:

> In the domains of application model, the attempt focuses on combining different theories specified independently, e.g. neoliberalism and constructivism, in the hope that together they may enhance our understanding of the real world. It deals with different empirical domains within a one-time frame. If the result is successful, the composite theory is deemed more comprehensive than each of the separate theories. This combination works best when the aim is to explain similar phenomena and the explanatory variables are complementary, i.e. they have little overlap – not interacting to influence the outcomes. The temporal sequencing model is similar to the domains of application but synthesizes theories that are temporally dependent, working together over time to explain a given domain. In this way, one theory is allowed to fill in the gap in the explanatory power of the other. In subsumption, one theory subsumes another when the latter constitutes a special case of the former so there is no scope of carrying out research under either of them separately.[39]

Although experiments have been conducted with the leading Western theories - of the English school, constructivism, liberalism, and realism (and their offshoots) - nothing hinders attempting the synthesis of other theories which do not fit into this conventional list or turning to non-Western models. Moreover, one can attempt to extract the rational grains from Western theories themselves, such as liberalism. For example, the opinion has been voiced that liberalism itself is not the exclusive property of the West.[40] The question is how to interpret liberal

---

38 Nikos Lekakis, Theory Synthesis in Sport and International Relations Research. May 26 2019, E-International Relations https://www.e-ir.info/2019/05/26/theory-synthesis-in-sport-and-international-relations-research/

39 Andreatta, Filippo and Mathias Koenig-Archibugi. 2010. 'Which Synthesis? Strategies of Theoretical Integration and the Neorealist–Neoliberal Debate'. International Political Science Review 31(2): 207–227.

40 Benazir Bhutto. Reconciliation. Islam, Democracy, and the West. Simon & Shuster, London, 2007. P. 261

ideas. If, for example, we take the notion of human rights, then several working frameworks could emerge. In the US, the interpretation of human rights arose out of the Christian teaching that God created all humans, and therefore all humans are equal. But what about traditions which reject creationism? In China, for instance, historically there has been no doctrine in the likes of monotheism. There is no God in Taoism, and there is no creation. Yet this does not mean that the Chinese tradition is amoral in its essence by virtue of its denial of equality between people. In the West, the question is regularly posed as to just how adequate the proclamation of equality has been in the spirit of the liberal political tradition. Karl Jaspers argued: "The notion of the equality of all people is completely, obviously false, given that such implies that the character and capacities of people are available for psychological study, and this notion is also false in terms of the reality of the social order, in which, only in the very best case scenario might people have equal chances and equal rights before the law."[41]

Finally, theory synthesis might be valuable to the extent that it provides for the first steps to be taken towards the rebirth of an holistic approach in the sciences, towards the rebirth of an holistic worldview.

Non-Western Theories of International Relations

In the late 1970's, Fernand Braudel wrote: "There is for one thing a 'historiographical' inequality between Europe and the rest of the world. Europe invented historians and then made good use of them…The history of non-Europe is still being written."[42] However, it would be another few decades before not only such a history, but also a non-Western school of international relations would begin. 2010 saw the publication of *Non-Western International Relations Theory: Perspectives On and Beyond Asia*, edited by Amitav Acharya and Barry Buzan, which lent an academic tone and broad circulation to this topic.[43] Buzan and Acharya

41 Yaspers C. Smisl I naznachenie istorii. Moscow: Politizdat, 1991. p. 453.

42 Fernand Braduel, Civilization and Capitalism, 15th-18th Century, Volume II: The Wheels of Commerce , (London/New York: William Collins Sons/ Harper & Row, 1982), p. 134.

43 Non-Western International Relations Theory: Perspectives On and Beyond Asia. (2010). Ed. by A. Acharya and B. Buzan. New York: Routledge.

proposed that non-Western theories of international relations do exist, but are kept out of Western discourse due to linguistic barriers and other problems, and therefore are still not being discussed on a global level. It is further argued that local environments have also not been conducive to the development of alternative theories, as only in democratic societies do there exist favorable conditions for broad debates and theorizing of international relations.

Yet in Lebedeva's opinion, contemporary interest in non-Western theories of international relations is related not only or not so much to the fact that at the end of the 20th and beginning of the 21st centuries international studies have begun to develop throughout numerous countries across the world, but rather the main impelling motive for the search for new theories of international relations, although unconsciously, has been the transformation of the political organization of the world (which remains Western at its core). Insofar as this transformation has covered all different levels, today we are witnessing a new, cardinal process of transformation of international political reality, thus stimulating the process of its conceptualization.[44]

What are these theories and with what countries and regions are they associated? First and foremost, attention should be paid to the Chinese school of international relations which has taken shape only in recent time, but which exerts definite influence on processes in world politics. However, in Yaqing Qin's opinion, there can be no such theory in the People's Republic of China for two reasons: firstly, due to the fact that the main ideas employed in practice have been taken from the West. Yaqing Qin demonstrates this by citing 63 books translated and published in China over time and under the aegis of different centers and publishing houses. Only one among them could, with certain reservations, be considered non-Western, namely, the Polish Professor Józef Kukułka's *Problems of International Relations Theory*, published in 1979. [45] However, for China such an author is relatively Western. Secondly, Qin argues that the term "international"

44 Lebedeva M. Nezapadnie teorii mezhdunarodnih otnosheniy: mif ili realnost? Vestnik RUDN. Seriya: Mezhdunarodnie otnosheniya, 2017 Vol. 17, No. 2. p. 246-256.

45 Yaqing Qin, Why is there no Chinese international relations theory? In Non-Western International Relations Theory: Perspectives On and Beyond Asia. (2010). Ed. by A. Acharya and B. Buzan. New York: Routledge. P. 29-31.

is not correct in terms of the Chinese view of the world. Historically, Chinese statehood developed along the sovereign-vassal model, as a result of which a tributary system took shape, at the center of which stood the emperor, while all the surrounding states were, from the point of view of the institution of sovereignty, dependent upon him. "In this unequal, quasi-international system called the Tributary System, China was the dominant power, maintaining stability and providing institutionalized mechanisms for interaction among states in roughly nowadays East Asia."[46] In this model, there was no room for "internationality", hence why this concept, typical of Western consciousness, simply does not correspond to Chinese thinking.

Nevertheless, this does not rule out the possibility of a particular, specifically Chinese approach to world politics. Qin proposes the "3G" model, consisting of Global Vision, Great Learning, and Grand Harmony. "Global Vision" means that "the Chinese that grow up in IR must have a global vision, rather than a mindset limited only to Chinese affairs." "Great Learning (Da Xue, 大学)", is named after one of the Six Books of the Confucian tradition which speaks of the need of "real-word-relevant learning", or the "inclusive" learning of things applicable to the "real world" and the integration of different ideas in reality. Great Harmony, in Qin's opinion, may sound utopian to Westerners, but for the Chinese is an approach and part of everyday life.[47]

As we pointed out earlier, in China various authors scrupulously approached analyzing changes in the world system in terms of the quantity and balance of poles even before the collapse of the Soviet Union. In addition, China is attributed the development of the concept of People's Diplomacy (*renmin waijiao,* 人民外交) and People-to-People Diplomacy (*minjian waijiao,* 民间外交).[48] This is partially related to the fact that when there were no ways to establish interplay on an interstate level due to the lack of official channels, Beijing resorted to the practice of "using the people as government officials

46 Ibid. P. 36.

47 Theory Talk #45: Qin Yaqing, November 30, 2011 http://www.theory-talks.org/2011/11/theory-talk-45.html

48 Casper Wits, The Transnational in China's Foreign Policy: The Case of Sino-JApanese Relations. New Perspectives on China's Relations with the World. National, Transnational and International, Ed. by Daniel Johanson, Jie Li & Tsunghan Wu. Bristol: E-International Relations, 2019. P. 105.

(*yimincuguan*)."[49] The expansive Chinese diaspora, especially in the Asian region, has aided the realization of this strategy.

To a certain degree, the New York Professor of Chinese heritage Lily Ling's[50] book *The Dao of World Politics*[51] might be considered part of the Chinese school of non-Western international relations. Ling endeavors to rely on the Taoist Yin-Yang dialectic to take world politics out of its current state of hegemony, hierarchy, and violence towards a more balanced system of cooperation through different means of equality, fluidity, and ethics. Ling's *The Dao of World Politics* also examines those aspects of world politics which are usually erased or overlooked in conventional international relations - for example, folk tales and popular culture - as well as how such factors influence, inform, and reinforce objective, rational political analysis. In essence, Ling's book presents a non-Western view on the Western, Westphalian type of international relations. However, Ling neither rejects nor excludes the latter. Rather, the book adheres to the teaching of the Dao: nothing remains as it was before, and everything comes from eternal truth. As follows, *The Dao of World Politics* proposes new means for formulating and acting in global politics in an inclusive and less coercive form. Only then, it is argued, will international relations allow for consciousness of what the Dao has always represented: a world of compassion and care.

At the same time, China has contributed to the development of a non-hegemonic theory of international order which emphasizes the maintenance of trade, yet in a manner differing sharply from that of European colonialism.

---

49 Ibidem. P. 108.

50 Attention should also be paid to another of Ling's works prepared jointly with an author of Greek origins: Anna M. Agathangelou, L.H.M. Ling, Transforming World Politics: From Empire to Multiple Worlds (Routledge, 2009). The latter criticizes neoliberalism and proposes both Greek and Chinese political theories as important components of a new, alternative approach to world politics. The work introduces the term "Worldism", a worldview whose main features and intellectual precedents are defined as constructivism, postmodernism, postcolonial studies, and Marxist and feminist contributions to history, philosophy, and revolutionary practice.

51 L.H.M. Ling, The Dao of World Politics: Towards a Post- Westphalian, Worldist International Relations. Routlege, 2014.

In India, meanwhile, an original theory has been advanced which examines the historical continuity and possibility of applying Advaita monism to international relations.[52] Amitav Acharya also argues that ancient sacred texts can be interpreted in terms of and for the sake of international relations. In Acharya's words:

> The philosophical texts that develop around the world's great religions, and not just the core scriptures like the Bible, Quran, Gita, or Tripitaka, carry important clues about epistemology, or how knowledge is produced, which is perfectly applicable to social science disciplines like IR. They represent conceptions of universalism that can either compliment or challenge the insights from Western philosophy, from which much of existing IR theory derives.[53]

Other philosophical concepts born on the Indian subcontinent have been analyzed through the prism of politics and in comparison with the Western sciences.[54] In the 20th century, the ideas of *Swaraj* and *Swadeshi* were widely employed throughout India. Whereas Swaraj reflects the idea of self-governance (and can literally be translated as "self-law"), Swadeshi is an economic strategy aimed at the achievement of self-sufficiency. Originally, Swadeshi meant the boycott of English goods, and was then appealed to as part of the Non-Aligned Movement.

The synthesis of religion and ethno-religious components can also be encountered in attempts at formulating an Islamic (Muslim) theory of international relations. Speculative Islamic theory of international relations does not speak of how states interact with one another or how the system of international relations influences the state, but rather presents a conceptualization of world order focused on relations between the Muslim/Arab and non-Muslim/non-Arab spheres, and how such can

52 Shahi D., Ascione G. Rethinking the absence of post-Western International Relations theory in India: 'Advaitic monism' as an alternative epistemological resource // European Journal of International Relations 2016. №. 2. P. 313—334.

53 Theory Talk #42 - Amitav Acharya, August 10, 2011 http://www.theory-talks.org/2011/08/theory-talk-42.html

54 Jones R.H. Science and Mysticism: A Comparative Study of Western Natural Science, Theravada Buddhism, and Advaita Vedanta. Bucknell University Press. 2016.

be attained. However, at the level of systemic analysis, Islam is rather difficult to interpret, insofar as it speaks of abstract notions such as the Ummah (community of believers) and *assabiya* (group feeling), and emphasizes the notion of supra-rational force. Nevertheless, these basic components, which make up the Islamic conception of world order, lend such a unique perspective. In recent time, especially with the rising significance of political Islam, such a theory of international relations is attracting more and more researchers in addition to previous attempts at similar analyses undertaken in the past.[55]

The question logically arises: is there a Russian theory of international relations? The Russian scholar Andrey Tsygankov argues that "over the past several centuries, Russia has developed an enormous, albeit scattered accumulation of theoretical knowledge which could by all means become the basis for formulating a Russian school of international relations theory."[56] However, "in order to develop international studies in Russia, deep knowledge of our own intellectual roots is needed, which is impossible without studying Russian thought."[57] In Tsygankov's opinion:

> The Russian theory of international relations that is taking shape today must appeal to deep and diverse Russian roots. It is important to take into account not only the socio-cultural uniqueness of the social sciences, but also the aspiration, organic for any theory, to overcome contextual dependency. A theory is made strong through attempts to rise above description and to reveal the general tendencies of the subject. As follows, it should be developed not only on the material of national debates, but also by way of constant comparison with the developmental processes of other schools of international theory. The optimal path for Russia is that of dialogue with the dominant and

---

55 См. J. Harris Proctor, Islam and I.R. N.Y: Praeger, 1965; Vatikiotis, P.J. Islam and the State N.Y: Routledge, 1987; Abo-Kazleh, Mahommed. Rethinking I.R. Theory in Islam: Towards a More Adequate Approach in Turkish Journal of International Relations vol.5 no.4 Winter 2006.

56 Tsygankov A. Rossiyskaya teoriya mezhdunarodnikh otnosheniy: kakoy ey bit? Sravnitelnaya politika № 2 (15) / 2014. pp. 65 - 83. https://cyberleninka.ru/article/n/rossiyskaya-teoriya-mezhdunarodnyh-otnosheniy-kakoy-ey-byt

57 Ibid..

> critical trends of international theory in both West and East. It is especially important to commensurate Russian reflections on the world with Western concepts and theories, insofar as the latter are the most systematized and analytically developed.[58]

Therefore, rethinking the legacy of the Slavophiles, the "Orientalizer current" (*Vostochnichestvo*), classical Eurasianism, as well as other philosophical doctrines ranging from Populism (*Narodnichestvo*) to Russian Cosmism and even Russian liberalism[59] promises to be fruitful.

Aesthetic Politics

If in antiquity politics was tied to the activity of the free citizens of the *poleis*, if in the Middle Ages the driving force of politics was religion, and if in the Renaissance politics began to be liberated from philosophical and theological notions - which led to an obsession with economics and ideology in Modernity and the rise of the bourgeoisie - then the circumstances of Post-Modernity have called all authorities and decision-making centers into question. Yet for all of these eras, one common detail has remained characteristic: a sense of beauty. Although many political manifestos and programs mention the need to strive for goodness and to create certain goods for citizens, external attributes, i.e. aesthetics, have conventionally remained secondary. Yet, the external side of politics - whether in the form of architectural constructs, court rituals, heraldry, or the commemorative depiction of battles and declarations - has often been an index of political supremacy or, vice versa, failure. Why, then, has aesthetics de facto been left outside of the Political?

Approaches to aesthetics can differ greatly from one another on the whole. Ronald Baker has emphasized the difference between the represented and representation.[60] A number of scholars have also conducted studies on the fixation of political moments in artistic

58 Ibid.

59 Of interest in this regard is P.V. Struve's remark that "Russian liberalism will become national not only de facto, but also consciously based in the Russian national element" See: Struve P. Nacionalnoe nachalo v liberalizme // Natsiya i imperia v russkoi mysli nachala XX veka. Moscow: Skimen, 2003. p. 235.

60 Pop-kultuta, v chem je ona horosha? Na samom dele, vo mnogih veshah! 10 Jan.

works and the subsequent use of art for political ends. In his books *Political Representation* and *Aesthetic Politics: Political Philosophy Beyond Fact and Value*, the Dutch political philosopher Franklin Ankersmit sought to re-conceptualize the legacy of Machiavelli, as well as deconstruct in detail and critique a number of Western political notions that have claimed universality over the past two centuries. In both works, Ankersmit uses the concept of *Virtu*, describing it as the ability of a state actor to immediately grasp any complex situation and to capture its essence. The subject of this analysis is the statesman who, analyzing a situation, understands in what direction he must act, and who wields personal power and charisma that compels others to react to his will and presence. Most importantly, the statesman subtly feels the right moment for political action. *Virtu* is closely tied to *Prudentia* (prudence) which classical authors such as Cicero considered to be the highest political virtue. In Ankersmit's words:

> "Virtu" and "prudentia" go beyond what ethics requires us to do, not in the sense that they are completely opposed to morality, but rather in that they see that morality is merely one of several considerations lying at the basis of political action. They are amoral or supramoral rather than immoral. Both are political or practical virtues in the sense that they require the politician to combine knowledge and action, instead of creating an insurmountable barrier between the two, as we have learned to do since Descartes and Kant.[61]

With the examples of Schumpeter and Smith, Ankersmit shows that "the transition from Stoic natural law philosophy to economics (and the social sciences), and the transition from a teleological to a merely instrumental Stoic reason (which has determined the nature of the social sciences down to the present day) is the consequence of a falling apart of the Stoic natural order."[62] Overall, Ankersmit's detailed description of various ideas, concepts, theories, and their interpretations in European political consciousness demonstrates that attempts at creating

---

2018. https://pluriversum.org/opinion/globalism/pop-kultura-v-chem-zhe-ona-horosha-na-samom-dele-vo-mnogih-veshhah/

61 F.R. Ankersmit, Aesthetic Politics: Political Philosophy Beyond Fact and Value (Stanford: Stanford University Press, 1996), 14.

62 Ibid., 80.

a political society or system entailing full consensus are doomed to fail, and such failures are frequently veiled with the need to respond to "new challenges" or "openness" to "political creativity." Aristotle also suggested that increasing unity leads to the disappearance of the state. This thesis confirms the aspirations of the globalists, whose vision foresees a global government that would, in all likelihood, represent a global corporation, not a unified political system.

For Ankersmit, politics requires friction, without which we would be idle. In his work *Political Representation*, Ankersmit argues that "The political party's point of departure should be the citizen's self-division after and because of the death of ideology, and the resulting conflict between short- and long-term interests and in how these conflicts can be expressed and articulated in terms of conceptions of the nation's future."[63] In *Aesthetic Politics*, this thought is formulated even more clearly: "Democracy will not work in a society or in a political reality that has no deep cleavages or in which these can insufficiently articulate themselves - or perhaps one should rather say, where they can no longer sufficiently articulate themselves, since it is the very purpose of democracy to achieve by a reconciliation of all relevant oppositions the kind of political order in which it will have condemned itself as a useless political construction."[64] Naturally, such an approach leads to the conclusion that in Western societies the state system and society itself are alienated from one another, evidence of which can be seen in the many crises which Europe and the US have faced. Ankersmit, for his part, concludes: "Order, peace, and the safety of citizens' lives and property are low on the state's list of priorities - if the state still thinks a list of priorities to be at all desirable."[65]

The theories of this Dutch philosopher are also useful for substantiating criticism of the bourgeois system and Western democracy as such. Ankersmit sees the bourgeoisie as usurpers, as the first to have created a "melting pot" out of different castes, or rather caste functions, who yet have remained incapable as a class of fulfilling their mission. Ankersmit writes: "This preeminently uncertain social class, the bourgeoisie, took upon itself a responsibility that no previous social

63 F.R. Ankersmit, Political Representation (Stanford: Stanford University Press, 2002), p. 132.

64 Ankersmit, Aesthetic Politics: Political Philosophy Beyond Fact and Value, 143.

65 Ibid., 160.

class would ever have dreamed of."[66] Further, in Ankersmit's words: "Indeed, the style of democracy is open and ironic, adverse to system and the seriousness of theory - and whoever wishes to imposes on democracy a high and sublime goal will try unwittingly to exchange democracy for an aristocracy ruled by the select group of himself and his own kindred spirits."[67] Such a thesis fits well for describing the US political system, in which democracy is more often than not mere demagogy for voters, all the while as the leadership of the country de facto belongs to a two-party aristocracy.

The study of the interrelationship between aesthetics and politics has also been the subject of several books of Roland Bleiker.[68] Bleiker suggests that "aesthetic sources offer us alternative insight: a type of reflective understanding that emerges not from applying the analytical skills that are central to the social sciences, but from cultivating a more open-ended level of creativity and sensibility about the political."[69] On this note it should be mentioned that, besides Plato and his notion of beauty and the beautiful[70], the founding father of aesthetic politics might be the Russian philosopher Konstantin Leontiev, who said that "higher aesthetics is at once the highest social and political practice."[71] Furthermore, Leontiev wrote:

> I believe aesthetics to be the best measure of history and life, for it applies to all ages and all localities...Statehood is strong only wherever there is much heterogenous aesthetics in life, so that this visible aesthetics is a sign of internal, practical, or in other words creative life...If visible diversity and the perceived intensity of life (its aesthetics) are in essence signs of the internal vitality of humanity, then their reduction must be a sign of the obsolescence of humanity and its near death (on earth).[72]

66 Ankersmit, Political Representation, 69.

67 Ibid., 157.

68 Roland Bleiker, Popular Dissent, Human Agency and Global Politics, Cambridge University Press, 2000; Divided Korea: Toward a Culture of Reconciliation, University of Minnesota Press, 2005; Aesthetics and World Politics, Palgrave, 2009; The Aesthetic Turn in International Political Theory // Millennium: Journal of International Studies, Vol. 30, No. 3, 2001.

69 Roland Bleiker: Aesthetics and World Politics, 2015 https://exploringgeopolitics.org/roland-bleiker-aesthetics-and-world-politics/

70 See dialogues Phaedrus and Symposium.

71 Leontiev K. Izbrannoe. Moscow, 1993. p .158.

72 Leontiev K. Pismo k V.V. Rozanovu от 13 aug. 1891.

Of no less interest in this regard is Leontiev's opinion on the existence of a form of logic that is different from rationalist logic. Leontiev noted that for the blossoming of any culture, a harmony between knowledge and ignorance is needed, since:

> Culture is not the spread of knowledge, science, and so on, but the aggregate of all those markers by which one civilization differs from another, and in this all the most ignorant beliefs, superstitions, and intransigencies play a significant and altogether largely useful role. Common knowledge, on the contrary, going beyond some kind of line that is elusive to reason, most strongly contributes to the destruction of living and unique cultures.[73]

Given that Konstantin Leontiev was a religious philosopher, the influence of Neoplatonism is lucid here, also given that such is implicitly present in Orthodox Christianity. This, in turn, speaks to the connection with Neo-Byzantinism, which might also serve as an orientation for developing an alternative political model, especially in those regions previously under the rule or influence of the Byzantine Empire, as well as where Orthodox Christianity continues to predominate to this day.[74]

Sustainable Politics

For many years, calls for the creation of appropriate mechanisms for a sustainable development model have been voiced from high tribunes, in particular by UN representatives. In these actors' views, such policies could lead to the eradication of conflicts and poverty in developing countries, as well as help to solve the problems of mass epidemics, access to social services, and halt the pollution of the environment, etc. "Sustainable development" has become part of the UN Millennium Development Goals program. Despite the resources expended on this and all the relevant declarations, many of these goals have not been reached, armed conflicts continue to flare up around

---

https://azbyka.ru/otechnik/Konstantin_Leontev/izbrannye-pisma-v-v-rozanovu/

73 Leontiev K. Leontiev K. Vostok, Rossiya, slavyanstvo. Filosofskaya i politicheskaya publitsistika. Duhovnaya proza (1872 — 1891). Moscow: Respublika, 1996. p. 696.

74 Ustyan A. Politicheskaya kontsepciya neovizantizma. Moscow: Institut socialnikh nauk, 2003.

the world, and greedy corporations still mercilessly exploit natural resources.

On this point, Corrado Poli has noted:

> The Sustainable Development approach has become the sole strategy available to deal with the environmental crisis and it operates as the proxy of a missing ideology. The removal of any alternative to environmental policy is paralleled with the elimination of a century old political dialectic between capitalism and socialism. This temporary lack of conflicting comprehensive political projects has impoverished the current intellectual and political debate.[75]

In Poli's opinion, "the elaboration of a political alternative - based on new social and political values related to a radically new covenant between humanity and nature - would help to recreate a new dialectic and the conditions for human progress." Russian authors have remarked on this matter that "only later has it become clear that, in addition to ecological security, it is important to include other characteristics of the real development process, i.e., the economic, political, legal, demographic, informational, and other dimensions."[76]

But the question is not only of the environment. Overall, neglect for the environment is rooted in Modernity, which gave birth to liberalism, fascism, and communism, all of which have, to different degrees, borne exploitative strategies aimed at the subjugation of nature. While liberalism provides for the exploitation of the working class through the usurpation of the means of production and the establishment of monopoly conditions, the other two theories entailed a certain subjugation of the animal and vegetal world, as the exploitation of natural resources and the acquiring of new knowledge are supposed to aid the establishment of a new society and serve the good of the nation or peoples. As shown in one of the preceding chapters, approaches to time have also influenced how society organizes its being, including political discussions and decisions. While apologists of liberal-capitalist ideology ceaselessly speak of progress supposed

---

75 Corrado Poli, Environmental Politics. New Geographical and Social Constituencies. Springer International Publishing Switzerland, 2015. P. 4.

76 Ursul A. Bezopasnost v kontekste globalnoy ustoychivosti // Information wars № 2 (46) 2018. p. 66.

to improve peoples' lives, the acute growth of industrial technologies has in fact seen peoples' lives worsen in terms of ecological criteria (air purity, access to clean water, the manufacturing of foodstuffs with organic components, the organization of living and working space, the utilization of wastes, etc.). If we remain within the paradigm of the liberal worldview, then despite all the UN debates and the adoption of various programs for the reduction of CO^2 emissions and fighting global warming, still no improvement shall follow.

If we consider nature to be part of us, then a respectful attitude towards nature can be realized only given the appropriate worldview. This demands confidence in a constant of some kind that will be adhered to not only by us, but also by future generations. In the political sciences, such a current is known as conservatism. Although conservatism is well known in many different incarnations, in our case it is worth mentioning the work of one of the leaders of the *Jungkonservatismus* movement in Germany, Arthur Moeller van den Bruck, whom we cited in chapter five. If political projects are pursued with an eye to eternity, then states and peoples will have different goals and means than those conceivable when trying merely to keep afloat or join in on economic competition with other powers. The consideration of eternity sets the tone for taking essential political decisions which can be flexible and meet primary needs. According to Arthur Moeller van den Bruck, conservatism is a workshop, not a collection of antiquities. In the opinion of this German thinker, traditional values retain a nation's ability to grow, and the acquisition of new values increases the vitality of a people. It is through the bearer of conservative ideas that the spirit of a nation acquires its image, as the conservative bases himself in traditional values as a unique identity.[77] Of course, for this an adequate understanding of tradition is necessary. In Eugen Fink's words: "Tradition is not only of an informative character. It does not simply inform what life is in all its rises and falls, how instincts and passions follow man, and how he is moved towards the noble and beautiful. Tradition has demands. It has many forms for its imperatives, such as the soft pressure of unspoken rules of decency, and such semantic structures as property, family, and state, sanctioned by human and divine law."[78]

---

77 Savin L. Arthur Moeller van den Bruck I mladokonservativnaya revolutsiya v Germanii // Russkoe Vremya, №1, 2009. pp. 62 - 65.

78 Fink E. Osnovnie phenomeni chelovecheskogo bitiya. Moscow: Kanon+, 2017. p. 43.

Unique identity is another important element for theorizing political sustainability, and this question has been raised not only in Europe, but beyond. The ideologist of the establishment of the modern state of Pakistan, Muhammad Iqbal, employed the term *khudi.* Although English translations of the Urdu frequently render such "Ego" or "Self Ego", which distorts the original meaning and more often than not introduces a certain confusion, *khudi* in fact means "selfhood", and is one of the key terms of Iqbal's philosophy. Although *khudi* appeals directly to Islam and is reminiscent of the view of Sufi mystics (as Muhammad Iqbal said: "*khudi* lives in your heart"), there is a collective version of this notion as well: *Ijtimayi Khudi.*[79] The latter is supposed to be appropriately integrated and organized into the political process, for which Iqbal uses the metaphor of music: the sound of instruments and singing must follow a certain system, or else there will be only cacophony.

When these respective thinkers were active in Germany and Pakistan, the challenges of Modernity demanded a certain reaction. In the first case, the remedy of Conservative Revolution was proposed, while in the second a rethinking of the Muslim heritage. Both ideas were born at a time when the major political currents of the era were attempting to build themselves into Modernity and become Modernist from within, thereby yielding furious attacks on traditional society and attempts at transforming society in line with their political goals.

The contemporary social dynamic, although under the sign of Post-Modernity, to no extent diminishes the mistakes of the past but, on the contrary, calls for their thorough analysis in accordance with contemporary challenges. The present social dynamic also highlights the importance of traditional values, hence the heightened interest in conservatism.

In the present situation, the abandonment of identity and the neglect of selfhood are leading to the weakening of the life forces of peoples to an even greater extent than happened under Modernity. The state is becoming vulnerable not only to Western liberal hegemony, but all sorts and forms of ideological simulacra and political derivatives.

---

79 Taimur Afzal Khan. Thoughts of Iqbal. Translation of Dr. Javid Iqbal's Urdu Publication "Afkar-e-Iqbal (Tashreehat-e-Javid)". Lahore: Ilm-O-Fann Publications, 2017. P. 31.

Before we can begin to speak about programs for sustainable development and sustainable economics, we must first establish a base for sustainable politics, and this is possible only upon appropriately appealing to conservative thinking and, as follows, traditional systems and metaphysical practices. This, in turn, highlights the significant place of the sacred in the life of peoples and civilizations. As one recent study has noted: "Whether religious or secular, sacred values are ideas, preferences or beliefs that people refuse to measure along material scales, typically evidenced by a refusal to trade off for economic (for example, money), social (for example, status) or other material benefits."[80] These values are persistently being preserved and transmitted from generation to generation, including even in Western countries despite the social erosion caused by globalization that has penetrated all distant corners of our planet. The hermeneutics of religious texts is also useful to substantiating a new approach to politics on the basis of conservative values. In the Bible, it is said in Isaiah 11:6 that "The wolf also shall dwell with the lamb, and the leopard shall lie down with the kid; and the calf and the young lion and the fatling together; and a little child shall lead them." Is this not an interpretation of the coexistence of cultures and civilization? Perhaps the main question on this matter remains how to correctly institutionalize the relevant political mechanisms in different societies for arriving at genuinely sustainable politics through consensus.

Dasein and the Fourth Political Theory

One relatively new, alternative political theory is the Fourth Political Theory, proposed by the Russian philosopher Alexander Dugin. The Fourth Political Theory is an open project whose ordinal number reflects the principle of its negational approach: it is neither the first, second, nor third theories, which it identifies as Liberalism, Marxism (Communism), and National Socialism (Fascism) respectively. All of the latter claimed planetary domination and wielded their own interpretations of time and the subject of history. As for the subject for the Fourth Political Theory, one of the key concepts of Heidegger's

80 Ángel Gómezl, Lucía López-Rodríguez, Hammad Sheikh, Jeremy Ginges, Lydia Wilson, Hoshang Waziri, Alexandra Vázquez, Richard Davis and Scott Atran, The devoted actor's will to fight and the spiritual dimension of human conflict.// Nature Human Behaviour. Vol 1. September 2017. P. 673–679. https://www.nature.com/articles/s41562-017-0193-3.epdf

philosophy has been proposed: *Dasein.* Often translated as "being-here", the French philosopher Henry Corbin translated this term as "human reality", but for the sake of genuine, complete understanding, this and many other of Heidegger's terms are best left untranslated. They should be provided in the original alongside something similar in one's native language. Other possible variations should also be considered. For example, *das Man* expresses inauthentic Dasein that has fallen into banality, whereas in authentic existing, Dasein has the property of "being-towards-death" – *Sein zum Tode* – which represents existential terror. Terror is counterposed to fear, which imbues the world with external things and the internal world with empty worries. Interesting to note in this regard is the fact that modern Western policies and liberalism as such are built on fear. This tendency dates back centuries and is directly related to the formation of Western (European) philosophy.

Let us add that another of Dasein's properties is spatiality, as space depends on Dasein, while on the other hand it is not a function of time. Dasein conditionally exists between the outer and inner, the past and present, the margin and the instant. Dasein has existential parameters – being-in-the-world (*In-der-Welt-Sein*), being-in (*In-sein*), being-with (*Mit-sein*), care (*die Sorge*), thrownness (*Geworfenheit*), *Befindlichkeit* (attunement, sofindingness, disposedness), fear (*Furcht*), understanding (*Verstehen*), discourse (*Rede*), and mood (*Stimmung*).

Another important element of Heidegger's philosophy is the Fourfold, encompassing Sky, Divinities, Earth, and Mortals – which are depicted in the following manner: the Sky in the upper left, the Divinities (immortals) in the upper right, mortals (people) in the bottom left, and the Earth in the lower right. An axis runs between people and gods and another between Sky and Earth. The center of the Fourfold is the most authentic modus of the existence of Dasein.

It should also be noted that Heidegger distinguishes between past and that which has passed, what is present and what is now, and the future and what is forthcoming. Dasein, according to Heidegger, must make a fundamental choice between the forthcoming and the future, i.e., the choice of authentic existing and directly confronting being (*Seyn*). Then the forthcoming will become the future. If Dasein chooses inauthentic existence, then the forthcoming will only be forthcoming, and therefore will not come into being. Overall, Heidegger's ideas are rather difficult to comprehend, insofar as he employed numerous artificial constructions intended to convey the real meaning of a wide range of phenomena. Describing all of these elements of Heidegger's philosophy in detail, Alexander Dugin poses the important question: can one speak of a specific Russian Dasein? What are its existentials? In what does it differ from the European Dasein? Dugin arrives at the conclusion that a special Russian Dasein does exist - and not only a Russian one, for at the heart of each civilization lies a particular "thinking presence", or Dasein, which determines the structure of a given civilization's Logos. It follows that every people (civilization) has its own special set of existentials. Dugin's interpretation of Heidegger's ideas is also tied to the history of Russian ideas, Orthodox Christianity, and a special path of state development including the theory of Eurasianism.

Heidegger's legacy is constantly criticized by liberals across the board, regardless of where and what the object of criticism is – be it Heidegger's work as a university professor, his interest in Ancient Greek philosophy and related interpretations of antiquity, or his relationship with the political regime in Germany before and after 1945. One gets the impression that liberals intentionally strive to demonize Heidegger and his works, yet the profundity and depth of this German philosopher's thought gives them no break. Clearly, this is because Heidegger's ideas harbor a message which is relevant to the creation of a counter-liberal project that can be realized in the most diverse forms.

In this context, it is necessary to take note of Heidegger's journals, famously known as the *Black Notebooks*, *1931-1938*, published under the title *Ponderings*. Therein, Heidegger criticizes liberalism in the following manner: "The 'liberal' sees 'connectedness' in his own way. He sees only 'dependencies' – 'influences', but he never understands that there can be an influencing which is of service to the genuine basic stream of all flowing and provides a path and a direction."[81] Another of Heidegger's most important entries reads: "The metaphysics of Dasein must become deeper in accord with the innermost structure of

81 Heidegger M. Razmishleniya II–VI (Chernie tetradi 1931–1938). Moscow: Izdatelstvo instituta Gaidara, 2016. p. 45.

metaphysics and must expand into the metapolitics 'of' the historical people."[82] As Dugin has pointed out, if early Heidegger assumed that Dasein is something given, then later Heidegger concluded that Dasein is something that must be discovered, substantiated, and constituted. To this end, it is necessary first and foremost to accomplish a serious intellectual process.

It is crucial to understand that although Heidegger's ideas are considered to be a kind of culmination of European philosophy (which began with the Ancient Greeks, a point which is symbolic in itself since Heidegger built his hypotheses on an analysis of Ancient Greek philosophers), Heidegger is also often classified as a thinker who transcended Eurocentrism. For this reason, during his lifetime, many of Heidegger's concepts were welcomed in regions that had developed critiques of philosophy with regards to the European heritage as a whole. For example, enormous interest in Heidegger's works could be found in 20th century Latin America. In Brazil, Heidegger's works were addressed by Vicente Ferreira da Silva, in Argentina by Carlos Astrada, Vicente Fantone, Enrique Dussel, and Francisco Romero, in Venezuela by Juan David Garcia Bacca, and in Colombia by Ruben Sierra Mejia.

Additional confirmation of this can be found in the words of the Iranian philosopher Ahmad Fardid to the effect that Heidegger can be seen as a figure of global significance, not merely as a representative of European thought. Interestingly enough, Fardid rejected the writing of texts, seeing this as a Western tradition, and only held talks with audiences. In a 1976 interview for Alireza Meybodi, it is clear that Fardid followed the philosophical line of the Sufi poet Hafez Shirazi. Fardid continued to actively develop the very important concept of another Iranian philosopher, Jalal Al-e-Ahmad, known as *Gharbzadegi*, or "Westoxification." Yet in Fardid's opinion, even in Iran this concept has been incorrectly interpreted.

Heidegger has had followers not only in Iran, but in many Asian countries as well. In Japan in the 1930's, Heidegger's student Kitaro Nishida founded the Kyoto School of Philosophy. Although in Japan Heidegger has largely been considered a bearer of the European spirit (following

82 Ibid. p. 140.

the Meiji reforms, Japan was swept with excessive enthusiasm for everything European, especially German culture and philosophy), it is interesting to note that Heidegger's notion of "existence" was redrafted in a Buddhist spirit as "true being" (*genjitsu sonzai*) and "Nothing" ("Oblivion") has been interpreted as "emptiness" (*shunya*). In other words, the Japanese interpreted Martin Heidegger's basic concepts in accordance with their own concepts, and they have also often blended his terms with the concepts of such European existentialists as Jean-Paul Sartre, Albert Camus, and Gabriel Marcel. Another Japanese philosopher, Keiji Nishitani, has adapted Heidegger's ideas to traditional Eastern models, as is so often done in the East. Parallels between traditional Eastern philosophy and Heideggerian analysis have also been drawn in Korea by Hwa Yol Jung.

In this situation, Russia and the study of Martin Heidegger's legacy form a kind of bridge between Europe and the East, between the rigid rationalism that has subsumed European consciousness since the Middle Ages, and the abstract contemplative thinking characteristic of Asian peoples. Let us say even more directly that Eurasianism and Heideggerianism are in some sense interconnected and spiritually close tendencies among contemporary ideological currents in Russia. Although these two schools can also be examined as independent philosophical doctrines, as is often done by secular scholars and opportunistic political scientists, any deep understanding of one can be had only upon grasping the other. If we take a radical[83] approach to the re-thinking political models, we find that the Eurocentric approach can be traced back to the Hellenic worldview. In his work on Heraclitus, Heidegger wrote: "We act…as if the determination of the human into a 'subject' were the most obvious thing in the world, when in fact such a determination is scarcely three hundred years old (though certainly during this time, as an incomprehensible frenzy of history, this determination has taken the essence of the human into its will)."[84] It is no coincidence that this cycle of lectures from 1935 (1943?) bore the title "The Inception of Occidental Thinking."

83 It should be remembered that the term "radical" comes from the Latin word radix, meaning "root." In the sense we employ here, "radical" has nothing to do with extremism or marginality, but rather with the remembrance of the ancient Latin proverb "Look to the root."

84 Martin Heidegger, Heraclitus: The Inception of Occidental Thinking and Logic: Heraclitus' Doctrine of the Logos (London: Bloomsbury, 2018), 99.

Of great importance is the very posing of the question of why the Greeks began to divide nature into subject and object, which ultimately led to a constantly renewing process of fragmentation and differentiation. Changes in social system over the course of history have led to a split between tactical and internal individuality (orientation towards good and what pleases one). The theory of the subject was later developed to solve the problem of instability in social use of signs and their vague references. Consequentially, the individual began to be divided according to the principle of positive and negative assessments of chances - the subject is contrasted to the home-copy as the person of the masses.[85] The object is also subject to change.

In his *Parmenides*, Heidegger said: "Modern man, the subject to whom the 'world' has become a uniquely uniform 'object,' consumes even time."[86] Further, Heidegger noted that the so-called "subjective" and the accompanying "objective" and their intertwinement are altogether dubious at the onset. A similar logic leads to the division into center and periphery, into "This" and "Other", which on a geographical scale sees the concentration of world history around Europe, whereas the geography of the marginal is filled in with dragons and barbarians, thereby justifying future expansion and the establishment of certain norms. If we adopt a radical approach to analyzing what the subject of history is, then perhaps the very denial of the posing of this question of division into subject and object, of this double-digit logic, is a necessary step in the direction of developing a new paradigm of politics and international relations.

In the opinion of the German sociologist Niklas Luhmann, the "dry veri-/falsified style of logical positivism which neglects other forms of expression, such as poetry and metaphysics, is no longer suitable"[87], and the fact that in Western circles which reject revolution people practice immersion into "consensus-oriented" discourses can, from a sociological point of view, hardly be regarded as a socio-political alternative. In other words, the imperative of a new political model is tied to departing from scholastic philosophy and appealing to other forms of knowing and interpreting the world, as well as revolutionary praxis.

---

85 Luman N. Differentsiatsii. Moscow: Logos, 2006. p. 191.

86 Heidegger M. Parmenid. SPb.: Vladimir Dal, 2009. p. 306.

87 Luman N. Самоописания. Moscow: Logos/Gnosis, 2009. pp. 280-281.

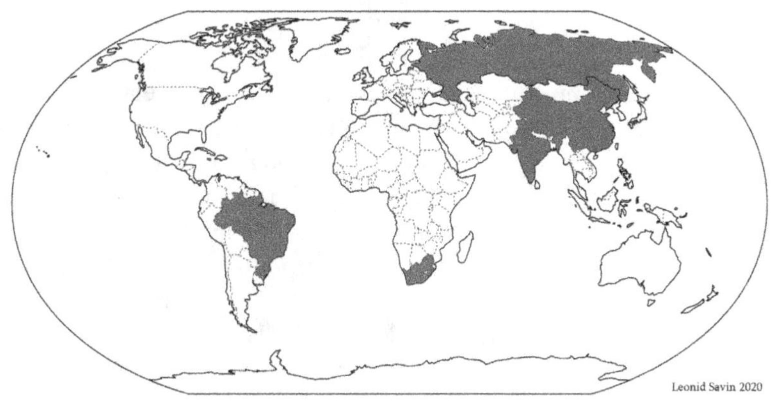

BRICS functions as an informal association of five states.

As a tool for developing a Fourth Political Theory, we can also adopt "generative capacity", which Kenneth Gergen characterized as "the capacity to challenge the guiding assumptions of the culture, to raise fundamental questions regarding contemporary social life, to foster reconsideration of that which is 'taken for granted', and thereby to generate fresh alternatives..."[88] In Gergen's words, generative theory "is designed to unseat conventional assumptions and to open new alternatives for action."[89] Gergen proposes to characterize people as "polyvocal subjects" capable of formulating numerous positions on the same question. This means demonstrating a certain level of similarity with one's supposed rival, in the form of a "revelation of one's counter-capacities" which "renders one 'part of the other.'"[90] Such a position allows for avoiding a Manichaean approach to politics in which divisions into "Us" and "Them" are artificially manipulated in favor of interest groups.

Overall, we can see that there already exists a number of conceptual and ideological tendencies which can claim to represent a certain alternative theory, and which are appropriate for realization on a global level. Some of them were first founded and developed in the early 20th century, while others are only beginning to be introduced in the form of political theories today. These tendencies are becoming

88 Kenneth J. Gergen, Toward Transformation in Social Knowledge. New York, 1982. P. 109, 142.

89 Kenneth J. Gergen, Social Construction in Context (London: SAGE, 2001), 163.

90 Ibidem. pp. 109-110.

evermore relevant alongside other geopolitical processes, especially given the reconfiguration of the world space that is ongoing through regional integration unions and new forms of interrelations, such as can be seen in the case of the BRICS club and in the growing number of bilateral agreements on transitioning towards accounting in national currencies, which are being signed on to by states wishing to free themselves from dependency on the dollar in international trade and therefore become more independent politically. Although such processes are taking place on different levels, they are intertwined and are vitally important to strengthening multipolarity.

13

Multipolar Praxis

In this concluding chapter, we will examine the emerging methodologies of interaction between those poles and relatively independent centers of power which are decisively influencing world politics. What are these methods? When it comes to the prospects of peaceful coexistence, there is ever-increasing talk of the need to establish dialogue between cultures and civilizations, to seek consensus, and to develop understanding on the most important issues. For a polycentric structure with multiple intersecting processes, it would be more appropriate to use the term "polylogue" or "multilogue." For instance, Richard Duke has employed the term "multilogue" in the context of communication and simulation gaming-training (including social and political spaces)[1], and the Soviet scholar M. Kagan spoke of "polylogue" to describe means of interaction.[2] In the opinion of contemporary Russian scholars, the technique of multilogue is by all means effective and adequate for structures typified by diversity: if dialogue is fraught with divergences, then multilogue allows for the development of different positions, acting upon them amidst their dynamism, and including all participants in communication processes in order to ensure access to consensus-forging technologies and techniques.[3] This term has yet to become widespread in political discourse, yet it has begun to be employed mainly by critics of liberalism and globalization. For example, in his work *After Liberalism*, Immanuel Wallerstein called for global multilogue to deal with current problems and to prevent lapsing into illusions and new mistakes.[4]

1 Duke R. Gaming: The Future's Language. N.Y.: Sage Publications, 1974.

2 Kagan M. Mir obsheniya. Moscow, 1988.

3 Zaitsev A. Multilog. Moscow: Akademia, 2001. p. 7.

4 Wallerstein I. Posle liberalizma. Moscow: URSS, 2003. p. 140.

Nevertheless, all of these ideas and concepts, despite their histories or relevance to contemporary political processes, remain fragmented and lack broader circulation in international discourse, largely because of the unwillingness of a number of states to lose their status as the "owners" of the terminological and scientific apparatus. The whole world remains virtually at the mercy of the Western point of view on world order, while the existing system of international relations remains unsatisfactory and in many ways unacceptable for the majority of countries and peoples.

This state of affairs must be changed. We cannot yet offer an unambiguous answer as to how new, future international interactions will be labelled, whether "multilevel polylogue" between communities, processes of "co-management" between cultures and civilizations, or some other term.[5] Moreover, it cannot be ruled out that old and forgotten concepts will once again re-emerge, or even that current theories will be rethought in new appropriate contexts. In the emerging reality, attention should be paid to new types of alliances, their subjectivity, and the phenomena of their interactions which are above all complex in nature.

Parallel Structures

One aspect of no small importance to the strategy of multipolarity is the inclusion of new actors into a broad coalition which rejects the unipolar dictatorship of the US. Naturally, every country will have its own motivations and interests, which may diverge at times, but multipolarity will serve more often than not as a platform for strengthening both bilateral relations and broad cooperation. For example, in the case of India this means more than just BRICS and SCO. The states which do not belong to these alliances also constitute the structure of multipolarity that is presently taking shape. As pointed out by Mohammad Samir Hussain of the National Centre of International Security and Defence Analysis at the University of Pune: "India and Germany also share the interest of preventing the emergence of the unipolar world. Both countries have a common stake in the quest for a multi-polar world. Being a member of G-4 countries, both countries

5 Savin L. Stanovlenie politsentrichnogo miroustroistva // Globalnie tendentsii razvitiya mira (Moscow, 14 June 2012 г.,INION RAN) Moscow: Nauchniy expert, 2013. pp. 371-380.

have committed to more power centers and are against the bipolar structure that existed during the cold war period. Both have protested against the U.S. or any super power dominance in the world."[6]

Of course, for the time being Germany remains a satellite of Washington and is hardly likely to actively insist on a new international paradigm. But this situation may change, and Berlin might then still be able to prove itself to be a fully-fledged sovereign actor. Indeed, there have already been proposals which might be called "draft sketches" for multipolarity, such as the concept of "anchor countries." The latter was developed by the German Development Institute in 2004 in response to the ambitions of the German Minister for Economic Cooperation to play a more active role in the world arena. Traditionally, this ministry had focused on countries and peoples on the periphery of the global economy or those who have been victims of globalization. The minister's team then believed that the noble goal of helping these target groups deserves a new approach. At the time, the German government did not support the US' unipolar approach (or that of its European ally Great Britain), but also recognized its own limited influence in the world. The concept of anchor countries substantiated the language and initial expeditiousness necessary to translating ideas into action. In this view, anchor countries were identified as bearing "economic weight and political influence" and as playing "a major role in their regions as well as on a more global scale in determining international politics."[7] Thereafter, the ministry began experimenting with this approach by assigning priority to six countries: India, Pakistan, South Africa, Indonesia, China, and Turkey. This concept also includes regional links as well: for instance, Russia and Turkey are seen as "anchors" for Europe and Central Asia; Argentina, Brazil, and Mexico as the anchors of Latin America; China, Indonesia, and Thailand for East Asia; Egypt, Iran, and Saudi Arabia for the Middle East and North Africa; India and Pakistan for South Asia; and South Africa and Nigeria for Sub-Saharan Africa. If we examine the composition

6 Mohammad Samir Hussain, India And Germany: Coming Together For A Multipolar World – Analysis, September 21, 2011. http://www.eurasiareview.com/21092011-india-and-germany-coming-together-for-a-multipolar-world-analysis/

7 Anchor Countries – Partners for Global Development, BMZ Position Paper 119, Bonn: Federal Ministry for Economic Cooperation and Development – Development Education and Information Division, 2004.

of this palette of states, we can see that the majority of them consider geopolitical multipolarity to be genuinely positive, boast natural and energy resources, have powerful armed forces (four of these states still possess nuclear arms) and, also of no small importance, these states also have certain political ambitions on the international arena.

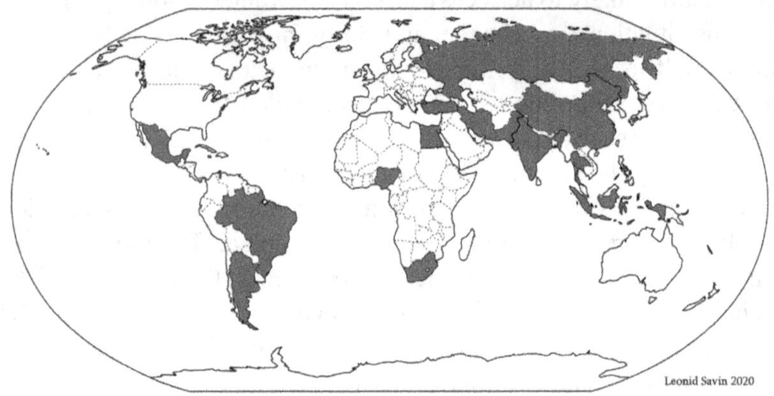

Map of anchor countries. 14 states with zones of geopolitical influence in six regions.

In 2006, a fellow of the BRIC[8] Research Institute of Japan, Takashi Kadokura, proposed the notion of VISTA, an acronym for the group of states including Vietnam, Indonesia, South Africa, Turkey, and Argentina. This bloc was seen as characterized by a high degree of political stability, high growth rates, large natural resource reserves, and a work force with significant training levels in addition to favorable conditions for trade expansion. Tsuyoshi Sato, an economist at Osaka International University, added that the VISTA countries are attractive for doing business. VISTA can be counted not only as a multilateral, joint "alternative", but also as representing a second, new wave with a more important role to play on the international arena. This bloc of countries presents enormous opportunities for the international integration of Argentina from a business standpoint, as well as for the establishment of a platform of cooperation in multilateral South-South alliances, a factor which confirms these entities' identities as dynamically developing countries. Also well-known is the N-11 or "Next 11" concept, which includes Bangladesh, Egypt, Indonesia, Iran, Korea, Mexico, Nigeria, Pakistan, the Philippines, Turkey, and Vietnam. In 2005 Goldman Sachs identified these countries as the "next

8 At the time, South Africa had not yet joined the club.

BRIC group." Even though over the past decade these three concepts have been consigned to the shadows in the face of other theoretical projects, the very posing of the question of new international alliances is of great importance and relevance.

The development of ties within BRICS will also contribute to the creation of a new global architecture. Great hopes have been pinned on this club, insofar as "by coming together, these countries had the potential to provide a geopolitical counterweight to the West."[9] Processes within this association have developed steadily, without political rush, which has helped smooth out possible contradictions and friction between participants while also allowing for the launch of new initiatives in various fields ranging from banking systems to science and education. Even the G20 might contribute to the development of an alternative global political architecture.

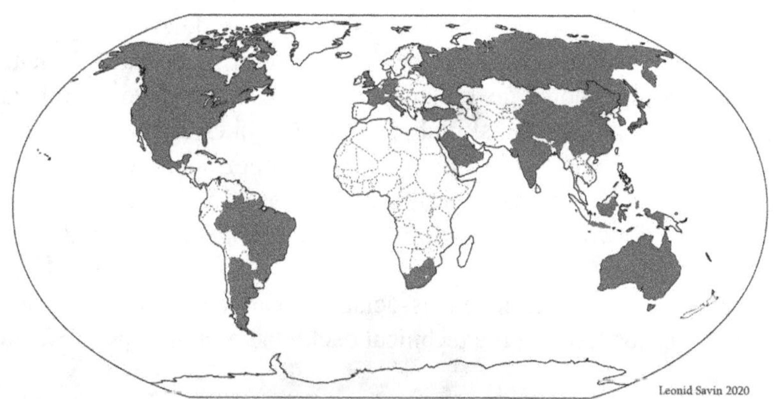

The G20 includes 19 states and the EU.

Initially, the G20 represented an attempt at creating a pool of global-scale crisis managers, and the origins of this club date back to the Asian crisis of the late 1990s, which affected Russia as well as a number of Eastern European, African, and Latin American states. In 1997, the G33 was formed, replaced by the G22 in 1999, only for the latter to last less than a year and quickly yield to the G20. Collectively, the G20 represents approximately 85% of global GNP and 75% of world trade.[10]

9 Elizabeth Sidiropoulos. BRICS in a multipolar world. July 26, 2018/ https://www.asiatimes.com/2018/07/opinion/brics-in-a-multipolar-world/

10 Savin L. Anatomiya Bolshoi Dvadsatki // Geopolitica.ru, 06.12.2018.

However, it should be taken into account that, firstly, this club is mixed: it consists of players who represent both the First and Second Worlds in terms of the classifications of Western political scientists. Secondly, a significant portion of its participants have if not cardinal, then still significant ideological and civilizational differences with the G7. At the same time, these differences exert a certain effect on planned agreements and discussions within the G20. Thirdly, G20 participants are not bound by a system of alliances and circumstances as are members of the G7. Non-Western countries also use the G20 platform to maintain constant contacts in discussions of various regional development projects. In particular, a parallel association on the level of foreign ministers has been established. In this format, the G20 group may benefit the development of multipolarity.

Along with this, the role of the US and even of interstate organizations is increasingly being called into question. The former Secretary General of Brazil's Ministry of Foreign Affairs, Marcos de Azambuja, has posited that neither the UN nor the US' unilateral actions are adequate mechanisms for global governance in the 21st century. De Azambuja also argues that any global club, such as the likes of the G-8, must necessarily include a Muslim country for both additional prestige and influence, as well as to establish a bridge with the more than 55 countries and two billion people who profess a Muslim culture.[11]

All of the above-mentioned associations can be seen as definite institutions constituting the technical backbone of a multipolar world order.

European Autonomy

One very important front for the creation of geopolitical multipolarity is shifting the role and function of the European Union as a collective actor consisting of the major political powers of the Old World. For now, the EU is still part of the Transatlantic zone, in which the most important geopolitical decisions are imposed by the US and, if adopted by European countries themselves at all, then only upon an exchange of glances with Washington. Nevertheless, certain changes

https://www.geopolitica.ru/article/anatomiya-bolshoy-dvadcatki

11 Marcos de Azambuja, Design for a Multipolar World, Global Governance 13 (2007), 307–323.

have already begun which point towards fundamental shifts in the field of foreign policy.

In 2017, the EU established the European Defence Fund (EDF), Permanent Structured Cooperation (Pesco), and the Coordinated Annual Review on Defence (CARD). In recent EU documents, such as the EU's Global Strategy programs for 2016, 2017, 2018, and 2019[12], the notion of "strategic autonomy" has been employed, which raises fundamental questions as to the role and influence of Europe's foreign policy. On the one hand, the roots of this concept can be found in the birth of the European community itself, while on the other hand it represents a continuation of the European Security Strategy of 2003, which emerged during a crisis of relations between the US and a number of European states. European autonomy has also come to be considered a complex issue, including "responsibility", "hedging", and "emancipation", on which point it has been asserted: "The ultimate logic of this vision of strategic autonomy has far-reaching ramifications for the EU and its relationship with the world."[13]

A special report on the interrelations of the EU's defense capabilities and strategic autonomy reads: "EU strategic autonomy can only be realised if the required military forces are available to provide a credible backup to political, diplomatic and economic action, and, if needed, to be deployed in support of such action. European strategic autonomy is as strong as its weakest link. Thus, strengthening European military power is the key to strategic autonomy."[14] In this context, we can recall the Franco-British summit of December 1998 in Saint-Malo, where the agreement was reached that the EU "should have the capacity for autonomous action, backed up by credible military forces, the means to decide to use them, and a readiness to do so, in order to respond

12 https://eeas.europa.eu/topics/eu-global-strategy_en

13 Daniel Fiott, Strategic autonomy: towards 'European sovereignty' in defence?, European Union Institute for Security Studies (EUISS), November 2018. P. 6. https://www.iss.europa.eu/sites/default/files/EUISSFiles/Brief%2012__Strategic%20Autonomy.pdf

14 European Preference, Strategic Autonomy and European Defence Fund, #22 - Report, The Armament Industry European Research Group, November 2017. P. 12. https://www.iris-france.org/wp-content/uploads/2017/11/Ares-22-Report-Nov-2017.pdf

to international crises."[15] All of these strategic formulations point towards the fact that the EU is still completely subordinated to the US, but might be able to act as another "West" by asserting itself as an independent force. As noted in a special study on this matter prepared by the German Institute for International and Security Affairs:

> Fundamentally, we understand strategic autonomy as the ability to set one's own priorities and make one's own decisions in matters of foreign policy and security, together with the institutional, political and material wherewithal to carry these through – in cooperation with third parties, or if need be alone. Strong strategic autonomy means being able to set, modify and enforce international rules, as opposed to (unwillingly) obeying rules set by others. The opposite of strategic autonomy is being a rule-taker subject to strategic decisions made by others: the United States, China or Russia. Germany can achieve strategic autonomy only in concert with its European partners.[16]

The section entitled "European strategic autonomy in a multipolar world order" reads:

> Europe has to develop and assert its strategic autonomy in a multipolar world order. It is therefore relevant how Europe shapes its relations with key actors – the United States, China and Russia as well as middle and emerging powers – and how these actors position themselves vis-à-vis a strategically more autonomous European Union.
>
> Relations with these actors range from alliance and partnership to rivalry and confrontation; from integration and cooperation to distancing and counter-balancing. These power relations

15 Margriet Drent, European strategic autonomy: Policy Brief. Going it alone? Netherlands Institute of International Relations, August 2018. P. 2. https://www.clingendael.org/sites/default/files/2018-08/PB_European_Strategic_Autonomy.pdf

16 Barbara Lippert, Nicolai von Ondarza, Volker Perthes (eds.), European Strategic Autonomy. Actors, Issues, Conflicts of Interests, SWP Research Paper 2019/RP 04, March 2019 https://www.swp-berlin.org/en/publication/european-strategic-autonomy/#hd-d14204e275

> are reflected in different degrees of symmetry and dependency between the different poles. Seeking strategic autonomy, Europe needs to define itself as a pole in a shifting multipolar world order that is increasingly determined by Sino-American rivalry...
>
> In a time of uncertainty about the course of US foreign policy and transformation in the international system it would be sensible for Germany to develop a policy of strategic risk hedging with its European allies and to expand its own foreign policy options. Even if increasing Europe's strategic autonomy is a long-term affair, the maxim of strategic risk hedging already points to certain conclusions for dealings with the United States today: Depending on the constellation of conflicts and interests, strategic risk hedging can result in a policy of economic and diplomatic hard balancing. One example would be the use of international institutions to rein in US unilateralism. A softer form of balancing could imply Europe showing international leadership itself in those policy areas where the United States tends to block rather than initiate, such as climate policy. Finally, strategic risk hedging can also mean bandwagoning with the United States in selected areas...
>
> With its close economic ties with Russia and its great weight within Europe, Germany remains Moscow's most important counterpart within the EU. This places special responsibility on Berlin for safely navigating these conflicts of interests in every step that Europe takes towards strategic autonomy. On the one side the dialogue with Russia needs to be maintained and meaningful cooperation continued. On the other, the coherence of the EU – including its eastern member states – represents the bedrock of foreign policy capacity to act. It is therefore important to always include the eastern neighbours in the dialogue with Russia. Germany's close relations with Russia in particular place it in a position to make the largest contribution to developing a strategically more autonomous Europe.[17]

This remark shows, firstly, that Germany recognizes at least three decision-making poles and, secondly, that Germany considers its capabilities on the international arena only as a totality in combination with other European

17 Ibidem.

players, particularly the EU as a whole, thereby essentially announcing the fixing of yet another pole. In addition, the document posits: "There are two fundamental options on the table: an *incremental approach* and a *true system transformation* putting a directorate in charge of foreign and security policy. These proposals pose the question of how cohesion within the EU would be preserved, and to what extent. Both options could be configured for compatibility with a – currently rather unlikely – shift towards a federal EU." The "incremental approach" or "reform option" means a "shift from unanimity to selective (issue-specific) majority voting in the CFSP [Common Foreign and Security Policy]. Further options include delegating the implementation of CFSP decisions to particular countries or country groups, and initiating contact groups and special formats that may be integrated ex post into EU structures or can be linked to these, such as the E-3. Groups of countries may also emerge to engage regularly around particular issues or regions." Further, the document postulates:

> All these paths and instruments could be used more frequently and consistently, and not least be developed further in response to crises and challenges. The drawbacks are frequently slow ad hoc solutions, unclear burden sharing, unpredictability and weakness. The advantages lie in flexibility, in the sense of either using the EU framework or operating outside it, or employing a combination…This option would also facilitate the engagement of third states like the United Kingdom, Norway, Turkey, Canada and others.

"System transformation", or the "directorate option", on the other hand:

> would represent the more radical move, involving a break with the equality principle in favour of a permanent differentiation of member states' rights to participation and decision-making in the CFSP/CSDP. This would require the establishment of new structures and considerable adaptation of existing ones, and would amount to a true system transformation. Specifically, a directorate, for example a European Security Council (EU-SC), would be established above the European Council as the nerve centre of the CFSP. The five largest EU member states – Germany, France, Italy, Spain and Poland – and the President of the European Council

> would be permanent members of this super-formation, joined by six other EU countries on a rotating basis; the Presidency of the Council of the EU would always be one of the non-permanent members. This arrangement could be organised broadly on the model of the UN Security Council. The permanent members qualify on account of their size and geographical location, but would also have to be willing to invest in *common goods* and shared capabilities and policies. They would have to accept joint decisions as binding and place external representation, to a much greater extent than hitherto, in joint hands. That cannot be taken for granted, but would be imperative for internal acceptance of the directorate. In this concept the full European Council would function as something like a deliberative plenary to discuss issues before the twelve-member EU-SC take decisions, but lose its role as the strategic centre and final instance on external policy. The entire underpinnings of EU external policy would have to be adapted, above all the Political and Security Committee, the European External Action Service (EEAS) and the office of the High Representative.

As we can see, for now the question of transforming the EU and its organs responsible for foreign policy has been treated only on the level of discussions. However these discussions themselves are of great importance, especially if we take into account the unwillingness of some EU countries to be US satellites and their aspirations to become independent decision-making centers. Further, we should take into account the latter German document's admission that contemporary security and defense policy is considered the most vulnerable spot in forging strategic autonomy. In other words, this concerns NATO, the command of which belongs to the US, not the EU. This recognition lends optimism to future reforms. Restructuring is already underway within PESCO and in EU Defense Fund financing, and Germany's promotion of the concept of strategic autonomy may be decisive for the EU's attaining of genuine independence. France as well is being drawn towards strategic autonomy - not only within the EU, but as an independent subject itself. One document on this matter reads: "What remains key to French autonomy is the country's capacity to lead operations on its own and to retain key capabilities allowing it to preserve a major influence on operations led with allies."[18]

18 Ronja Kempin and Barbara Kunz, "France, Germany and the Quest for

Subjectivity and Sovereignty

In one of the preceding chapters, we examined the complex phenomenon of sovereignty. The future reorganization of political associations will in one way or another also concern such questions of sovereignty. We can see two possible tendencies here. If we take the present situation in Europe, for example, some see the establishment of the EU as a systemic mistake, whereas others see it as merely an intermediary step towards the further disintegration of nation-states and the creation of a global civil society. These two points of view are manifest in the current European crisis, and the further development of events depends on which point will be that of geopolitical bifurcation. We propose to examine two concrete case studies in this regard. For comparison, we will take the ideas expressed in two works with similar titles: *The Breakdown of Nations*, published in 1957, and *The Breaking of Nations*, published in 2003.

The first work was written by a lawyer, economist and political scientist of Austrian origin, Leopold Kohr, who held the position of Professor of Economics and Public Administration at the University of Puerto Rico and was also inspired by the Small is Beautiful movement. Kohr called himself a philosophical anarchist, although he never advocated anti-state activities. He was an opponent of large projects, including European integration. In 1941, Kohr predicted not only the fallacy of creating a supranational system in Europe, but also the collapse of the Soviet Union. As long ago as World War II, he analyzed the balance of ethnic groups and came to the conclusion that both the Nazi and Soviet regimes were doomed. As we can see, his analysis turned out to be quite on the mark, although few scholars have paid attention to his theoretical postulates.

Kohr's approach to the Swiss Confederation can be seen as quite concise: Kohr considered it to be not a confederation of ethnic and linguistic groups, but a confederation of regions. As he wrote in his "Disunion Now: A Plea for a Society based upon Small Autonomous Units"[19]:

European Strategic Autonomy: Franco-German Defence Cooperation in A New Era", Notes du Cerfa 141, December 2017, p. 12.

19 Leopold Kohr. Disunion Now. A Plea for a Society based upon Small Autonomous Units. The Commonweal, September 26, 1941 http://www.

> In fact the basis of the existence of Switzerland and the principle of living together of various national groups is not the federation of her three nationalities but the federation of her 22 states, which represent a division of her nationalities and thus create the essential precondition for any democratic federation: the physical balance of the participants, the approximate equality of numbers. The greatness of the Swiss idea, therefore, is the smallness of its cells from which it derives its guarantees. People who argue for a union of nations in Europe because they believe that this kind of union has been realized and thus proved its practicability in Switzerland, have never based their wonderful schemes on the principle of cantonal or small-state sovereignty. The national idea has so much troubled the minds of the political thinkers, in contrast, the notion of the state is so much more flexible, adaptable and multipliable than that of the nation, that it has most completely gone out of use. For virtue has been seen only in great and greater while smaller entities have been thought and taught to be the source of all mischief and evil…We have learned to praise the unification of France, Britain, Italy and Germany in the belief that they would give birth to a unified humanity. But they created only Great Powers.

Kohr upheld the principle of sovereignty for the smallest, not the largest state subject, or the *Kleinstaaterei*, as the Germans say, even remarking that no one knows what the term "humanity" really means or why one should die for such.[20] Unionism and colossalism, in his opinion, would not result in anything good, as Unionism is just another expression of totalitarianism, a one-party system transplanted into the international sphere. Kohr writes:

> Not only history but also our own experience has taught us that true democracy in Europe can only be achieved in little states. Only there the individual can retain his place and dignity. And if democracy is a worthwhile idea, we have to create again the conditions for its development, the small state, and give the glory of sovereignty (instead of curtailing an institution from which no one wants to depart) to the smallest community and to as many

panarchy.org/kohr/1941.eng.html

20 This formulation is reminiscent of the similar adages voiced by Carl Schmitt, Ernst Junger, and Karl Jaspers.

> people as possible. It will be easy to unite small states under one continental federal system and thus also satisfy, secondarily, those who want to live on universal terms. Such a Europe is like a fertile inspiration and a grandiose picture, although not a modern one which you paint in one dull line. It will be like a mosaic with fascinating variations and diversity, but also with the harmony of the organic and living whole.[21]

This is practically the very idea of a Eurasian confederation, merely expressed in other words!

In his most famous book, *The Breakdown of Nations*, Kohr proposed a number of philosophical, political, cultural, economic, and administrative arguments in favor of small state actors. In the section entitled "The Physics of Politics: The Philosophic Argument", he says:

> This is no accident, for smallness is not only a convenience. It is the design of God. The entire universe is built on it. We live in a micro-cosmos, not in a macrocosmos. Perfection has been granted only to the little. Only in the direction of the minuscule do we ever come to an end, to a finite, a boundary, where we can conceive the ultimate mystery of existence. In the direction of the colossal we arrive nowhere. We may add and multiply, and produce increasingly vaster figures and substances, but never an end, as there is nothing that can not always again be doubled, though doubling in the physical sense soon means collapse, disintegration, catastrophe. There is an invisible barrier to size beyond which matter can not accumulate. Only non-existing mathematical shadows can penetrate further. Division, on the other hand, brings us eventually to the existing, though unseen, ultimate substance of all things, to particles which defy any further division. They are the only substances which creation has endowed with unity. They alone are indivisible, indestructible, eternal. Lucretius has called these the first bodies or primal particles and, in an unsurpassed piece of reasoning, has argued in the Nature of Things.

Although at first glance it may seem that Kohr is appealing to

21 http://www.ditext.com/kohr/5.html

Democritus' idea of atomism and the individual (which, in a sense, can be translated into the practice of liberalism and multiculturalism), this is not the case. Unfortunately for many anarchists who are nihilistic materialists (especially followers of Peter Kropotkin, who tried to provide scientific examples of anarchy), Leopold Kohr always spoke of God and His will as necessary to understand from the perspective of state organization:

> There are two ways by which equilibrium and order can be achieved. One is by means of a stable and the other by means of a mobile balance. When in their proper element, both are self-regulatory. The stable balance is the balance of the stagnant and the huge. It creates equilibrium by bringing two objects into a fixed and unchanging relationship with each other such as a house with its ground, or a mountain with its plain. Instead of creating harmony, it moulds its diverse parts into unity. Being the balance of the rigid and fixed, it could be conceived as a universal principle only if the universe were still, non-moving, lifeless. Then the existence of only a few large bodies would make sense and, for that matter, even the existence of a single one. But in the bottomless vastness of the abyss of creation, it could be maintained only by the ever-conscious will of God Himself who, in order to prevent it from dropping into nowhere, would have to do nothing less than hold it perpetually in His hands. Since this was obviously not His intent, He created instead a moving, breathing, and dynamic universe, maintained in order not by unity but harmony, and based not on the stable balance of the dead, but the mobile balance of the living. In contrast to the stable balance, this balance is self-regulatory not because of the fixity of its relationships but because of the coexistence of countless mobile little parts of which no one is ever allowed to accumulate enough mass to disturb the harmony of the whole.

Kohr associated this political system with the idea of internal democracy, which relies on the community: "A small state in its inner nature is democratic. The rulers of small states could be considered as neighbors of citizens..."

Although Kohr's ideas are not quoted widely, the example of Switzerland could serve as proof of his ideas' validity. Furthermore, it might be added that the majority of today's nation-states of Europe are also in need of being "defragmented" in order to completely eradicate the bourgeois spirit and erroneous bases of the nationalism from the Enlightenment which have so severely destroyed the traditions and cultures of the peoples of Europe, imposing bureaucracy in their place.

Now let us turn to the second above-mentioned book bearing the similar title, *The Breaking of Nations: Order and Chaos in the Twenty-First Century*, by the British diplomat and strategist Robert Cooper. When this work was published in 2003, Cooper was serving as Director General for External and Political-Military Affairs at the General Secretariat of the EU Council.

Despite the identical titles, the ideas and approaches in these two works are completely different. If Kohr proposes to strengthen sovereignty from the bottom up, then Cooper, on the contrary, believes that sovereignty should be completely destroyed, asserting: "The sovereignty of the post-modern state is the right to a place at the negotiating table."[22]

Much of Cooper's work is in fact contradictory. For example, Cooper states that "Liberalism and nationalism can go together today just as they did for 18th and 19th century states emerging from one or another form of imperial rule."[23] But how is this possible? By permanently destroying national culture or manipulating movements and parties that appeal to national identity? Cooper seems to have both in mind. In the second part of his work, he declares that "most people are subjugated by ideas rather than by force"[24], only later on, in the same chapter, he states that "European institutions strengthen international cooperation by strengthening sovereignty...the EU security of public order agreement provides for police action in other countries". Yet where is the rule of law and ideas if "member-states of the EU have lost the exclusive right to the adoption of laws"?[25]

Cooper speaks fearfully of Islam as potentially becoming the basis

22 Robert Cooper. The Breaking of Nations: Order and Chaos in the Twenty-First Century, 2004. p. 62.

23 Ibid., 29.

24 Ibid., 40.

25 Ibid. 61.

for a new imperialism, and he mentions the Pacific region as where the question of a union might also be raised. Both of these scenarios, according to Cooper, pose a threat not only to Western interests, but ultimately to the West itself.

Consequently, Cooper defends Western hegemony and its transformation into something new. For him, the post-modern state is the quintessential idea of Liberalism, which has hitherto opposed any forms of collective identity, be it class, national, race, or state. Cooper argues that both Communism and Fascism were attempts at containing the effects of the modernization of society caused by the ideas of the Enlightenment and the technological innovations of the Industrial Revolution.[26] Hence his certainty that all industrial and post-industrial countries have the potential for post-modernity.

In the end, Cooper reveals his cards and confirms the need to celebrate the individual: "Chaos is tamed by empire; empires are broken up by nationalism; nationalism gives way, we hope, to internationalism. At the end of the process is the freedom of the individual".[27] On the same page, he clarifies that he has in mind the "open society", which is in fact identical to post-modernity. In other words, this is practically the same thing that George Soros has spoken of and tried to realize in practice through various projects.

In addition, Cooper confesses to US interests and the difference between American and European perceptions of reality: "European countries are based on nationality and history. History is nonsense for Americans. They aim not to colonize space, but colonize time, in other words, the future space".[28] This colonization has been successfully implemented in Western Europe through a system of political, economic, and military dependence on Washington: "The American plan consisted in developing a global community of open markets and international institutions in which the United States would play a leading role...In general, the United States has managed to achieve the stated goals through the Marshall Plan, the creation of the European Union and international

26 Ibid., 70.

27 Ibid., 98.

28 Ibid., 65.

financial institutions, particularly the IMF and the World Bank".[29] Let us take note of the phrase "the creation of the European Union". Did European countries, starting with the Coal and Steel Community, understand that the Americans were behind all of this? Certainly some of the actors must have benefited from such an association, but for just how long? The fragility of the European Union has already manifested itself in Brexit, in an inability to cope with migration problems and terrorist attacks, as well as in some of its countries' dependence on the dictates of financial commissioners. What does Robert Cooper offer as an immediate political agenda? "In politics it is necessary to restrain manifestations of the pre-modern or foreign; interests can be reconciled with the modern state, but lasting peace can only come with the confluence of postmodern identities", he writes.[30] For the EU, this means the continued erosion of the cultural code of all peoples and countries. As a result, a new type of *Homo Politicus* should appear. Yet Cooper's theory has diverged from the practice of recent years as, in reality, weak identities yield to stronger ones, and amidst protracted crisis the situation stands only to worsen on the whole.

The World as a Complex System of Systems

The works of Robert Cooper and Leopold Kohr focused on political subjectivity and their relevant structures. It is obvious, however, that Cooper's proposal is hardly possible in the coming decades, even as supporters of neoliberal globalization continue to insist on their agenda. Kohr's ideas, on the other hand, can be adapted to the contemporary situation, adjusted to different regions, and might be fully applicable as a technocratic instrument. What, then, would be the most adequate description of the global political architecture, if it will be not monolithic, but rather consist of interconnections between different actors which must be taken into account? Have there been historical precedents for such a description?

Fernand Braudel suggested that civilizations organize space on the same grounds as the economy, that is to say they can coincide with one another, but also differ insofar as a culture has its origins in the endless past. "Culture is the oldest character in human history: economies

29 Ibid., 161.

30 Ibid., 178.

succeed each other, political institutions crumble, societies replace each other, but civilization continues along its way…At the heart of every civilization, religious values are asserted: this is something that goes back to the very earliest times…[Culture] is at the same time society, politics and economic expansion." Further: "World-civilizations and world-economies of course join hands and help each other."[31]

On the Mediterranean and, more broadly, Europe, Braudel emphasizes: "This was not one society then but several, coexisting, resting on each other to a greater or lesser degree; not one system but several; not one hierarchy but several; not one order but several; not one mode of production but several, not one culture but several cultures, forms of consciousness, languages, ways of life. We must think of everything in the plural."[32]

Here we can see several levels of interaction and layers mutually penetrating one another. This heritage is still alive in the European consciousness. While liberal rule has sought to forge the project of multiculturalism, claiming a diversity of views and traditions, this project has turned out to be a failure due to its lack of ontological depth, to its appeal only to banal everyday problems which liberals have proven incapable of solving.

How can this view be applied to emerging multipolarity? First of all, a scientific basis is needed. If we proceed from theories of international relations, then it is necessary to mention institutionalism, which is one of the foremost schools of this field, and one which initially appealed more to socio-political theories. The main dogma of institutionalism is the primacy of laws and normative acts, and the necessity of the actors of international relations arranging their policies on the basis of these laws. According to institutionalism, the international system in practice has implicit and explicit structures which determine how states act within this system. Institutions are the rules by which decision-making processes are organized, and on the international arena such institutions are interchangeable with "regimes." According to Krasner, such "international regimes" are "principles, norms, rules,

31 Fernand Braudel, Civilization and Capitalism, 15th-18th Century, Vol. III: The Perspective of the World (London: Collins, 1984), 65-66.

32 Fernand Braudel, Civilization and Capitalism, 15th-18th Century, Vol. II: The Wheels of Commerce (London: Collins, 1983), 465

and decision-making procedures around which actor expectations converge in a given issue-area."[33]

In international relations, institutionalism is overall often understood to refer to not one but several different theories, such as the functionalist approach, regime theory, and state cartel theory. All of the latter are united by their emphasis on the structures of the international system, while the methods of these schools essentially differ. "Neo-institutionalism" is often used to denote integration processes within the EU and therefore can be applied to the integration of other regions as well. In particular, one of the most visible theoreticians of neo-functionalism, Ernst Haas, argues that neo-institutionalism is built on strict scientific grounds and is of universal geographical applicability, up to the point of employment for typologization of integration processes the world over.[34]

Moving forward, it is also necessary to examine in more detail the very notion of "system" as applied in institutionalism. In his 1973-1974 lecture course "The Making of the Historical World", Raymond Aron suggested that the use of the term "system" in international relations should be accompanied by the qualification that there can be no dominant power in such a system, but rather the unification at once of sub-systems, i.e., participants or states, each of which is under a certain central control.[35] Aron was departing from Morton Kaplan's work *System and Process in International Politics*[36], which proposed six types of systems - two historical systems: the first termed "balance of power" as expressed in the concert of European powers, and the fragile bipolar system reflected in the dualism between the USSR and USA with their respective satellites - followed by four models which exist only in theory: a rigid bipolar system, a universal system (a global federation in which all participants are subordinate to

33 Krasner, Stephen D. 1982. "Structural Causes and Regime Consequences: Regimes as Intervening Variables." International Organization 36/2 (Spring). Reprinted in Stephen D. Krasner, ed., International Regimes, Ithaca, NY: Cornell University Press, 1983.

34 Haas, E.B. The Uniting of Europe (Stanford University Press, 1958). Haas, E.B. Beyond the Nation-State (Stanford: Stanford University Press, 1964).

35 Aron R. Izbrannoe: Izmereniya politicheskogo soznaniya. Moscow: Rosspen, 2004. p. 397.

36 Morton A. Kaplan, System and Process in International Politics, New York, 1957.

recognized rules), a universal hierarchical system (global state), and a unit veto system structured in the likes of the Polish Sejm, where every state would have veto power over all other states.

Systems theory can by all means be applied to international relations. One of the pioneers of this field was Lars Skyttner, whose monograph *General Systems Theory: Ideas and Applications* served as the basis for defining the very laws of a system's functioning. There are fifteen such rules.

1. The second law of thermodynamics. Although Skyttner refers to the redistribution of heat between bodies within a closed system, according to a number of authors this law is applicable to complex systems which are fundamentally open.

2. The law of complementarity.[37] In systems theory, this law appears as the following: any two projections or system models allow one to acquire knowledge about one of the systems, as any two systems are by no means fully independent or compatible. Accordingly, Paul Feyerabend and Nicholas Maxwell's ideas on the existence of competing and alternative theories possess no less of a convincing base of evidence. Undoubtedly, different integration associations, alliances, and projects can be subject to numerous descriptions, sometimes even contradictory ones.

3. Holism. According to Skyttner, a system is composed of holistic properties which do not manifest themselves in any of its individual parts or interactions, while its individual parts consist of wholes which do not necessary appear in the system as a whole.

4. The "darkness" principle states that a system cannot be entirely known inside and out. Firstly, a given system's elements themselves cannot be totally conscious of themselves and, of course, each one will be responsible for the information available to it in political processes. The neoliberal system attempts to solve this problem by homogenizing cultures and peoples, creating a single market and index of norms. For us, this principle is a most important function which is associated with secrets.

37 In the context of Eurasianism, Lev Gumilev theorized the laws of complementarity between peoples.

5. The "80-20" principle, according to which the behavior of a system is formed 20% by its elements, while the remaining 80% is fulfilled by the stabilizing functions of the system, i.e., a kind of protective service. This in fact confirms the well-known theory that the minority is always behind both the establishment and death of states. The remaining masses are led by this simple minority (the "passionaries" according to Gumilev).

6. William Ashby, who deals with questions of cybernetics, i.e., administration, was involved in the formulation of the law of requisite variety. According to this law, the variety of elements governing a system should be no less than the variety of perturbations input into the system. In other words, the greater the diversity of a system's possible operations, the easier it will be to deal with possible deviations. Although this law is quite straightforward, some actions of the current leaderships of a number of countries and alliances display a distinct inability to think in complex categories.

7. The principle of hierarchy. The word hierarchy immediately brings to mind either the pyramid of castes relevant to the agrarian period of human history, or the layers of political and bureaucratic ladders that reflect the principle of a state's functioning in the industrial era. Hierarchies are based on natural phenomena and consist of several integrated systems on each level. Thus, in complex systems hierarchy represents a rather complex process instead of a single structure consisting of separated blocks. An example of this in international relations is presented by supra-state structures which need their own managerial language differing from the model used in the states themselves.

8. Modularity. Any system is divided into a certain number of modules. Researchers have noted that the spontaneous emergence of modular organization is peculiar to critical networks. The presence of such modules produces a system in which so-called "walls of resistance" appear which impede the passage of signals. This resistance can be posed by parties, bureaucratic officials, or the specific interests of regional or national elites. Modules are horizontal structures while hierarchies (as mentioned above) are vertical structures in complex systems which help one to better understand and instrumentally use a system, i.e., manage it.

9. Redundancy of resources. Such a requirement is needed for ensuring stability under circumstances of disturbances as discussed in the description of the law of requisite variety and the 80-20 principle. It should also be noted that an important condition of the information age is that supplementary channels of communication are needed for the obtainment of proper information and its robust protection. Information leaks or the intentional incorrect interpretation of information can be used to destabilize a system from within.

10. The principle of “large density flow” is also connected with the previous point. If the flow of resources through a system is large enough, then more resources will be available for coping with disturbances. This all seems quite simple, but in addition to the tasks of ensuring the stability of a system, the questions of quantum leap, development, and evolution might also arise, i.e., those societal imperatives for the realization of qualified policies and new achievements in science and technology.

11. Lars Skyttner’s principle of sub-optimization is defined in the following way: even if all subsystems are individually designed to operate at maximum efficiency, this does not mean that the system as a whole will operate at the same efficiency. Vice versa, it is possible to develop the most effective model for a whole system, but its individual elements might not live up to such. This brings to mind certain thoughts associated with the unification and standardization of administrative decisions and processes. According to this principle, it follows that there is no single organization or collective which will be effective at all levels of a hierarchy. Hence the conclusion can be drawn that adequate staffing and proper organization is necessary for integration and political processes.

12. The next principle, which also bears relevance to the previous one, refers to the redundancy of potential control. In order to achieve a desired approach, it is necessary to possess a sufficiently thorough understanding of a system.

13. The principle of causal negative and positive feedback, which is also a staple of physics, is linked to the equilibrium of systems. With the presence of negative feedback, the equalized state of a system remains invariant to a wide range of initial conditions.

Lorenz's strange attractor also fits the description of this principle. Positive feedback produces the opposite effects. This phenomenon is also called the law of creativity since the consideration of a social system depends on examining different results from all groups at once with the most similar initial parameters possible.

14. The principle of relaxation deals with the following: if the relaxation time of a system is less than the average time between disturbances, then a system is likely to be stable. This is directly relatable to integration processes seeing as how the latter mean essentially the rearrangement of economic, legal, political, and social mechanisms. If this re-organization goes too fast, then it will fail to adapt to and "digest" previous impacts. Of course, the sheer overlay of impacts creates uncertainty as to which decisions should be taken to arrive at certain results. In light of the issues of modernization which remain relevant to countries of the Second World, it would be fully logical to ponder which reforms are good, how they can be presented, and how long the "breather" between reforms should last.

15. The principle of spotting is a quite interesting postulate proposed by Skyttner which says that systems constructed on restrictive rules, where what is permissible and what is not are specified in advance, are less stable than systems which develop randomly. At first glance, this might appear to be a quite paradoxical idea, yet the collapse of the USSR and similar experiences have shown that rigid, inflexible systems fall apart sooner than chaotic ones. This is due to the change in the external environment of a system which drives the system to spend too many resources on following its single, pre-planned model of approach. This is rendered even more difficult when external players understand this and contribute to such from the outside. North Korea is perhaps the most exemplary such political model. The absence of strong dynamics in contrast to a rapidly changing context is particularly evident in this example. But in Russia and, more broadly, the countries potentially engaged in the Eurasian Union, the opposite is happening. In Latin American countries as well, this is the case. Actions which might be contrary to accepted norms can often be directed towards the survival of a system and its effective functions. Of course, such a thesis is not an excuse for inconsistencies in foreign policy nor justification for the efforts of oligarchical clans in the countries

of the future Eurasian Union to defend their narrow self-interests veiled under national and integration projects.

We have briefly described the fundamental principles proposed for complex systems by Lars Skyttner. Yet there are still a number of attributes. On the basis of interdisciplinary studies, scholars at the Santa Fe Institute developed methods for controlling complex, adaptive systems and other definitions. For example, the issue of emergencies inherent to the phenomena which we have discussed, albeit in regards to emergent states, was first discussed and described by them in examining the political processes which collapsed the Austro-Hungarian and Ottoman Empires. At that time, the major players in Europe preferred to balance issues using suppressive methods against the disturbances which arose in newly-forming states. Balancing between order and chaos, which necessarily arise out of the properties of complex systems, and the pluralistic and non-linear thinking characteristic of their descriptions will be useful not only for explaining the changes already underway, but will also aid in designing the new reality of large spaces. The main task is choosing the right equivalents between current geopolitical perturbations and theories of complex adaptive systems.[38]

In support of the latter hypothesis, we can cite influential American scholar with experience working in the IMF, the World Bank, the US State Department, and USAID, George Mason University Professor Hilton Root, who points out: "Scholars aren't sure what the right model is, but there is no longer a general consensus about the direction of social and economic change. The race is on for an underlying intellectual framework that will help us to understand the change processes we are experiencing and to conduct policy analysis amidst greater uncertainty." Unlike his compatriots and colleagues of (neo) liberal views on the organizational aspects of world order, Root notes: "We can place the political economy of global development on a new footing of complex adaptive systems. This new foundation will enable scholars and policymakers to better understand the past; to identify the change cycles of a far longer duration than previously considered; and to engage with the interconnected, multidimensional risks and uncertainty we face today."[39]

38 Savin L. Evraziyskoy soyuz i teoriya slozhnih sistem // Geopolitica.ru, 22.06.2013. https://www.geopolitica.ru/article/evraziyskiy-soyuz-i-teoriya-slozhnyh-sistem

39 Interview – Hilton Root, E-International Relations, Feb 26 2019.

In his book, *Dynamics among Nations: The Evolution of Legitimacy and Development in Modern States*[40], Root began to advance the idea that international relations constitute an adaptive, complex system, suggesting that international relations, like other complex ecosystems, exist in a constantly changing landscape in which hierarchical structures yield to systems of networked interdependence, a process which changes each and every aspect of global interactions. Consequently, a new means of understanding the process of changes is needed by politicians, on which point Root proposes that the study of complex systems offers an analytical basis for explaining unforeseen developmental disruptions, governance trends, and shifts in the contemporary global political economy. In his new work, *Networks in Economic Transitions: A Complex Systems Approach to World History*[41], Professor Root develops this hypothesis further. Although Root's many years of professional experience have been dedicated to economic policy instead of political philosophy, such an approach seems wholly adequate insofar as it is consonant with the ideas which we have examined in previous chapters.

While some such official postulates of different states may appear to be eclectic, contradictory or even chaotic, it is necessary to take into account both the differences in the initial starting positions between cultures and traditions as well as the very nature of complexity. In and of itself, "chaos is inherent to complex systems, it is their indelible quality"[42], and "it is simply impossible to protest against complexity."[43] Amidst the shift in the international order that is underway today, these factors must be taken into account, given that "amidst restructuring, the actualization of new forms of collective, cooperative interactions between elements leads to morphogenesis, that is the formation of new, stable sub-systems which, despite their complex internal structure, act as a unified whole."[44]

---

https://www.e-ir.info/2019/02/26/interview-hilton-root/

40 Hilton Root, Dynamics among Nations. The Evolution of Legitimacy and Development in Modern States, Mit Press, 2013.

41 Hilton Root, Networks in Economic Transitions: A Complex Systems Approach to World History, Cambridge University Press, 2019.

42 Malkov S. Sotsialnaya samoorganizatsiya i istoricheskiy process: vozmozhnosti matematicheskogo modelirovaniya. Moscow: Librokom, 2009. p. 15.

43 Luman N. Differentsiatsiya. Moscow: Logos, 2006. p. 297.

44 Malkov S. Sotsialnaya samoorganizatsiya i istoricheskiy process: vozmozhnosti

Multiplexity and Relationism

One interesting opinion on the international structure presently taking shape has been expressed by the professor of international relations at American University in Washington, Amitav Acharya, in his book *The End of American World Order*. Acharya believes that the unipolar moment in international relations has already passed, and suggests that the new world order will be neither bipolar, i.e., between China and the US, nor multipolar. Instead, in Acharya's opinion, this new order will be "multiplex", as a comparative metaphor for which the author evokes a multi-auditorium movie theater, where different films can be screened simultaneously in different auditoriums. No one can monopolize the attention of the audience, which decides for itself what film it wants to go see. A multiplex world, therefore, will consist of a number of key actors whose relations will be defined by complex forms of interdependence. As an historical example of such, Acharya cites the parallel existence of different empires across the space of Eurasia. However, it should be taken into consideration that Acharya understands multipolarity to be little more than a concert of powers, particularly in the likes of the states which preceded the Second World War. This remains a rather Eurocentric view, although there were objective reasons why, at the time, many states in Asia, Africa, and Latin America did not participate in global politics.

Nevertheless, Acharya argues that the United States is no longer capable of establishing rules and dominating global institutions of governance as was the case for most of the post-Second World War period. Instead: "A multiplex world would have multiple layers of authority and leadership. Especially important are the role of regions, regional powers and regional institutions."[45]

Still, the comparison to a movie theater compels the remark to be made that such multiplexity presupposes the presence of a kind of supra-national, global regulator: after all, even if a cinema has numerous auditoriums and films, the functioning of the establishment's systems must be ensured by a single engineering network. In the case of political actors, this concerns the coordination and security of resources needed for states' activities.

---

matematicheskogo modelirovaniya. Moscow: Librokom, 2009. p. 14.

45 Amitav Acharya. From the Unipolar Moment to a Multiplex World. July 3, 2014. https://yaleglobal.yale.edu/content/unipolar-moment-multiplex-world

Moreover, the similar opinion has already been expressed that "viewed from the perspective of American strategic relations with Europe and Asia, the central feature of international relations today is not American unipolarity — but the once popular notion of interdependence."[46] In other words, "the period of the indisputable dominance of one 'superpower', in the face of the US, striving to impose its will onto other states (including by means of intervening in the internal affairs of others), has turned out to be short-lived."[47] The trade wars between China and the US and their effects on other countries only serve to confirm this postulate.

If we examine nation-states or alliances as sub-systems of one system or as systems in their own right within the global system, then the question arises of how to establish an effective mode of interactions: "The task of effectively governing sub-systems by means of 'chaoticizing' dynamics consists of creating an optimal structure of ties between these sub-systems which translate such into a synchronized state."[48] After all, society itself is a system of interactions, an autopoiesis (operative closing) of communication.[49] Further, any one given state has a number of interconnected levels.

Achieving such stability requires multilateral polylogue and proper feedback communication between different levels, insofar as "organizations become segmented in various ways - geographically, functionally, hierarchically - so do they generate multiple centres of meaning making. We may configure the organization, then, in terms of a range of relational nuclei, each striving to coordinate internal meaning." These "relational nuclei", according to Kenneth Gergen, "should be multiply enmeshed with other nuclei, engaged in dialogues in which multiple intelligibilities are shared, interpenetrate, modify, concatenate or act with critical reflection on each other."[50]

---

46 Sherle Schwenninger, The Multipolar World Vs. The Superpower. December 5, 2003 https://www.theglobalist.com/the-multipolar-world-vs-the-superpower/

47 Kokoshin A. Nekotorie makrostrukturnie izmeneniya v sisteme mirovoi politiki. Tendentsiina 2020-2030-e godi. Polis. Politicheskie issledovaniya. 2014. № 4. p. 53. https://www.politstudies.ru/files/File/2014/44/2014-4-KOKOSHIN.pdf

48 Malkov S. Sotsialnaya samoorganizatsiya i istoricheskiy process: vozmozhnosti matematicheskogo modelirovaniya. Moscow: Librokom, 2009. p. 190.

49 Luman N. Differentsiatsiya. Moscow: Logos, 2006. p. 247.

50 Kenneth J. Gergen, Social Construction in Context (London: SAGE, 2001),

This flexible administrative model by no means rejects conservative, traditional practices, but rather calls into question their interpretations' adequacy to current challenges and corresponding application in practice. Such requires a special type of functionaries differing from the modernist type of bureaucrat or postmodernist technocrats.

Gergen also points to the necessity of aspiring towards new forms of articulation and, as an example, proposes the concept of "systasis" or "systase": "an organization without an absolute centre, around which order - as a patchwork of language pragmatics that vibrate at all times - is continuously being established and threatened."[51] The latter term was coined by the Swiss philosopher Jean Gebser in his book *The Ever-Present Origin*.[52] In the explication of Ed Mahood, Jr.:

> This is a subtle and difficult concept to understand completely and in all its ramifications. It has in common with system building that the end result is a greater or better comprehension than at the outset of the process. System, however, deals always with parts, not with the whole. Also, system deals primarily with the product rather than the process. Gebser goes on:
>
> "[Systasis'] acategorical element is the integrating dimension by which the three-dimensional spatial world, which is always a world of parts, is integrated into a whole in such a way that it can be stated. This already implies that it is not an ordering schema paralleling that of system. We must especially avoid the error of considering systasis — which is both process and effect — as that which is effected, for if we do we reduce it to a causal system. We must be aware that systasis has an effective character within every system. Systasis is not a mental concept, nor is it a mythical image (say) in the sense of Heraclitus' panta rei ("all things are in flux"), nor is it a magic postulation of the interconnection of everything to and with everything else. And finally, it is not integral, but integrating."[53]

145-146

51 Ibid., 164

52 Jean Gebser, The Ever-present origin (Authorized translation by Noel Barstad with Algis Mikunas. Athens, OH: Ohio University Press, 1986). P. 130 http://www.gaiamind.org/Gebser.html

53 Jean Gebser, The Ever-present origin (Authorized translation by Noel Barstad

Gebser is also responsible for another important notion of practical utility to political theory and international relations: Synairesis. "Synairesis comes from synaireo, meaning 'to synthesize, collect,' notably in the sense of 'everything being seized or grasped on all sides, particularly by the mind or spirit.'" In Gebser's words: "Whereas synthesis is a logical-causal conclusion, a mental (trinitary) unification of thesis and antithesis (and falls apart because it becomes itself a thesis as a result of the dividing, perspectival perception), synairesis is an integral act of completion 'encompassing all sides' and perceiving aperspectivally…The synairesis which systasis makes possible integrates phenomena, freeing us in the diaphany of 'awaring' or perceiving truth from space and time."[54] Further:

> By introducing systasis into simple methodology, we are able to evince a new "method" which is no longer three-dimensional. This new method is four-dimensional diaphany; in this what is merely conceivable and comprehensible becomes transparent. Diaphany[55] is based on synairesis, on the eteological completion of systasis and system to an integral whole, for integrality is only possible where "temporal" elements and spatial magnitudes are brought together synairetically. The concept which makes possible the "comprehension" or, more exactly, the perception of the "temporal elements" is that of systasis. If we also take into account the systatic concepts, the mere methodology of systems is intensified to synairetic diaphany; and this must be achieved unless we are to remain caught in the three-dimensional scheme of thought.[56]

If a conglomeration of political structures can be called a "system of systems" or systasis, then to describe the process of interactions between the latter we can use the term Ordo. Although at first glance this may give the impression of an association with "whole", unlike Order or *Ordung*, Ordo "first and foremost means harmony against

---

with Algis Mikunas. Athens, OH: Ohio University Press, 1986). P. 130 http://www.gaiamind.org/Gebser.html

54 Ibid., 311, 312.

55 Diaphany in Aristotelian philosophy it means essence or nature as encapsulated in a mental construct.

56 Ibid., 334.

inequality."[57] Ordo is order in the sense of a sequence of numbers, each of which is of equal importance but different signification, and any deletion of one means that the existing order is destroyed.

A pluriversal, harmonious order of a complex and polycentric system of systems perhaps most approximately expresses the ideal which the overwhelming majority of the planet would like to see in political incarnation on the global level.

57 Luman N. Differentsiatsiya. Moscow: Logos, 2006. p. 112.

Afterword

The theory of multipolarity has developed shoulder to shoulder with critiques of the hegemony of the United States of America. Even outside of this context as well, many authors have been wary of the US' efforts to preserve its leadership. Each has had their own opinion based on specific indices and methodologies. With regard to Asia, for instance, it has been said that "The US unilateral hub-and-spoke system, then, does not seem to be a perfect match for the region."[1] It has been also been noted that China and Russia's cooperation over the past decade and their common opposition to US unipolarity has incited some people in the West to predict a clash between a Chinese-Russian alliance and the United States.[2]

But the problem of the US ruling elites' perception of the world has remained: in the change of role or status of other countries they have always seen attempts at establishing hegemony, whether regional or global. It is as if the advice of the most astute Western scholars and political scientists has gone unheeded.

Ivan Krastev and Mark Leonard, representing the European subsidiary of the Council on Foreign Relations, wrote in a joint publication in 2011:

> Instead of being a "concert of powers," the European Union should develop a "concert of projects" to breathe life into multilateral arrangements for managing the continent's security. Rather than transforming all of Europe into E.U. member states, the new European order should help Europe's state-building projects live together in peace..[3]

---

1 Chika Yamamoto. The United States in Multilateral East Asia Dealing with the Rise of China. Strategic Studies Quarterly, Winter 2011. P. 120.

2 Susan Turner, Russia, China and a multipolar world order: the danger in the undefined. Asian Perspective, Vol. 33, No. 1, 2009, P. 164.

3 Ivan Krastev, Mark Leonard. Multipolar Europe. The management of interdependence should define the new European order // IP-GE January/February 2011

Further, the authors proposed the consolidation of Russia's post-imperial identity in its current borders and encourage Turkey's ambitions to become a regional power with global influence. This idea may have looked good, but this scenario clearly did not suit the globalist hawks. In the same year began the Arab Spring which led to the destruction of statehood in Libya, the transformation of government in Egypt and Tunisia, and the beginning of intervention in Syria's internal affairs. Then came the coup in Ukraine with the support of the US and EU. What ensued would be unprecedented pressure on Russia and other countries advocating the idea of a multipolar world order. This is hardly a coincidence.

As has happened many times before in history, the year 2020 has presented humanity with yet another surprise: within a matter of months the closely intertwined systems of the globalized world have been transformed by the novel coronavirus, which has grown from a few cases in China into a global pandemic.[4] The COVID-19 epidemic has brought its own amendments to international political processes. Comparisons have already begun to be made with the global crisis of 2008 which led to the emergence of the BRICS bloc, the creation of the IMF during the Second World War, and the emergence of the G-7 after the oil shock of 1973. The present crisis will inevitably lead to the emergence of some kind of new configuration.

Meanwhile, the agitated globalists are crying out that a new wave of nationalizations has begun across the whole world.[5] In the US it has been predicted that the coming economic crisis will be even worse than the previous one and will raise the unemployment rate in the country to 20%.[6] Indeed, the collapse of the American economy has begun to be compared to the Great Depression of the 1920s.

---

4 David Steven, Alex Evans. Planning for the World After the Coronavirus Pandemic // WPR, March 18, 2020. https://www.worldpoliticsreview.com/articles/28611/planning-for-the-world-after-the-coronavirus-pandemic

5 Alitalia To Be Nationalized, March 16, 2020. https://airwaysmag.com/airlines/alitalia-to-be-nationalized/

6 Jeremy Diamond, Mnuchin warns senators lack of action could result in 20% unemployment rate, source says // CNN, March 18, 2020 https://edition.cnn.com/2020/03/17/politics/steven-mnuchin-unemployment-warning-coronavirus/index.html

Former Assistant Secretary of State for East Asian and Pacific Affairs, Kurt Campbell, in a publication from 18 March 2020 co-authored with the director of the Brookings China Strategy Initiative, Rush Doshi, remarked that although the "geopolitical implications [of the novel coronavirus pandemic] should be considered secondary to matters of health and safety, those implications may, in the long term, prove just as consequential — especially when it comes to the United States' global position."[7] Campbell and Doshi compared the current pandemic to a "Suez moment" posing another test for all elements of US leadership. Whereas China acted quickly and even turned to aid other countries, the same cannot be said of Washington. According to official statistics, in early March 2020 the US had only one percent of the needed number of medical masks.[8] As for ventilation systems, only 10% of the amount needed for the conditions of an epidemic were in supply. At the same time, 95% of antibiotics on the US market are of Chinese origin and the majority of their ingredients cannot be produced locally. Overall, 80% of the US' basic medicinal components come from China and India.[9] By and large, in order to pull itself out of this situation, the US would need to solve this problem at home, begin to supply socially important goods and services on a global level, and coordinate (and, ideally for them, lead) a global campaign to fight the pandemic and mitigate the consequences of the impending economic crisis. Obviously, this is not going to happen.

The US is not the only one with such problems. Italy, which was the first to face a wave of fatalities, turned out to be unprepared for such a turn of events. Moreover, it was unready for the position taken by other EU participants, who abandoned the country to its fate. Meanwhile,

---

7 Kurt M. Campbell and Rush Doshi. The Coronavirus Could Reshape Global Order. China Is Maneuvering for International Leadership as the United States Falters // March 18, 2020 https://www.foreignaffairs.com/articles/china/2020-03-18/coronavirus-could-reshape-global-order

8 K Oanh Ha. The Global Mask Shortage May Get Much Worse // Bloomberg, March 10, 2020 https://www.bloomberg.com/news/articles/2020-03-10/the-global-mask-shortage-may-be-about-to-get-much-worse

9 Yanzhong Huang, The Coronavirus Outbreak Could Disrupt the U.S. Drug Supply, March 5, 2020. https://www.cfr.org/in-brief/coronavirus-disrupt-us-drug-supply-shortages-fda

unprecedented aid came from China, Russia, and Cuba. Many Italian politicians - and not only from among the ranks of Eurosceptics - have started talking about the possibility of an Italexit, or Italy's departure from the EU following the example of the UK. Perhaps such remains a rhetorical proclamation insofar as in economic terms Italy is far from Britain, but the EU will no longer be the same as it was before.

The EU and US remain two major poles of global geopolitics. They remain linked by the decades-old tradition of neo-Atlanticism. Now the present crisis is exposing the vulnerabilities of the whole complex of the politics, ideology, and geopolitics of economic neoliberalism and Western democracy, which has degenerated into a cartel-clan corporation of oligarchs.

To return to the opinions of the globalists themselves on this issue, altogether telling is a recent article in the publication of the Council on Foreign Relations which assesses the actions of the US as the driving force of globalism. The authors of the article write:

> As policymakers around the world struggle to deal with the new coronavirus and its aftermath, they will have to confront the fact that the global economy doesn't work as they thought it did. Globalization calls for an ever-increasing specialization of labor across countries, a model that creates extraordinary efficiencies but also extraordinary vulnerabilities. Shocks such as the COVID-19 pandemic reveal these vulnerabilities...The result may be a shift in global politics. With the health and safety of their citizens at stake, countries may decide to block exports or seize critical supplies, even if doing so hurts their allies and neighbors. Such a retreat from globalization would make generosity an even more powerful tool of influence for states that can afford it. So far, the United States has not been a leader in the global response to the new coronavirus, and it has ceded at least some of that role to China. This pandemic is reshaping the geopolitics of globalization, but the United States isn't adapting. Instead, it's sick and hiding under the covers.[10]

This sickness will prove to be very difficult for the US, both literally

10 Henry Farrell, Abraham Newman. Will the Coronavirus End Globalization as We Know It? The Pandemic Is Exposing Market Vulnerabilities No One Knew

and figuratively. The visible fragility of the most technologically advanced state will affect the revaluation of both domestic and foreign policy. The citizens of the US and other countries will increasingly demand political stability, access to key decision-making, and the removal from the levers of power and punishment of those who profited from this crisis and manipulated it in favor of personal or corporate interests. This will grant further chances for the introduction of the ideas of multipolarity and their realization not only by the opponents of unipolar hegemony, but within the West itself, insofar as this becomes a question of the West's very survival. For the non-West, another window of opportunity is opening in global geopolitics for casting off the last chains of neocolonialism and building a future on the basis of authentic ideas, the principles of good-neighborliness, and mutually-beneficial cooperation.

Existed // March 16, 2020.
https://www.foreignaffairs.com/articles/2020-03-16/will-coronavirus-end-globalization-we-know-it